The Universal Machine

consent not to be a single being

The Universal Machine

FRED MOTEN

DUKE UNIVERSITY PRESS   DURHAM AND LONDON   2018

Printed and bound by
CPI Group (UK) Ltd, Croydon, CR0 4YY
Designed by Amy Buchanan
Typeset in Miller by Westchester
Publishing Services

Library of Congress Cataloging-in-
Publication Data
Names: Moten, Fred, author.
Title: The universal machine / Fred Moten.
Description: Durham : Duke University
Press, 2018. | Series: Consent not to be a
single being ; [v. 3]
Identifiers: LCCN 2017036792 (print) |
LCCN 2017056619 (ebook)
ISBN 9780822371977 (ebook)
ISBN 9780822370468 (hardcover : alk. paper)
ISBN 9780822370550 (pbk. : alk. paper)
Subjects: LCSH: Black race—Philosophy. |
Blacks—Race identity—Philosophy. |
Philosophy, Black. | Racism—Philosophy.
Classification: LCC HT1581 (ebook) |
LCC HT1581 .m6846 2018 (print) |
DDC 305.89601—dc23
LC record available at https://lccn
.loc.gov/2017036792

Cover art: Thornton Dial, *Monument to
the Minds of the Little Negro Steelworkers*,
2001–3. Steel, wood, wire, twine, artificial
flowers, ax blade, glass bottles, animal
bones, cloth, tin cans, paint-can lids, and
enamel; 38 x 76 x 46 inches. © 2018 Estate
of Thornton Dial / Artists Rights Society
(ARS), New York.

CONTENTS

ACKNOWLEDGMENTS

Earlier iterations of some of the writing collected here appeared in the journals *African Identities*, *Criticism*, and *South Atlantic Quarterly* as well as in the following books: *The Oxford Handbook of Critical Improvisation Studies*, ed. George E. Lewis and Benjamin Piekut (Oxford University Press); *Hannah Arendt zwischen den Disziplinen*, ed. Ulrich Baer and Amir Eshel (Wallstein Verlag); and *Fanon postcoloniale: I dannati della terra oggi* (Ombre Corte).

PREFACE

The Universal Machine is a monograph discomposed. Riding the blinds gone
way off the rails. Though a certain movement might be discerned from object
to thing to no-thingness, in general, and in the generative absence of a teleological principle, what you have here is a swarm. I hope it's also a party cum
polygraph, establishing truth by feel(ing) despite juridical and philosophical
inadmissibility. The swarm has no standing, troubles understanding's proper
subjects and objects, even when both are radically misunderstood as things.
It is not so much antithetical to the rich set of variations of phenomenological regard; rather, it is phenomenology's exhaust and exhaustion. On the one
hand, phenomenology's comportment toward the thing itself (as given in
experience, as consciousness) is deformed by an insufficient attention to the
thing itself; on the other hand, phenomenology's assumption of thingly individuation renders no-thingness unavailable and unavowable. What remains
of phenomenology in this fallenness and being-thrown? The social life of
no-things bumps and thuds and grunts in plain song. When phenomenology is exhausted, no-thing insists on social life. Frantz Fanon's adherence to
phenomenology's possibilities is given as a kind of manifesto for sociogeny
expressing disbelief in social life, wherein the new discipline he invokes and
practices takes the form of an autopsy report. It is pathontology (as opposed
to paraontology—W. E. B. Du Bois had already discovered the necessity of an
improvisation [a movement; a dehiscence; a quickening] of ontology for the
study of social life, as Nahum Chandler teaches us) and therefore relatively
unattuned to (what) remains, the exhausted, its marked breath and black
lung.[1] High lonesomeness is both an effect of and a remedy for coal dust,
which is moved ground. Edmund Husserl, too, is phenomenology's exhaust,
as are Emmanuel Levinas, Hannah Arendt, and Fanon, among others. This
is to say that phenomenology's spirit, its song, its animation, its aspiration is
its exhaust, the thing that it expels, that it abjures, as disorganized, as an anarchic principle of disorganization or constant reorganization, the enformal,

presence in motion, generative incoherence, black matter in black operation. Idle talk gathers around things in their diffusion, the internal and external sociality of things-in-themselveslessness. It's not that there's no such thing as things-in-themselves; it's just that such things are other than themselves. Such (dis)appearance is deep and not to be trifled with.

What if phenomenology were improperly, generatively (mis)understood as a set of protocols for the immanent critique (degeneration, corrosion, corruption) of its object, namely the transcendental subject of phenomenology? Let's say that deconstruction is the ongoing history of this misunderstanding, this refusal to understand. If we wanted to broaden this out, take it outside the proper philosophical enclosure, identify this movement's historicity in and as something that is both more and less than a performative mode, we could call it improvisation rewound—it might sound out something of that recursive predication that George Lewis calls "Toneburst."[2] Phenomenology is there beside this irruption that places phenomenology beside itself. The soloist refuses to be one and this consent not to be single worries the joint composure of phenomenology, ontology, and politics past the point of distraction, where the lineaments of an aesthetic sociology await their incalculable arrangements. This swarm is on the way, and wants to help make the way to that rendezvous, happily consenting to such diffusion while counting on you to push it along.

More generally, the swarm is always only on the way. Its *Unmündigkeit*, translated as "minority" or "immaturity," is, more literally, unprotectedness or, perhaps, what it is to be ungoverned, as what is out of hand or unhanded (as if Spillers's echo anticipates this) in having been handed; not in hand, not in good hands, ungrasped, unowned, passed around.[3] What is it to go from hand to hand, like a honky-tonk angel? What is the relationship between fallenness and minority? What is it for no-thingness to have fallen into the world of things, to have fallen into a state of radical inauthenticity insofar as our talk is idle and our relation to things is one in which we do not grasp them, as if their showing is, in the first instance, not for us—as if, instead, world was always being reconstituted as a mutual showing? There are a whole bunch of questions for Immanuel Kant, for which these essays are a kind of preparation, or maybe just a kind of massive *Ausgang* through an opening he makes and sees and is determined not to see, the one in which unprotectedness, insecurity, danger, and chance are given in and as whatever "autonomy" is supposed to signify—the general gift and consent of the ones who are out of hand, unowned, ungrasped, fallen, falling; the ones for whom "toppling the vertical plane" of representation is lived as the birthright of the dispossessed."[4] But the tricky part is that the word Kant uses carries the trace of what it appears, at first, to want to escape. If *Unmündigkeit*, minority, is "the incapacity to use one's intelligence without the guidance of another," and if it is self-imposed insofar as one does not lack intelligence, then what we're talking about is what it is to be self-guided, in submission of oneself to one's own protection.[5] What is this submission, this fealty, of self to self? What is it to own oneself; to keep oneself in hand; to grasp, and thus also to know, oneself? The ecstasy of Nathaniel Mackey's "Dolphic Oracle" is not supposed to be in play here.[6] In order not to fly off the handle, not to have his hand or head fly off in some anti- and ante-analytic traversal and retraversal of every Königsberg bridge, Kant pulls back from the general impropriety, the general expropriation, that he also gestures toward or opens onto—the dark time or black time of the enlightenment's commonunderground, the double edge of the fact that modern times have only ever been dark. This *longtemps* of darkness and its black light, its open and general obscurity, is seen by everybody but the overseer in his blindness. Kant wants us to get a hold of ourselves. But why don't we let ourselves go? See, in spite of all this omnipresent law enforcement, because we want to hear and taste and smell and feel, we can't go very long without trying to talk about some art.

The Universal Machine offers three suites of essays on Levinas, Arendt, and Fanon, key figures in a certain dissident strain in modern phenomenology. Dissident strains usually operate under the shadow of a question concerning the humanity they cannot assume. Such dissidence often stretches out in the direction of a displacement of the human that appears to exert gravitational force as if it were a body. What's at stake is not just the strangeness of displacement's capacity to attract but also a more general unease regarding the very idea and, as Gayle Salomon puts it, assumption of a body. Jan Patočka can, with some confidence, proclaim that

> we arrived at the conclusion that the world in the sense of the antecedent totality which makes comprehending existents possible can be understood in two ways: (a) as that which makes truth possible for us and (b) as that which makes it possible for individual things within the *universum*, and the *universum* as a sum of things, to be. Here again the phenomenon of human corporeity might be pivotal since our elevation out of the world, our individuation within the world, is an individuation of our subjective corporeity; we are individuals in carrying out the movements of our living, our corporeal movements.

Individuation—that means movements in a world which is not a mere sum of individuals, a world that has a nonindividual aspect, which is prior to the individual. As Kant glimpsed it in his conception of space and time as forms which need to be understood first if it is to become evident that there are particulars which belong to a unified reality. It is as corporeal that we are individual. In their corporeity, humans stand at the boundary between being, indifferent to itself and to all else, and existence in the sense of a pure relation to the totality of all there is. On the basis of their corporeity humans are not only the beings of distance but also the beings of proximity, rooted beings, not only innerwordly beings but also beings in the world.[7]

On the other hand, in the wake of phenomenology's distress, Levinas, Arendt, and Fanon will have never fully arrived at that conclusion, having been forced to speak from, if not always of, a corporeity under profound relative distress. Their speech and thought produce powerful and profound echoes—perhaps most intensely and shatteringly in the work of Frank B. Wilderson III as it engages with and follows from that of Hortense Spillers—that explore the unlivable, postlivable, yet undercommonly lived experience of that distress up to the point where relative deprivation opens out onto absolute chance. If "in their corporeity, humans stand at the boundary between being, indifferent to itself and to all else, and existence in the sense of a pure relation to the totality of all there is," then these essays tend toward the exploration of chance outside of the relation between self and world. Chance is the way of all (irregular) flesh as it breathes and bears the palpable air of buried, undeniably anearthly life whose terrible beauty has been the aim and essence of black study all along.

So I want to argue, or move in preparation of an argument, for the necessity of a social (meta)physics that violates individuation. Critical discourse on the Shoah and on racial slavery, even in their various divergences, rightly align mechanization (or a kind of mechanistic rationalization) with de-individuation while also recognizing that de-individuation—the theft of body—is a genocidal operation. Mutually dismissive analytics of gratuitousness notwithstanding, the slave ship and the gas chamber are cognate in this regard and, in their separate ways, jointly end at the convergence of death and utility (for only one of which either one or the other is supposed to stand). There's a question concerning the requirements of preserving and fostering an entirely mythic national-subjective hygiene and worldly maturation, which emerges at the intersection of extermination and fungibility.

At that intersection, individuation and de-individuation orbit one another as mutual conditions of im/possibility operating in and as the frigid mechanics of an indifference machine. The genocidal erasure of entanglement and difference is the culmination, and not the refusal, of the metaphysics of individuation. The serial presentation of outlined, isolated black bodies, sometimes alone and sometimes in logistical formation, or the brutal merger of emaciated Jewish bodies in collective graves or clouds of ash, is an extension of that regulative compaction and dispersive de-animation of ensemble (swarm, field, plenum) whose inauguration is subjection's all but interminable event. If Levinas is accidentally right to say that violence is done to the individual, the one, whose sovereign Otherness remains invisible despite whatever instance or activity of graven imaging, then Arendt is accidentally wrong to say that violence is an act of the individual who renders himself invisible and inaudible in whatever inarticulate and unseemly petulance manifest as simultaneous withdrawal from and invasion of orderly public/private détente. It's not just about the brutal actions of the state, or the brutality of the individuals who stand (in) for the state; it's also about ensemble's violent care. If genocide is the disavowal of incompleteness's differential entanglement, then violence is differential entanglement's improvisational activity.[8] Aunt Hester's violence, the gift she gives and is given, which is given again and again all throughout the history of the social music it animates and that animates it (as Levinas would say were he both consistent in his analysis and proficient in his dancing), must—in the most terrible of ironies—keep faith with the incalculable while accounting both for (what Arendt would see, were she both consistent in her analysis and sufficient in her reading, as) the rapacious weakness of the master's response and the reactionary, totalitarian power of racial, global, state capitalist mastery that sanctioned him while he symbolized it. The music will mess you up but that fails to constitute an alibi. Where did the savage breast come from? To figure that out, in accordance with the refusal of the unique figure, we need a difference engine, recalibrated. Fanon reinitiates this cryptographic operation with militant affection. The anti-genocidal renewal of ante-genocidal violence is his concern, and ours, and even against the grain of a certain cryptonymic impulse that phenomenology bears, we feel the obscurity of a disorder, an incompleteness, that which rearranges the rendezvous, across every deathly boundary, in the flesh. We say blackness and the imagination are none. How soft that softest darkness bends the light. *consent not to be a single being* is meant to bask in that light, available, like a monument you see through.

chapter 1

There Is
No Racism Intended

Emmanuel Levinas: I always say—but under my breath—that the
Bible and the Greeks present the only serious issues in human
life; everything else is dancing. I think these texts are open to
the whole world. There is no racism intended.

Questioner: "Everything else is dancing"—one could naturally think
of Nietzsche.

E.L.: Yes, but you know television shows the horrible things occurring in South Africa. And there, when they bury people, they
dance. Have you seen this? That is really some way to express
mourning.

Q.: It, too, is an expression.

E.L.: Yes, of course, so far I am still a philosopher. But it supplies us
the expression of a dancing civilization. They weep differently.
—**EMMANUEL LEVINAS**, "Intention, Event, and the Other"

Dedication to the movement of hips requires asking whether Emmanuel
Levinas's refusal of dance is anything more than a moment in the ongoing,
unintended, anticipatory recording with a difference of racism's last word.
It's not only that one wants to avoid the conclusion that Levinas was as
devoid of funk as Hendrik Verwoerd; for so far as one still desires philosophy
one is compelled to ask if philosophy's representative man—the perennial in-
sider who stands as if he were outside, enthralled by his authentic mirror
image; the one who thwarts impediment and enters, and always more fully
inhabits, always as if saving and returning; the one who declares the end—is
necessarily prone to that brash, invasive stillness that has enforced the openness of the whole world to the Bible and the Greeks. This question invokes
an incalculable rhythm, moving in and out of measure like a fugitive. It concerns the locale and the age of elusion, a spatiotemporal coordinate that is,

as we'll see, beneath the underbreath. Consider that a tempo-topology of flight is offered, in its greatest intensity, as a problematic of crossing and gathering, of the bridge, of translation not only as distance and traversal, but also as scar and transverse city. This, too, is Levinas's transport. So that the one who with such sad clarity expresses the fixation of unintended racism is also the one who would forge and enact a philosophy of escape. One of these things is not like the other, a condition requiring some choreatic intervention. For Levinas, the example of Franz Rosenzweig is decisive: fateful in the linkage of translation with true vocality as the protection and projection of things; fatal in the exclusivity of what is valorized as exemplary and worthy of translation.

> The true goal of the mind is translating: only when a thing has been translated does it become truly vocal, no longer to be done away with. Only in the Septuagint has revelation come to be at home in the world, and so long as Homer did not speak Latin he was not a fact. The same holds good for translating from man to man.[1]

The ethical imperative of translation—more fundamentally, the figuring of the ethical as translation—bears, in breath, a utopian social weight, the heft and density of a rematerialization of the city from deep outside. But how will the outside have irrupted into the incorporatively exclusionary nexus of the Bible and the Greeks that is implied in Rosenzweig and amplified in Levinas? And what does that nexus tell us about the project of philosophy as Levinas defines it, the danger of philosophy as he diagnoses it? What if we trace the decaying orbit of his commitments by way of their own units and methods of measure? Meanwhile, there remains the possibility of another geometry, another dynamics of the bridge, the dispersed and dispersive thing, (the laws of) its movements and its loads, its choreographic madnesses, its phonographic flights and descents (and fights and dissents), its pornographic restraints and licenses: perhaps we can go from a restricted to a general economy of translation.

Reading Levinas requires some attempt to both account for and disrupt the trajectory between the following passages, the first from 1934, and the second from 1986:

> How is universality compatible with racism? The answer—to be found in the logic of what first inspires racism—involves a basic modification of the very idea of universality. *Universality must give way to the idea*

of expansion, for the expansion of a force presents a structure that is completely different from the propagation of an idea.

The idea propagated detaches itself essentially from its point of departure. In spite of the unique accent communicated to it by its creator, it becomes a common heritage. It is fundamentally anonymous. The person who accepts it becomes its master, as does the person who proposes it. The propagation of an idea thus creates a community of "masters": it is a process of equalization. To convert or persuade is to create peers. The universality of an order in Western society always reflects this universality of truth.

But force is characterized by another type of propagation. The person who exerts force does not abandon it. Force does not disappear among those who submit to it. It is attached to the personality or society exerting it, enlarging that person or society while subordinating the rest. Here the universal order is not established as a consequence of ideological expansion; it is that very expansion that constitutes the unity of a world of masters and slaves. Nietzsche's will to power, which modern Germany is rediscovering and glorifying, is not only a new ideal; it is an ideal that simultaneously brings with it its own form of universalization: war and conquest.

But here we return to well-known truths. We have tried to link them to a fundamental principle. Perhaps we have succeeded in showing that racism is not just opposed to such and such a particular point in Christian and liberal culture. It is not a particular dogma concerning democracy, parliamentary government, dictatorial regime, or religious politics that is in question. It is the very humanity of man.[2]

I think that Europe is the Bible and the Greeks, but it is also the Bible that renders the Greeks necessary. . . . The great problem would consist in asking, what is the relation between the two traditions? Is it simply the convergence of two influences that constitute the European? I don't know if it is very popular to say this, but for me European man is central, in spite of all that has happened to us during this century, in spite of "the savage mind." The savage mind is a thinking that a European knew to discover, it was not the savage thinkers who discovered our thinking. There is a kind of envelopment of all thinking by the European subject. Europe has many things to be reproached for, its history has been a history of blood and war, but it is also the place where this blood and war have been regretted and constitute a bad conscience of Europe, which is also the return of Europe, not toward Greece, but toward the Bible. Old or New Testament—but it is in the Old Testament that everything, in my opinion, is borne. This is the sense in which I will answer your question: am I a religious thinker? I say sometimes: man is Europe and the Bible, and all the rest can be translated from there.[3]

What's in question, in the question of racism, is the very humanity of man. That question opens this series: How is European man discovered? How does he discover? What is such discovery's relation to expansion and envelopment? How does Levinas come to embrace expansion under the rubric of envelopment? How does he come to include himself within the category of the European after "all that has happened to us"? What does "all that has happened to us" have to do with discerning the most authentic modalities of "savage thought"? Us? Who? What is the relationship between racism—detached, if only for a moment, from its question and attached, if only for an apparently interminable moment, to a certain interplay of discovery, expansion, and envelopment—and "the very humanity of man," and what ought to be the implications of this relationship for one who speaks not just of the centrality of European man, but of man *as* Europe, Europe *as* the Bible and the Greeks? Who or what can be translated from this standpoint? How does a kind of sneering dismissal of "what one calls decolonization and the end of a dominating Europe" (reduced here to a mere object for structuralist thought) emerge from the thinker of the terrible interplay of universalization and force?[4] What philosophical task propels the movement from the latter to the former? What other philosophical tasks, what other possibilities of and for thinking, are forgone in that movement? How does Levinas's arrival at the cusp of a clear vision of the end of philosophy as decolonization, as an abolition both internally and externally directed in its relation to what he will come to speak of under the rubric of "escape," turn into another version of the same (racism), however unintended?

Consider this essay's epigraph, a passage from another late interview in which the appearance of the question of intention demands retracing our steps to consider Levinas's attention to the topic of intentionality in an early text. It would be wrong to attempt to debunk or discredit Levinas by locating and exposing him at his worst; and it would be fruitless either to evade or obscure him by dwelling on work that some would argue lacks his distinctive and mature signature. But Andrew McGettigan requires us to acknowledge that Levinas's signature bears a sustained, practically originary distortion. In taking up the fact that "those who have sought resources in Levinas for a project of anti-racism have been confounded by some of his comments about non-Western cultures," relegating them to an exoticism for which he has no "nostalgia" and that is marginal to European centrality, and in considering that "many of his advocates have been confused by the metaphysical apparatus of the 'face' (*le visage*)," McGettigan moves beyond the tendency to understand these features "biographically or as functionless remnants of religious beliefs and personal prejudices," arguing instead that

> the two problems—metaphysical apparatus and unpalatable comments—are fundamentally connected through Levinas's conception of transcendence. The failure to foreground paleonymy in his writing means that the systematic reconfiguration of terms such as "face," which transforms its everyday sense, goes unaddressed. The "face" is not a physical countenance; it is an interpretation, beyond philosophy and phenomenology, tied to a particular historico-cultural formation: the "culture issued from monotheism." This has the consequence that the special idea of the "face" of the Other (*Autrui*), as encounter with the idea of the Infinite, in drawing from one particular culture, is not open to all other cultures: it is not a universal possibility.[5]

In declaring that the very animation of those texts Levinas says are open to the whole world are, in Levinas's fully elaborated estimation, subject to a culturally determined closure enacted through a certain problematic technology of facial recognition, McGettigan directs us toward the consideration of openness and the open and what these mean that must also move through the reinstantiation, in Levinas, of the universal(ist) exclusion. It requires recognizing that, for Levinas, flight is from being, a matter to which we must return by way of the demand that we recognize, along with McGettigan, that "there is a misapprehension when 'alterity' in Levinas's work is understood simply as difference. For him, it marks a positive plenitude that breaks with being."[6] In this regard, intra-ontic difference would be encompassed by knowledge and is, therefore, merely part of "the Same." Intra-ontic difference in the human field, determined already by a larger discrimination in the worldly surround between humans and things, is easily given over to a violent, regulative understanding of a certain faulty, inhuman simulation of European man whose exclusive suitability for instrumentalization is posited in a vast idiomatic range of justifications by Man, the end, in subjection. More particularly than Hegel, Levinas links difference in human sameness to history. Here the difference is between those who are "with and without *sacred history.*" A specific and exclusionarily Judeo-Christian monotheism, understood by Levinas as (something that is at once the essence and the destiny of the) European, characterizes those who are given to sacred history, those whose historicity is structured by a relation to the Other as infinite and transcendent. "The transcendental," in McGettigan's words, "is no longer understood as universal."[7] Instead, relation or nonrelation to it constitutes the difference between humanities. The cultural/spiritual stranger does not stand in for or instantiate alterity or exteriority. She is, rather, degraded precisely insofar as she cannot stand *in relation to* alterity, which McGettigan glosses as "a presence that is not integrated into the world, a presence that can be effaced by 'humble chores' and 'commonplace talk.'"[8] Idle chatter is aligned, here, with the pagan "who seeks the satisfaction of the self before the other," the one who is "rooted in Being and Fate."[9] Here, idle chatter has a differential function not unlike the one it takes up in Heidegger. The difference is that in Levinas it is aligned with a fall into being; in Heidegger it is aligned with a fall from being. In both, concern with earthly affairs indicates thingly incapacity. A predisposition for being-instrument, given in the absence of that ethical "self-control" that is manifest both as submission to the Other and dominion over the other, is interinanimate with a certain predisposition toward servility. Again, the stranger's, the other's, ethical disability—her intra-ontic difference from and within the same (a standard that is born/e, as it were, in the guise of Judeo-Christian, European Man)—does not simply mark her radical difference from the Other but also marks her radical inability to encounter Him. She is a maid, from Thokoza, say, or Thrace. Dangerously given to the Other's effacement, she is an invasive instrument, bearing the capacity to breach an exclusive totality of the breach with profane and common song and dance. This effacement and its corollary refusal of ethical subjection (to and in the form of a *transcendent intention*) are understood as emerging from an inability to intend.[10] She bears but does not exercise capacity. The ethical subject must deal with what he has posited as impossible. He must, moreover, attend to her domestication, which he has also declared impossible as a matter of law and impenetrable, originary sexual and cultural difference. The impossible domestic was always a household terror. Her thingly presence in the European's place in the sun (which will have been whatever imperial zone either at home or in the settler colony, whose difference from the metropole disappears the more we come to recognize that the history of, say, Paris, is two thousand years of conquest) is nothing other than violent usurpation, an immanence whose most shocking manifestations are always also a terpsichorean disruption of mastery, an unruly student's fallenness in refusal of the master's standing, breaking the substitutive transcendence of His face, revealing, as McGettigan shows, the pre-phenomenological insistence on the very idea of a "master who does not belong to my 'plane.'"[11] If the epiphany of the master's, the Other's, face opens humanity or produces a whole new experience of humanity, it does so precisely by instantiating intra-ontic difference in the human, now understood as mastery's representational field, within which fraternity's hierarchical drama is staged after the fact of "the propagation of an idea" (of sacred history) that "creates a community of 'masters.'" The tragedy that is marked by and attends "the unity of a world of masters and slaves" that Levinas presages is only a concern within the European reserve, which is defined by its expansionist opening of the world, its intrusive imposition of its sacred texts on the divided world that it opens. In 1934, the capacity to conjure pre-Hitlerian Europe as a community of masters without slaves is as chilling as the unity of a world of masters and slaves that Levinas presages for Europe's immediate future. That chill is intensified with every dismissive reference Levinas makes to decolonization and redoubled by every refusal to acknowledge it that is offered by his devoted readers. And it is important to remember that what they refuse to acknowledge is not just a series of unfortunate misstatements that are extraneous to the proper philosophical work. They are, rather, restatements of a theme that is constitutive of that work. The theme does not sanction a dismissal of Levinas or a justification for not reading him. Rather, it sets the terms for an ever more rigorous engagement with his work, something McGettigan both argues and enacts. It is in and by way of such a reading that one recognizes, along with McGettigan, that Levinas's "idea of fraternity is premised upon the monotheistic concept of alterity *as* height, the [Euro-]human [master] as potential image of God, in opposition to a notion of alterity *as* difference that would be premised upon a 'saraband of innumerable and equivalent cultures.' Western thought is privileged in so far as it contains the germ of this value given to the individual as the finite site of the incarnation of the infinite."[12] McGettigan adds: "Levinas concludes that desire for exteriority and the beyond, as found in monotheistic culture, provides [a single orienting] sense in the midst of the variety of cultural totalities: 'the [presence of the] Other dispels the anarchic sorcery of the facts.'"[13] McGettigan convincingly argues that this single sense, this image of single (transcendence of) being—the hopelessly and delusionally self-reflective picturing of alterity in and as individuation, which then performs as teleological principle's regulation of the "anarchic sorcery" of differentiated, differentiating swarm's swoon-inducing, profligate, (de- and re-)generative facticity—is the instantiation of Levinas's sense of the generosity of Western thought as well, manifest not only in its objectification of cultures that had heretofore "never understood themselves," but in its masterful instrumentalization of the ones who will have given themselves over, in any case, to a whole other theory of the instrument, some wholly other vernacular disruptions of whatever mastery. McGettigan concludes that Levinas's disturbing views of the intra-ontic human other "whose sheer frequency should be underscored, do not 'run counter' to Levinas's ethics—if Levinas's radical, *metaphysical* transformation of that term is appreciated." He continues,

> Indeed, I have argued that the "idea of the face," the spur to ethics, is fundamentally tied to a theory of separated cultural totalities which circumscribe the particularity of its obligating force. Levinas fears a valorization of alterity that would not orient around the transcendence resulting from "Sacred History" distilled into ideas. To repeat, the alterity of height is distinguished from an alterity of difference. For Levinas contiguity without orientation will lead to wars worse than those witnessed in recent history.
>
> In light of this, I can share neither Bernasconi's suggestion that Levinas's work "contains the most promising resources for addressing the enigma of persecution, hatred and violence," nor Judith Butler's idea that Levinas can help to reanimate the "human" in the "humanities": the structure of "what binds us morally" can find in Levinas only a representation of a specific religious tradition. . . . His philosophy evinces the easy, armchair belief in superiority which is constitutive of prejudice and discrimination.[14]

Presumably, McGettigan also cannot share Paul Gilroy's capacity to include Levinas in "that odd collection of humanist and antihumanist voices that ranges across the spectrum of formal politics" who "have been bold enough . . . to approach the metaphysical potency of racism, and to become engaged by what the history of its expressions shows about the constitution of sovereign power, the diminution of justice, and the functional articulation of rationality with irrationality."[15] According to Gilroy, that odd collection also includes W. E. B. Du Bois, Mahatma Gandhi, Eric Voegelin, Jean-Paul Sartre,

Frantz Fanon, Michel Foucault, and Giorgio Agamben.[16] But if Levinas is to be included in it, after taking into account what McGettigan's reading demonstrates, then his text, and the new anthology it helps to form, must also be open to the whole world. Perhaps then it will be possible to amplify certain radically important insights that emerge in his thought and which are always in danger of receding into what he would teach us to call the thinglike solipsism of the unintended, the unintending, the nonintentional. Perhaps, more precisely, it is possible to consider whether the ongoing accumulative disavowal of the thing that animates certain essential strains of Western philosophy manifests itself in the accidental reversion to the very state (which one might characterize as the emergency of an authoritarian shutdown of intention and extension) that Levinas attributes to the thing.[17] What is the relation between racism—as that nonintentional or unintended turn or return to what Levinas would call the state of a thing—and the ongoing denigration of the thing? What would an unintended racism be? What would a nonintentional racism be? Can there be racism outside of intentionality? Would such racism be a part of the structural endowment of European mind or man that must, as such, be understood as savage? Could a phenomenologist, whose work is animated by a prephenomenological "experience," ever speak of such a thing? Would such speaking have been, as it were, unintentional?

Implicit in these other questions to Levinas is the necessity of an encounter of the unintended failure to escape racism's decaying orbit and a more properly, textually grounded understanding of Levinas's understanding of the thing. Levinas writes, "If things are only things, this is because the relation with them is established as comprehension. As beings, they let themselves be overtaken from the perspective of being and of a totality that lends them to a signification."[18] Coming early in Levinas's philosophical trajectory, this formulation demands that we consider the dual relation between nonintention and letting oneself be overtaken and lent to signification. This is to say that Levinas requires us to consider the interplay between the unintendedness of racism in philosophy and subjection to comprehension or envelopment, even as racist expansionism and letting oneself be overtaken by it both operate within an assumption of intent. Simultaneously, Levinas encourages us to wonder whether a certain thingly resistance to the status of mere thing plays itself out precisely as a resistance to signification, as the irreducible phonic materiality of unique accent whose richly internally differentiated singularity, disruptive of the very idea of the unique (word), given in its fullness, as Levinas himself requires us to understand, in detachment from an origin that is not one, is indicative of another agency altogether that turns out to be translation's nemesis, its condition of possibility and its drive. It is therefore important to note in early Levinas a refusal of the denigration of affect that is almost as striking as that of the denigration of tonalities, a refusal that will disappear in the late interviews when singing joins dancing as the very figures of the nonserious and, when weeping differently, when degraded mourning, will have marked the unruly irruption of accented, affective spectacle back into that nexus of Europe/Man/The Bible/The Greeks from which they had been (always unsuccessfully) banished. To think, or even to imagine, the content of such spectacle is not even a question for the later Levinas so, once again, we're left to wonder how he moves from resistance to enforcement of the ban.

Meanwhile, the discovery of such accent, affect, and what Guattari would call the "a-signifying economy" they intimate places formidable demands on the reading of racism in Levinas and in general.[19] This is to say that if racism is also to be understood as an aggressive and expansive drive to comprehend the other and thereby to reduce the other to what Levinas would call a thing, it must also be understood—precisely in its unintendedness—as a submission to comprehension that immediately places an ethical demand on those who read it, we who must both disavow a certain temptation to comprehend, envelop, and reduce the racist's or philosophy-as-racism's field precisely by engaging what remains truly thingly and otherwise—a certain phonochoreographic performance—in Levinas in particular and in the text of philosophy more generally. We want to resist comprehension in order to get at, to allow some passage to, to translate, the thing in Levinas. We want to get at things—at the things themselves that evade us precisely to the extent that our attempt to get at them is an authentic gesture of incomprehension, an authentic expression of our own residually evasive thingliness—to get everything and everything else in Levinas, not for envelopment's sake but to remain open to the possibilities that attend letting the Levinasian thing continue to get to us. This openness demands recognizing that Levinas becomes the thing he denigrates in his disavowal of the thingly by way of a liquidation of the thingly in his own work that cannot be fully accomplished. Perhaps the thingly is the animative madness of Levinas's work and of the necessarily unfinished works that compose—the irreducibly disruptive (non)works that do, or at least initiate—the work of philosophy. We must appeal to another way of thinking of things that is offered in the social aesthetics of black radicalism and its improvisatory protocols. Perhaps some critical inhabitation of the other, dancing civilization black radicalism is and calls, some consideration of how that other thinking animates the whole history of mourning, of goodbye, of farewell's relation to (antepolitical/antipolitical) morning, is the disorder that is in order here. Abiding with and in this boogie-woogie rumble—this underground, outskirted, fugitive deferral and differing—will constitute something like an out-of-tune and out-of-round so long to Levinas from near and far away; an ante-solo long-song and an antiphonal love song, antinomian to him and to itself; something like a burial with music that is open to ascension, to repetition of and with the animateriality of *différance*, which is what blackness is (and ain't).

This is to say that maybe it will be possible to read, without comprehending, a resistance to racism in some early texts of Levinas that is prior to and critically anticipatory of the racism of his later interviews. If this disruption of Levinas's trajectory from resistance to racism is also a disruption of a similar trajectory in the history of philosophy, then perhaps this task of reading—by way of a rigorous differentiation of its techniques in the face of every difference that it engages—can be brought to bear on the general encounter with the text of philosophy, as Jacques Derrida's work, insofar as it is and bears the trace of Levinas's, constantly shows. I will move, then, by way of the deferral and distancing that Derrida enacts in and on the interiority of (the ends of) philosophy and (the ends of European) man. In short, this is an attempt to show how deconstructive, black reconstructive attunement to the accent/affect of things comes between Levinas and Levinas, translating, as it were, man to man. One finds, in translation, that Levinas's unintended racism is an effect of philosophy as he himself came to understand. It is the unintended effect of philosophy's denigration and comprehensive disavowal of earthly things, its ongoing reticence toward a fugitive withdrawal, as Adrian Piper would have it, into the (external) world of things. Meanwhile, to sound or resound the question of the thing is, as Michael Inwood suggests, "to bring the whole world into play."[20]

The Bible, the Greeks: What is the nature of these texts' openness to the whole world? On the one hand, for Levinas, they are available to the whole world; on the other hand, they *are* the whole world. The whole world is in these texts and the refusal of these texts, the failure to enter into them is also a failure to enter into the world, to naturalize oneself—as it were—outside of the natural, to become a world-forming world citizen. This failure is to exclude oneself from the world, to deny oneself (the) world. It is to place oneself in a state of poverty or even destitution and to submit oneself to, or to let oneself be overtaken by, whatever implications attend such states of statelessness. At the same time, it is also clear that the whole world that constitutes and is constituted by these texts in and as their openness is Europe. The whole world is Europe and Europe is the Bible and the Greeks. Europe is the world of the ones who are capable of world. Europe is the world of man; Europe expands into and envelops the world of things. And here is where the distinction between racism and humanism, racism and a certain universalism, breaks down, as Levinas himself understands in his early work. Those texts that are open to the whole world (to the ones who inhabit the world, who live—as opposed to stay in the world—in a manner that bespeaks what is supposed to be their capacity for world; as opposed to those who, in their incapacity, will have never occupied the world to which those texts are open) must then also be understood as texts that have been deployed in the opening of another world and in the theorization and justification of that opening.

One way to characterize modern philosophy is as the ongoing task of honing and clarifying the difference between—or repressing the irreducible inter-inanimation of—(the world of) man and (the world of) things. Edmund Husserl's work is decisive for Levinas in this regard, as both example and object, not only in its isolation and elaboration of phenomenological method but also in its intuition regarding the proximity to a fundamental crisis of the difference between the lifeworld (the zone of the immediately given in which things appear in and to signification; the horizon of experience that is the common ground of subjects and experience) and an underworld of things that lies buried within and on the edge of the lifeworld—a zone of geographic abandonment and topographic incapacity, of eternally subpolitical and interminably prephilosophical nonhistoricity; a radical absence of developmental form. Things barely or nakedly appear in the lifeworld—as its border, as its core, as the very possibility of its spatiotemporal orientation—while inhabiting the underworld. The citizen/subjects of the lifeworld comport themselves toward things by way of comprehension, envelopment, and expansion. If Frantz Fanon is right, there are (black) things who could be said to experience, in their inability to experience, this worldlessness, this absence of a common sociality, where they bring neither ontological resistance nor philosophical self-assertion to the conceptual scene. Dancing is often understood to be the funked-up essence of such constitutional nonseriousness, the mark of a nonbeing that is both more and less than poor in world. On the other hand, to comport oneself toward the things themselves, and thereby to inaugurate phenomenology's reinaugurating disruption of philosophy, is to posit (phenomenological) critique—or, in Husserl's terms, "teleological-historical reflection upon the origins of our critical scientific and philosophical situation, to establish the unavoidable necessity of a transcendental-phenomenological reorientation of philosophy"—as "the natural ground for the so-called specific philosophical sciences."[21] And philosophy, when so placed on properly phenomenological ground, is the concentrate and elaboration of such comportment. At the same time, philosophy, as the critico-experiential direction toward the things that are in, if not of, the world, constitutes a racial difference in its experience of what it posits as a racial difference. Or, as David Carr puts it, "with philosophy thus placed at the head of European culture, a teleological-historical reflection on philosophy becomes a teleological reflection on the history of the European spirit as such."[22] It is from this position that Levinas will come to arrive at what might be (mis)understood as an inevitable conclusion in which European spirit is understood as the very historicity, the very humanity, of man insofar as the immediate givenness of the lifeworld, its manifestation in/as mental acts and the intuition of those mental acts, is only available to those who move within "a voluntary epoché of all natural practice," thereby activating a theoretical attitude that constitutes scientific capacity. They are members of "a new and intimate community . . . of purely ideal interests" that "develops among men, men who live for philosophy, bound together in their devotion to ideas, which not only are useful to all but belong to all identically."[23] Those ideas, within the context of forceful, envelopmental humanity and its exclusionarily acquisitive operations, are in a technical sense open to the whole world whose openness to invasive expansion they help to instantiate and justify.

The irony is that Husserl puts forward this meditation on European historicity in response to the very crisis that will have led to his own radical exclusion, placing himself and his project at the very center and as the very exemplars of the spirit of European man, upon which his claim was interdicted. The teleological-historical reflection on the origins of what he calls "our situation" allows the refiguration of a tradition to which Husserl can be assimilated after his having radically broken (from) it in order properly to define and ground it. Perhaps certain fundamental questions of transcendental phenomenology can now be rearticulated in light of this dialectic of rupture and irruption: How do "we" abstract "ourselves" from a tradition that we might understand its essence? How do "we" remove "ourselves" from "our" history that "we" might grasp its historicity? How do "we" step back from the spirit of European humanity that "we" might grasp its essence? How do "we" enact that difference which structures "us" as European man? The crisis of European spirit is precisely this step away from European spirit in order to step to its essence. That crisis of European spirit is the difference that constitutes European spirit. This raises two corollary questions: How do "we" move through the illusion of the radical break? How do "we" move through the illusion of an inevitable contiguity? In short, how do "we" break through the opposition of the punctual and the durative as it becomes manifest in the interconnection of philosophy's historicity and the essence of (theoretico-European) humanity? This question is, of course, intimately connected to some others: Must the constitutive difference of philosophy always be physically embodied? Must that embodiment always lead to a second philosophical maneuver, a figuration, an embodiment of the difference of philosophy in the other, given as the natural or the animal or the thingly? Must that figuration lead to a second appearance—a second sight or seeing or *theoria*, of the physical—namely that radically repressive violence that enacts a dialectic of exclusion and assimilation that is manifest materially in language, as world?

The dialectic of membership and dismembering is the precise position of Husserl's text: that dialectic is always in crisis *as* crisis. Husserl recognizes this as a teleohistorical phenomenon even as it is activated in his own exclusion, an exclusion he replicates and regrounds (in the poignant efforts he makes to formulate a line in which his own work takes the multiply paradoxical place of a central, epochal extension) in the reformulation of the natural (attitude). The Crisis (of European Man) *is* Husserl. Meanwhile, what Heidegger will understand as Husserl's failure to submit consciousness to thought—an uncompensated detour in the return to *die Sache* that is manifest as an old ante-hermeneutic inattention to *das Ding*—is perhaps best understood as precisely that unconscious double consciousness that black radicalism audiovisualizes in an anticipatory critique of the desire for, necessity of, and resistance to assimilation. Such audiovisuality is always also manifest as a kind of movement. Such movement, is, in turn, often denigrated as just another manifestation of the absence of volition, as if the bodies of the persons in (perpetual) question are nothing other than driven by inclination substituting for interiority.

In 1929, Levinas begins to publish his early understanding of the pathbreaking significance of Husserlian phenomenology's reinitialization of the question of the human. In contradistinction to a thinking that applied "the categories of exterior things to man" and thus "considered human facts to be like things," phenomenology, in a reversal as striking as it is subtle, turns inward-turning sensationalism toward outward-turning intentionality in a way that once and for all marks the boundary between the world of man and the world of things.

Phenomenologists understood their first task to be the determination of the true nature of the human, the proper essence of consciousness. We know their answer: everything that is consciousness does not turn in upon itself, like a thing, but *tends* toward the world. What is supremely concrete in man is his transcendence in relation to himself— or, as the phenomenologists say, intentionality.

This is an apparently paradoxical thesis. That theoretical knowledge tends toward an object, and especially that this tension is synonymous with the very existence of knowledge, will perhaps be granted. But feelings—love, fear, anxiety—are, in their intimate warmth, directed toward nothing. They are, according to psychologists, subjective states, affective tonalities, and seem entirely contrary to intentionality. Feeling is not knowledge—this is what this objection means. But neither do the phenomenologists maintain such an absurdity. On the contrary, their fundamental idea is to affirm and respect the specificity of the *relation to the world* that feeling brings about. But they firmly maintain that there is a *relation* there, that feelings "want to get some place," and *as such* constitute a transcendence with respect to ourselves, our inherence in the world. Phenomenologists consequently maintain that the world itself, the objective world, is not produced on the model of a theoretical object, but is constituted by means of far richer structures which only these intentional feelings are able to grasp. . . .

Thus *intentionality* is the concrete element starting from which the world must be understood. A consciousness consisting of sensations deprived of meaning, not aiming at anything, turned in on itself— Taine's "polypary of images" or even Bergson's *duration*—cannot make us comprehend the world, which is not a content of consciousness. Here intentionality opens up possibilities to us. And concrete geometry, rather than being ridiculous, will be one of its first achievements. The *concrete* situation that reveals extension to us is *our presence in space*. This presence is not reducible to a simple inherence of an extended thing in another more extended thing which envelops it.

It is, above all, a *complex of intentions*, the sole type of intention appropriate to intending space—just as sight alone discovers light and anxiety alone apprehends nothingness.[24]

The object toward which theoretical knowledge tends is "the true nature of the human" or "the proper essence of consciousness." This is to say that the proper object of theoretical knowledge is the way theoretical knowledge tends toward objects. Levinas takes up the phenomenolgist's interest in the object of intentionality—the object of an individual and affective life that tends toward objects, that does not turn in upon itself but toward the world—precisely insofar as that object is intentionality figured as "a transcendence with respect to ourselves, our inherence in the world." But what is, or who has, an individual and affective life? Are there persons who are not, or who do not have, this? Are there persons who, in a way that is far more problematic than failing to transcend objecthood, refuse to attain objecthood? Can we describe—phenomenologically or otherwise—the convergence of personhood and thingliness or, perhaps more precisely, thingly objection? Is it possible to understand the meaning of the being of that convergence?

This aporetic complex is the vanished ground of a series of questions. What is it to refuse or to deny to the object parts that are integral to it, thereby refusing the object its constitution? What is it for the failed or abortive object to take up or to claim the refusal of objecthood? What is it *not* to intend? What's the relationship—if any—between the unintentional and the nonintentional? What's the relationship between a certain accidental racism and the mere accumulation of "facts" that can be attributed to a grasping natural science or assimilated by an expansive natural history? What's the relationship between the constitution of the object and what might best be understood as recognition of the thing's inhabitation of—as opposed to placement in—world? How is this recognition both different from and apposite to submitting the thing to "the very atmosphere of comprehension into which [for instance] the ideal objects of mathematics had to be reintroduced in order to be understood"?[25] Can something more be said about the *a*ppositional relation between the recognition of worldly inhabitation and envelopment in the "atmosphere of comprehension"? Another understanding of the thing is held within the space of that apposition, one that thinks the thing's relation to personhood precisely by way of the modalities of abstraction and escape.

Levinas's unintended racism manifests itself precisely as a refusal to intend the thing of his "thinking." He renews grasping as a repetition of abandonment and so denies the thing its constitution (which is to say its self-exception, its standing over against itself), those parts that are integral to it, that are its constitutive categories. But perhaps this denial, in the very violence of a long duration that Levinas extends but by no means initiates, is a blessing. Perhaps this refusal is anticipated by another, by an escape—not from being but from subjection—that is given in the failure to attain object-hood. That which is grasped can neither be grasped in its role as object nor achieve what might be called the intentional subjectivity of grasping. That which is most integral to the object is its (relation to) exteriority, a certain capacity for intentionality. Can Levinas's denial of that capacity to the thing be understood as something on the order of a collapse of the intentional field? Is it a failure—activated, as it were, by a denial—of world? Is such an unintended effect the very essence of racism?

The relationship between racism, the failure/denial of world, the collapse of the intentional field, and the denigration of things remains to be thought. And there is a question concerning racism as the unintended, the noninten-tional, and the perennial interinanimation of the crisis and persistence of the European in Levinas's work—in particular, the trajectory between his essays of the late twenties and early thirties and his interviews of the late eighties and early nineties—that remains to be thought as well. If what is supreme in man is his transcendence of himself, his intentionality, his becoming-object unto subjection, then what does it mean to speak of the unintendedness of racism? Perhaps one becomes an object, enters into subjection, becomes rac-ist, becomes human, only insofar as one grasps, only insofar as in so doing one submits oneself to (an already given capability of) earnest grasping, to an economy of comprehension. Meanwhile, how does the one who has been consigned—as opposed to the one who submits—to the grasp, the one who refuses what he or she is posited as incapable of, elude the grasp? Is racism the failure of autotranscendent intentionality to transcend itself? Is it a kind of fallenness not so much into the world of things as to the state of the thing or, more precisely, of what has been reserved for the thing? Can racism in its fundamental unintendedness, its failure to tend toward the world and to ascribe the world to things as the most integral part of things, also be under-stood as a failure of the accentual difference (emergent only in what singing and dancing do to speech in their animating constitution of it) that demands and allows a necessarily translational articulation as opposed to the ineradi-cable detachments and envelopments of force? The racist is a failed man; racism is a failure of man but is also linked in profound and disturbing ways to the very essence of man, which is to say to the fundamental Europeanness of man in the fateful and fatal convergence of what that man would call a thinglike turning in on himself and his forceful and undetached envelopment of the thing-as-Other. This is to say that racism is the necessary failure of European man, an inescapable Levinasian implication that emerges most fully in his work in its tendency to fail, in its own failed tendencies. And it is, finally, necessary to recalibrate this rhetoric and this language. For the failure of man is bound up in a refusal of the world to things, a refusal of what is most integral to the thing, that can be characterized in this way: in refusing what is most integral to the thing, racism denies the thing its humanity and denies humanity its thingliness; the racist is thereby reduced precisely to that which racism would reduce the thing. Or, more precisely, the racist becomes that which he had defined as the thing and is redeemable only by way of the thing's catalytic and catastrophic resistance, the thing's own ante-intentional, transcendental inherence in the world, the thing's own refusal of the racist's refusal of world to the thing. Can the world of the thing, the thing's irreducible embeddedness in a world, which is to say in a world of things, be understood also as that which is integral to the thing, that which constitutes, as it were, the thing's interiority?

Under the influence of Heidegger, Levinas will come to understand phenomenology as a mode of rigorous investigation of what had been thought to be or had been called psychological states as modes of being determined by *Geworfenheit* and *Entwurf, thrownness* and *projection,* into being. Perhaps Levinas's early trajectory can be characterized in this way: from the commitment and submission to the Heideggerian recovery of the question of the meaning of being (as the authentic mode of our reorientation in being, our authentic inhabitation of thrownness/projection into being against what is understood as a kind of fallenness into the world of things or into the modes of presence that are exemplified by things—not just readiness-to-hand but a kind of technological attitude) to the escape from what he understands to be a certain thralldom of/to being that determines Western philosophy. Levinas's escape is enabled and demanded by the discovery of the "there is," *il y a,* which not only reveals being as horrific plenitude and anonymity but understands being within that negative determination of thing as without world.[26] This is to say that Levinas flees from the propagation and detachment he had earlier valorized in his critique of Hitler's philosophy. That ecstasy, in which "the idea propagated detaches itself from its point of departure" and, "in spite of the unique accent [or affect: whatever phonochoreographic singularity of affect or gesture] communicated to it by its creator, . . . becomes a common heritage" in its fundamental anonymity, is forgone precisely in the rejection of the thingly materiality—the projected embodiment—that makes such communication possible. Instead, Levinas commits himself to a kind of flight from being in its thingly materiality, though such flight, such escape, might be better understood, in Levinasian terms, as expansion rather than evasion. So that Levinas's direction is by way of and through both Husserl and Heidegger: from essence as an object of contemplation to an understanding of existence embedded in the affective, productive, and material modalities of everyday life to the face-to-face encounter of human existents in their fugitive irruption from being-in-anonymity. Being's envelopment of existence leads to a kind of forgetting of beings that Levinas would reverse in order to escape the interinanimation of the anonymity of being, universality, and racism as "the very humanity of man." However, Levinas's recovery of beings, his commitment to the particularity of a given visage, is structured by severe limits on his capacity to recognize. His face-to-face encounters are mediated by a highly circumscribed textual canon and by whatever force is deployed to open the world to the texts that he declares are open to the world.

Let's follow Levinas's trajectory more closely. Here is a long and central passage in an early reading of Heidegger:

> If, in the first place, philosophy is an understanding of being and of human being—of existence (for it is existence that has the privilege of understanding being), philosophy does not come about *in abstracto*, but is precisely the way in which *Dasein* exists; it is a *possibility of existence*. Philosophizing thus amounts to a fundamental mode of *Dasein*'s existence. But, as such, philosophy is a finite possibility, determined by dereliction [throwness; *geworfenheit*], by the project-in-draft [projection; *entwurf*] and by the fall, that is, by the concrete situation of existence that philosophizes. Now, when, in our fallen condition, we usually understand ourselves, then all the categories with the help of which we try to seize *Dasein* are borrowed from the world of things. The reification of man, the absence of the very problem concerning the meaning of the subjectivity of the subject (an absence that characterizes all traditional philosophy): none of these phenomena are contingent errors owing to the blundering of this or that philosopher; rather, they come from the fall, from the very situation of philosophizing *Dasein* established in everyday life. But also for that reason

the analytic of Dasein, appointed to *adumbrating the authentic pos-sibility* of human existence, consists above all in *getting one's bear-ings again* [*remonter la pente*] and, in the first place, in ontologically clarifying the very situation of the fall into which *Dasein* is initially plunged. Moreover, this tendency toward the authentic understanding of the self—that is, toward a mode of authentic existence—does not issue from an abstract and intellectual principle, but is manifested in the form of a call that *Dasein,* fallen and dispersed amongst things, hears, and which, for Heidegger, amounts to the originary phenom-enon of moral consciousness [*conscience morale*] (*Gewissen*).

The importance and necessity of the analysis of "everyday existence" is thus explained. *Dasein* is always already fallen, and philosophy, as finite possibility, takes everyday life as its point of departure. Also the *via negationis,* followed by phenomenologists in order that they may stand before the phenomenon in question in order to describe it, is not a contingency of method. It is determined by the fundamental structure of the fall, by the chatter and the equivocation which comprise it. In virtue of the very state of things, Heidegger conceives of the history of philosophy as a *destruction* [*destruktion*], namely, essentially as an at-tempt to get back one's bearings after the fall. For this reason, also, the history of philosophy thus conceived is not a simple aid to systematic philosophy—whether in the form of information or of critique of errors in the tradition—but the historic element is a constitutive movement of systematic philosophy itself. The second volume of *Sein und Zeit* was proclaimed in advance to be dealing with this de[con]struction, and we can say now that this will not be a matter of the *history* of philosophy but of *philosophy.* On condition, however, that this mere history becomes a *destruction* and that it is not restricted to exposing and critiquing errors in the tradition; it is a question, in fact, of destroying something more profound than error by returning from the fall to authentic existence.

We will understand, finally, that Heidegger's constant preoccupa-tion with "everyday life," whose conditions in existence and authen-tic time he ceaselessly investigates, is not due to a simple interest in vindicating supposed abstractions to common sense. For we could ask whether, in Heidegger's thought, the fact that the philosopher feels obliged to start from common notions or to return to them is not bet-ter explained than by a simple invocation of the commonplace that all abstract truth must conform to the facts of experience. The alleged evidence of this dictum becomes contestable if we understand by "experience" the vague experience of our everyday life. If, nevertheless, it is such experience that philosophers mean to take as their point of departure, then philosophy is not at heart contemplative knowledge about which one must pose such and such a question of method, but, conforming to Heidegger's ontologism, it is, in its most intimate essence, a possibility of concrete existence already in progress, as Pascal would say, always already fallen, finite possibility in the most specific and most tragic sense of the term.[27]

The task that Levinas sets for himself, a setting that is only possible via Heidegger (which is to say via the intensity of Heidegger's engagement, however intermittent or appositional, with Marx's recovery/discovery/invention of the question of being as a possibility of concrete, economical existence already in progress), is one that is both peculiar to his time and is something set for his time, set for the time of modernity in general, a task that is of the history of philosophy and that is that history's end, the end of that history *as* the end of the history of philosophy, which is to say the end of philosophy. It is a task that is both recognized and necessitated by philosophy and is continually recycled in the history of philosophy as the history of a fallen modernity or contemporaneity. When the history of philosophy is theorized by Heidegger as the history of the being of beings, the history of the being of Dasein, of Dasein's concern with being, this fallenness of the contemporary, the lived fallenness in the world of things, becomes an explicit theme but its force is always there as an ever more conscious inhabitation of the problematic of the modern, the problematic of our contemporaneity. Levinas is aware of this structuring force of the contemporary problematic in Heidegger even as he fails to understand the perennial nature of this philosophical thematic which we might come to understand, by way of the very irruption of the thing, as the city, the market, the ongoing mobility and morphology of a given epoch's capital and of the capitols of epochs, in all of their uncontrollable impurity, which are disseminated as the impurities of song, dance, and animation, of processions and parades, of passages to Indian shawls, of the irruptive choreography of musicals, of the natural history of the theater, of opera, of work and of the work of art, of the painting, of work in the painting, of work and the commodity and desire in the painting, of the fetish character of Olympia and Olympia's maid and Olympia's cat and their secrets in all of the evasiveness of their natal occasion, all the insistence of their previousness, all the way back to Kant and before, all the way back to the irruption of race war in Europe which was always also a war of accent. Levinas is attuned to Heidegger's contemporaneity in all the force of its returning but not to the Heideggerian echoes emitted from his own historically situated recall: "The return to the original themes of philosophy—and it is in this that the work of Heidegger remains striking—does not proceed from a pious decision to return finally to who knows what *philosophia perennis* but from a radical attention given to the urgent preoccupations of the moment. The abstract question of the meaning of being qua being and the question of the present hour spontaneously reunite."[28] What is the question of the present hour? It follows the eternal assertion that there's something wrong (with us) right now that is a function of the way we are here right now, the way we live now. This is a perennial theme of philosophy. And the perennial task of philosophy is to save us from the way we are right here right now; from the impurities of the way we live now, the impurities that determine the way we live now. Which is to say that the way we are right now is necessarily impure, the impurity at the very heart of European self-constitution. If that self-constitution is one of ever more intense accumulation and expansion—grasping—then, say, Mr. Melmotte is the embodiment of impurity as both degradation and animation. Of course, Marx understands this self-consumptive, self-deconstructive expansion that is Europe better than anyone though it takes other perspectives to recognize that the European obsession with its own self-endangerment is the very essence of an *omnicidal* drive. And the question of this "we" arises immediately. Not only at the level of the abstract and perennial division between "who" and "what" that Derrida inhabits and elucidates (is the "we" a person or a thing?), but also at the level of an immediate question of race and sex that becomes the very language through which the who/what distinction is articulated. Is the whole ethicopolitical problematic of neighbor/stranger (or friend/enemy) (which structures and defines the relationship of self/Other by way of another surreptitious detachment [wherein the neighbor is not but nothing other than the self]) some more fundamental register for this racial/sexual problematic? I don't think so. Which is to say it is not prior to but is a modality of it. These terms are already racialized and sexualized even if in ways that are other than the ones we recognize in "our modernity," here and now. At any rate, there is a we or an us that must be saved and we look to philosophy for the method through which we might save ourselves (from ourselves, from our fallenness, from a fallenness that is also a having fallen into a certain kind of philosophy, a philosophy of forgetting, a philosophy overdetermined, as it were, by the presence of [raced and sexed] things).

At stake here, finally, is that this being saved is an intra-European phenomenon: the crisis is a European crisis, a crisis of European sciences, European spirit, European man. This goes back at least to Kant, where a certain metaphilosophical consciousness, a discourse on the laws of thinking, emerges in a necessary relation to questions of difference and inequality that are only articulable through the question of genesis; where teleological principle is understood as a condition of possibility of thinking that is itself only possible by way of the convergence of genesis and race, both figured as (law's) originary criminality. This structure is implicit, with certain interesting fissures, in Heidegger; it is explicit and, at the same time, hopelessly broken, in Husserl and Levinas. This is to say that Heidegger is open to the Kantian ambivalence—what Gayatri Chakravorty Spivak might call the Kantian honesty—of a certain necessary opening or incompleteness of European man (as *lunatic* reason or the madness of the necessarily unfinished, if never absent, work) that Husserl and Levinas tend to refuse. At the same time, like Levinas's emergent refusal in the recoil of the Old Testament as the originary infusion of otherness that constitutes the essentially European, Heidegger's openness is always also and most fundamentally a closure at the level of an insistent German philological return to the Greeks as originarily European. Such recoveries of original Europeanness are always put forward as the answer to the question of our problematic, fallen contemporaneity. The ongoing and loopy production of the task of saving European man is Levinas's task as well. But the only thing European man has to be saved from is the ongoing task of an always already impossible *self*-preservation. It is a savage irony that this task, which is the essential task of modern philosophy, is also the task of what Levinas calls "the philosophy of Hitlerism." In his reflections on that philosophy Levinas recognizes this irony and inhabits it, if only for a moment. The question, then, is how the disavowal of and/or escape from being come to be submitted to the commitment to the European. How does the Weimar Republic come to be read as the very locale and polity of fallenness (this will have been Adorno's perspective)? It's as if Jewish intellectuals in Europe are given the task of saving a culture that has, on the one hand, disavowed itself, no longer knows itself and, on the other hand, never knew itself, never recognized this moment of fallenness and disavowal as its most authentic possibility. This is the task: to save Europe from itself in its unhappy sojourn in the world of things.

Some alternative speculations, not decreed but sung: What if escape, which will have become the specific modality of the task of saving/reauthenticating European man that Levinas embraces, is more im/properly understood to be the fundamental and irreducible disunity of the world of masters and slaves? What if the task of saving/reauthenticating European man produces the ideal of an escape from being as a kind of ruse, a sort of reenveloping entrapment? What if the need or desire for an escape from being emerges from a fundamental misunderstanding, one tied, finally, to something like an ongoing disavowal of fallenness, an ongoing disavowal and devaluation of things, of falling into the world of things, of withdrawal into the external world, of the unrecognized relation between fallenness (burial [with music]) and ascension, immanence, and transcendence? What if the escape from being that Levinas prescribes is just another moment in the history of the refusal of thingliness? What if being is a kind of interinanimation of thrownness, projection, and fallenness? What if fallenness is integral to being, is the very essence, the very authenticity, the very *destruction,* of being? What if fallenness *is* escape, the fugitivity of being in/as things? What if being, the humanity of man, the anonymity of a certain crossing over, translation, transcendence, exteriorization, or intention, is escape? What if escape, or fugitivity, were encoded in idea and expression as the very accentual singularity that guarantees their anonymous, anti-imperial, and nonexclusionary universality? (One thinks, here, of Derrida, of the other's strained, strange, estranged monolingualism, of the irruption of accent and improvisation in the unintended racism of the same [who is, therefore, not the same].) What if being, as life, always escapes, as Foucault says? And what if racism is the eternal drive—the authentic iron systemic rhythm—of the pattyroller? Racism is neither being, nor anonymity, nor universality, nor an eternally open and foreclosing question internal to the very humanity of man; it is, rather, the power that responds—immediately, as it were—to these resistances, these fugitivities, these flights. Racism is a basic modification and another mode of propagation of the very idea (of universality). It is violence done to the unique accent that is both the very emanation and the condition of possibility of becoming-common (or, perhaps more precisely, of being-in-(the)-commons, of living in the world of fugitive and common things. Tom Sheehan says that the problem with Levinas is that, unlike Reiner Schürmann, he would evade being rather than meet it head on.[29] Perhaps it's a matter of the mode of evasion, the specific materiality of appositional torque or torsion, a kind of dance, a move, a (drop) step, a pivot.

The question of song and dance (of cinema and theater) in Levinas's late interviews ought to be understood, finally, in relation to the nonintentional, unintended racism that animates, paradoxically, what might be called European philosophy's drive to hold, to intend, and to disavow that which evades the ontological grasp while failing to escape being:

Q.: Let us imagine, Emmanuel Levinas, that a student who is about to graduate were to ask your definition of philosophy. What would you tell him?

E.L.: I would say to him that philosophy permits man to interrogate himself about what he says and about what one says to oneself in thinking. No longer to let oneself be swayed or intoxicated by the rhythm of words and the generality that they designate, but to open oneself to the uniqueness of the unique in the real, that is to say, to the uniqueness of the other. That is to say, in the final analysis, to love. *To speak truly, not as one sings*; to awaken; to sober up; to undo one's refrain. Already the philosopher Alain taught us to be on guard against everything that in our purportedly lucid civilization comes to us from the "merchants of sleep." Philosophy as insomnia, as a new awakening at the heart of the self-evidence which already marks the awakening, but which is still or always a dream.[30]

Q.: We live in a society of the image, of sound, of the spectacle, in which there is little place for a step back, for reflection. If this were to accelerate, would not our society lose humanity?

E.L.: Absolutely. I have no nostalgia for the primitive. Whatever be the human possibilities that appear there—they must be stated. Though there is a danger of verbalism, language, which is a call to the other, is also the essential modality of the "self-distrust" that is proper to philosophy. I don't wish to denounce the image. But I contend that in the audiovisual domain there is considerable distraction. It is a form of dreaming which plunges us into and maintains the sleep of which we were just speaking.[31]

At issue is the possibility and desirability of avoiding song which is associated with intoxication, sleep, lack of seriousness, the technoprimitivity that attends modern audiovisual distraction, accompanies the ongoing inability to escape being, and is, ultimately, aligned with The Worst. This avoidance would not be a total disavowal of the performative since, finally, Levinas thinks the ethical encounter as staging, as mise-en-scène; but it is a rejection of any non- or extradiscursive theatricality particularly insofar as such theatricality is understood by him (in a way that Judith Butler and, before her, Nicole Loraux make it impossible for us now to understand) "outside" of the classical discursive field. This complex is interarticulate with a profound sexism that Luce Irigaray reads in Levinas.[32] This is Levinas's phal-logo-euro-centrism. In the meantime, European man is revealed as nothing other than the unintended effect of the task of saving European man. Who will save European man from (saving) himself? Who will save European man from his disavowal of his own endangerment? An address of these questions is made more accessible by considering Levinas's (and, by extension, Husserl's) relation to a tradition of thinking the dialectic of exclusion and assimilation that Eric Santner characterizes as a German-Jewish discourse "on creaturely life." There is a vessel carrying a set of differences that will constitute the surplus when it is broken. By way of Santner, I want to move toward some consideration of *that* thing.

> In his eighth *Duino Elegy,* Rainer Maria Rilke famously distinguishes human life from the way of being of what he calls, simply, *die Kreatur.* In the elegy, written in 1922, Rilke praises the capacity of plant and animal life to inhabit a seemingly borderless surround that he names, as the environmental correlate or sphere of the creature, *das Offene—* the Open: "With all its eyes the natural world [die Kreatur] looks out into the Open."
>
> Because human life is essentially reflective, mediated through consciousness and self-consciousness, man's relation to things is crossed with borders, articulated within a matrix of representations that position him, qua subject, over against the world, qua object of desire and mastery:
>
>> Only *our* eyes are turned
>> backward, and surround plant, animal, child
>> like traps, as they emerge into their freedom.[33]

Santner describes the relation between the Rilkean notions of die Kreatur and das Offene and the difference between these terms, as well as their relation to one another and the terms *man* and *world* and their relation to one another. Das Offene is the environmental correlate or sphere of die Kreatur— plant and animal life, the natural and its attitude. Die Kreatur inhabits das

Offene, "a seemingly borderless surround." Surround denotes immediate environment—"environmental correlate or sphere"—but it also denotes border. Santner speaks of a borderless border that surrounds. Die Kreatur looks out, with a natural attitude as opposed to a theoretical one, onto the borderless border that surrounds it. Man does not inhabit this borderless border; rather, his world is crossed by borders that he produces, borders that could be said to attend grasping at the intersection of owning and knowing. For in man's backward, self-directed gaze is enacted a surrounding, an envelopment, a masterful, desire-driven grasping, the scientific-acquisitive attitude that defines subjectivity. On the other hand, die Kreatur inhabits its surround—though there's something off about this phrasing insofar as inhabitation seems not quite fully to bear a certain dehiscence that prompts the question of whether or not it's possible to inhabit what surrounds. There is a barely conceptualizable offset—a disturbance at the rendezvous of the inhabiting subject, the surrounded object and the constantly escaping thing that demands a general recalibration of agency and personhood—nagging such spatial orientation. Perhaps this offset at the heart of creaturely inhabitation intimates or prefaces the difference that sets off human life from die Kreatur. Alternatively, perhaps this offset is what remains when that difference dematerializes.

Santner shows how das Offene, the borderless border, the surround of die Kreatur, is referred to by Rilke as the freedom of die Kreatur, something held by or belonging to plants and animals as they emerge or irrupt into it, which is to say into that open that surrounds and envelops them. But the way that bordering and surrounding animate the spheres and the modes of inhabitation of both man and die Kreatur remains troubling. Perhaps the mediation between man and world that is manifest as the inward, backward gaze and the immediate, outward look of die Kreatur into das Offene are disrupted in a way that intimates an irreducible indirection at the heart of every directed glance. This is to say that the inward look or representational protocol that intervenes between man and world is cut, before it cuts, by a centrifugal detour of any inward turn or return; that the outward gaze of plant and animal life into the borderless border that surrounds them is subject to a concentric veer toward representation. The offset between man and die Kreatur, backward and forward, inward and outward, is given to a migrant curve. In this troubling of the articulable difference that sets off human life from creaturely life lies precisely that inarticulable, irreducible offset between inhabitation and being surrounded which must be attended. Where are the ones who are surrounded, enveloped, bordered, held? Where do they live? This is a question concerning the fugitivity and the insistence of things, their resistance to the representations their resistance instantiates. To ask this question is to offset or appose the setting off or differentiation that Rilke proposes and Santner takes up. The offset will constitute an underground counterpoint to Santner in my reading of him—a persistent transgression of and transportation across the borders that separate man and things and provide an axiomatic structure to which Santner adheres; an irruption of the thing into the discourse of the object from which it had been excluded and which it had made possible; a fantastic interinanimation of smuggling and fantasy; a refusal of a certain labor that is reserved for man and imposed upon him; a dissent from the mandatory work of mastery that animates the descent of the captive.

Let's begin again by way of Santner's examination and enactment of that task:

> Man is forever caught up in the labor of the negative—the (essentially defensive) mapping and codification of object domains that allow for certain sorts of desire and possession but never what Rilke posits as the unimaginable enjoyment of self-being in otherness manifest by the creature:
>
>> Never, not for a single day, do *we* have
>> before us that pure space into which flowers
>> endlessly open. Always there is World
>> and never Nowhere without the No: that pure
>> unseparated element which one breathes
>> without desire and endlessly *knows*.
>
> Man, instead, is condemned to the ceaseless production of mediating representations (in German the word for representation, *Vorstellen*, literally means to place before, in front of, over against the agent of representation):
>
>> That is what fate means: to be opposite [*gegenüber sein*],
>> to be opposite and nothing else, forever.[34]

It makes you think of Trane, who wanted to be the apposite, precisely in apposition to anything like Rilke's conception of man's fate. (I've got this fantasy about High Point vowels and how they migrate, another collusion of o and a in the interview, amplified in a Barakan invocation that has already happened and hasn't happened yet, analogous to that anarkestral migration from o to a that Sun Ra serially announces in his enactment of it.) Trane keeps irrupting into and erupting out of that self-inflicted, rendering condemnation of man who had seemed to make such ruptive motion impossible, determined to keep returning to—or to keep turning in—that exhaustively locomotive breaking until he comes round right. What if man escapes the labor of the negative via self-inflicted release into the thingly, a simple auto-dispossessive gift of self to instrument that resets both self and instrument in an ongoing, general recalibration of any and every such relation? (This is a hard question. You have to come around again and start all over and hope that what you do gets close to what you're trying.) Rilke asserts that plant and animal life inhabit a "borderless surround" that Santner calls "the environmental correlate or sphere" of die Kreatur. However, taking into account that "surround" denotes an immediate environment but also an area or border around a particular thing or place, what's the relation between this "borderless surround" and certain border zones: between the environmental correlates or spheres of plant and animal life, on the one hand, and things, on the other; between that of things, on the one hand, and man, on the other? Deeper still, what can be thought by way of the notion of a borderless border that constitutes an immediate environment or sphere? One wonders what it would mean to investigate, by inhabiting, the surround that comprises composite border zones—bridges, crossings, passages that define spheres of inhabitation. Let's call that surround (that field or plain of borders, of border zones, that borderless border) the slave quarters or the (s)crawlspace; a cistern or a pallet on the floor; a space by the side of the road; an unowned mine; a cell; a common underground. This is where the trace of, and the trace that is, the speaking commodity, the talking thing, lives. (Her name, as we'll see, is Nandi.)

There, in that space, lies a massive question concerning the (open) circle that all one can do is keep circling: Are die Kreatur and das Offene not but nothing other than the same? Does their relation intimate the thinglike material blur that is essential to relations between man and world, die Kreatur and man? These are questions concerning the relation between *polis* and *metoikos*, city and out$_2$law (the one who is outside the law's protection; the one who is before the law, who is the disorderly condition of im/possibility of the law; the one who is, therefore, doubly out, out from the outside). What's the relation between the world, the open, and the city? Is to be in the open to be poor in world? Is it to be on the outskirts of the city? Is it to partake of the double stolenness of the out$_2$law? Is there an extrapolitical sociality of the city's edge, or of its opening, held in the way a contraband broken vessel carries herself? Is there a world on or under a bridge, a secret location on the Lower East Side or her lower left arm from which some things are compelled, periodically, to issue certain bent communiqués?

We assemble the party, bring the jam, and kick it out. At stake here, again, is the shape (the geometry, geography, and topography) of relations. Does a new analytic of shape call the very idea of relation into question? An analytic of ensemble's shapeliness is required. Inside/outside blows up in this (non) relation between the open and creaturely life. If this ruption is borderless, it is also a border zone, a border/less zone that is, on the one hand, (not-in-) between, and, on the other hand, what surrounds, the open, the world, the city. It is the encircled open circle, the open's broken circle unenclosed, the city's outskirts, the external world in play. It is a zone of circulation and nervous, muscular occupation. Santner wants to locate the one who is not but nothing other than man in her surroundings or, to be more precise, within a geotopographic economy of surrounding. I'd like to show how this is a question concerning the realm of things.

According to Rilke for man "always there is world." Man never has before him "that pure space into which flowers endlessly open." Man never has the open, into which flowers endlessly open, before him. Man never stands before the open. To stand before would be the opposite of standing against— the opposite of being opposite, of rendering oneself opposite and nothing else. Man, who stands against or stands opposite, is the opposite of that which stands before. Man opposes that which stands before. Man positions himself opposite that which stands before. (Unlike Trane,) man *opposes*. In opposing, man is rendered—renders himself rather than *is*—the opposite. Man poses. Man is posed. Man makes himself stand against. Man imposes this on himself. In standing against, man renders himself and what he stands against. Man renders himself, and what he stands against, an object, constantly mapping and codifying object domains upon his world and his own person. Man submits himself to his own manmade borders. Such mapping objectifies the open as well as what opens into the open, and what opens in the open, and what becomes the open, and what objects to mapping and bordering, codification and calculation. Man does not open (into the open, in the open). Man makes world and stands against the open and himself. Man made the boat for the water like Noah made the ark. Man brings objects into the world and stands against them. All this is part of what it is to be unable, in Santner's words, "to relinquish that fateful oppositional posture that inhibits access to the open" (3). The oppositional posture or pose must also always be understood in its relation to possessing, enclosing, bordering, grasping. Meanwhile, for every question Santner addresses concerning the difference between world and the open, between man and creaturely life, we must throw illumination and shade by (super)imposing the question of the thing. Where do things stand in all this?

Michael Inwood says, "The question of the thing brings the whole world into play." Perhaps this means that what opens the world to play, what brings the world out into the open (secret), is the question *and the questioning* of things that have been brought into the closed world of their exclusion, those who have been incorporated by way of that which has been made open to the world. Taken out of the dark, brought into light but shadowed, brought out by shadow, dark to themselves, things are thrown into shade by shade throwing shade. The ones who have been brought into the world by way of that which has been made open to the world are excluded from the world, are given over to the world as poverty and dereliction. They remain outside of the world into which they have been brought. They are outside of the world into which they have been thrown. From there they open the world, bring it out into play. They bring the world out into the open from outside the world into which they have been brought, thrown, bought. They unmade the world of the ones who belong there, the ones to whom they belong, the ones who brought them, threw them, bought them. By way of the ones they threw, the ones who possess and belong made the world into which they threw them. But the ones they threw into the world, so that the world they withheld from them might be made, unmake that world. Perhaps the world the slaveholders made is the text of impossible origins. The Bible and the Greeks are the world the slaveholders made. "Europe is the Bible and the Greeks." "Man is Europe and the Bible, and all the rest can be translated from there." All the rest can be transplanted there. All the rest can be transported there. All the rest can be transforming there.

The Bible and the Greeks. These texts are Europe. Europe is man. This is not but nothing other than to say that Europe is man's "environmental correlate or sphere." Isn't this also (not but nothing other than) to say that Europe is world or is the world? So what does it mean to say that these texts, which are the world, are open to the whole world? Would it not be more precise to say that these texts stand against the open and that they would envelop the open in standing against it? If these texts are open they are so in the interest and in the shadow of an impossible enclosure they will have carried out but for the fact that they are unmade by the invaginative play of what they stand against. Europe is unmade by what it stands against. Man is unmade by what he stands against. But perhaps it would be more precise to say that these texts are not open to the world but to the open. That they do not stand against the world but stand before it. That to stand before is to be the apposite of whatever reduces these texts to man-as-Europe.

Meanwhile, things stand out from the outside. To be turned toward the world of objects is to be turned inward, to be enclosed in an inner theater of representations. Separation from the maternal, material sphere is that distance from things that attends their transformation into the objects one grasps and that attends the reduction of one's self or the consciousness of one's self to the status of object. At the location of this "new, dual object" also lives the relation between Kantian purposiveness—which, again, he defines as "that the existence of which seems to presuppose a representation of that same thing"—and Husserlian intentionality—understood as consciousness tending toward the world that is given to consciousness in the forms of things, a tending that is manifest as the representational transubstantiation of things into objects.[35] Questions of theater, of the theoretical or spectatorial attitude, and of the relation between these and the limits of being-political return here with great severity. Permit me to quote the onset of Santner's engagement with Heidegger, Carl Schmitt, and Agamben at length.

> Martin Heidegger, the twentieth-century philosopher most associated with the analysis and critique of—or perhaps better: diagnosis and therapy for—the spectatorial attitude Rilke identifies with representational thinking, has himself argued that Rilke's elegy is fundamentally implicated in the stance to the world from which the poem ostensibly seeks to gain a distance. He accuses Rilke of participating in a movement of thought that produces "a monstrous humanization of the 'creature,' i.e., the animal, and a corresponding animalization of man," thereby perpetuating the popular biological metaphysics of the end of the nineteenth century which, in the wake of Schopenhauer and Nietzsche, posits the instinctual will of animal life as a primordial and uninhibited ease of movement through the elemental spheres of existence. Because he identifies human life with the capacity for—and curse of—representational thought, "a consciousness of objects . . . that is conscious of itself and is reflected onto itself," Rilke is compelled to conflate the ostensible lack of self-consciousness of animal

life with freedom. To cite [Robert] Pippin . . . , what Rilke's conception seems to preclude is an understanding of "reflective absorption as *an intensification of such absorption,* not a thematizing and ultimately theatricalizing distancing." Pippin adds that this sort of "theatricalizing might be said to occur only when something like the normative structure of such mindedness begins to break down, fails to sustain allegiance, becomes a *reflected object of inquiry,* not a *mode of life.*"

. . . As Heidegger sees it, Rilke's "creaturely" understanding of the Open blinds him to the true ontological distinction of human being, one that cannot be captured by the language of consciousness, self-reflection, subject-object relations. Grounded as it is in a forgetting of the ontological distinction between being and beings, Rilke's understanding of the Open as a locus of unimpeded motility forecloses the possibility of thinking "the free of Being, and it is precisely this free that the 'creature' never sees, for the capacity to see it constitutes what is essentially distinct about man and consequently forms the insurmountable boundary between animal and man." As Heidegger continues, "The open" in the sense of the unceasing advance of beings in the realm of beings and "the open" in the sense of the free of the clearing of Being in distinction from all beings are verbally the same, but in what the words name they are so different that no oppositional formulation could suffice to indicate the gap between them.[36]

Santner goes on to describe the uniqueness and exclusivity of the human relation to truth in its Heideggerian understanding as "unconcealedness," as "the emergence into presence of beings in their Being." Only humans can claim that relation, which Santner describes as being "'on to' things in a way that is responsive, indeed *beholden to,* what and how they are—in a way, that is, that necessarily includes the possibility of being right or wrong about them" (7). This being "on to" is the free that the creature never sees. The creature never stands before this free. What's the difference between being exposed to the alterity of things, to the effects of captivation, of being taken, of being (dis)possessed, on the one hand, and, on the other hand, being responsive to the otherness of entities in a way that requires a kind of judgment, that one be right or wrong? How to speak of this being right or wrong? And what's the relation between this judgmental comportment and enveloping? At stake is that Santner's reading of Heidegger reveals the trace of phenomenology's distant or distancing relation to things. That distance is structured by the desire for a certain purposiveness that representation would retroactively confirm and it turns out to animate even Heidegger's attempt to recover an authentic, hermeneutic nearness to things from a transcendence of them that the phenomenological subject enacts in his transcendence of himself. Consider the fatal relation between world forming and judgment, representation and transcendence, as that which Piper calls "aesthetic acculturation," which is how she would denote what Santner calls "the historical field of man's understanding of Being."[37] This crossing is where judgment shows up precisely as a paradoxically invasive and acquisitive xenophobia, an antiperformative or antitheatrical enactment of racialized attraction to and repulsion by song and dance as fugitive effect and affect. But what if beauty were understood—in a way that is irreducible to seeing though seeing is irreducible in it—as the sensual alterity that ruptures judgment, the material difference of another, heretofore unimaginable interiority of things, whose unlocatable loci are the quarters, territories, borderlands, passages, bridges, cisterns, and tunnels that reveal the very structural openness of the polis in and by way of the scars that mark its always incomplete historical closures? According to Santner, Heidegger understands that "human life unfolds in an articulated space of possibilities embodied in the forms of life into which one contingently comes to be initiated, the practices that define one's historical community" (7). But what if there is a form of life—an unknown, unowned form of things—that is not but nothing other than human, that is marked but not defined by such thrownness? I'm interested in what there is before the throw, before the call. Whatever force there is in a certain being-problematic comes before posing. I'm interested in what comes before any positioning—the absolutely fugitive punctum.

(If human speech is an archive and a locus, then what is human song? Song and dance touch on the realm of the animal but more than that they break off from the realm of man. This broken archive lies before Heideggerian "speech" and Levinasian "saying" [as something also on the order of a certain highly restrictive repertoire moving in relation to a very specific and equally restrictive textual trove]. This is to say that part of what's at stake in inhabiting this border between thing, animal, and human is a challenge to a certain distinction between archive and repertoire, a challenge to its adequacy rather than its legitimacy, and to its hidden grounding in another distinction, that between speech and writing, which it might imagine itself to have transcended.)

What Santner, commenting on Heidegger, characterizes as the "instinctual captivation" of the animal in contrast to human world forming, is to be understood in its alignment with being-driven, possession, hysteria, an iron-systemic noneurhythmics, a "traditional" autopositioning outside of Europe, which is to say its ur-texts, which now are open as and by way of envelopment, as much as with some contingent thrownness, into a specific historical situation. But this must be clarified. What are the histories of thrownness? What would it mean to have been multiply thrown, to be continually thrown outside of Europe, in and from its migratory interiorities and busted headings, as its structuring possibility as well as the possibility of its deconstruction? Song and dance are the graphic marks of an ongoing refusal of what has been refused under the sign and the authority of an open Europe, that enveloping lie. Levinas also speaks in these terms, in terms of the openness of a world, which is to say a Europe, whose openness to the world is expansion in the world; an *Abendland*, whose openness is defined by closure and expansive envelopment. One could say that both before and after Heidegger, by way of an Heideggerian bridge that both would disavow in their crossing, Husserl and Levinas cleave to this conflation of Europe and world and, more specifically, enact that cleaving as a kind of seeing, where intentional comportment is given as a kind of visual attitude, where being beholden to what and how things are is manifest as judgmental beholding, which, it turns out, is not nearly as distinguishable from will and representation as Heidegger would have liked. In the meantime, one still remains interested in, or captivated by and with, attuned to the movement of, some moaners, certain pipers, different drummers. What if one *bears*, while also responding to, the otherness of entities? How does such bearing shape one's response? How does one know what and how entities are in their otherness? This is an ethical question that cuts the visage, or what we might call the sight, of the human. I'm trying to get way into some questions concerning the difference between the Open and enclosure, world and envelopment.

The possibility of representation (of relating to something else as present at hand), of handling, is withheld from animals that are, therefore, taken, held, handled. To be taken is to have what apprehends withheld from one and to be, in that withholding, held by that which is withheld. One is interested, here, in the intensity of the denial—the intensity of a certain refusal to own being dis/owned, being taken by things, being taken by something else, especially a something else that is defined by its being taken. It might be asked of Heidegger, as too of Santner's commentary, what would it be to inhabit the position of the not but nothing other than man? To take on a certain thingliness that goes with being taken, with a kind of doubled or multiple thrownness? Would this inhabitation or activation of an animality and thingliness of man that constitutes man's disruption and, perhaps, fulfillment reinitialize possibilities for other comportments toward things? What kind of being-open would this being taken be? What bulwark against envelopment would this being taken be? What rupture of enclosure? What would it mean to deal with the thingly in oneself, to attend the possibility of being-captivated, to think from the position of the captive and thereby to enact possibilities of escape that, in the end, are irreducible to seeing either the free of Being or the face of the Other or whatever trace of will and representation haunts Heidegger, and whatever trace of Heidegger haunts Levinas, in and through their phrasing, their embeddedness in an archive, the heliocentrism of their European attitudes? One wants a genuine investigation, as it were, of interiority's essential criminality to initiate a being-historical that Heidegger thinks he found. I'm trying to think the genuinely and at the same time multiply problematic (the multiply thro*wn* field of a certain problematization of humanity and of man), a critique, we might as well say, of Western civilization. This field or feel is the break that bridges being-captive and being-fugitive. This is the modality of escape-in/as-being.

Santner reads Agamben and Heidegger in order precisely to discuss being-captive as animality. This discussion is manifest most clearly in his particular attention to Agamben's insight regarding a certain discomfiting proximity between animal and human life. Here is Part III of "On Creaturely Life":

> Agamben's crucial contribution to this "debate" between Rilke and Heidegger as to the meaning of "the Open" in animal and human life has been to underline a profound ambiguity in Heidegger's own position. Agamben points to the ways in which Heidegger's very insistence on the radical ontological distinction between animal and human life— one conceived, precisely, in opposition to Rilke's still "metaphysical" understanding of the animal human divide—brings the two kinds of life into an uncanny proximity, one duly noted by Heidegger himself. That is to say, for Heidegger, man's freedom and destiny as "world-forming" includes a dimension—I am tempted to say: a traumatic dimension—that brings him into the proximity of the animal, that renders him, in a certain sense, creaturely.

Interestingly, one of the points at which this proximity begins to register in Heidegger's argument is where he refers to the Pauline conception of a longing for redemption immanent to creaturely life itself, to the haunting vision of creation groaning in travail (Romans 8:18–22). Paul's words suggest to Heidegger that the *"animal's poverty in world [is] a problem intrinsic to animality itself."* In its captivation by a narrowly delimited functional environment, the animal "finds itself essentially exposed to something other than itself, something that can indeed never be manifest to the animal either as a being or as a non-being." But precisely such exposure, writes Heidegger, "brings an *essential disruption* [*wesenhafte Erschütterung*] into the essence of the animal."

For Heidegger, it is this disruptive dimension of animal captivation that stands behind Paul's evocation of suffering creation (the word Heidegger uses, *Benommenheit,* translated here as "captivation," already registers a dimension of shock and thus could just as easily be translated as "benumbedness"). Heidegger furthermore suggests that the phenomenology of profound boredom—a mood Heidegger posits as that of contemporary Dasein—provides a crucial site for the elaboration of the proximity of animal and human forms of exposure to alterity. In both animal captivation and human boredom, which Heidegger characterizes as an *"entrancement [Gebanntheit]* of Dasein within beings as a whole," the being in question is delivered over to an *arresting opacity. "In becoming bored,"* as Agamben summarizes Heidegger's claim (one that the latter unfolds over the course of some two hundred pages),

> *Dasein is delivered over* (ausgeliefert) *to something that refuses itself, exactly as the animal, in its captivation, is exposed* (hinausgesetzt) *in something unrevealed. . . .* In being left empty by profound boredom, something vibrates like an echo of that "essential disruption" that arises in the animal from its being exposed and taken in an "other" that is, however, never revealed to it as such. For this reason the man who becomes bored finds himself in the "closest proximity"—even if it is only apparent—to animal captivation. Both are, in their most proper gesture, open to a closedness; they are totally delivered over to something that obstinately refuses itself.

The conclusion to be drawn from this proximity of animal *Benom-menheit* and the human *Gebanntheit* that registers itself above all in the fundamental mood of boredom, is, in its own way, quite stunning: "The jewel set at the center of the human world and its *Lichtung*," Agamben writes, "is nothing but animal captivation; the wonder 'that beings *are*' is nothing but the grasping of the 'essential disruption' that occurs in the living being from its *being exposed in a nonrevelation* [my emphasis]." But this means, Agamben continues, that "*Dasein* is simply an animal that has learned to become bored; it has awakened *from* its own captivation *to* its own captivation. This awakening of the living being to its own being-captivated, this anxious and resolute opening to a not-open, is the human."[38]

By way of Santner's reading and interpolation of Heidegger one approaches, again, that open set of questions regarding refusal that phenomenological description of the human limit, from Europe's always already crossed border, makes unavoidable. At the human limit, at Europe's edge and interior frontier, at their illicit and constitutive proximities to the outsides they take in and cannot admit, it is possible to imagine the improper gesture of a refusal of the refusal, the closedness, to which one is given. This requires, first of all, imagining captivation not as the boundary that separates the human and the animal but as an internal boundary crossing the human. Moreover, one must then consider that internal boundary not in its relation to boredom but to the morbid drudgery or insupportable exhaustion of a kind of necropolitical labor redoubled as a kind of domestication or exclusionary assimilation in which life is given over to a proximity to death but in which proximity as being-toward is shadowed, as it were, by itself as being-apposite.[39] Life up, against, or under the shadow of death is life that shadows death, life apposing death. Imagine, in other words, that blackness lives this life; that it lives in and is a certain revelatory mode, not unlike that to which "Dasein is delivered over," that resembles the animal's captivation. This revelation of being exposed in something which is unrevealed is understood by Heidegger as boredom (an analytic formulation taken to its height in Walter Benjamin's *Passagen-Werk* but still, in a sense, captivated by a certain disrespect for things, a certain inability to be on to them in another, perhaps nonjudgmental way, a thinglike or animalistic solipsism of the unintended, the un- or nonintentional) and is, more to the point, understood as manifest in "something [that] vibrates like an echo of that 'essential disruption' that arises in the animal from its being exposed and taken in an 'other' that is, however, never revealed to it as such." To live in that revelation, in whatever attends or accrues to such revelation that is as unavailable to man as it is to the animal, is what blackness has to offer as escape. Meanwhile, Heidegger speaks of being left empty, like a vessel. But the empty vessel contains possibilities, as Heidegger will explore later in an analysis of the thing. Emptiness is an interiority. And what if the vessel, the bottle, is broken? What if the real issue is not boredom but violation as the essential and irreducible disruption? Emptiness will have always been the impossibility that masks what is dismissed as an absence of possibility. Meanwhile, there are traces of perfume that vibrate like an echo. They constitute (the shadow of) an essential disruption that attends being exposed to alterity, being taken by an Other. Blackness knows something about that. Can we now cut the opposition between that being exposed to alterity that attends being taken and being—in the free of Being, in the Open—on to things? It's not about boredom as a fateful proximity of humanity and animality-as-captivation; it is, rather, about escape and refusal within that proximity. Imagine what it means to say (with reference, perhaps, to the fucked-up natural history of intended or unintended racism or the fucked-up intended or unintended natural disaster of a hurricane): I ran from it and was still in it. The revelation that is, after all, in question, is not knowledge of boredom as an effect of being taken; it is, rather, flight. The vessel is not empty but broken. The vessel breaks. What of being-fugitive? Being-criminal? What if being-fugitive bears the possibility of a recalibration of the human, a reopening of, rather than an opening to, the not open? New world. New world.

As Levinas says, what is in question is the very humanity of man. But perhaps the very humanity of man is given in what Santner calls, after Heidegger, that "'essential disruption' that renders man 'creaturely.'" Santner says that disruption has "a distinctly political—or better: *biopolitical*—aspect, [that] names the threshold where life becomes a matter of politics and politics comes to inform the very matter and materiality of life" (12). If so, then the very humanity of man is given in the creaturely, in the thingly that inhabits man, and that man inhabits; the thingly and the creaturely that is manifest in and as vibratory echo, a fugitive phonochoreography in a certain step of the dance, as Derrida would say, in relation to which Levinas suffers a pronounced nonattunement. Meanwhile, what is given in the very humanity of man is given in and as the political. This is to say that "the 'essential disruption' that renders man 'creaturely'" emerges in and as the "'strife between unconcealedness and concealedness' that is at the core of human existence [as political life]," [and] "indeed . . . defines the very space of the *polis*." Santner adds, "Agamben has suggested that for Heidegger 'the originary political conflict between unconcealedness and concealedness will be, at the same time and to the same degree, that between the humanity and the animality of man.' By contrast, I am proposing that the emergence of the political *generates* a uniquely human form of animality or creatureliness" (13n22). This seems to me, however, to miss the point. What would it mean genuinely to investigate and inhabit the not but nothing other than man is, first and foremost, to demur from formulations that would envelop animality (or thingliness) in the human? The whole complex that is held within the confluence of terms like "the Open," enclosure, World, the empty, envelopment, border, interiority, concealedness, and unconcealedness is not an effect of the political but is, in a certain sense, that prehistory of the city of which Marx speaks. What Heidegger understands as a binary strife, in other words, has to be looked at again as, and by way of an optic of, a massive ensemble of differences.

This gets us more squarely to the question of the city, of (the space of) politics. The Heideggerian understanding of the tension between concealedness and unconcealedness as the very condition of possibility of politics and of the polis is what Agamben recalibrates and brings to bear on Schmitt as that interplay between animality and humanity that accompanies the essential disruption that renders man creaturely—being exposed in a nonrevelation, being delivered over to something that refuses itself. The difference in which I am interested arises from possibilities that are given in such fateful deliverance. Again, I want to consider politics as the refusal of that which is refused, and to consider as the exemplary political moment the phonochoreographic response to the vibratory echo that is of and that attends the essential disruption constituted by exposure to radical alterity. But this requires understanding that disruption/exposure as nonoriginary, noninitiatory, and attuned to a call and response without origin or end.

For Schmitt, the political abides in the possibility of the extreme case, the state of exception, wherein juridical normativity is suspended so that it can be protected. The distinction between friend and enemy is where that possibility, that constant interplay of danger and preservation, lives. Hence the friend/enemy distinction is the condition of possibility of politics. The key point here is that what initiates everything, for Schmitt and Agamben and the German-Jewish tradition Santner wants to illuminate, is the originary power of the sovereign. But how do we analyze the originary power of a figure that depends on the originary violation of the normativity that guarantees that power? If sovereign power is not subject to analysis, perhaps its vicissitudes open a pathway onto something that remains, for Santner and the tradition upon which he makes a claim, both incalculable and impossible: the exception to the state of exception; the one whose being is constituted by a refusal of what is refused. At stake, therefore, is the derivation of some sense of an exception to the rule of law *and* to the suspension of that rule that is, as it were, before that rule. The difficulty of analyzing an originary sovereign power whose foundations are originarily disturbed begins with the realization (which Santner expresses by way of Agamben) that the external border that separates friend from enemy presupposes an internal border within what might be called sovereign ground between law and an outside that will turn out to have been immanent to the law. This immanent outside is always understood as an internality that has been rendered ecstatic insofar as it must break the law that it safeguards in order to make the law safe. At the same time, the ecstatic-belonging given in the sovereign's rupture of the law that structures his authority can be called an etiolated exteriority. The immanent outsider has been rendered or, as it were, unmade in an activity that we might call the self-making of sovereign power. And because there is no analytic for the unmaking—the first refusal—to which sovereign power answers, no sense whatever of something like an anoriginal fugitivity to which the rule of law responds (insofar as sovereign power, in its capacity to suspend that rule for the sake of that rule, can withdraw its protection from this or that so-called friend), the question that Santner suspends, or overlooks, remains: *To what tradition can we turn for a thought of the outside?*

The unlikely answer—Kant's tradition—is made both more improbable and fantastically exact when that tradition is called by its most (im)proper name, which is the object of its most proper and appropriative disavowal: black radicalism. Part of what there is to be loved in (the devoted hatred of) Kant is his acknowledgment, which is inseparable from his racial conception, of the imagination in what he calls "its lawless freedom." If Agamben and Santner are right to suggest an interplay, at the border, between inside and outside, then perhaps it would be, as it were, *more right* to consider that the internal and the external presuppose one another within the general field—or, if you will, the borderless surround, the common underground—of the out from outside. My point is the necessity of imagining a productive difference, a political differing, a differential city or city-ing, that is irreducible to the distinction between friend and enemy. Such wondering gives significance to Schmitt's exposure of the law's paralegal transgression of its own limits, its law's extralegal essence or mystical foundation, and provides a clue regarding the inextinguishable possibility of a city that *is* its constitutive out$_2$side. At stake here is the relation of Schmitt, Agamben, and Santner to a Kantian tradition of the outside that was dark to Kant himself. This is to say that fundamental to that tradition of the outside is the play, or the absence, of its own desire for the outside (which is to say for that which is out from the outside). How can a tradition, which is necessarily defined (at least in part) precisely by some protocol for belonging, be given in the ceaseless activity of belonging's edgy, immanent critique and in the desire that persistence marks?

We can take up this question in the form of some contemplation of the history of the exception to the state of exception—the fugitive; the outlaw, the impossible domestic, the incorrigibly, promiscuously questioning maid; the one whom Cedric Robinson calls the "internal alien," she who disrupts the originary force of the very state that her choreographic refusal of assimilative exclusion (her ecstasy-belonging) guarantees.[40] If Santner's brilliant and suggestive characterizations are accurate, then what distinguishes the black radical tradition in its broadest conception (against the grain of something Levinas would never have bothered to develop into its summary dismissal) from the German-Jewish tradition of the discourse of "creaturely life" is a refusal of the inaugural force of sovereign power. The difference this refusal marks can be characterized as a sort of animism, an animagraphic exception, a phonographic swerve, a preservation—by way of cut augmentation—of what Robinson, again, calls the ontological totality. Such movement is to be distinguished from a thinking that assumes and submits itself to what Santner reads in Schmitt as

"the specific 'creativity' associated with such *ecstasy-belonging*:

> The exception is that which cannot be subsumed; it defies general codification, but it simultaneously reveals a specifically juridical formal element: the decision in absolute puprity. The exception appears in its absolute form when it is a question of creating a situation in which juridical rules can be valid. Every general rule demands a regular, everyday frame of life to which it can be factually applied and which is submitted to its regulations. The rule requires a homogeneous medium. This factual regularity is not merely an 'external presupposition' that the jurist can ignore; it belongs,

rather, to the rule's immanent validity. There is no rule that is applicable to chaos. Order must be established for juridical order to make sense. A regular situation must be created, and sovereign is he who definitely decides if this situation is actually effective. All law is 'situational law.' The sovereign creates and guarantees the situation as a whole in its totality. . . . The decision reveals the essence of State authority most clearly. Here the decision must be distinguished from the juridical regulation, and (to formulate it paradoxically) authority proves itself not to need law to create law [*daß sie, um Recht zu schaffen, nicht Recht zu haben braucht*]. (14)

After his citation of Schmitt, Santner continues, crucially:

What I am calling creaturely life is the life that is, so to speak, called into being, *ex-cited*, by exposure to the peculiar "creativity" associated with this threshold of law and non-law; it is the life that has been delivered over to the space of the sovereign's "ecstasy-belonging," or what we might simply call "sovereign *jouissance*."[41]

Black radicalism—the life that moves in the break between the thingly, the animal, and the human—may have been delivered over to "sovereign *jouissance*" but it is not called into being by exposure to that force. Blackness is present at its own making—it is the autopoeisis of imagined, imagining things. This is to say that the "peculiar 'creativity' associated with this threshold of law and non-law" has been subject to a massive historical mislocation (15). More precisely, the movements and directions of fit within that threshold (which is the constitutive outside of every household, every [moral or political] economy), the common animation in response to the forces that it anticipates and calls into being, are the active and anoriginal refusal, within that borderless border, of the imposition and denial of the regular situation that regulative power would institute. I am insisting on a distinction between being delivered over or being exposed to and being called into being by the sovereign power of the state of exception. Extraordinary rendition—by way of whatever point or door of no return and in the interest of whatever protection of whatever particular determination of the proper—might very well be understood as the most extreme example of the state's interpellative, violently transportive call, but that call is not a call into being. And if this is so, it means that the refusal of that call does not require an escape from being or from the question of its meaning. At stake, rather, is the question and the sociality of *being*'s escape, its essential fugitivity. This is not just about being excluded from the "regular situation" that one's irregular presence guarantees; it's about recognizing that the decision that creates the regular situation must be created and exists only in response to the everyday irruption of imagining things, "the anarchic sorcery of the facts," that calls it into being and cuts it. It is inaccurate and probably unfair to place Levinas in— let alone make him exemplary of—the German-Jewish tradition of which Santner speaks. And yet Levinas's work, especially when seen in its relation to that of Husserl, calls upon one to consider what it means to pledge oneself, as it were, to the "homogeneous medium" that the rule of law requires, the regular situation that it demands and withholds, the abstract and general equivalent that is called Europe and its texts, that field that exists and is open to the whole world only insofar as it moves within a violent rendering of the whole world open to itself and its expansive force.

My concern, then, is with the one whose guarantee of the situation places it in the gravest and most irrevocable danger; the one who ruptures normativity precisely by way of the captivating force of her having been captured by and excluded from it. This dis/possessive force of dis/possession is resistance to the decision; the refusal of the very verdict that one is subject to and gives; the gestural critique of judgment. There is an insistent previousness that evades the natal occasion of the state's interpellative call. One faithfully heretical translation of this Mackeyan poetic is Butler's temporal paradox, the unfadeable persistence of the question of who and what the state calls into being. This poetic and this paradox intimate what is revealed in a chain of reading that extends from Marx to Foucault to Michael Hardt: that resistance is prior to power. It's not about being called into being by—and in one's exposure to—sovereign creativity; it's about (the) being (of) whatever (creativity that) calls such creativity—that epiphenomenal interplay between decision and regulation—into being. This anarchic, jurisgenerative principle is blackness, whose open and transformative preservation turns out never to have been miraculous but merely a quotidian dispersion and predication of the miracle.

Meanwhile, Santner cites Schmitt's recognition that the jurisprudential state of exception is "strictly analogous to the concept of *miracle* in theology." As such, the state of exception is repudiated by Enlightenment rationalism even as it is linked to Santner's tradition by what Santner calls, again, "a dimension of the miraculous" (15). However, Santner here tries to articulate a difference. For that "dimension (in the ethico-political realm) . . . will pertain not to a repetition, not to a new instantiation of the topology of the sovereign exception, but rather to some form of its suspension, some way of *uncoupling from the mode of subjectivity/subjectivization proper to it*. It will involve, in a word, an intervention into the realm of "creaturely life" and the processes of its production" (15–16). Perhaps the suspension of the state of exception involves an intervention into the realm of "creaturely life," an uncoupling from subjection, a counterecstatic disavowal of that passionate attachment to it that Butler theorizes.[42] Is there a significant difference to be explored between "intervention into" and the intervention of that which has already been inhabited? This question arises in response to Santner's elaboration of the concept of the miracle, which moves by way of Slavoj Žižek: "In a discussion of the Israeli-Palestinian impasse, Žižek has suggested that such a miraculous dimension opened up with the gesture of the so-called refuseniks, those Israeli soldiers who refused to serve in the occupied territories. By way of such a gesture, the creaturely aspect of those subject to the ongoing state of exception that characterizes so much of life in the occupied territories is transformed into that of the *neighbor*" (16n28).

This elaboration, in turn, prompts further questions. What prevents the Žižek/Santner example from being another act wherein sovereignty differs from itself in the interest of maintaining itself? Is that miracle something other than the state of exception's mirror image, its self-representation, its autopositioning as opposed to autopoesis? What's the relation between autopoesis and the interplay of refusal and response? Isn't the auto-poetic neighborliness of the Israeli Defense Force soldiers' refusal a response to or echo of a history of refusal of the ones who have been refused, delivered over to enjoyment, made subject to an expropriative expansion that moves by way of the imposition of the proper? Isn't the refuseniks' refusal in response to an uprising? This is to say that what keeps it from being merely another sovereign act (a gesture of benevolent power) is that it is a response to an ongoing socioethical upheaval, an enactment of enjoyment against being enjoyed and enjoined. Hence it disrupts whatever presumed priority accrues to external boundaries or internal walls. Perhaps prayer is a kind of uprising to which the miracle is a response. Perhaps *intifada* is a kind of prayer, or *al-masha* the interinanimation of uprising and appeal, an eruptive performance of impossible translation and transportation best understood as the persistent insistence of a Palestinian everyday, of Palestinian social life. Perhaps the Palestinian everyday, under the present conditions to which it has been made subject but which do not call it into being, is a durative phono-choreographic operation of mourning, of a different weeping, in the interest of another morning. A Palestinian thing Levinas would not understand.

Such incapacity of (the regulative) understanding can be further illuminated through Santner's invocation and analysis of Benjamin's notion of natural history (*Naturgeschichte*), its placement against the backdrop of Kant's notion of natural history which it not only echoes but also prefigures. Santner writes:

> In Benjamin's parlance, *Naturgeschichte* has to do with . . . the breakdown and reification of the normative structures of human life and mindedness. It refers, that is, not to the fact that nature also has a history but rather that the artifacts of human history tend to acquire an aspect of mute, natural being at the point where they begin to lose their place in a viable form of life (think of the process whereby architectural ruins are reclaimed by nature). This paradoxical exchange of properties between nature and history that constitutes the material density of natural historical being, can be thought of in exactly the opposite way as well. Because human beings not only have natures but also *second natures,* when an artifact loses its place in an historical form of life—when that form of life decays, becomes exhausted, or dies—we experience it as something that has been *denaturalized,* transformed into a mere relic of historical being. To put it yet another way, natural history is born out of the dual possibility that life can persist beyond the death of the symbolic forms that gave it meaning and that symbolic forms can persist beyond the death of those that gave them human vitality. Natural history transpires against the background of this space between real and symbolic death, this space of the "undead."[43]

Ruins are, in this sense, analogous to the bare facts that Kant attributes to mere natural description in its difference from a natural historiography guided by principle.[44] This is to say that a further analogy is implied, that between teleology and viable forms of life. Consideration of that analogy demands some investigation of the interplay between a cultural and social formation—a communal mode of existence—and the imaginative construction of a historical trajectory that conveys upon every manifestation of communal activity not only its significance but its animation. Santner is interested in the interplay of naturalization and denaturalization that attends the human artifact's loss of place within a historical form of life. What transport or displacement is supposed to reduce to mere fact loses its voice and becomes a thing of nature that is, precisely in the severity of that transformation, irreducibly unnatural. At stake, Santner adds, in this homelessness and statelessness of the artifact is its persistence, the insistent fugitivity of its life in the underground, the outskirts, the borderless border zone between "real and symbolic death":

> Natural history, as Benjamin understands it, thus points to a fundamental feature of human life, namely that the symbolic forms in and through which this life is structured can be hollowed out, lose their vitality, break up into a series of enigmatic signifiers, "hieroglyphs" that in some way continue to address us—get under our psychic skin— though we no longer possess the code to their meaning. For Benjamin, natural history ultimately names the ceaseless repetition of such cycles of emergence and decay of human orders of meaning, cycles that are, for Benjamin—and this is where the Schmittian background can be felt—always connected to violence. It furthermore provides the key to the symbolic mode privileged by the baroque dramatists who experienced life in seventeenth-century Germany as one of irremediable exposure to the violence of natural historical temporality: *allegory*. Allegory is the symbolic mode that most vividly engages with man's thrownness into the "bad infinity" of natural historical "progression" (think here of Benjamin's own allegory of the angel of history staring helplessly at the wreckage of such "progress").[45]

What's the relation between the loss of vitality Benjamin diagnoses, and which he describes as a kind of broken series whose message seems lost in the pathological discontinuity that paradoxically characterizes their continued address, and that which Kant might be said to consider a fall from the discovery of the purposive to that form of impoverished instrumental rationality that constitutes "empirical groping"?[46] Perhaps this: that for Benjamin natural history is best understood as the interplay between the animation of unmethodical observation by what Kant calls teleological principle and the constant return to, and invention of, things taken for inanimate natural facts. Insofar as Benjamin understands natural history as a repeating cycle of "emergence and decay," wherein forms of life are disrupted by the radical violence of representational seizure, his notion of natural history could be said to incorporate what Kant would understand to be the failure fully to achieve natural history. For Kant, purposiveness animates the theoretical attitude, thereby creating a dilemma for the phenomenologist whose antipathy to teleological principle must somehow be made to correspond with a historical trajectory that brings metaphysics and the metaphysical people to life. Allegory is the privileged symbolic mode for attending to this dilemma and its violent, attendant history. Benjamin theorizes the relation between allegory and violent history and requires us to consider that allegory be understood as a form of violence itself to the extent that it enacts the seizures it intends.

At the same time, Kant's defense of "the use of teleological principles in philosophy"—which turns on the distinction between natural history and the indeterminate cataloging of the things of nature—can be understood also as a defense of allegory where it is understood, in something like Benjamin's concept, as the petrification of historical movement, its reduction or concentration into a skull, a dead artifact. More precisely, Kant's defense could be understood as a kind of antecedent mirror image of that to which Benjamin attends. While Benjamin is concerned with that allegorical seizure of history that the fossil implies, Kant seeks to justify an anticipatory animation of that fossil by the narrative/meaning it will retrospectively be said to embody. Somehow, the animative force must be deanimated—or at least placed in an irreducible proximity to the loss or absence of *anima*—to carry out its proper operations.

Deeper still, it is race that exists, for Kant, as the exemplary teleological principle insofar as it indicates "a radical particularity that announces a common descent," is animated by that descent against the force of its own thingly congealment or fossilization, and thereby organizes a collection of differences or natural facts into a meaningfully developmental ensemble.[47] For Kant, the differences between "the Negro and other humans"—between that exemplary fossil or stilled natural fact who is being given over to a preintentional complex of impulse that is and works a seemingly empty interior as if from outside and the self-possessed subjectivity that human bodies are understood as being meant to carry—are too great to be attributed to "a simple play of nature" or a "merely accidental" imprint.[48] This irreducible difference or *differend* that marks and is the Negro, that constitutes the Negro as the necessarily (un)gendered embodiment of race as the teleological principle par excellence, punctuates the natural history of man, is and confers its rhythm. Those differences—which place the Negro on the utopographic or subterranean outskirts of the human that turn out to constitute the very interiority of the human—are animated by an analytic of purposiveness, are brought to life, as it were, by the kind of allegorical assertion that Benjamin reads as most clearly revealing "man's subjection to nature" but which might also be read as man's subjection to subjection. Kant might say, as if after both Benjamin and Santner, that man's relation to himself is crossed with borders, that there is something like a racial crossing—manifest in and as the strife Kant recognized between natural history and empiricist catalog that, for Benjamin, *is* natural history—in the nature of things or which, more precisely, constitutes the passage over the asymptotic gap between the world of things and the political mise-en-scène in which object and subject animate one another under the sign of (necessarily European, necessarily masculinist) man.

It's important to note again that what lies beyond Levinas is a form of mourning that is, for him, unworthy of the name insofar as it bespeaks impulse rather than intention. Indeed, Levinas could be understood as implying that a dancing civilization is, as it were, an improper form of life. It is left for us to ask to what natural history mournful dance belongs? Perhaps one that reinitializes and then disruptively transcends that fateful interplay of Kantian progress and the arrhythmic force of the state of exception that is the very structure of the political space-time known as Europe (or The [necessarily European] World). In this instance mournful dance must also be understood as something other than that refusal of loss that constitutes melancholia. Once again we are brought to the threshold of considering the ethicopolitical implications of a refusal of sovereign power's "right" to dispossess that is enacted by way of a claim upon, an owning of, dispossession.

However, for Santner, allegory, melancholia, and the creaturely are bound to one another by what might be called the natural history of violence:

> Allegory is . . . the symbolic mode proper to the experience of irremediable exposure to the violence of history, the rise and fall of empires and orders of meaning, the endless cycle of struggles for hegemony; it is furthermore what defines the posture of melancholy, the affect so intimately linked to the dimension we have been calling "the creaturely." One should add that the "posture of melancholy" had, both for Benjamin and the cultural tradition at issue, a quite literal meaning. The allegorical sensibility associated with the melancholic disposition and "immersion in the life of creaturely things" bent the back forward, drew the gaze earthward: "Everything saturnine points down into the depths of the earth. . . . Here the downward gaze is characteristic of the saturnine man, who bores into the ground with his eyes."

. . . To bring it to a formula, creaturely life is just life abandoned to the state of exception/emergency, that paradoxical domain in which law has been suspended in the name of preserving law. And once again, what is included in the state of exception is not simply outside the law but rather inside an *outlaw-dimension internal to the law*, subject not to law but rather to sovereign *jouissance*.[49]

What's at stake in the reduction of creaturely life to that which is abandoned to the state of exception? Again, what if there is another agential mode—not the sovereignty of the state of exception and of the outlaw dimension internal to the law but the agency of an other outlaw, the one who is abandoned to the law even as she is abandoned by the law, the out$_2$law who is not internal to the law but out from the law's outside? These questions are at issue in Levinas's trajectory in that he begins with an articulation against the sovereign decision, the re-creation of the regular situation in its inevitable relation to the state of exception (as Benjamin most clearly and particularly understands that relation), only to succumb to that situation in his embrace of the homogeneous medium—the abstract and general equivalent known as Europe or European Man. Santner is interested in the life that is abandoned to the state of emergency and he justly understands the German/Jewish tradition he seeks to illuminate as the long inhabitation of that abandonment—the creaturely form of life. My interest is in a mode of life that I'll uneasily, perhaps temporarily, call *thingly* insofar as it is determined not by abandonment to the state of emergency but by envelopment in the regular situation. What is implied here is that a fundamental and irreducible difference obtains between, on the one hand, the "now dispersed, now chronic" state of exception in which erstwhile subjects melancholically refuse the loss of the citizenship and subjectivity they never had and, on the other hand, the pointed, targeted grasp of the regular situation that is refused by the things to whom subjectivity and citizenship were always refused. To say that the suspension of law in the name of the law's preservation *is* the regular situation is to erect a rickety bridge between forms of life whose historical nonconvergence defies the commerce between them. At the same time, the break, the borderless border that divides and surrounds them, might constitute the field in which radical particularity announces a common dissent. That field is a common underground—the irregular situation.

Now, having unjustly attached Levinas to the tradition Santner studies, I am relieved finally to arrive at Santner's principal invocation of him. Santner will bring us round, by way of a kind of replication, to the border that crosses Levinas's work.

In a 1935 essay on shame recently published under the title, "On Escape," Emmanuel Levinas has suggested (in a still Heideggerian vein) that shame does not simply refer to one's reduction to one's animal nakedness, but pertains rather to the dimension where one is, as Levinas puts it, *riveted to oneself*, placed in that (non)relation to an opacity that is one's own being: "Nakedness is shameful when it is the sheer visibility of our being, of its ultimate intimacy. And the nakedness of our body is not that of a material thing, antithesis of spirit, but the nakedness of our total being in all its fullness and solidity of its most brutal expression of which we could not fail to take note." To flesh out the nature of the materiality at issue in this abandonment to oneself, Levinas refers to the famous scene in *City Lights* in which Chaplin's tramp swallows a whistle at a party given by his benefactor; every time he hiccups, one will recall, a whistle emanates from his body. As Levinas puts it, the whistle "works like a recording device, which betrays the discrete manifestations of a presence that Charlie's legendary tramp costume barely dissimulates. . . . It is . . . our intimacy, that is, our presence to ourselves, that is shameful" (40–41).

The insight Levinas attains here is of a shame made apparent by way of irregular and unregulatable sound. This is sound mediated by a kind of technology, sound irreducible to words, to speech; bodily presence is cut and augmented by a technological irruption, by something on the order of an invasion of an interior instantiated by that interior, or by the outside that it has taken in. The shameful notice or notation or excess of notation that marks the material irruption of our presence to ourselves is given in/as sound. It disrupts, and is given in the disruption, of a relation: a scar, a rivet, or the mark of a rivet or being riveted which is the mark, in its turn, of something Lacan would call an irreducible "dehiscence at the very heart of the organism," an interinanimation of bridge and chasm.[50] The whistle, in its technomateriality, its performative reproductivity, defies enclosure. This is what Levinas attends, hears, disavows. But what is that opening? How is it to be understood? This goes back to the question of exposure and what it reveals of the regulative attitude to an insistently previous aperture. One wants to inhabit the break, the broken vessel. Meanwhile, the clear-headed, the clear-eyed, can only understand the open(ing) as a ruse, a cunning of enclosure.

Meanwhile, one desires something as problematic as a kind of Heideggerian revenge that requires turning the Heideggerian imagining of the imagining thing against Heidegger's seal. Meanwhile, for Santner, creaturely life is enclosed in the status of "a by-product of exposure to what we might call *excitations of power*, those enigmatic bits of address and interpellation that disturb the social space—and bodies—of his protagonists" (24). Meanwhile, in the premature and postexpectant colonial situation, the song and dance of thingly life prompts certain engines of exposure like a ring. Here is Santner's mediated gesture toward the prompt to which he (and, of course, Levinas) cannot quite respond:

> In a brilliant essay on Shakespeare's the *Tempest*, Julia Lupton has re-
> ferred to the same German-Jewish tradition I have been invoking here
> to capture the structural and historical specificity of that most famous
> incarnation of creaturely life in the Western tradition, the figure of
> Caliban. It is precisely the concept of creaturely life she develops there
> that allows her to chart a new course of interpretive possibilities be-
> yond the binary opposition that has framed so much of the scholarship
> on the play; that is, humanist universalization, on the one hand, and
> culturalist particularization/postcolonial historicization, on the other.[51]

What does it mean to dismiss so cavalierly, as the underside or under-ground of a binary, postcolonial historicization (as opposed to humanist universalization), especially insofar as Santner has established the necessity of being-historical (of, more precisely, natural history as the violent, cyclical emergence and submergence of forms of life) for the analytic of the creaturely? What is eschewed, in the interest of a kind of transhistorical appeal to the history of the state of emergency, is the no less problematic history of the regular situation that remains unthought or relegated to the outskirts of an other-wise intense thoughtfulness of Santner's work. This dismissal of the postco-lonial historicization of the regular situation is business, not personal. It's encoded in Santner's procedure; especially in the invocation, at which we'll glance shortly, of Freud's universalizing claims. This procedure presupposes the absence of a universalizing tendency in postcolonial or, more properly, anticolonial critique. This is, of course, upon perfunctory reading, an impos-sible case to make.

What's at stake, here, is a precision given in the blurring of the creaturely, the thingly, and the human. When Lupton charts the decline of the under-standing of the creature—"anyone or anything that is produced or controlled by an agent, author, master, or tyrant" (cc 1)—what comes into relief is a congealment of creative process in the material figure of the inert slave that merges with Kant's understanding of the thing as that to which nothing can be imputed (except, perhaps, inclinations which, on the one hand, she is subject to and, on the other hand, are not only imputed to the thing by Kant himself but constitute the irruption of a kind of lawlessness that will threaten the subject himself). The thing—in a supposed absence of any capacity for spontaneity that is troubled by inclination; against the grain of that regulation of inclination that interdicts the autonomy it is meant to protect; doubly outside, therefore, the subject's constitutional state of emergency—could be said enigmatically to inspire the paradoxically enveloping and prophylactic force of universalist/humanist comprehension. As Santner reiterates,

> Once again, it is not the mere fact of being in a relation of subject to sovereign that generates creaturely "non-nature" but rather the exposure to an "outlaw" dimension of law internal to sovereign authority. The state of exception or emergency is that aspect of law that marks a threshold of undecidability proper to the functioning of law/sovereign authority: the "master's discourse" in the state of exception marks a *sanctioned suspension of law*, an outside of law included within the law. Creaturely life emerges precisely at such impossible thresholds.[52]

But what of the outlaw that prompts the apparatuses of exposure? The thingly, the ensemble of imagining things, emerges in the recognition that she who is relegated to the status of the creature is present at her own making. To be present at one's own making, to exist in and as unmaking presence, is to operate (within) a certain fundamental inability: to see the face or the eyes of the one who is outside of thought. This disability, this specific blindness to the abject other's visage, is the moment of a politics (of sound) before ethics. When this incapacity is claimed it can be said to approach a more proper naming as an attitude European assertion will have rendered wholly inappropriate: that what one sees is that there is no one who remains outside of thought. That claim is a moment of identification in the radical disidentification with the violence of the sovereign *and* the benevolence of the righteous man. It's the cramped and capacious room of a political scene of overhearing, the sound barrier's opening, an out attunement to a *Sprechgesang* that had been thought impossible. At the bar you tap your foot, secretly, inside your shoe, for now. In the club, in the gap, in the band, you get a hump in your back. (Caliban's) cramps respond to a capacious choreography, body writing what will write on it, a new kind of kick or some kind of kicking played out by a thousand twangling instruments, like a mobile ensemble of banjos. Lupton is at least hip to Caliban's eternal internal alienation from his maternal home as, precisely, "the possibility of another type of subjectivation," in Santner's words. Can the concept of the creaturely approach the dispossessive essence of the thing of darkness that the broken sovereign must acknowledge as his own?

Such acknowledgment confirms "an avidity for the reason of things" (32). Santner quotes this phrase of Lacan but there is nothing to be made of it. It occurs in Lacan's text within a counterfactual construction as that with which the child is unconcerned in all of his questioning, all of his *whys*. Rather, the child, according to Lacan, is testing the adult, seeking fissures and cracks in the discourse of the Other since it is in the break that the Other's desire can be apprehended. My engagement with this phrase would not only release it from its oppositional function but also recalibrate its internal stresses insofar as what remains to be thought, outside of the Cartesian elaboration, is the *un*reason of (thinking) things. I'm interested in this phrase—which places *cogito* in that history of madness that takes place on an other shore where Descartes, Foucault, and Derrida gather together as a choir to discuss it—as if it were a detachable component, part of some modular calculus of the incalculable. This is what I hope my *whys* reveal precisely in their response to a discourse whose envelopment and expulsion of me and all my friends only repeats its relation to things inside and out. In this regard, Santner's invocation of Jean Laplanche's notion of "internal alien-ness maintained, held in place by external alien-ness; external alien-ness, in turn, held in place by the enigmatic relation of the other to his own internal alien" harkens to Denis Diderot's invocation of "the hideous blackamoor" who occupies normative interiority, on the one hand, and Robinson's critical praise song for the internal aliens of the black radical tradition, on the other.[53] In the end, this is Santner's fullest, clearest, and most invested definition of creaturely life: "Unconscious mental life gets mobilized around such enigmatic signifiers that can never be fully metabolized, translated into the projects that make up the life of the ego. They persist as loci of signifying stress, excitations linked to but not absorbed by our life in the space of meaning. It is the excess of pressure that emerges at such sites—really a kind of life in excess both of our merely biological life and of our life in the space of meaning—that I am calling *creaturely*" (34).

This seems to me a severe and sad reduction. It's not that it's not true but that one feels here the residue of the loss of history. Reduction to Freud's Euro-universalist frame is Santner's genuine area of concern. He wants to investigate "the threshold where life takes on its specific biopolitical intensity" and to consider "the creaturely life manifest in . . . cringed bodies," perhaps in the interest of that redemption Benjamin hoped could be attained by passage through creaturely life (34, 25). In conclusion, Santner invokes Paul Celan, Benjamin's devoted reader and the last in the line that Santner is trying to extend: "In his famous speech given on the occasion of receiving the Georg Büchner Prize in 1960, Celan offers an account of poetic discourse as one addressed, precisely, from and to the creaturely dimension of human life. In the speech, Celan develops his conception of the poet's task by way of a reading of Büchner's prose and plays, which he locates within the field of tensions between the high artificiality of art—of *Kunst*—and what Celan refers to as 'the angle of inclination'—the *Neigungswinkel*—of man's creatureliness" (36).

> Celan is very likely alluding here to Benjamin's remarks about the bent backs—the constitutive cringe—of so many of Kafka's figures. But toward the end of *Malte*, Rilke provides a scene that Celan may also have had in mind when he wrote these words. In it Rilke's protagonist finally encounters the blind newspaper salesman he had worked so hard at avoiding. What he encounters is, we might say, a fellow creature: "Immediately I knew that my picture of him was worthless. His absolute abandonment and wretchedness, unlimited by any precaution or disguise, went far beyond what I had been able to imagine. I had understood neither the angle of his face [*den Neigungswinkel seiner Haltung*] nor the terror which the inside of his eyelids seemed to keep radiating into him." It is, of course, crucial that Malte experiences this moment as a kind of revelation, one that seems to involve the elevation of the creature to the status of *neighbor*: "My God, I thought with sudden vehemence, so you really *are*. There are proofs of your existence. I have forgotten them all and never even wanted any, for what a huge obligation would lie in the certainty of you. And yet that is what has just been shown to me."[54]

Why is it that when Celan alludes to a particular historicization it is raised to the level of the universal, as if the colonial occasion were, on the one hand, necessarily less than that of the *Shoah* and, on the other hand, fundamentally detachable? This is the date to which we must remain attuned. Levinas and Santner are linked by a shadow bridge, a kind of procedural span: the dismissal of a certain hope for the postcolonial future. They share the attentiveness of the one who recognizes, and fails to recognize, the ongoing failure of envelopment. At the same time, they are inattentive to what coalesces at the intersection of the creaturely, the thingly, and the human. Let's call it a certain anticolonial angle (of incidence or inclination). Meanwhile, did blackness make the German-Jewish discourse on the creaturely possible in Weimar Germany in ways that are not unlike how it makes the criminal imagination/teleological principle possible for Kant? This is a question that must, for now, remain suspended even as I remain interested in blackness as a kind of *metoikic*, if not psychotic, enclave outside of a doubly etiolated sense of a certain possibility in and for personality in man. I'm interested in the straightening of bent backs; in the little girl who sells the sun and the one who carries her, not Rilke's blind newspaper vendor or the one who encounters him. I want to identify not with creaturely life but with the stolen life of imagining things. It's not enough for poets to encounter the creature as the mirror of their own heretofore avoided powerlessness; not enough to encounter the cringe as one's own; at stake, rather, is the straightening, the resistance, the interiority behind the eyelids of what is projected on to them, all of which move, perhaps paradoxically, by way of cants and curves, extensions, broken angles, cut circles. This movement is on and in the serrated edge of a history whose relinquishment enacts the loss of history in general.

It is in his attention to the demand for German-Jewish assimilation which "was at some level structured as an 'impossible interpellation' . . . that involved an exposure to an arresting opacity that could only be experienced as a persistent disruption and disorientation . . . in the self-understanding of those Jews who tried to assume the demand," that Santner comes to approach the borderless border, the "biopolitical *animation*" that distinguishes the human from the animal (39). That border is the zone of things grasped and disposed; blackness is the insistently previous animation of that which will have been serially, cyclically rendered inanimate (as the dead, as the [reified] thing) *and* brutally, invasively revived. But there is a second aspect of the process of assimilation in which Santner is more interested:

> For secular Jews, that is, the laws of normative Judaism—the commandments of the Torah—were themselves experienced to a very large extent as a set of opaque rules—enigmatic signifiers—with which

they could no longer identify even if they did not fully cease to feel addressed by them. It is against this background that we can understand Gershom Scholem's characterization, in his correspondence with his friend Walter Benjamin, of the status of Holy Writ for Kafka as the "nothingness of revelation." He writes, in a now famous letter to Benjamin,

> You ask what I understand by the 'nothingness of revelation'? I understand by it a state in which revelation appears to be without meaning, in which it still asserts itself, in which it has *validity* but *no significance* [*in dem sie gilt, aber nicht bedeutet*]. A state in which the wealth of meaning is lost and what is in the process of appearing (for revelation is such a process) still does not disappear, even though it is reduced to the zero point of its own content, so to speak.

This understanding of the distinctive predicament of the secular Jew as an exposure to a "valid" yet empty revelation might be seen as a late variation of the Pauline trope of the distinction between letter and spirit; the Jew is exposed to the "dead" letter without spirit and thus "writes" the letter on the surface of his body in the form of circumcision (rather than take it up into the spiritual depths of his heart). Indeed, from the perspective of the secular mind, there may be no more powerful image of "validity without significance" than this cut on the body in the name of the Law.[55]

What this second aspect of assimilation reveals can then be understood as something already rehearsed by secular Jews—namely "the psychic—or better, creaturely—complexities of life abandoned to the validity or force of law beyond any meaning or signification" (41). In a footnote, Santner justly points out what he predictably calls "one of the most stunning performances of Jewish self-hatred in modern letters," Otto Weininger's definition, in *Sex and Character*, of Jews (and women [and, of course one wonders about other groups who failed even to bring themselves to Weininger's attention]) as "beings who fundamentally lack access to this dimension of practical reason as conceived by Kant" in which self-legislation and, if you will, self-understanding constitute the capacity of "entering into a true social contract, of . . . forming a genuine state as a union of . . . beings with reason" (40n62). It is my contention that "an avidity for the reason of things" makes possible an appositional response to Weininger's vicious Kantianism. What about the defiance of self-legislation as the terminally repeating instant of the state of exception rather than the implied protest that one has that capacity? What kind of city is imagined in such dissent? In the face of Weininger's assertion, and the philosophical line that animates it, one must resist the urge to cringe. Instead, and by way of another mode of animation altogether, *dance*. This is to say that one must—against the massive range of difficulties that accompany ossified, exclusionary habits of thought and the expression and repression of guilt those habits engender—attend to what had been dismissed as the impossible signification or empty revelation of an inappropriate and abject, as opposed to sovereign, *jouissance*. How do we think the aesthetics, ethics, and politics of enjoyment offered by a civilization that dances and suffers? Eventually by way of a detour into the realm where mechanical reproduction and animation mix in a form of "stone-age" filmmaking (that the artist himself describes as primitive even as it jolts the meaning of that term into whatever borderless border surrounds modernity), a zone of fantasmatically irreducible instrumentality where things figure things, where certain animative offices of the unburied dead refresh what is already given as not but nothing other than a certain surreal(ist) awakening, where the question of history is invoked in order that we might appose ourselves to it.[56]

On the question of a certain modality of unintended racism, South African artist William Kentridge writes: "White guilt is much maligned. Its most dominant feature is its rarity. It exists in small drops taken at infrequent intervals and its effects do not last for long."[57] This statement invokes one of the subjects of Kentridge's work: that ongoing, irregularly disrupted avoidance of looking at oneself that is always accompanied by the knowledge that one is nevertheless seen by someone else, that the mirror translates that truth about you that you hide or can't show and that only you are supposed both to see and not to see. To have one's eyes sounded, to be deeply regarded in reflection, from behind, from outside, by an absent one given as the third (non)person, mis/taken for the appositional impropriety who props up that face-to-face drama of self and other and who is assumed to make no observations, distilled into the thing who in her absence fills the world: this particular form of theater, this particular scene of being seen, articulated across a range of manifestations, is the ethicopolitical essence of Kentridge's work. As he says, this politics is one of ambiguity and contradiction, where confusion lurks behind the clarity of rhetoric; and as Rosalind Krauss might not quite say, the open-endedness of Kentridge's medium and form parallels the open-endedness of an ethicopolitical aesthetic in appositional proximity to a range of histories of enclosure.[58]

One way to approach Kentridge's events and things is as the unfinished but countermelancholic constitution of an ethical sociality and sociology of improper mourning, where what you are in the mirror is the one you love, the ones you desire, the one you lost, the ones who see you, obliquely, as if from another shore inside you. To pose that looking into one's own eyes is always also looking into the eye of the I as another than the others—this is a paradox of self-portraiture within which Kentridge moves. For Kentridge, self-portraiture, however mediated, implies a kind of dispossessive self-possession—an owning up, an owning of the self and its actions, a taking of responsibility however intermittently, however glancingly, that moves by way of a renunciation of the privileged impossibility that has accrued to normative conceptions of the self. So that to speak, here, of a kind of glancing, deferred, layered, disrupted self-possession is also always to speak of what happens when you look straight into *her* eye. Ultimately, the task will have been to devise a scene of objection played out in the resonant, resistant insistence of things; to face up to the challenge of this intermittent guilt, this particular being white and its other$_2$, with new forms of theatricality for the new city, in which being there together is enough, like some final and broken soliloquy of the interior paramour, the hidden blackamoor, who came from some world up ahead of us to bring the city magic, joyful noise. There is a gaze, by way of mirror and bridge-like mutual telescope between two worlds, and then the singing starts and then the parade of the mirror world resumes, machinery of the orange circle, penetrated eye, procession of the world of your dark, hidden continent that looks at you from being looked at like an outsider. I'm very interested in Kentridge's work, in part, because of the space that something out from the outsider takes there and the truth and beauty such pre/occupation produces.

In working through the attention Krauss pays to Kentridge's interinanimation of drawing and cinema, one must take note of the great importance she assigns to his understanding of South African history and the moral imperatives it produces as "the rock" whose escape is the job of the artist: "To escape this rock is the job of the artist. These two constitute the tyranny of our history. And escape is necessary, for as I stated, the rock is possessive, and inimical to good work. I am not saying apartheid, or indeed, redemption, are not worthy of representation, description or exploration. I am saying that the scale and weight with which this rock presents itself is inimical to the task."[59]

The rock looms, like and as some Friedian thing whose objective, objectional incompleteness is mistaken for etiolation. It is explicitly distinct, according to Kentridge, from subjects (of art) whose origins lie outside a particular object, which is to say a particular sociohistorical construct, a particular historical sediment or geological occasion whose lunar demand is the absorption of all available light. The rock is an anthropomorphic monument with the weight and scale of an unavoidably aggressive (which is in part to say animated or reanimated or reinspirited) body whose presence, both subterranean and extraterrestrial, might easily be mistaken for the dead or, more precisely, the unanimatable. The rock is ordinary, the everyday spectacle of subjection that is horrible precisely because it gets in our heads and in our ways and in our eyes and in our images of ourselves like dust, threatening to subordinate art and the desire for art—threatening to subjugate "the imagination . . . in its lawless freedom" to the force of subjection's strict exchanges.[60]

The formulations Kentridge makes regarding the rock are also crucial especially in their resonance with a phrase heard quite often in the late 1980s and early 1990s as the anti-apartheid struggle rose in intensity in the United States. It was a phrase uttered in tribute to black South African women engaged in that struggle and it said—simply, roughly—that when you strike a black South African woman you strike a rock. I want to think about the commerce between these choruses of the rock by way of some questions Kentridge raises regarding the provenance and destiny of the figure called Nandi, a black woman who surveys the traces of blood and trauma that mark and are hidden by the South African landscape and whose irruption into the mind and eye of Felix Teitelbaum is so fundamental to Kentridge's *Felix in Exile*. Felix is a central character in Kentridge's projected drawings. He is often seen from the back, naked, gazing into a landscape that reveals to him the bodies it hides or into a mirror that reflects the intensity and ecstasy of the already given impurity that animates his person. The character's resemblance to the artist is often remarked and perhaps they can both best be understood as part of a tradition of thingly animation that demands a more thorough consideration of the interplay between these two formulations of the rock. Such consideration is crucial not only to addressing those questions about Nandi but to understanding something fundamental to Kentridge's work in its inhabitation and expression of—and in its being possessed of and dispossessed by—that singing, dancing, differently mourning civilization that Levinas could neither think nor imagine.[61]

More precisely, I would like to think about the ways the figure of Nandi could be understood as moving in resistance to the notion of the rock that Kentridge puts forward and that his critics take up without further geological (which is to say sociological; which is to say aesthetic) investigation. Nandi moves from outside and in the name of and as another rock in resistance to the rock. Such resistance demands that we consider that the job of the artist might be to escape by both resisting and being the rock, but we have to take care in understanding the significance of the term *resist*. We may speak of the resistance of the artist and we may speak, after Levinas + Kentridge, of the "propagation" of "*fortuna*" in the artwork as the mark of the resistance *to* the artist, a kinaesthetic irruption of ensemblic anonymity that emerges in conjunction with that resistant work *of* the artist that moves, finally, in an improvisational scarring of the idea of the work itself and the normative subjectivity who intends it.[62] This chain of resistances is at the heart of Nandi's seemingly mysterious itinerary. To think Nandi as not but nothing other than the rock is to demand some consideration of the rock's subtle theatricality, a thingly appositional proximity in the political scene that stems from no simple, undifferentiated presence. Apartheid and the moral imperatives that continue to arise from it are no mere monoliths. The problem is not in the thing—as if it had no difference, no syntax; as if redemption were not always already broken, resisted. Fortunately, the artists and critics we admire (like Kentridge and Krauss) do not and cannot foreclose this performance—this resistance of the object given in the insistence of things—that animates and discomposes the artwork.[63] Kentridge says he works in the narrow gap where optimism is kept in check and nihilism is kept at bay. But Nandi—the pool of her lost body, the fluidity of dust, the absence that fills the world—does not remain there. Rather, by taking the space of the outside/r in the work, she enacts a kind of transportation whose effects cannot be contained. This off-stride irruption—what it is to stumble, what it is to shave too deeply—is the gift, to both Felix Teitelbaum and William Kentridge, of Nandi's complex presence for which we still must attempt to account.

Speaking of the provenance of *Felix in Exile*, Kentridge writes:

> The third and central starting point was a series of police forensic photographs of murder victims. In fact, the starting point was not the photos, but a friend's description of having seen these photos of bodies in landscapes. In fact, nearly all of the photos are of bodies in small rooms or small open spaces, alleys, corridors. But in my head, sight

unseen, the description of them as bodies in landscapes was prior. The photographs served as references for drawings that in a sense had already constructed themselves. In the end, the photographs I used were ones which came closest (in most, not all cases) to these prior images I had of corpses in landscapes. Which if I think back now, have their roots in the body lying on the ground in Goya's painting *Tres de Mayo* (*The Third of May, 1814*).[64]

By way of a series of receding origins that is iconic of the very idea of tradition, Kentridge gives us a glimpse of his understanding of the hard, heavily weighted place that stands in opposition to the rock of South African history and its moral imperatives—the tradition of image making of the European masters that he describes as "visions of a state of grace, an achieved paradise" that "is inadmissible to me."[65] That tradition stands, in its weightiness, as a problem for Kentridge because of what he sees as its valuation of formal innovation above content and the dangers in content of sentimentality and certainty. Such presentness is not Kentridge's terrain; he traverses the theatrical space between the rock and a hard place. However, I would like to consider that terrain as a borderless border rather than a circumscribed in-between. Nandi is not-in-between. Kentridge continues:

> As with all the films, the process of construction is one of moving backwards and forwards from images as they emerge. After about a week of drawing, there are approximately forty seconds of film. When these rushes are viewed, the first hypothetical film is formed around them, and the next few weeks' work is based on this. When this new work is in turn put onto the editing table, and inter-cut with the first material, new pressures and values are put onto the first images. Things tangential to the film suddenly become central to it. Other elements that I had thought of as vital do not maintain their place in the film. In this way, for example, the Cassandra figure, Nandi, found her way into the film. Initially, she was simply one of the corpses about to be absorbed by a landscape; as the weeks progressed, it became clear that she was very central to the film. Quite who or what she is, finally, in the film, I am not certain myself. In a sense I am still waiting to do a film with her in it that will fit earlier in the cycle of films.[66]

What is the shift in fortune that brings Nandi back to life? Here, in a way that Krauss describes, the temporal nature of Kentridge's method creates a kind of opening through which Nandi reemerges like a comet, the pre-objective anobjectional thing as an event both unprecedented and annular, neither fully hidden nor completely buried. By way of Nandi's instantiation of "the event of the thing," the history that the terrain or the traversal of the terrain of the work would submerge—as if in some unavoidable repetition of the burying of bodies—is resurrected. This is the living, an ecstatic interiority given in not belonging, that the rock makes. It produces, finally, the charged space of a mise-en-scène of thingly objection, a field of dissent descended from two traditions, where exile, reflection, and resistance are one. The rock is possessive and it disposseses; possessed, in the broken fatality of colonized life, she now possesses both Felix Teitelbaum and William Kentridge by way of an endless drive, a processional, open, aleatory encountering. Perhaps Kentridge awaits what already happened in *Sobriety, Obesity, and Growing Old*, another of the projected drawings, where Mrs. Soho Eckstein, neglected wife of the character who embodies the brutality of South African capitalism in the films, reminds us of the figure who hadn't happened yet but who, as the rock and in the very time of the rock, is as prior as the first image of the history of the making of the image. Who or what Nandi is in the film is tied both to the history of Kentridge's own image production as well as to the racialized history of the production of the image of the object of desire. In other words, Nandi bears the burdensome richness of the history of the rock *and* the history of the hard place; of the history of apartheid and the history of art (which some might say amount to the same thing), the history of the last word and of its interminable and aninaugural creaking. But she is not-in-between. Rather what she brings from outside, which can be spoken of as a kind of music or musical theater, that of the chorister whose c preceded the choir, is a tone and step that throws off stride Kentridge's traversal of the space between (camera and paper, optimism and nihilism). That objective and objecting weight—as the danger and saving power of the thing—determines the structure and method of *Felix in Exile* as extended and impossible self-regard that, because it is given through the eyes of a separated Other, is anything other than self-absorptive envisaging. For his openness to the improvisational good fortune of that objection and the fall it brings (as the chance of reconstructed identity, reconstructed seeing, reconstructed responsibility) we should give Kentridge—and everyone to whom he is indebted—thanks since such opening makes speech, the self-disruptive movements that accompany it, and the auto-interruptive sounds that compose it, possible.

This is to say that Kentridge is aware of the good fortune that issues from his indebtedness to the unaccountable forces that constitute Nandi's animation. One way to think, if not calculate, that force is as a taking responsibility for a debt never promised not only to the ongoing history of colonialism, not only to the history of art, but also to the history of philosophy. Antonio Negri, after Reiner Schürmann, refers to "the perverse continuity of the theme of eugenics throughout the history of Western metaphysics" in order to imagine a biopolitics determined by "the will to let forms [of life, in all their impropriety or, as Santner terms it, their "essential disruption"] flourish."[67] Is it possible to disown the violent project of saving European man, which is Heidegger's project and Hitler's project, and, alas, also Husserl's project, Levinas's project, the project of Santner's tradition insofar as the biopolitical intensities or animation it thinks or inhabits is given over to (the repression of) the regular situation? Perhaps, if one considers, under the cover of blackness, the way Kentridge does not escape from but through being by way of a disruptive augmentation of intention whose thinking/drawing/dancing staves off the unintended that remains residual in and disruptive of the figure of the artist. In this respect Kentridge, even if against his own grain, offers a kind of model for (what might emerge from) the philosophical realization that being tends toward escape, in a fugitive practice of animation; that the city and its practice, which finally can be reduced neither to a word nor a concept, is the continual enactment the anatopographical bearing of the trace that holds off every insistent arrival and every irreducible departure; that being's essential run toward fugitivity *is* the city, the ongoing history of the common underground. In that model and its models lie hope for the refusal of the perennial repetition—intended or unintended—of the philosophy of racism; in that refusal lies the mournful, joyful aesthesis of a whole other socioethical party.

chapter 2

Refuge, Refuse, Refrain

The External World

Activated in refusal, refuge might take the form, depending on a range of chances, of a kitchenette or a small bungalow; of a project, or the projects, or a range of fantastic, variously violent projections; of a field of discrete but proximate, secretly interarticulate and publicly antagonistic, societies. Some find a haven for thinking in exclusive zones, surrounded by others who live the buried life of study out in the open, unprotected from the hawk, in zones for the excluded, who have been enclosed. Chicago, which is to say, more specifically, the University of Chicago, which is in but not of Chicago, was for a time a refuge for Hannah Arendt. It was also a crossing or, more precisely, the initial site and nodal point of an encounter, which does and does not take place, between Arendt and another refugee intellectual named James Forman. I'd like to restage this encounter (a nonstarter that will never have been finished) by way of a couple of its exhaustive iterations—those between Arendt and Curtis Mayfield, Arendt and Anthony Braxton.[1] Beyond reviving the shadow duet in ways that confirm its structural limitations, I would also remove it to a broader social plain, a transverse social dance with a rope in the middle, where everybody's giving it up, though some are trying not to refuse, where everybody's praying, though some are trying not to attend. Places like that are effects, and sites, of planning, belief, and study. I'm interested in one such place, which is of but not in Chicago, under and above and on the outskirts of that and every other sweet home. Holographic images of the black student are projected from this other Chicago—they offer collective, space-time separated testimony in the form of deconstructive gathering, destroying, and rebuilding, profane and sacred space blown up and out from the inside, surreptitiously; sorry, but I can take you.

There's a kind of musical offering that argues for what it is to plan to believe, something Arendt constantly theorizes and performs, but which, by way of a story of it that is for her both insistent and unintelligible, she once indirectly described as "half-illiterate fantasy."[2] I want to amplify that argument and will do so while recognizing that much contemporary devotion to Arendt figures her as the embodiment and constant assertion of a supreme, and even supremacist, intelligence. In the field in which I study, "supremacist" can't help but bear the echo of another modification, "white"; this implies (and this essay will not avoid) an antiblackness that infuses and animates Arendt's work, something perhaps not best understood as belonging to her, but rather as that to which she, along with many others, both black and white, neither black nor white (more than merely), belongs.[3] Neither antiblackness nor its mere denunciation fully signifies independently of a more general belief in the supremacy of a certain mode of intelligence and the supremacy of anyone who could be said to carry it. Fuck that intelligence; exercise, instead, some disruptive, phantasmatic, antepolitical phonography to extend a tradition of discursive violence that passeth understanding. There's a heretical Kantianism, which turns out to be essential in and to Kant, and to which Arendt is ambivalently attuned, as well as a heretical Fanonism, which turns out to be essential in and to Frantz Fanon, to which Arendt seems unambivalently deaf despite its resonant relation to the stakes and methods of her work—take that; let's be taken by that sound of joy, get elevated five or six stories on down to subChicago. We can step not only to the violence that Fanon argues must attend national liberation but also the more fundamental and fundamentally disruptive violence, insofar as it is manifest as an essential nonviolence, that attends the liberation, or at least escape, from the very idea of nation—a canted, mottled cosmopolitanism in flight from the Kantian reserve. In the luxuriously ascetic cells in which such heresy is practiced in rarefied, clarified, ensemblic solitude, the interplay of graphophonic deconstruction and perpetually reconstructive peace is an object of constant study.

To be committed to such study and to the fresh air it requires and emits as subterranean breath in a brutal atmosphere is to feel no "moral obligation to be intelligent" in the way that Arendt and her disciples might recognize and deploy.[4] Standing in this refusal, as if in refusal of standing, might seem all the more risky since we live the perpetual dawning of the age of intelligence and its equally apparently timeless Other, a moment Arendt, the political philosopher, in the constancy of her establishment of it, must fear given her sense that a pseudoracial conflict between the intellectually disadvantaged and advantaged must ensue, with its attendant resentments and demagoguery on the one side, and tyranny and despotism on the other.[5] There is a relation between the underground ascent of a certain (non)violence and the irruption into, and more importantly out of, (nationalist) politics by what has been excluded by and incorporated into thought under the never fully articulated rubric, or given in the black and supposedly inarticulate (pre) figure, of ante-intelligence.[6] At stake here is a sociology and sociality given in or as the shadow of a third term—whose inherent profligacy will have turned out to be innumerable—with which Arendt, in her American sojourn, tries to come to terms, in an elevated version of the task the refugee seems destined to perform as an obligation of naturalization, of the upwardly mobile path to the status of "voluntary" immigrant and then citizen, namely the putting of black people in their place. Arendt's managerial concern, then, is with the differential relation between the recurring vulgarity of a nonintelligent pro- vocateur and the uncivil obedience he rouses (for which Arendt expresses a certain magisterial distaste) and what she sees but can never precisely name as the more dangerous ante-intelligence of the irreducibly ensemblic black solo and what they carry in their gig bag, or their book bag. In the end, it is not the one who uncivilly obeys the genocidal dictates of naturalized nativ- ism that troubles Arendt; it is, rather, the civil disobedient's proximity to who or what shows up as the effectively, if perhaps not essentially, oxymo- ronic black student that requires her to pay attention to ante-intelligence's antagonistic disruption of the illusory conflict between the smart and the dumb. From Arendt's detached viewpoint, in her intelligent (super)vision, nonintelligence must be allowed to Trump the ante-intelligent black study to which it responds. (It's not that she would have supported him; it's just that she would have supported the ones who did—both in their assumed right to social segregation and in their suspicion of the cult of policy and adminis- trative expertise where a kind of velvet painting of black study had come to symbolize the suspension of the former and the hegemony of the latter.) For Arendt, violence in America at the end of the 1960s, at the time of the publi- cation of her essay *On Violence*, is black study. Only secondarily and by way of the most minimal gesture of implication, if at all, can Arendt apply the term *violence* to the genocidal regulation of such study. This is both a scandal and a chance. Black study, in its turning over of the very ground of the distinc- tion between intelligence and its Other; which is to say black presence, in its continual displacement and deferral of here, now, and the subject which they determine and by which they are determined; which is to say blackness, which in its communicability is not reducible to the black people whom

Arendt rightly understands to have borne and protected it, seems to emerge most problematically for Arendt in the call for what Bayard Rustin calls (and Arendt echoes this naming's slanderous accuracy) "soul courses," which is to say black studies or black (brown and beige) study, the vast amplitude (certain starry heavens above and bottomless bottoms within that are *still good*) and chromatic range of whose manic depressive solo flights (soul's courses, its studious movement) is reduced by her to moodiness.[7] You're embarrassed for Arendt (and Rustin), now, when you realize that for her soul courses are a greater danger to the so-called life of the mind than, say, a George Wallace stump speech. But let's engage, here, neither in the vindication of such study nor in some corrective attempt to detach illegitimately undifferentiated blackness from violence; rather, let's acknowledge and engage Arendt's deeply disagreeable but theoretically productive misunderstanding of that connection, which is, it turns out, black study's animation as well as its aim. Let's throw some black light on these matters by way of music.

Consider *Rolling Stone* critic Jon Landau's review of Mayfield's classic album *Curtis/Live!*, recorded in Greenwich Village at the famed folk music venue The Bitter End in January 1971.[8] This was Mayfield's first solo recording after years leading the Impressions, one of the most studied and studious musical ensembles in the history of soul. In his review, Landau negatively evaluates Mayfield's emergent solo act, accusing him of ignoring his "melodic gifts," of abandoning "the fabulous harmonics" provided by Sam Gooden and Fred Cash, his partners in the Impressions, and of self-indulgently concentrating on lyrics that "have become increasingly political and pretentious." Landau compares Mayfield to Eddie Kendricks, formerly of the Temptations, and Smokey Robinson, formerly of the Miracles, two other singers who are seen as having left what is thought to be a kind of harmonic security. However, their work had always been driven by a kind of abandon—a release, held paradoxically in their falsettos, of an urbanized version of those deformations and/or reformations of speech that Frederick Douglass ambivalently referred to as "plantation peculiarities."[9] What Douglass so indexes is not simply grammatical and accentual differences but also a kind of furtiveness, the tonal presence of a plea that sounds a strangely aggressive deference, an evangelically apologetic charge, an ungendered (which is to say unmanned) assertion, a challenge held in the rhythm and rhetoric of the unrequited, that bore in what was heard as its brutally imposed submissiveness the elusive static of an encrypted maternal lecture, which the falsetto in and of itself only indicates (because the falsetto is always more than in and of itself). At stake is an affective speaking that comes out of nowhere, as if said by no-body, as if about nothing; an irruption, in lieu of manly action in the polis, of that catastrophic, counterstrophic (non)violence of which and in which I have been trying to speak, in the open secret code and tone of an objectional, thingly prefiguratively counterintelligence and its necessarily artificial inva-sion, from the inside, of the human differential. Harmonic insecurity is the hallmark of the group for whom the soloist is message more than messenger.

What Douglass tries to convey, invoke, and sublate in literary language is made available to us by way of mechanical phonography. We are thereby able to consider, say, Charlie Patton's eerie vocals and vocalized guitar, clearing and tilling an obscure common underground on the constantly traversed bor-der separating the Dockery Plantation and Parchman Prison Farm in 1920s Mississippi, as a migrant Chicago thing reconfigured in the 1950s by Cabrini Green's Committee on Alternative Social Thought, a unit of presumptively feeble-minded, unqualified black students that Mayfield chaired. Against the whole history of such singular (an)arrangement and argumentation, in which the soloist's differential integrity in and to the unit, his perpetu-ally contrapuntal declaration of independence, is the soul student's open thesis, Landau desultorily claims that Mayfield (as well as Kendricks and Robinson) "sound best as part of a blend," thereby revealing his gross mis-understanding of the theory of harmony. Mayfield's voice, argues Landau, "lacks punch and dynamic range," therein magnifying (by way of his limited phonoptics) Mayfield's violation of common sense understandings of appro-priate meter, tone, and enunciation in standing out in an already ecstatic vocal sociality. Moreover, Landau is particularly annoyed by the fact that the songs "seem to go on forever lyrically," instantiating the emphatically over-spoken word's rhythmic adventures, which show up for him in *Curtis Live!* as "frequent moments of embarrassment, such as when Curtis offers us this unthought-out piece of wisdom" in "I Plan to Stay a Believer":

> We're over twenty million strong
> And it wouldn't take long to save the ghetto child
> If we'd get off our ass
> $10 a man yearly think awhile.
> Twenty million times $10
> Would surely then put our brothers free.[10]

I have corrected Landau's mistranscription, whose carelessness is surely bound to his fruitless hope that Mayfield "will find his artistic self again," presumably back in the small group where he left it behind in order to assert and call for a renewed manifestation of an expansive black sociality. One is left to consider, by way of Landau's inability to endure the groove, that Mayfield goes on so long because he continues to offer Landau, among others, a choice of colors, a saturative chromatic expansiveness and infusion in blackness, black presence, black study—articulate with a belief in an on-going overcoming—that Mayfield autocritically asserts is available "if you'll only listen to what I have to say."[11] As we've seen and as we'll see, Mayfield's interminable indulgence in "half-illiterate fantasy" is echo and dub.

When something Arendt calls the "idiocy of political 'believers'" con-verges with the temerity to plan, it proves too much for Landau to bear.[12] He reacts, in Arendtian fashion, to a (non)violent interinanimation of musical and political discourse that he experiences as an irruption of undercommon sense into the necessarily separate scenes of legitimate musical and politi-cal reason. This sound's migrant curvature, repressed but all too precedent, is eccentric, enthusiastic, differentially ensemblic expression whose broken and irruptive lyricism cuts politics with what is presumed to be an irratio-nally serrated edge. The regulation of the edge, and of the ones who live on it, always begins again with the assertion that it is neither the effect, nor is it worthy, of thought. Regulation takes the form of a virtual relegation—the sharp, close edge is viciously and myopically mistaken for what it is: a zone (let's say of "occult instability") where the spare materiality of Mayfield's ir-regular, uncontained, prophetic vocality can only either please or displease, where its disturbance of what Paul Guyer, in his reading of the interplay of aesthetics and morals in Kant's philosophy, calls the "intersubjective valid-ity" of judgments of taste (which is, for Arendt, the very ground of a necessar-ily restricted, restrictively necessary political consensus) is quickly filled with the dangerous animus that must exist between warring intellectual classes.[13] Mayfield's falsetto is poor musical theater staged in an interval off the charts; arte povera straining against constraint, alienation, expropriation, and being-accumulated. For Arendt, the social space cleared by such a thing is a vestibule for terror, where deviant oratorical flourish mobilizes the many as an instrument of violence for the one *and* demobilizes the many by way of a "hypnotic effect . . . [that] put[s] to sleep our common sense."[14] Bearing sep-aration, as distinct from contemplative isolation, the high lonesome sound of blackness is paradoxically communicable and both bespeaks and helps constitute deviant sociality. When it puts to sleep our common sense, it deac-tivates a capacity for discrimination that common sense allows—something

Arendt understands by way of Cicero as the capacity to discern and judge differences in rhythm and pronunciation that convey the tenor of unintelligent demagoguery.

This sedation of the sensus communis, which is lulled by the sedition to which it pays such vigilant inattention, and an accompanying disruption of the *consensus universalis* can be traced back to the dangers embedded in the accent of a deviant nonparishioner—for instance, the uninvited's disruption of a Riverside Church service in 1969, when Forman recited "A Black Manifesto," in reference to which Arendt coins the phrase "half-illiterate fantasy," in anticipation of Landau's dismissal of Mayfield's "unthought-out . . . wisdom." Here are two passages from that manifesto's preamble:

> We the black people assembled in Detroit, Michigan for the National Black Economic Development Conference are fully aware that we have been forced to come together because racist white America has exploited our resources, our minds, our bodies, our labor. For centuries we have been forced to live as colonized people inside the United States, victimized by the most vicious, racist system in the world. We have helped to build the most industrial country in the world.

> We are therefore demanding of the white Christian churches and Jewish synagogues which are part and parcel of the system of capitalism, that they begin to pay reparations to black people in this country. We are demanding $500,000,000 from the Christian white churches and the Jewish synagogues. This total comes to 15 dollars per nigger.[15]

Arendt misjudges the (non)violence of the coordinated study in which Forman is engaged and from which his singular expression emerges. Her misunderstanding of this musical continuum of organization in the improvisation, rather than rejection, of principles is an error of the common sense that is shared across a wide spectrum of the universal consensus and applied to a broad array of black expression. I want to move with Forman's bearings, to Mayfield's accompanying gestic music, in the underground they air out after the fact of Landau's and Arendt's attempts to bury it. Such attempts produce unintended effects: refusal of that extrapolitical quickening power that serially animated (even newly made black) churches or nonattunement to the deconstructive singularities that kept (even newly made black) joints jumping between ascension and descent (pronounced dissent) resulted in involuntary and uncharacteristic pseudocritical gesticulation. Arendt and

Landau are trying not to hear the sound to which they are trying not to move—instances of imaginative flight, propelled by recalibrated rhythm and tone that distill a diverse schedule of brutalities requiring reparation. Wherever it takes root, even in purportedly oppositional ground, common sense—as Kara Keeling and, before her, Wahneema Lubiano have shown—if it manages partial avoidance of the deleterious effects of gendered, queered, blackened, musicked speech or new musical language, recognizes the dangers inherent in such knowledge for the already existing state of affairs and remains committed to whatever allows us to recover what Arendt refers to as "our mental organ for perceiving, understanding, and dealing with reality and factuality" as they already stand.[16]

When Forman got up to testify there were things in the air that he both echoed and anticipated. He was accompanied by the history that sent him and that he, in turn, was about to send. For political common sense, or normative political intelligence, the history that animates Forman's intervention should be known only insofar as such knowledge is subject to immediate dismissal lest it be allowed to preface, and even determine, action. When a plan for action (Forman, for instance, wants reparative funds partially devoted to the establishment of a black university in the South, requiring us to consider what the relationship is between that and the takeover of the university in general) accompanies a recitation of the acts and conditions that demand action, the polyphonic force of such utterance is difficult to assimilate. Such music cannot be read at sight. The one who would do so often mistakes richness for evidence of a deficit in compositional skill. Forman's speech is (non)violent because it sounds destruction and reconstruction with equal emphasis. Such sound trumpets a desire not simply to level the (church and the) university but to replace its administration—and deeper still, the administered world—with another mode of organization altogether. He wants to take it over, by way of the interplay of separation and communicability, which is the form (of life) that bears, insofar as it is inscribed by, the music's content. Arendt recognizes the Fanonian badness of it all; she has a common sense of this danger, as this excerpt from a letter to Mary McCarthy, to whom *On Violence* is dedicated, demonstrates. "Today the situation is quite clear: Negroes demand their own curriculum without the exacting standards of white society and, at the same time, they demand admission in accordance with their percentage in the population at large, regardless of standards. In other words, they actually want to take over and adjust the standards to their own level. This is a much greater threat to our institutions of higher learning than the student riots."[17] Negroes want to take over. Their leaders announce that this is so in oratorical flights whose wings need to be severely clipped by the understanding, which takes the form of the exacting standards of white society. The Negro community moodily and openly indulges in fantasies of fantasy, where difference and desegregation converge, where the set of integrated singularities maintain their integrity, thereby modifying commonness on the fly, as if some alternative consensus, which could never hope to claim universality insofar as that is a white preserve, held in and holding together what Arendt refers to as "our institutions," became operative in corrosive, melodramatic *Sprechgesang*. Perhaps I am wrong to think that for Arendt, the ones who utter such burning, ceremonial speech—such amplified perpetration of implicit and potential violence—are indistinct in the mental rogue's gallery in which she holds them. For instance, from *that* luxuriously ascetic cell, which is also another open secret space carved out in Riverside Church, Martin Luther King Jr. provides a prefigurative accompaniment to Forman on April 4, 1967, in which his too-deliberate condemnation of the U.S. invasion of Vietnam is accompanied by urgent prophesy, which envisions, without quite calling for, the paralytic fracturing of American power. Forman's example is most on Arendt's mind in *On Violence*, but that very appeal to exemplarity gives the overwhelming sense that to her they were all the same. The way such a judgment will have been right is all but obliterated by the way it will also have been wrong.

What was, in fact, at stake in the radically new curriculum Forman was planning was a platform for social equality that would be manifest in the extreme differentiation within black social life from which Forman's plan emerged. What seems all too easily to have been dismissed as a kind of harbinger of monolithic and irrational counterviolence is much more accurately understood as the desire for another language that would express, by way of a genuinely collective socialization, the capacity for difference that elsewhere Arendt so insistently valorizes as natal individuation. It bespeaks a communal diffusion of singularity—the disruption of whose given chorus is in the interest and in search and in expression of another, experimental band. In this light, one might hear the echo of Forman, Chicago native and first executive secretary of the Student Non-Violent Coordinating Committee (SNCC), in the compositions of Braxton, another Chicagoan and longtime member of the Association for the Advancement of Creative Musicians (AACM).

The acronyms SNCC and AACM are talismans for anyone concerned with the history and possibility of social and aesthetic advancement in the present century as well as in the last. They are loci for a contribution to such advancement that was always predicated on the deepest commitment to study, one that certainly, violently disrupted already given standards in the interest of other standards whose high notes remain, at least for some, unreachable. The invaginated circle of Braxton's breathing, his movement out into extensions of the alto horn that remake it or, at least, reconstruct what had been given as its capacity, is a solo that inhabits the upper registers, augments the upper partials, always in more than one voice. The harmonics that animate *For Alto* reveal an already given preoccupation with the contemplative, an already expressed commitment to the revaluation and reinvigoration of standards, in a field where the study and the forging of language are one another's articulation. Such language is, necessarily, one of trade, of exchange, of commerce and of the *commercium*, whose jurisgenerative grammar, an ongoing anarchic improvisation of principle, is instantiated materially by way of dirty, impure, mongrel sounds whose aesthetic sociality is manifest, finally, as black music discomposed, ancient to the future. The history of that pitch, its great enterprise and continuing moment, its law-breaking and law-giving grammar, is what Braxton is after in the études that make up *For Alto*. It was, again, something that migrated from Mississippi to Chicago, like Braxton's father, in order to be taken back home, as it were, on a kind of relay or feedback loop in the voice of Forman, before Mayfield projects it out, which is to say back, to the world in a more than perfect expression of the jurisgenerative grammar that Arendt hears as a broken standard.

When a Stranger Appears

Black students, committed to the project of black study, must be mindful that in either case Arendt is deeply skeptical of the very idea. She must be spoken of in the present tense because she remains here, on the scene that is supposed to be the American political and intellectual field, and now, when the ubiquitous cry of and for hope reveals its almost complete absence. Perhaps Arendt is what remains of political thought in the absence of hope or, perhaps more precisely, her work is what stands in for political thought when it is properly understood as the remains of hope. If, as this implies, hope cannot be kept alive, this need not lead to despair since what is beyond hope, in terrible enjoyment, is an absolute sufficiency, an irreducible optimism, given in more in less, in everything in nothing, as scheme and variation, critically anticipating, speculatively accompanying, on the edge of arrival, never to return.

An imago of the black student, herself a message from black study to black study, and a judgment of her devolution that follows from the assumption of her impossibility, is a decisive, if necessarily peripheral, element for certain voices and forces that speak through Arendt. The imago displaces that holographic image of the project to which I earlier referred, and while *On Violence* is its own occasion for thought, that text must be read in close relation to another that accompanies it as propelling force or prefatory undertow, Arendt's 1959 essay "Reflections on Little Rock."[18] In those reflections the imago takes the form of a photographic image that prompts but finally remains outside of them: the appearance of a face on their edge, seen but not seen, visage of another imagining—Elizabeth Eckford in the gauntlet, on her way to school. Here is the opening of Arendt's essay:

> The point of departure of my reflections was a picture in the newspapers showing a Negro girl on her way home from a newly integrated school: she was persecuted by a mob of white children, protected by a white friend of her father, and her face bore eloquent witness to the obvious fact that she was not precisely happy. The picture showed the situation in a nutshell because those who appeared in it were directly affected by the Federal court order, the children themselves. My first question was, what would I do if I were a Negro mother? The answer: under no circumstances would I expose my child to conditions which made it appear as though it wanted to push its way into a group where it was not wanted.[19]

The collateral object of Arendt's critique is my primary aim; I want to resound the depths of something serial representation threatens to reduce to one dimension.

Neither the "Negro girl" nor her actions appear to Arendt. Eckford is unseen because she is neither seen nor heard to see. More precisely, something remains unseen in Arendt's reflection(s), something given in and by Eckford's alternative vision and the revisionary passages through which she is seen. Arendt does not see what she sees and so the photograph is a speaker through which Arendt's own voice is projected. This is to say that Arendt understands Eckford to bear mute, however eloquent, witness (as if her face, submitted to the rigors of portraiture, were the blood on a hand both murderous and suicidal, a shown confusion of manipulation and complicity, self-infliction and nonintention, violence and impassivity) to what Arendt already knows. Perhaps this is because Eckford's eyes are obscured by shadow and by sunglasses, which could be mistaken for a blindfold; on the other hand, perhaps this is because Eckford's eyes are hidden—in plain sight, in sight made plain by sound or song, in muted speech, in a seeing and on a scene that must be heard—in having been trained on something else, in having something or somewhere else infused in them. Not against, not substituting for the brutal time and place of her seeing, of her being unseen in being seen, Eckford appears, to those who want to feel, to place her eyes and thoughts elsewhere. Elsewhere, which is the nature of her (refusal of) time and place, is in her eyes as she strides, strives, in and toward earth in and out of the world, which is already given beyond whatever movement of assertion or insertion and which, nevertheless, continues to be given in action and enactment, in and as (a black woman's) nonperformance, which bears the story, the ongoing history, of an already existing alternative. Let's call this nonperformance black history (and women's history), an object by decision as well as default of women's studies (or black studies). It remains for us to study this moment in the history of art, this instance of what Laura Harris would call "aesthetic sociality" in its experimental defiance of and recursion to documentation, so that we can learn how it is that Elizabeth Eckford falls to earth; how her being elsewhere is manifest in and as engagement with this fallenness and with this locale, at its worst, in the interest of it, for the love of it.[20]

By way of what remains unseen and unavailable to her reflection/s, Arendt imagines herself to be "a Negro mother." But what is the thing she imagines herself to be? Arendt diverts this question, addresses it obliquely, as if it were worthy neither of a direct articulation nor a direct address (Who are you? How do you feel? What do you think?) to one who also fails to appear. An answer emerges, in the avoidance of the question, as a relation: between the etiolated empathic mobility Arendt bodies forth in her act of imagining and the thing she indirectly imagines, in having imagined herself to be its fulfillment, to be incapable of such movement, such being-moved.[21] In diverting the question of (and to) a Negro mother (or in assuming it to have been asked in, and unanswerable but for, her own intervention), Arendt's imagining (herself to be) a Negro mother capable of imagining herself to be a Negro daughter (one who is exposed and in pain; one in need of parental protection and a proper home; one who is—therefore, and deeper still—preternaturally prenatal in this supposed parental absence) is a revision of what she's already seen, a re-veiling of what she chooses not to see (by way of that structurally determined [non]association of the free to which Arendt is privileged to cling). In a moment of profound misrecognition that seemingly could only accompany a vision of the wholly Other, Arendt sees herself in (imposition, substitution, and supercession of) Eckford's face; and so Eckford, and her seeing, and her choosing not to see, remain unseen. Moreover, Arendt infuses Negro motherhood with her own (in)capacity—the regulated imagination, the purified worldview, of the clear-eyed. The clear-eyed ask: How could one expose one's child to the (deadly) social cold, where everyone has the right (not) to associate with whomever they choose? Or, in substitution of my inadequate paraphrase, take Judith Butler's, given by way of other objects, in other contexts: "What happens to the child, the child, the poor child, the martyred figure of an ostensible selfish or dogged social progressivism?"[22] This kind of lament, which Arendt offers without ambivalence, let alone irony, is immediately bound up with a sense of the violation of a certain national character as well as with the disruption of the very constitution of the polity. A violent overturning is presaged in the irruptive, collectively individualized pushiness of the ones who shoot a Negro girl, like a bullet, or a virus, into the crowd and its venal, simple, static, state-sanctioned code. Such linkage is understood by Butler to be centered "not only on the question of what culture is and who should be admitted but also on how the subjects of culture should be reproduced." She adds: "They also concern the status of the state, and in particular its power to confer or withdraw recognition for forms of sexual alliance." Finally, in Butler's words, "the question is not only which relations of desire ought to be legitimated by the state but also who may desire the state, *who may desire the state's desire.*"[23] But recognize, also, that another question lurks here, one concerning the modes of personhood that have been desired by the state as an object of incorporative exclusion and the general and generative field and force of impersonation who have not desired that desire, who have refused what has been refused to and imposed upon them, as well as that refusal and that imposition. What Arendt sees is the collateral damage that accompanies an illegitimate desire for recognition; and Eckford, the black student, is the symbol of that illegitimacy. What Arendt fails to see is a refusal not only of the state's desire but also of the brutally exclusionary desire of a society whose civility is manifest always and everywhere as hostility.[24] Her substitutive defense of the right to marry across racial lines, which is often invoked by her devotees as balancing and justifying her attack on the movement for school desegregation, is severely weakened by the absence of an analytic of (the refusal of) that desire and its violently miscegenative history, which is woven through with appeals to the shadowed complex of states' rights, parental rights, and heteronormative parental responsibility, where Arendt's reflections also linger.

According to Arendt, an inadequate theory of society, in its distinction from and place between the public and the private, along with a more or less venal desire to climb socially appear to have rendered at least one black mother incapable of seeing the reality that is clearly visible to Arendt in Eckford's face, which has become, for Arendt, nothing but a mirror. What undergirds Arendt's critique of pushiness—an innoculative anti-anti-Semitism projected outward into a more general notion of nonbelonging as slur—is common sense, or submission to a common seeing; for her, Eckford's humiliation is visible ("How," she must have asked, "can anyone not see it?"—this effect of maternal endangerment and abandonment); and when Arendt imagines herself to be a Negro mother, moving in a reparative fantasy, that common sense remains with her. It is the undercommon sense of this scene (its backstage or offstage, meta-melodramatic, extrapolitical theatricality) that remains unseen and unsounded for and by Arendt. There is much in that open secret venue that strains against regulation. You could call it the antipolitical antepolitics of children and their impossible mothers; an intelligibility given and made in the shadow of political common sense and its crude, common sensibilities; a plan for, that emerges from, a beautifully horizonal, anexpansively horizontal, fantastic social life in the hold. Arendt cannot see and cannot think this other seeing, this other thinking; instead, she sees and thinks herself. Arendt asks, "Can't you see her suffering, which is mine?" Eckford answers (in anticipation of the question), "You can't see our plan," her tone enriched by invitation and demand, set off in overheated choir, infernal congregation, in her sunglasses, so she can feel cool, so she can see while seeing otherwise, somewhere else, something else. (Perhaps she sees Arendt. Perhaps she asks, "Who are you? We've never seen you. You're a whole new thing, dark to yourself. We're the old-new thing. Can't you see?") The clear-eyed can't imagine the criminally jurisgenerative, antematernal imagination of black maternity; her governed fancy is stuck on its own autoempathic theater, methodically performing an Other while remaining, finally, unalterably, who and what she is. What is instantiated, in such imagining, beyond an already given and assumed privilege? Nothing more than the inability to imagine the diffusion of black maternity as thinking and acting out (of) something other than that pathological imposition of authority and danger that normative understanding takes to be its essential and illegal drive. Such thought and action move in and against an interdiction such that impossible motherhood enables a general, rather than a restricted, natality that emerges in and out of constriction as claimed, photophonochoreographic dispossession. The child, earthly alive in the world of the dead, is disruptive of mere belonging. She does not belong to her mother, is unheld by her father's protection, is estranged even from the limits of the singular personal pronoun. They, which is to say Elizabeth Eckford, are neither subject to nor the object of either the mother's sacrifice or the father's heroism precisely insofar as they are infused with what the terms *sacrifice* and *heroism, mother,* and *father,* devotedly misname. Elsewhere in her work, Arendt eloquently sounds her attunement to the irreducible interplay of the natal and the stranger, but here she is unable to valorize its enfleshment and the ethical imperative it brings. It is as if the alienation that must attend whatever natality is much too much for Arendt to bear, an interinanimation of rupture and excess that carries the terrible gift of a whole other mode of social bearing. In this, and against her own grain, she anticipates Orlando Patterson's full and fatal disavowal with her own uncanny dismissal of something other than belonging that black (non)performance fleshes out while inadvertently echoing Theodor Adorno, who, when he said that jazz is not what it is, sensed, in and as the music's depths, that which he could not imagine—the revolutionary, paraontological power of natality in its alienated, alienative essence—a dissonance, before emancipation, grounded in the rhythm of working but working out, flying but not home. Passing through the world, but never at home in it, because home is always bound up with homelessness in Little Rock; because in Little Rock there is no home sweet home; because Sweet Home is on its outskirts, over the edge of the polity, in the outwork of its broken circle, hidden in its unseeing, all-seeing eye; because home is (or always bears) a plantational, planter-national enclosure; because they were already embedded in a structure without a Little Rock Central, Elizabeth Eckford's passion and passage is the ongoing, annihilative condition of politics. They are, however, not prepolitical, but ante- and antipolitical, though this condition that is before and against politics might become something akin to what good people have desired under the rubric of politics. This terrible beauty works its wounded kinship to politics, cut and out of round for the people, by themselves in their selflessness, in the open curriculum of black study's invaginated and irregular shape as form, an ensemble—the Little Rock Nine (Elizabeth Eckford, soloist)—before, which is to say way up ahead of, politics and the totalitarian (in)versions that it bears, still-moving like the breathing, breaking, unbroken circles of Braxton on the alto horn or Probe on the afro horn.[25]

Ultimately, you can't get at what's going on in "Reflections on Little Rock" or On Violence *without dealing with Arendt's attitude toward the essential and constitutive violence of un/held* Phantasie *in its black, ungendered nothingness. The pride of regulated political* Einbildungskraft *in "Reflections on Little Rock" and the slander offered to black study in* On Violence *go together.* The imagination's wings were clipped by a misunderstanding of what it is to be without standing and of what it is to stand, anyway, outside, as a field of objection. It is never possible for Eckford to withdraw from the zone in which they are unwanted because that zone is the place in which they are serially and brutally subject to a violent and obsessive desire. *Pariah* is neither the right word for, nor the proper conceptualization of, what they are. At the very moment of the photograph, surrounded by and in flight from the inescapable substitution of a patriarchy protecting them from itself, as well as in a range of moments proximate to and beneath that moment—both in relation to and in spite of their insurgency—they are wanted. How do we deal with this vicious dialectic of desire and aversion, protection and endangerment? How we and dem a-go work this out? It demands imagination—a richly internally differentiated antiworldliness that is given in abundance, against method, in a certain poverty of theater at Max's Kansas City where Adrian Piper restages Eckford's untitled performance.[26] Here is how Piper describes it:

> Max's was an Art Environment, replete with Art Consciousness and Self-Consciousness about Art Consciousness. To even walk into Max's was to be absorbed into the collective Art Self-Consciousness, either as object or as collaborator. I didn't want to be absorbed as a collaborator, because that would mean having my own consciousness co-opted and modified by that of others: it would mean allowing my consciousness to be influenced by their perceptions of art, and opening my perceptions of art to their consciousness, and I didn't want that. I have always had a strong individualistic streak. My solution was to privatize my own consciousness as much as possible, by depriving it of sensory input from that environment; to isolate it from all tactile, aural and visual feedback. In doing so I presented myself as a silent, secret, passive object, seemingly ready to be absorbed into their conscious-

ness as an object. But I learned that complete absorption was impossible, because my voluntary objectlike passivity implied aggressive activity and choice, an independent presence confronting the Art-Conscious environment with its autonomy. My objecthood became my subjecthood.[27]

In a gauntlet that replicates with differences the blurring of Art-Consciousness and Race-Consciousness that Eckford's passage turns out already to have revealed, Piper desires a kind of extremity in her sensorial self-protection that was unavailable to Eckford's absolute, empathic, availability; nevertheless, a certain capacity for self-projection is enacted precisely in its relation to Eckford's enabling incapacity for self-protection. What accompanies the savage ritual of Eckford's exclusionary assimilation into what Piper elsewhere refers to as the "external world" is a kind of visitation, an earthly projection of self in selflessness, that we might come to think of, with Piper and Allen, as withdrawal but also as something Hortense Spillers has called being "available in the flesh," as when entrance bends toward trance in an interstitial, black existential drama of wordlessness.[28] At stake are the roots, the rootlessness, and the routes of the "tree of anger" to which Spillers attends in echo of Audre Lorde's tending to them. Arendt rightly sees such self-projective non-protection as aggressive, even violent passage through the world while refusing to acknowledge that this mobile inherence is also the ecstatic announcement and defense—given in openness, not fortification—of the stranger: a birth announcement, if you will, in the form of an anticipatory biotopographic assertion into and out of a given history of incorporative exclusion. If, in her "Untitled Performance at Max's Kansas City," Piper simultaneously resists and reveals assimilation into the fatally political mechanism that requires and allows her to see herself as "an object in the world among others," then Eckford's untitled nonperformance at Little Rock Central is consent not to be a single being.[29]

The world Piper enters and inhabits, where Eckford is held while passing through, is phenomenological. It is structured by desire, which sanctions an impossible regard for the one who finds meaning rather than her own objecthood. The self is the epiphenomenon with which phenomenology is obsessed. It is that object among other objects that will have been elevated in its rendezvous with the subject, implying a line of thought that precedes Kant and succeeds Fanon, who are its stanchions. Piper offers no proper citation for the phrase but its closeness to Fanon's famous finding of himself to be "an object in the midst of other objects" in the world into which he came is striking.[30] If to come into the world is to enter into objecthood there is an immediate problem of cost and benefit that accompanies a no less urgent problematic concerning the nature of that which enters. To have written "the one who enters," or to have assumed that such entry is the task of a subject bound to his ongoing constitution, will have been to (en)close those problems at the very moment of their articulation and, therefore, to accept the boundary of the phenomenological world and to accede to its gravity. A certain paralegal alienation might be given here—something that, in detaching entry from subjectivity, makes escape velocity possible. We ought to be concerned with the nature of an entrance that occurs under the name of Elizabeth Eckford insofar as generative propulsion and annihilative exit are held there. In Eckford, Piper, and Fanon assimilation prompts recess, declension, withdrawal.

Try saying to yourself and others, after having assimilated the external world of assumed interiority: "We ain't thinking about you." The relative absence that is established will have been all there is. But an appositional code is embedded in the movement of Piper's and Fanon's silent partner. It says, history sent us, desire brought us, to where they say we are not wanted. Having been sent by ourselves in selflessness, from selflessness, our place in history is now secure, if it makes anybody feel better or, on the other hand, honor us. It was never so that we could go where we are not wanted. There is no such place. We are wanted, as it were, everywhere; needed, one might even say, dead or alive. This is the condition of the fugitive, sleeping with one eye open, one hand on their gun, beneath the advertisement that graphically declares they are wanted everywhere, in every there, right where they are, right here, right now, amid and on the scene of their exclusion. The dialectic of being-wanted and being-excluded is the background against which Eckford emerges into the instant world where Arendt is a Negro mother, unsuccessfully trying to move herself against herself, in brutal empathy. (At stake, here, is the way heteronormativity and antiblackness inform one another by way of an operation in Arendt that is unknown to Arendt, a secret operation she does not intend. It would only be in our attendance to this opening in/of Arendt that her disciples want kept close or closed that we might find some other thing in her work, some black operation mobilized in and through that work, that sounds anempathic and anticipatory counterpoint and countermeasure to the murder that she does intend. It's not as if we haven't heard that double melody before. It takes something unnatural to be able to play it right.)

It was never so that we could go where we are not wanted. We had already been captured and regarded by that prize. We want to avert our eyes from that acquisitive aversion and its gaze to look elsewhere, to withdraw into the external world of things, of dreams. We do so, again, out of love for the world. We are out of love with the world and that love, this imagining, does not emanate from the conscious pariah or, for that matter, from her unconscious or her unconsciousness; it is an effect neither of legitimate, sanctioned intelligence nor unintelligence. This exhaustion of love is strange, in ways that are akin to and against the grain of something Arendt once wrote to James Baldwin regarding the apocalyptic ending of "Down at the Cross: Letter from a Region in My Mind," an essay that would later appear in *The Fire Next Time*. Baldwin writes:

> When I was very young, and was dealing with my buddies in those wine- and urine-stained hallways, something in me wondered, *What will happen to all that beauty?* For black people, though I am aware that some of us, black and white, do not know it yet, are very beautiful. And when I sat at Elijah's table and watched the baby, the women, and the men, and we talked about God's—or Allah's—vengeance, I wondered, when that vengeance was achieved, *What will happen to all that beauty then?* I could also see that the intransigence and ignorance of the white world might make that vengeance inevitable—a vengeance that does not really depend on, and that cannot be prevented by any police force or army: historical vengeance, a cosmic vengeance, based on the law that we recognize when we say, "Whatever goes up must come down." And here we are, at the center of the arc, trapped in the gaudiest, most valuable, and most improbable water wheel the world has ever seen. Everything now, we must assume, is in our hands; we have no right to assume otherwise. If we—and now I mean the relatively conscious whites and the relatively conscious blacks, who must, like lovers, insist on, or create, the consciousness of the others—do not falter in our duty now, we may be able, handful that we are, to end the racial nightmare, and achieve our country, and change the history of the world. If we do not now dare everything, the fulfillment of that prophecy, re-created from the Bible, in song by a slave, is upon us: *God gave Noah the rainbow sign, No more water, the fire next time!*[31]

To this, Arendt responds:

> Your article in the New Yorker is a political event of a very high order, I
> think; it certainly is an event in my understanding of what is involved
> in the Negro question. And since this is a question which concerns us
> all, I feel I am entitled to raise objections.
>
> What frightened me in your essay was the gospel of love which you
> begin to preach at the end. In politics, love is a stranger, and when it
> intrudes upon it nothing is achieved except hypocrisy. All the charac-
> teristics you stress in the Negro people: their beauty, their capacity for
> joy, their warmth, and their humanity, are well-known characteristics
> of all oppressed people. They grow out of suffering and they are the
> proudest possessions of all pariahs. Unfortunately, they have never
> survived the hour of liberation by even five minutes. Hatred and love
> belong together, and they are both destructive; you can afford them
> only in the private and, as a people, only so long as you are not free.[32]

Perhaps what Arendt also responds to—in partial acknowledgment of the
marriage of love and hate, in nonacknowledgment of Baldwin's awareness
of what must not merely accompany but constitute the humanity of an oppressed people—is this passage from earlier in Baldwin's text:

> It probably occurred to me around this time that the vision people
> hold of the world to come is but a reflection, with predictable wishful
> distortions, of the world in which they live. And this did not apply to
> Negroes, who were no more "simple" or "spontaneous" or "Christian"
> than anybody else—who were merely oppressed. In the same way that
> we, for white people, were the descendants of Ham, and were cursed
> forever, white people were, for us, the descendants of Cain. And the
> passion with which we loved the Lord was a measure of how deeply
> we feared and distrusted and, in the end, hated almost all strangers,
> always, and avoided and despised ourselves.
>
> But I cannot leave it at that; there is more to it than that. In spite of
> everything, there was in the life I fled a zest and a joy and a capacity for
> facing and surviving disaster that are very moving and very rare. Perhaps
> we were, all of us—pimps, whores, racketeers, church members, and
> children—bound together by the nature of our oppression, the specific
> and peculiar complex of risks we had to run; if so, within these limits we
> sometimes achieved with each other a freedom that was close to love.[33]

What love? We must ask that question of Baldwin, whose writing requires us to do so, in the wake of Arendt's not having faced the risk that the question of love poses to the very idea not only of an American public but also of American privacy. Is the love in question a general derivative of that sovereign affect and affection, in fear and distrust, that Baldwin calls love of the Lord? Or is what's at stake something that will have been, in excess of being, near to but distant from that love and what that love opposes— something fallen before and beyond but not in love, something more and less than love, something disruptive of love's normative arithmetic and geometry? This something (else), this something other than some thing, this something other than that same thing, will have been as nothing, as neither of nor for the stranger, which is a predicate common to what the world conceives as selves and others, whose rapprochement in the world to come is, as Baldwin says, the wishful distortion of a necessarily political theology. Who or what bears this insolvent and insovereign love (in black and blue or bloom or blur) is more and less than a stranger in the public-private world of Arendt and her friends, who are the ones, according to her, that (she) can love. To consider the appositional relation of "the nature of our oppression" and "the specific and peculiar complex of risks we had to run" is to consider not only that these are not the same but that the latter is not strictly derived from the former. This more and less than derivative complex of risk, and the subsequent flight that flows from and through it, brings into relief the temporary and therefore illusory achievement of freedom—within limits, within unfreedom, bounded, bordered, chained to a fucked-up struggle. The achievement of that country, or of another one, is *close to love*, says Baldwin.

Elizabeth Young-Bruehl famously publicizes a private sentiment, expressed to Arendt's friend and mentor Karl Jaspers: "I've begun so late, really only in recent years, truly to love the world. . . . Out of gratitude, I want to call my book on political theories [*The Human Condition*] 'Amor Mundi.'"[34] Is there a reason why one comes late to such love? Is such love necessarily belated? Perhaps it must follow not only the voluntary exodus into the political but also the involuntary expulsion from the political. Within a certain relegation to the private that is given in the form of rescue, perhaps this sentiment toward the public can only be expressed in a sealed envelope. Young-Bruehl intimates that Arendt's arrival at this feeling is a matter of naturalization, of a certain overcoming of "European fearfulness," which manifests itself not simply in becoming an American citizen but in discovering for oneself the allure of American political renewal, wherein the country that Baldwin reminds us has not been achieved can be imagined to have returned to the absolute fullness of what it was before.[35] As Arendt puts it to Jaspers in the apparent waning of McCarthyism, "the political tradition of the country has come through again; and we—thanks and jubilation be to God—were wrong."[36] On the one hand, you weren't wrong. On the other hand, who is "we"? The crisis in Little Rock had yet to become apparent to Arendt and when it did, what was at stake for her was the necessity of protecting "the political tradition of the country." Arendt's quietly expressed love of the world is woven into the fabric of her brutal misprision of Eckford, which is manifest in their being held under political theory's cold and exclusionary jurisdiction. In this regard, love of the world is tough.

Does Baldwin love the world? He wants to change it, requiring us to consider that the Marxian opposition between interpretation and change remains operational. But what if the only way to change the world is to bring it to an end? What's love got to do with that? To be sure, something occurs for Baldwin in and by way of the love of another person. But if love of the world is manifest in its maintenance through interpretation, then what might be the relation between transformation and hatred of the world? Is love, in Baldwin, the improper name of *that* relation? It's difficult to imagine that Baldwin's love (of the world) is the same of which Arendt writes. Perhaps there is both deficit and excess in Baldwin while Arendt's global affection can be smoothly and evenly rounded and derived from the necessary exclusions of her public/private regime. If a book on political theories bears the writing of the love of the world, where is the necessity of transforming it to be intoned? Such intonation is a nasty, metaphysically aberrant harmonics animating Baldwin's work, to which Arendt remains unattuned. Baldwin himself describes it as "something ironic and violent and perpetually understated in Negro speech."[37] It's "something tart . . . authoritative and double edged," he later declares, before echoing Douglass's analytic of the incommensurability of tone and sentiment in black song.[38] To think, more specifically, this incommensurability not only as an effect but also as a mode of violence is crucial insofar as it helps us index love's destructive, revolutionary force. In this regard love is not what makes the world go around, like some hermeneutic rotary engine whose tightness initiates, maintains, and confirms the world's proper motion. Rather, love brings the world to an end, which is a formulation given most emphatically in a black economy—a "specific and peculiar complex"—of risk where everything is dared.

As the photographs of Eckford and Piper show, risk aversion takes the form of rapture as well as terror. Perhaps Arendt's response to Baldwin is nothing more than a declaration that she is not prepared to risk it all, and an admission that somehow, despite the brutalities she endured, she feels no need to do so. Arendt is, in this respect, not so much free, but, as it were, chained to the struggle for freedom, where to be a subject and a citizen is to be held off, always in suspense, from something just out of reach. On the other side of that freedom, love emerges as an explosive whose destructiveness both Baldwin and Arendt recognize. But Baldwin recognizes, and remains with, what Arendt cannot—this entanglement of bondage and freedom, where "one must accept one's nakedness."[39] Baldwin thinks this entanglement by way of the event wherein one falls in love with another. In that event, nakedness disrupts the interracial frame, which is unknown "to those who have never covered, or been covered by, another human being."[40] The relatively conscious are covered in the explosive beauty of blackness, which is to say that this covering, of one by another, in small groups of relatively conscious ones and others, is an upheaval not only of the regime of racial opposition but also the metaphysics and mathematics of individuation-in-relation. Love might then be configured here as an absolute violence where achievement, transformation, and destruction (of world, of country) converge. When one and another are set beside themselves in radical generality, "the senses become theoreticians in their practice."[41] In this radical disruption of coordination and global positioning, "the world changes then, and it changes forever. Because you love one human being, you see everyone else very differently than you saw them before—perhaps I only mean to say that you begin to *see*—and you are both stronger and more vulnerable, both free and bound. Free, paradoxically, because, now, you have a home—your lover's arms. And bound: to that mystery, precisely, a bondage which liberates you into something of the glory and suffering of the world."[42] If we begin to see, and hear, where what it is to be liberated into is inseparable from what it is to be liberated from, then we enact a fugitive consent. No word, no world. The violence of the instrument is social, coenobitic. When mo'nin' breaks, the soloist walks away.

Therefore, what if the love that must be opposed to politics—however much it is held in politics' gravitational field, however much it is achieved and felt by what and who are subject to/subjects of politics—is the inadequate index Baldwin uses to point to a love that is beside itself in and as ante- and antipolitical sociality? Perhaps this love-in-exhaustion, this love at the end or over the edge of breath, brings a certain tumultuous derangement, a certain noise, an undercommon graining of the legitimate image. My reflections on Arendt's reflections are predicated on the assumption that this would be a good thing, given and made in and as the supposedly impossible irruption of a black thing everyone can apprehend, but which political theory's cool reason cannot comprehend. Baldwin is not a political theorist. He is not concerned with political thought. When Arendt speaks disparagingly (lowly, as if under the fullness of her breath, taken in the open air of public speech) of love, she is speaking of love for a people, of the love of something peculiar to or particular in a people. But Baldwin is speaking against the determination of whatever notion of exclusivity of such beauty. He does so, therefore, in the interest of a love that is, finally, in excess of the love of a people though such love is given in and manifest as the capacity, against just about all the pressure the world can muster, to love a people who have been understood to be incapable of love and being-loved, of sensing and instantiating beauty. Baldwin's thinking is encompassed neither by (Arendt's dismissal of) the love of a people nor the law of peoples, which the love of which he speaks, and his supremely loving, antisupremacist speech of and out of that love, anticipatorily, jurisgeneratively breaks. Perhaps there is a certain univocal speech of the love of a people that enacts what Arendt might call the unconscious pariah. It is in contradiction to this figure that the conscious pariah doesn't love, but merely belongs, to a people. It is belonging such as this that blackness cuts. Besides, the question of what survives liberation is still not, at this particular moment, our concern. The fugitive remains, in love, out of love. This remainder, which Chandler speaks of in a different register under the rubric of exorbitance, is costly, perhaps unaffordable, but we've lived this experience of pricelessness-in-value for this long. Our refusal of privacy has always been disruptive of the public, our secrecy forced out into an open underground, our business put in the anonymity of the street. The intruding stranger, in flight from their estrangement, inhabits the disruption they bear, as its enactment and its object, like a mobile asylum. We remain in and as irreducible fugitivity, troubled, of hopeless words, never to return, refusing to arrive, as what we can't afford. Harriet Jacobs couldn't afford herself. At any rate, the history of the bought and sold, of a certain soul that is the special charge—a luxurious, extravagant, theatrical, and theoretical poverty—of the black student, is priceless. And so, they ask, openly, in silence, Will you come with us? Come be who we are and what we perform? Come go to school with us, she says. Come go to the school we tore down and rebuilt for all of us, where we study what it is not to be. The questions heard through Eckford's face, the voices imagined as anarranging counterpoint to and refusal of the terror that surrounds it, are articles of faith, expressions of planning, resonances of study: the fantastic, fugitive étude of we who carry, in the way we carry ourselves in giving ourselves away, our refuge with us. We are not a free people.[43]

When, in her 1968 essay "Civil Disobedience," Arendt invokes the authority of Alexis de Tocqueville, who recognizes black presence as "the most formidable of all the ills that threaten the future of the Union," it is so that his words might sanction her understanding of the black student, offered here in *On Violence*, as carrier of a violence, alloyed neither by knowledge nor genuine power, to which the morally disinterested white student is particularly vulnerable.[44]

> Violence has remained mostly a matter of theory and rhetoric where the clash between generations did not coincide with a clash of tangible group interests. . . . In America, the student movement has been seriously radicalized wherever police and police brutality intervened in essentially nonviolent demonstrations: occupations of administration buildings, sit-ins, et cetera. Serious violence entered the scene only with the appearance of the Black Power movement on the campuses. Negro students, the majority of them admitted without academic qualification, regarded and organized themselves as an interest group, the representatives of the black community. Their interest was to lower academic standards. . . . It seems that the academic establishment, in its curious tendency to yield more to Negro demands, even if they're clearly silly and outrageous, than to the disinterested and usually high moral claims of the white rebels, also thinks in these terms and feels more comfortable when confronted with interests plus violence than when it is a matter of nonviolent "participatory democracy."[45]

Their lowering of academic standards is, again, not only manifest in their presence but in the fact that such presence is invoked in the interest of illegitimate (black) reconstruction, or the institutionalization of counterinstitutional black studies, which is exemplified, for Arendt, by what she regards as the self-indulgent nonstudy of a mongrel trading language, one marked from the very beginning by the history of its use in the historical brutalization of the ones who would now learn it (she is referring not to English but to Swahili). When black presence is understood as a localized but communicable dissatisfaction, and when such dissatisfaction is understood potentially to lead to a radical transformation of the universal consensus that structures and animates the university and the national community, then the option to reinforce an already given segregation, beyond the mere possibility of exercising the individual right and duty to discriminate, must remain operative for Arendt at the convergence of personal choice and public policy. In *On Violence*, Arendt recognizes and mobilizes against a perceived danger, and the ambivalence or nuance that marks her understanding and strictly limited defense of civil disobedience and student civil disobedients as *vulnerabilities* does nothing whatever to prevent an understanding of her as a representative figure of the dominant strain of American intellectuality.

Blackness as violence, in a communicability that, again, will have always already exceeded the very idea of what are imprecisely called black bodies and the bounds imposed on black people when they are constrained to bear those bodies as loss; blackness as a refusal of a polity or community structured by refusal; blackness as a form of social thought in social life is the irreducible, antifoundational danger to which legitimate American intellectual work responds. Let's call that danger abolitionism in order to index Louis Menand's discovery of the emergence of the American ideology as antiabolitionism.[46] Arendt's antiabolitionism comes neither naturally nor as a function of naturalization. It is a Kantian signal transmitted in and through her that, when she enters into American public discourse, is detached from black and contrapuntal abolitionist noise as a function of the redactive intellectual remix Menand describes. The Kantian serration on the edge and at the heart of Arendt's voice, a rough and paradoxically foundational parergonic ornament, is submitted to the regulatory and refining force of an already given attitude toward the specific structures and effects of abolitionism in the United States. It is, more specifically, by way of Stanley Elkins that Arendt confirms her acquisition of the tone that makes it possible for her to be taken seriously by serious men. Arendt echoes Elkins in her commitment to a comparativist view of the plantation and the Nazi death camps; to the thesis of black infantilization and cultural inferiority as a function of extended bare existence outside the protection of the law and organized society; and to an understanding of abolitionism's origins, in the radical absence of black social life, as a debilitating transcendentalism whose dependence on absolutist abstraction and principle structures its refusal or inability to think institutionally in the interest of the reform of certain aspects of "the peculiar institution."[47] The constant insurgent irruption of black (non)performativity as abolition, the constant danger of an airborne contagion, always induces a doubly dismissive reaction: on the one hand, evidence of black planning is only ever evidence of deficit and inability, the unlearned effect of an already given and intransigent constraint; on the other hand, such planning always bears the trace of an extremism calibrated to dismantle the tacit consensus that excludes it.

Arendt's extension of Elkins's misrecognition and critique of abolitionism manifests itself as the commitment to institutions that are founded on the exclusionary essence of the supposedly universal consensus, itself an effect of the most egregious abstraction of them all, the fiction of the general interest. If abolitionists condemn American institutions, they do so because those institutions gave their tacit consent to slavery and to the *consensus universalis* upon which it was founded. That condemnation is manifest primarily as a range of refusals whose primary object is the preservation of the refusal of enclosure. Because exclusion from the tacit consensus did not mean being excused from the obligation to consent; and such obligation did not mean the presumption of an ability to consent or to join and participate in the tacit consensus. Arendt's understanding of "welcome" having not been extended to the enslaved by a general institutionality whose structures the enslaved precede is undermined by her having left unthought the force and trace of being desired and accumulated. What does it mean that nonwelcome takes the form of incorporation? Note, too, that her insistence on the promise (to engage in conduct that is not violent to the already given institutional structure) as "the prepolitical condition of all other, specifically political, virtues" and her yoking of that insistence to the eternally dangerous black example is nothing less than the reimposition of the obligation to consent (to one's own violation).[48] This reimposition will have been justified insofar as refusing the obligation, however violently imposed, however unaccompanied by some reciprocal promise, is to relinquish one's claim to a polity and, therefore, to humanity. In *The Origins of Totalitarianism*, Arendt argues that

> Even slaves still belonged to some sort of human community; their labor was needed, used, and exploited, and this kept them within the pale of humanity. To be a slave was after all to have a distinctive character, a place in society—more than the abstract nakedness of being human and nothing but human. Not the loss of specific rights, then, but the loss of a community willing and able to guarantee any rights whatsoever, has been the calamity which has befallen ever-increasing numbers of people. Man, it turns out, can lose all so-called Rights of

Man without losing his essential quality as man, his human dignity. Only the loss of a polity itself expels him from humanity."[49]

To be expelled from humanity is to be reduced to the bare nakedness of being human. Such reduction is understood by Arendt (and Elkins) to be the dubious rhetorical *achievement* of abolitionism. Slavery, on the other hand, free of such ideology, antithetical to such abstraction, confers upon the slave a place, a home (Sweet Home). And if the slave, in the interest of the abolition of slavery, which is understood by her not as a goal but as an ideological commitment, relinquishes that place, flees that "home," then not only is she expelled from humanity but she is also guilty of a violence fundamental to the tacit consensus (imposed upon her in the absence of any protection of her personhood and in the oppressive fullness of its protection of her acquired thingliness) in which and from which that home is constructed. Perhaps Arendt doesn't understand what it is to have rather been expelled, to have rather been displaced or to claim and own an already imposed displacement and dispossession. Or, more precisely, perhaps she only understands such preference as violence. I'm here to echo the ongoing claim to that violence, which animates civil disobedience in the name of those who never intended murder.

Meanwhile, antiabolitionism is serially manifest in the murderous brutality with which it checks the planners, the believers, the enthusiasts, and the rampantly illegitimate (re)productivity of their thinking. The cult of intelligence—whose moral obligations are imposed on the ones who are faithful to an already given decision from which they derive benefits in exchange for themselves, and which adorns itself in its attendant ceremonial dress, which calls attention to itself as the supposed opposite of some others' supposed nakedness—administers this eugenic project. While Arendt can be invoked today in the interest of checking uncritical exuberance, one must still wonder if her own hopes would have been unduly raised in the current conjuncture precisely because what we see in *On Violence* is her having made a preferential option for the very nonexuberance out of which the current uncritical exuberance has emerged. It is her response to an exorbitance of, a vile participation in, democracy. This is to say that for all its rhetorical grace and erudition, its movement against the social scientistic nonlanguage of the nonthink tank, Arendt's identification of the *Crises of the Republic* (of which *On Violence* is a crucial component) is the anticipatory companion of *The Crisis of Democracy*, a 1975 text commissioned by the Trilateral Commission, written by a group of "first world" intellectuals led by Samuel Huntington whose thesis, put simply, is that the crisis of democracy is too much democracy. To my mind, Arendt's post-68 texts (against the grain of more radical impulses that compose the underground of that work and of her work in general) blaze the trail for the noxious mixture of neoconservatism and neoliberalism that now authors hope and manages participation. This is, then, not to say that any invocation of Arendt in the critique of the features and contours of the current conjuncture is thereby rendered illegitimate; it's just to say that such invocation threatens to render itself both illegitimate and irrelevant if it doesn't acknowledge and come to terms with Arendt's placement within the dominant intellectual apparatus of this conjuncture, where antiabolitionism meets the end of ideology. In this particular figuration of the ongoing national crisis, what intelligence discovers is not simply the serial exposure of the nation's originary civil hostility but the fact that the true object of abolitionism is not only slavery but the structure that establishes its inseparability from citizenship as well. Having been submitted to constant misjudging, apposition to citizenship (the open, secret voluntary association that is blackness, black social life; the refusal of refused and therefore tainted citizenship) emphatically claims itself as the expression of the political idiocy of the ones who plan to stay believers, motherfucker. Soul music, which is to say soul studies, as Mayfield exemplifies, extends abolitionism's unfinished, fantastic, superliterate project, clearing and inhabiting a kind of movement-space. The oppositions of power and violence, the many and the one, association and loneliness, beauty and terror, politics and love are broken down by the music of strangers, who are conscious and more, but not strictly pariahs, because they have been so brutally and insistently desired. They imagine and have already claimed and enacted something more than to be free.

In her 1970 *Lectures on Kant's Political Philosophy*, Arendt distinguishes herself from Kant by declaring her disbelief in the pure productive imagination. Kant, on the other hand, thinks that pure productivity as a function of impurity, a recognition, perhaps, that *Einbildungskraft* bears the trace and taint of *Phantasie* in its heart, as its wings, which would propel it on its free and lawless way were it not for the regulatory understanding. The common sense of Kant's distinction between these very different senses of the imagination proceeds by way of a racial logic that animates Arendt's work as well. What she loves in Kant as foundational, what in him she veers away from emphatically but respectfully is denigrated elsewhere in her work under the rubric of the illiterate and in his work under the rubric of the criminal, both of which operate, as I have tried to show elsewhere, in an irreducible relation to the philosophical concept of race which is, according to Robert Bernasconi, Kant's invention.[50]

There is an echoic update of Kantian antiblack racism in *On Violence* that any cursory reading must confront. There is, at the same time, a trace in Arendt of a racial difference internal to Kant, manifest as the interplay of productive imagination and abolitionism. The antiabolitionism to which she submits herself (the American self-image; the American ideology) all but buries that difference, attempting to suppress its dynamism with the name blackness. But that which blackness now names survives in and under that cover. And so it is of some interest that Arendt, in a brief reading of his "Perpetual Peace," approvingly portrays Kant as an abolitionist (of war), with all the disruptive absolutism this term elsewhere implies. She remarks on his advocacy of an unrestricted and general communicability in resistance to enclosure that is always already embedded "in an original compact, dictated by mankind itself," and it is worthy of note that Arendt would return, via Kant, to the supposedly discredited distillate of naked humanity, "an idea of mankind, present in every single man," one capable of being expressed singly and in combination. Arendt's citation of Kant is unadorned and uncut: "If such an original compact of mankind exists, then a 'right of temporary sojourn, a right to associate,' is one of the inalienable rights." Rights, here, are acknowledged as inextricably bound to principle and the absolute enactment of the original compact. As Kant says, and Arendt quotes, "the common right to the face of the earth . . . belongs to human beings generally." Like all such ownership, it is only ever fully enacted in its having been relinquished. Such autodispossession is the (*first*) common right. Resistance to enclosure is its vehicle. But why is Kant's abolitionism fathomable for Arendt when black abolitionism, or blackness/black power as abolitionism, is not? Perhaps it is because black abolitionism recognizes that any promise made to or in the name of the tacit pseudouniversal consensus violates and, in practical terms, denies or seeks to render impossible and inoperable "the sheer fact of being human" that "is one's cosmopolitan existence" and which constitutes one's membership in a world community in which acting and spectating, politics and study, cooperate (if not cohabit). Such assertion of world community is the essence of black radicalism/black abolitionism. Its productive imagination moves to make present what has not already been here; but this is to say that it makes present, presents in the open, the original compact that was always already here. It makes it present by enacting it, against all claims and impositions of impossibility. It does so in study, against sequestration, in always open unison.[51]

The soloist's emergence in attentive enactment of the open collective head is the form of scholarship to which black students, Chicago's underground urban planners, have been long devoted. They emancipate dissonance in a conception of sociality hinged on dispossession, where one is bereft but for the specifically human, irreducibly necessary possibility of enacting new social forms, into which one disappears. (We hear that disappearance in audition's improvisational incursion of the song form. In listening so hard and so judgmentally for Mayfield's separateness, Landau fails to get an impression of expansive ensemble Mayfield had always been coming from, always already all the way live.)[52] They exercise a preferential option for such poverty, plumb the depths of its history, descend into its surreptitious canons. Their improvisation of social forms should be our constant study. We must inhabit such study, and the poverty of the student, like St. Jerome in his cell or St. Anthony in the desert or Woody Guthrie in his boxcar or the impossibilities—in their devotion to the impossible—who are preoccupied in monastic projects or occupy the mobile hermitage of an ark(estra). We have to study what it is to study, as Forman does, as Mayfield and Braxton do, so that what is at stake here is something far more than the entirely justifiable and necessary, but narrowly interested and insufficient, reassertion of the honor of the black student. It's not about what it is to live under the shadow of a falsifying disregard, even when it reveals a threadbare aspect of an otherwise sumptuous life of the mind; the thing is that lived, luxuriant mindfulness that such disregard brings inadvertently into relief: the collective head, the hydratic passage, hydraulic story that is the refuge and fugue(d) state of the stateless, the refusers, the refugees, which we share in common where blackness and study are in play. It's not whether anyone could ever stand in for the many that are gone, and that still come, to send Elizabeth Eckford. At stake, in the fact and question of her neglect and regard, is whether we can feel (with) her in having seen (through) her.

Elizabeth Eckford's Passion

When Patterson says the slave is not part of a human community that is, of necessity, political, he diverges from Arendt but not to the extent of differing from her sense of the necessity of such belonging. Against the backdrop of this theoretical kinship, Elizabeth Eckford's passion comes into a kind of relief. In an attempt to correct Arendt, and refute Patterson, while adhering to the valuation that structures their categories, Danielle Allen seeks to provide that passion political context and justification. It's impossible to separate the passion from its aftermath. "After being mobbed," Allen writes, "Elizabeth slipped inside herself, remaining there wordless during all of the news reports in the following days, screaming at night in her dreams."[53] At the same time, the passion's aftermath is inseparable from its preparation, from the fact that Eckford had been prepared for something as if she were an instrument. It is as if she were accompanied by the host that sends her; or as if she were the nonperformance through which that host performed. All this bespeaks a grammatico-mathematical confusion that can't be spoken. We see through one to the other until their separation disappears. Can we remain there wordless, worldless? Brilliantly, Allen attempts to clear up that confusion, so we can get our bearings; but what if we require blur and disorientation?

Allen regards Eckford's passion, her passage, as an entering of the world that can also be located in the world. Such geographical desire demands topological explanation. Certainly, Eckford endures wrenching duress, unto the point of collapse, or even vanishing. And it is not so much at that point but through it, where perspectival singularity turns out to have been uncountable propulsion all along, that a set of questions takes retrospective form. If she must enter the world that she is in, which implies she is neither in nor of it, where in the world is Elizabeth Eckford? If her work is placed in the desire for worldliness, citizenship and sovereignty, nothing could be more natural or unobjectionable than such entrance. But what if worldliness, citizenship and sovereignty jointly form a general impossibility reserved for the one who will have always remained obscure in what is otherwise misconceived as a place in the (political) sun? What if Elizabeth Eckford is inseparable, in what appears to be her loneliness, from the company that sent her? Wordless, worldless, where do they remain?

If wretchedness is given in the longing to belong where such belonging guarantees single being, then damnation is embrace in (the constantly, centrifugally fallen outness of) alternative study. Embrace implies alternative pronominal, mathematical, metaphysical, antipolitical arrangements. Damnation might be described as fallenness; it might be described as foldedness, too. It might be conceived as a kind of topographical and numerical irreality, this coming down to earth which is also a veering off line, something become more and less than itself in nothingness. Given the dark times that are said to prompt it, damnation may be only human; but if the darkness of time(s) were constant perhaps it will have been due to the human eclipse of earth. In any case, will someone have been sent to tell of this undercommonness? Will they tell us with human speech or some slap-tongued, tongue-tied, more+less than human speechlessness? Sacrificial crucifixion will then have been an epiphenomenon of symposium, piercing it with the point to which concept, body, and soloist tend. She is sent as a chance to resist her own allure—in renewal of general sending, of studious descent. One is sent in silence to tell us there is none. Perhaps there is a kind of violence, to be sharply distinguished from cruelty, that is required in order to see such terrible ecstasy, and to work the difference between sacrifice and selflessness, which is given as study, in care. Allen approaches that violence, with a political theorist's proper and rigorous caution, by way of Ralph Ellison, author of black literature's most celebrated public speaker.

> Ellison recuperates the term "sacrifice" as critical to understanding how politics works and what law is in a democratic society. *Invisible Man* is fundamentally concerned with the nature of democratic political action, and in it Ellison argues, through the movement of the narrative, that a legitimate account of collective democratic action must begin by acknowledging that communal decisions inevitably benefit some members of a community at the expense of others, even in cases where the whole community generally benefits. Since democracy claims to secure the good of all citizens, it is the people who benefit less than others from particular political decisions, but nonetheless accede to those decisions, who preserve the stability of political institutions. Their sacrifice makes collective democratic action possible.[54]

What is, and who determines, benefit or sacrifice? What is the ontological, or ontomathematical, ground of such determination? What does Allen mean by communal decision? What are the mechanisms, operations, and institutions through which such a decision is made and acceded to by those who dissent? Can we believe in the easy transition from a notion of the commune to a notion of the political? What if the political is a structural operation of division within and dereliction of the commune, wherein a failure to tear (given at the convergence of incorporation and exclusion) becomes the twists and turns that serially initialize anticommunal decision? Then we would require an understanding of the relation between accession and imposition; then we would require an understanding of sacrifice as externalization of cost in its relation to internalization of benefit. Sacrifice implies prior individuation. You not only have to have but also to be something in particular in order to sacrifice or to be sacrificed. Can the noncitizen, the nonsubject, sacrifice if sacrifice is a capacity belonging to the sovereign? What if those who are defined and who live through and by way of the definition of themselves as insovereign move within and by way of a set of collective resources that can be studied precisely so that the impossible collectivity of the sovereign, which will have legalized and justified the privatization of communal wealth, can itself become an object of critical scrutiny? Consider that the only thing the white men and women of Little Rock lost in desegregation was the epidermalized illusion of their sovereignty, a sacrifice that was, according to Arendt, far too great to impose upon them. Consider the importance of the commitment to this illusion, this "possessive investment."[55] Consider the importance for stability of the right to claim it—the right but also the capacity, literally, to speak this claim within the exclusionary grammar of a common language uttered in properly sanctioned public enclosure, according to rules and protocols established in ritual re-enactments of an inaugural (communal) political decision. Consider how terrible it is to come to know the undetectable difference between what it is to be the subject of and what it is to be subject to political decision. Consider, finally, that the alternative, held in a hold far below and deep outside either compensation, repair, or redemption, remains external to political decision, its benefits or its losses. Ellison tells us this in frequencies lower (and higher) than normative speech can achieve, as another metaphysics to which the interplay of one and many can only inadequately gesture. Some uncountable and unaccounted for ensemble is always saying something else, he says. Recall that in avoidance of proper political theory, Baldwin writes of "something ironic and violent and perpetually understated" in such speech and in the life from which it emerges while taking note of Ellison's extraordinary use of it.[56] What secrets about democracy's unlivable limits are, in the violence of black life, held open to the violence of black speech? Beyond that, what is given in and as black speechlessness?

These are questions Allen amplifies, in the interest of whatever collective democratic action is supposed to mean or bear, in seeking emphatically and explicitly to establish the politicotheoretical pathway between benefit and loss. Arendt, Allen argues,

> is adamant that the law and democratic political structures should
> leave to citizens the right to control their private life and household,

including their choice of whom to marry, and also their social spaces. Arendt had argued in *The Human Condition*, published in 1958, that participating in the world consists of the ability to construct a common world, the ability to speak qua men and not qua members of society. It also depends upon a citizen's ability to "fight a full-fledged political battle," to articulate one's "own ideas about the possibilities of democratic government under modern conditions," and to propose "a transformation of the political institutions." In contrast, advocacy of interest positions and participation in "interest parties" is work we do as members of society. For Arendt, the parents of the Little Rock Nine were acting as members of society and not as political agents.[57]

Allen continues,

> All citizens must, as a part of their political education, learn how to negotiate the experience of political loss, which is felt personally and socially.
>
> African-American parents therefore feel obliged, according to Ellison, to teach their children the lesson that the political and legal worlds are imbricated in a social context (sometimes of terror) that constrains the possibilities for action supposedly protected by law. These African-American parents simultaneously taught their children that they would have to pay a social price for exercising the democratic political instrument provided to them by legal institutions and that both the use of the democratic political instrument and its preservation were worth that price. The concept of sacrifice pinpoints the relation between the social world—the realm of custom and citizenly interaction in which one suffers mental, physical and economic harm from other citizens— and the political world, the institutions and practices for the sake of which one may be able to master that harm. Moreover, the ability to make such a sacrifice constitutes, for Ellison, "the basic, implicit heroism of people who must live within a society without recognition, real status, but who are involved in the ideals of that society and who are trying to make their way, trying to determine their true position and their rightful position within it." As Ellison describes them, the African-American parents were, over the course of their struggle, articulating and acting on ideas about how a democratic community might best organize itself. Moreover, they were giving rich lessons in

citizenship. They were, therefore, on Arendt's own terms, pursuing in the public sphere a properly political battle.[58]

Allen seeks to establish that the parents of the Little Rock Nine were acting as political agents and that their contribution to collective democratic action is made in and as sacrifice. But what if we say—by way of Arendt, within and against the resonance of her slur, and in light of her capacity to recognize white sacrifice while overlooking what Allen asks us to consider as black sacrifice—that those parents were socializing, in dissent and in descent? Let's say, more precisely, more starkly, though again by way of Arendt's disdain, that beneath (her) notice they (were) moved not as interested parties but as a party without interest concerned not with the transformation but with the liquidation of existing political institutions. What if the (under)commonality movement, which proceeds outside of normative political agency but is also illegible to and disruptive of already existing society in its constant regulation of sociality on behalf of the political, was not about sacrifice or accession but about revolution, if by revolution part of what is meant is the ongoing refusal of the artificial boundary between sociality and publicness whose maintenance was, for Arendt, the politicotheoretical justification for school segregation.[59] This is to say that corollary to insistence on a variation of Arendt's distinction between the social and the political is the rupture of the dividing line between private and public.

What was at stake in Little Rock, what was being asserted insofar as it was being defended, was free association (though perhaps the term *fugitive sociality* is more precise), which politics and the family, the public and the private, all are meant to regulate. Free association, in this regard, manifests itself in desegregative planning, not integrationist achievement. Separation's constant and violent assault on equality is always most emphatically an assault on black social life. Segregation is the modality through which that assault is carried out. And if black social life can only be defended in its continual practice, then part of that practice is and always has been planning and enacting the resistance to segregation. Allen frames this practice as it is carried out communally in black Little Rock, bringing it into sharper relief even as it is displaced when she, after Ellison, asserts the involvement of that community in the ideals of American society. What Allen takes for sacrifice to or for the law might then be better imagined as mutual instrumentality, consent not to be a single being (for it is single being, possessive individuality, that is the fundamental assumption of this theory of sacrifice as well as the irreducible ideal of the society), beyond category (in Duke Ellington's ethicoaesthetic sense) and its imperatives. What if Eckford's solo, sent in and by and for and through her parents—whose sending, which is terrible and beautiful, renders them transparent—is *unentitled nonperformance* of a contract for destruction and rebuilding, rather than the determination of a true and rightful position? Then the soloist who is not one violates Arendt's more natural(ized) sensibility precisely because of who and what they bring. Their (meta)physical loneliness is troubled and plexed. It blurs the line that separates involvement from endangerment, as Arendt clearly sees, even as her antiblack refusal to see black political subjectivity makes black refusal of political subjectivity more evident.

The jurispathic character of every natural history of the political is ruptured by something like the improvisational, jurisgenerative theatricality of the study group in constant meeting. Elizabeth Eckford—the force that was sent to defend what sent them—requires and allows the exposure of a ge(n)ocidal calculus the categories of the individual, the family, and the state operationalize and obscure. This force, and the exposure it demands, remain unspeakable for Arendt. Her citizenship—her allegiance to a given politics, its constitution and its institutions—inclines her not only to reject whatever disrupts these institutions but to characterize such disruption as unnaturally anti- and antepolitical. The one who is newly naturalized can assert rights of public speech for which those she sees as unnatural, and who were forced to perform the underlabor of her welcome, in their neglectful parenting or social climbing, show themselves to be unfit. Her defense of the abstraction "politics," which is manifest in the allegiance to an already given materialization of politics, reveals an impropriety proper to the abstraction—the degraded sociality that is both constitutive and disruptive of every political instance. The essence of the political, which any given body politic must exclude and disavow, is a necessarily social impropriety. Perhaps if Eckford hadn't come along, Arendt would have had to invent her. It's just that what Eckford brings, the force that sends her, cannot be contained by Arendt's intervention. The social extension of love beyond the figure whose protection and sacrifice are a matched pair, the social perversion of speech at the intersection of impediment and refusal, and the conditions of incarcerated flourish that structure their apposition are generally unspeakable even though they're all that political theory can talk about.

And the valorization of speech that is given in and as political theory quickly becomes the ground of discrimination between kinds of speech.

Allen writes of the distinction between dark speech (rumor, gossip, a kind of un-authored and unauthorized speech whose origins cannot be traced, thereby placing it in a kind of illegitimate adjacency to divine power) and speech whose origins are visible, in the light of day, emerging from a place in the sun in which the rights and obligations of publicness, and the power to be seen, can be assumed.[60] In this regard privacy implies privation as well as deity, something proximate to that poverty in world that Heidegger attributes to the animal. Publicness is elemental to the human condition and dark speech is like some current that alternates between divine plenitude and a kind of destitution that, itself, oscillates between wildness and docility. Such destitution bears, as it were, an absence of volition, an incapacity for self-control, where darkness of speech tends toward wordlessness as a kind of limit. Across that boundary, one supposes, is the realm in which the ones who are not one enact a necessary failure of coalescence, composure, completeness—the personal and the political body falls apart or, more precisely, is always already fallen.

The relative silence of a certain darkness of speech constitutes something like the underbreath of the polis, threatening the normative order the city can be said to have agreed upon. Allen's analysis of this speech moves by way of her engagement with Sophocles and Machiavelli, each of whom are concerned with how such speech is to be regulated insofar as even in its privacy, such speech remains dangerously political. In remaining political, the danger dark speech bears for already existing order remains circumscribed, how-ever, insofar as the basis of that order is the concept of the political, itself, which is enacted in speech by way of the exclusion of a range of subpolitical utter-ance and non-utterance. In other words, there is something that defies the political constitution of the word itself—something below even dark speech and its circumscription, something beneath the political underbreath, some-thing correspondent to what Arendt characterizes as illiterate and which she recognizes as a more absolute danger to the political even if it is beneath her recognition. This constant drama of broken words—words ruptured by utterance or left incomplete in being unuttered, stunted by musical lysis or stretched in lyrical extension, said in the absence of standing or unsaid in ambulatory mutation of standing—is like a regenerative grammar of muted, mutant, worldless jurisdiction. If, on the lowest frequency, Eckford doesn't speak for you; if, in the highest register Mayfield and Forman aren't really talking to you, there is a kind of communicability that remains in the relative absence of communication. The full range of wordlessness, which is given by

Allen as the preparation for and aftermath of Eckford's passion, is inadvertently illuminated in Arendt's reductive understanding of it insofar as it is almost immediately relegated to the realm of the social, marking that realm as outside and disruptive of the public/private partnership that constitutes the political. That which is called illiteracy (which we might think along lines established by Erica Edwards, as *charismata*, the gifts of a kind of common, sociotheoretical spirit), in the musicopoetic force of its enthusiasm, is an irruption through speech of unsanctioned presencing, constituting, at once, violent incursion of and militant flight from the field of behavior the political sanctions and sacrifices.[61]

This is what the "Untitled Performance at Max's Kansas City" restages, against the grain of a common self-understanding that Eckford and Piper will have come to share and which I have come, with the greatest possible respect, to misunderstand. You could say that I must misunderstand abuse, again, not because it can be reconfigured as the source of resistance (and whatever one might want to valorize by aligning it with resistance so conceived as reactive) but because it reveals to us something about resistance as source or, more precisely, as resource. At stake is the massive problematic of where Eckford is coming from, which is more precise than inquiring where in the world she is. Why is the political exalted over the dislocation from which Eckford emerges and to which Eckford returns? This is a question concerning the sound of anti- and antepolitical silence. Edwards requires and allows a reading of Allen's narration of the aftermath of Eckford's passion, which recites Daisy Bates's recitative on "the long shadow of Little Rock," as a non-fictional analog to

> the vanishing spectacle in civil rights fiction as a narrative of black radicalism, in which the charismata (the gifting of the many) overtakes charisma (the gifting of the one) and in which the nature of the black radical tradition—which Cedric Robinson argues has historically tended to be more surreal than real, more sensual and spectral than material, and, most importantly, "more charismatic than political"—is narrativised as silence and disappearance. The decolonization impulse cannot be represented in either sense of the word—"spoken for" or "illustrated." Rather, it appears as an expression of what Lindon Barrett calls a "sly alterity."[62]

Sly alterity—something tart, something double-edged, "a something-else-ness," as Edwards puts it—comes from somewhere.[63] This unspeakability that lies below speech, as speech's dislocation, is a serially dissed location. It is a privation at the heart of privacy, which disrupt's privacy's partnership with publicness. It is not apolitical but it is ante- and anti-political. In the recitational chain that links Eckford to Bates and Allen (and Edwards), charismata doesn't overtake; it sends: a gifting, a presentation, a presencing, that is, in turn, given retrospectively. "When she began to talk again," Allen writes, "she described the morning of September 4. Her focus is on her parents."[64] Must we take this focus on her parents to be on the way to a political, juridical sacrificial understanding of disappearance? Or is Eckford the vanishing point through which alternative metaphysical arrangements are envisioned and enacted? Before and after Eckford's lonely, annihilative walk, she is with her parents, according to Allen. Their presence frames what is supposed to be Eckford's abandonment, which Arendt decries as a violation of the political and which Allen justifies by declaring it to be political.

> Elizabeth's parents obeyed [Pulaski County, Arkansas School] Superintendent Blossom's instructions not to accompany their daughter, and they did so in order to support the rule of law and the institutions that were purportedly available to all citizens to obtain their democratic rights, and which claimed to offer all citizens equal protection. The result was psychological terror for them and for their daughter, which was endured for a future good: this constitutes sacrifice.[65]

It's not that the gauntlet Eckford walked that day didn't induce psychological terror; it's that the gauntlet and the result can only be understood as intensifications of previously existing conditions. It's not that her parents did not accompany her to school on September 4; it's just that they did accompany her, too. What if the political is nothing other than a public slippage into the self that black selves—inoperative in the face of juridical and philosophical impediment, impossible given the constitutionally brutal enforcement of the law of selves—are constrained to perform with sly, deformative alterity? What if that alterity is ensemblic, social, such that what shows up as abandonment is better understood as abandon? What if where Eckford came from, and where she slipped to, was this unworldly charismatic field in which wordlessness and screams are signs not only of individuated mental distress but also animaterial assembly? The double edge of terror and enjoyment, as Saidiya Hartman teaches us, is double-edged.[66] Where in the world is Elizabeth Eckford? Nowhere, such absolute woundedness being also an absolute blessing. It's not that charismata are given in sound *and* silence—it's that charismata refuse the efficacy of that opposition. In this regard, Eckford and Forman, Piper and Mayfield, Bates and Allen, Edwards and Hartman, engage in a mutual accompaniment whose sexual division of labor demands analysis when coming into voice is tantamount to entering the world while defying analysis when the breaking of speech is earthly inhabitation. Either way, manly, human speech-in-action in the polis is both denied and denied.

Allen, like Piper, assumes estrangement as a kind of ontological condition. At the same time, slipping inside oneself is understood, properly, to be a function of abuse rather than the originary condition that is elsewhere assumed to be the ontological foundation that requires everyone else in the world, ultimately, to be understood as a stranger. The public and its institutions, which can be said to foster the speech that constitutes them, are supposed to mediate between strangers. And to be excluded from the public is, in a sense, to be excluded even from the claim one makes on estrangement. Allen speaks of dark speech, of a dark word, whose illicit truthfulness—often adversarial to dominant structures, or to forms of abusive dark speech that thwart the positive evolution of publicness—must be made public in the public interest. But dark speech and wordlessness are not the same; and wordlessness implies a worldlessness that proper individuation cannot bear. How can Eckford be said to have gone inside a self that will have only existed in the public that refuses her? Can her withdrawal be better understood as part of a general refusal of that relay between self and world to which her access has been barred? How can we understand the entanglement of desegregation and the flight of the accidental soloist—she who was never (meant to be) alone? The interpretation of her wordlessness and her screams strictly as a slipping inside herself betrays metaphysical assumptions that bear the all but immediate implication of the political. But where had Eckford gone and how do we think the wordlessness and worldlessness of her condition? This is something Piper attempts to investigate. In the meantime, to consider where Eckford had gone where she'd been coming from, is to raise some fundamental questions concerning sociality as it concerns not only political phenomenality but consciousness more generally, when it is understood either as the condition of possibility or the constitution of experience. Natalie Depraz helps to advance this questioning.

> To talk of "transcendental phenomenology" is, at one and the same time, to talk of the close link between Husserl's philosophy and Kant's critical philosophy, and also to rupture this link. For Kant, "transcendental"

designates the level of the conditions of the possibility of all possible experience, most eminently represented by the pure concepts of the understanding. The categorial conditions of the possibility of experience apply to the latter, take account of the latter, but without ever depending upon it. In the same way, for Husserl too, "transcendental" refers to the a priori level of the structures constitutive of all possible experience; but by contrast with Kant, (1) these structures do not have the exclusively formal character of the Kantian categories, their constitutive origin being of the hyletic (material) kind; as a result, (2) they are given intuitively and are therefore capable of appearing as such. To uphold the rights of a transcendental phenomenology consists in bringing to light the very *constitution* of the experience of an object for a consciousness by showing how the object is, in this way, given intuitively to the consciousness. Unlike constitution, condition of the possibility maintains the duality between the phenomenal and that which conditions it. Constitution, on the other hand, rejects such a duality by engaging phenomenality on the level of its original constitution.[67]

To engage the phenomenality of the nation on the level of its original constitution is, in some sense, what occurs in the illuminative relay between self and world. However, what is for some a pathway is, for others, a dislocation. For Allen, this is what it sounds like on the path to citizenship;

> We've had the Constitution since 1789. . . . Last night they came into our neighborhood and rocked our homes, breaking windows, and all that. We've taken a lot because we didn't want to hurt the chances of the Negro kids, but I doubt whether the Negroes are going to take much more without fighting back. I think I'll take the rest of the day off and check my shotgun and make sure it's in working condition.[68]

Allen describes the words above as emerging from "a language of sacrifice"; and given a need for sacrifice that appears to be constant, the path to citizenship may well be endless. But what if the passage above is more accurately described as the sound that comes from nothing, indicating a radical detachment of passage from arrival? As Allen says, "the public language of political theory, which can directly interact with policy, did not reflect such a precise awareness of the particular sacrifices involved in the production of democratic agreement and laws. As a result, political theory was not in a position to offer a full account of democratic citizenship or of the full range of potential citizenly action. It could not responsibly engage the subject of law."[69] Allen feels no need to establish the particularity or location of this citizen of Little Rock even though the language renders simple interpretive identification impossible. This citizen is simply "on the ground."[70] But who came into whose neighborhood? Whose homes were rocked? Who was going to check the working condition of a violent instrument? And was that instrument the constitution or a shotgun? Insofar as the chances of the Negro kids are invoked we can all but assume that this citizen of Little Rock is black, and that their claim to citizenship is, therefore, radically interdicted. A certain retrospective naturalization is projected onto the appositional anonymity of the noncitizen. Perhaps Allen seeks to acknowledge the force of law but without that distinction between jurisgenerative principle and legal systematicity that helped to underwrite and justify Robert M. Cover's critique of the statist legalism whose foundations Allen seeks to fortify.[71] She understands black insurgency as having taken up these fortifications, turning the music of (non)violent insurgency into the language of sacrificial loss. This is to say that Allen understands the communal to have been constituted in regulative agreement and legally imposed sacrifice rather than in differentiation and in the disruption of whatever legal systematicity asserts the right to impose loss as a regulative tool.

But what appears to be the strife between two theories of constitution cannot be allowed to obscure the difference between constitution and condition. What if political theory also always depends upon the underlying presence of formal categories, "most eminently represented by the pure concepts of the understanding"? And what if the disruptive folds and bends of constitution exert a more than merely material force on the understanding so that a radical and irreducible generality can be said not only to resist but to recondition the constitutional? At stake is not so much what constitutes political experience but what antepolitical forces remain in the wake of political reduction and regulation. It's not simply that Eckford's passion cannot be explained or contained within the framework of the political, just as Arendt asserts; or that her passion constitutes a danger to the political, just as Arendt fears. It's that if Arendt's assertion is true, which it is, and if her fears are justified, which they are, it is because Eckford's passion is a function of a social imagination of which the political is derivative. This belated, repressive degradation of sociality is the overflown and overflowing proscenium in which sociality appears and then is viciously disappeared. Eckford is neither subject to nor the subject of political loneliness. Her name sounds what her silence shows: radical accompaniment, of which incursions into the fortifications of the political, which seeks to envelop both what constitutes and what conditions it, are modalities of selflessly self-defensive care. If desegregation is more accurately thought as anti-genocidal, anti-geocidal resistance—rather than as the attempt simply to enter a polity whose regulation and accumulation of difference in the name of individuated conformity is given in the incorporative exclusion of those who are constrained to stand in for difference in general—then Eckford's passion will have been not merely seen, but seen through. Deeper still, the redactive appearance of her loneliness is not only displaced by the visionary company of love which sends her but also that which sees through her shaded eyes, having thereby joined her. In such assembly another metaphysics is implied, one which transcendental phenomenology won't imagine and hermeneutic phenomenology can't contain; one which constantly escapes political theory into the poetic sociology that surrounds it.

This problem for political theory is an open secret. Wendy Brown might say, why appeal to the state that is your undoing, whose very constitution is predicated on your exclusion?[72] Allen might reply, in order to reconstitute, or to renew, that constitution. And here, maybe in a kind of turning back on her own phenomenological training, Arendt might say, this isn't about constitution but condition of possibility, as if the very political phenomenality of the nation were separate, finally and irrevocably, from the blackness, the sociality, the thingliness, the nothingness, whose exclusion conditions it. Allen might argue that Arendt doesn't understand that sacrificial injury is the essence of being-political, that it is a mode of political assertion too easily mistaken for social appeal. But what if these arguments in political theory are flawed insofar as they apply intentional analysis to irruptive sociality? Allen then seeks to identify, out of the flux of sociality, intentional political subjects whose actions can be understood from within the terms and conceptual apparatuses of an already given political order. Sacrifice becomes the primary object of this intentional analysis, and it is supposed to allow us to understand the actions of blacks in Little Rock, Eckford's actions and those of her parents, *as actions* that are constitutive of a political order that is, paradoxically, already given and (to Eckford, her colleagues, and her family) denied. But what if one goes against the grain of Allen's assumption of Husserl's Kantian echo in order to delegitimize intentional analysis and its assumption that "an essentially necessary conformity of type prevails and can be apprehended in strict concepts"[73]? Here, Husserl asserts an essentially Kantian conceptualism—a universal idea, a regulative and teleological principle, that asserts the unity of objective sense even against the grain of its own Hericlitean flux. Jean-Michel Salanskis puts it this way: "[Husserl's] text in fact tells us that the field of consciousness is the Hericlitean flux and expresses in its own terms its nondiscrete nature ('Processes of consciousness . . . have no ultimate elements or relationships, fit for subsumption under the idea of objects determinable by fixed concepts'). The text poses as the problem of phenomenology the success of an *intentional analysis* capable of extracting from this flux a noematically describable element, itself the result of an intentional integration of the flux."[74] Husserl, too, believes in the requirement of a strong, transcendental force that holds things together, that ameliorates what he can only view as a paradoxically general estrangement. On the one hand, like Kant, Husserl assumes the necessity of regulation. On the other hand, unlike Kant, he believes that what necessitates regulation can be understood finally as internal to the phenomenality that it conditions. So we must consider the difference between saying that the imagination is the condition of possibility of the understanding and saying that the imagination constitutes the understanding. Similarly, we must consider the difference between saying sociality is the condition of possibility of politics and saying that sociality constitutes politics. To consider these differences is to consider what duality allows—the idea of an alternative; the thought of/from the outside. Allen writes, "The relation of law to sacrifice brings to the fore the fact of *law's necessary forcefulness*. In a democratic context, where full consent is the guiding aspiration, acknowledgment of this forcefulness is troubling. Indeed, the project of many recent democratic theorists (e.g., writers in the deliberative democracy tradition) has been to seek methods of pursuing full and enthusiastic consent, and such efforts might be seen in part as pushing against the necessary fact of law's forcefulness in order to allay our worries about it."[75] What does Allen mean by "full consent"? The full consent of single beings rather than consent not to be one? The forcefulness of law is exerted on individuals in the realm of the social as well as in the interdiction of their being political. But what if we consider the relationship between jurisgenerativity and consent not to be single? Who sacrifices to the law, to its forcefulness? What do they sacrifice? Is consent not to be single best understood as sacrifice? Certainly it is incompatible with the particular interplay of uniqueness and plurality that Arendt envisions—a plurality of single beings that has, also, to forgo a discourse on the internal differentiation of whatever singularity. The difference between consent and sacrifice will emerge out of another analytic of force and its relation not to statist legality but to jurisgenerativity. If there is a nonsacrificial nonidentity of the subject then there is no subject of self-forgetting. Ellison's notion of sacrifice, which Allen valorizes, goes back to his analytic of the relation between soloist and group in jazz. But that analytic is faulty precisely insofar as it axiomatically posits the priority of the individual even if the individual must subordinate himself to the rule of law. You could say, by way of Walter Benjamin, that Allen and Arendt are on two points in the movement between law-making and law-preserving forms of activity. And it is Allen who understands that those activities are, in any case, violent or forceful, requiring consent or sacrifice. This insight comes, again, in her comparison of Ellison and Arendt.

> Arendt fears that what she sees as a struggle for social equality will jeopardize the political instrument that has made the struggle possible. Although she does not use a language of sacrifice, she nonetheless proposes that democracy needs a social sacrifice for the political end of maintaining the rule of law. She asks for sacrifice, but slyly, and here her distinctions between social and political are all important.
>
> The distinction is primarily ethical. That is, Arendt's arguments outline how those who wish to gain honor in the polity can best do so: They must refuse to allow their social interests to affect their political choices. They must, in other words, make sacrifices. Her strong opposition between social and political is, among other things, an exhortation for citizens to give up some things (pursuing economic interests in the public realm) for others (glory and the greater wholeness of the whole). Where Ellison uncovers sacrifices and asks that democratic theorists attend to the way in which citizens negotiate their losses, Arendt simply insists that citizens sacrifice the social to the political. But sacrifice is not something to be insisted on, Ellison argues; it is something to be negotiated, discussed, recorded, and reciprocated. Rather than insisting on sacrifices, citizens should work to develop practices of and conversations about equity that will surround the polity's political institutions and provide a backdrop to its decisions. Because Arendt does not acknowledge the importance of requests for sacrifice to her own argument, she leaves herself without the conceptual resources and analytical grounds to address the full ethical implications of collective public decisions.[76]

Technically, Arendt insists on the sacrifice of the noncitizen, the non–full citizen, the nonnaturalized, the unnatural who gains honor in the polity by accepting her exclusion from it. It's not that such sacrifice is imposed upon the one who is excluded; it is that exclusion constitutes the sacrificial activity of the citizen as he ritually makes of the excluded a sacrificial offering to the state. Moreover, and this is Arendt's point, the rule of law, in the interest of its own preservation, insists precisely on the sacrifice of the noncitizen. While Allen seeks citizenship for the excluded by positing her as the agent of her own being-sacrificed, what remains clear is that the metaphysical foundations of Allen's and Arendt's political theories are the same. Arendt understands that the public space of the political as well as the category of the citizen are structured by exclusion. By definition, the one who is excluded, whose exclusion is the condition of possibility of the polity from which she is excluded, cannot sacrifice that from which she is excluded. She is, however, what can be seen to have emerged from the consent not to aspire to such membership. She is the lens through which that consent is manifest in all its incompleteness. This is to say, against Allen's reading of Arendt, that the political instrument has not, in fact, made the struggle possible. If Arendt fears for the rule of law, for normative political instrumentality, it is because she sees that the threat it is under comes from something that is, paradoxically, outside of and essential to it. This, too, is a problematic of the surround. She makes frequent reference to original sin, original crime, though what is at stake in and by way of the presence of blackness is a transubstantial power that might be better understood as the interplay of anoriginal criminality and jurisgenerative force. There is a wayward instrumentality, maybe something along the lines of what Benjamin imagines as a politics of noninstrumental means, that is both essential to and disruptive of whatever political instrument. These things have to be established from before the beginning. Failure to do so means that Allen's argument that in Arendt's reticence to acknowledge the necessity of sacrifice in some general way—a way that would require some general ethical investment in the equal distribution of sacrifice—she is willing, more or less uncritically, to privilege the rule of law over the sacrificed, particularly when the sacrificed mobilize against the unequal imposition of sacrifice, is applicable to Allen as well. To recognize the law's forcefulness is not to argue in some definitive way against the rule of law. Moreover, what must also be recognized is that access to the public space of citizenship is unequal in ways that necessarily taint negotiation and reciprocation with force. Politics is the war zone within which inequality is maintained through negotiation.

What remains, if we are guided by the example Ursula K. Le Guin offers in "The Ones Who Walk Away from Omelas," and by Elizabeth Povinelli's analyses of Le Guin's story, which shares important features with Allen's reading of Arendt, is an "ethics of abandon" predicated on the irreducible entanglement, which we might imprecisely say that Eckford bodies forth, of the fugitive and the held. [77] What's the relation between brutal incarceration and exilic mobility? Why does this question remain necessary? What can and must we imagine of the social life of that girl who is not one? Eckford has no honor in the polity, according to Arendt. This is a matter of necessity. Eckford has, rather, a kind of degraded natality tainted by simultaneously overbearing, neglectful, impossible maternity. In that maternity, and in the exile that accompanies it, sociality persists. Already existing democracy and its various implied ontologies are the limits of Allen's steadfast resistance to Arendt. Consent not to be a single being is not where one is lost, but rather where the irruption of difference is staged in the appearance of singularity.

Is the world that which arises between people? Is it what surrounds people? By "people" one means individuals. Is multiplicity or relationality the same thing as "world"? If this is what Édouard Glissant means by "one world in relation," does it require the priority of the individual? Does any*one* consent not to be a single being? Do we speak of the priority of that to which one consents or the priority of the one who consents? These are questions Allen, having been taught by Arendt, teaches us to ask.

In *Men in Dark Times* Arendt writes:

(1) Everywhere . . . the public realm has lost the power of illumination which was originally part of its nature.

(2) For what was wrong, and what no dialogue and no independent thinking ever could right, was the world—namely, the thing that arises between people and in which everything that individuals carry with them intimately can become visible and audible.

(3) History knows many periods of dark times in which the public realm has been obscured and the world becomes so dubious that people have ceased to ask any more of politics than that it show due consideration for their vital interests and personal liberty.

(4) Then a brotherly attachment to other human beings . . . springs from hatred of the world in which mean are treated

"inhumanly." For our purposes . . . it is important that human-ity manifests itself in such brotherhood most frequently in "dark times." This kind of humanity actually becomes inevi-table when the times become so extremely dark for certain groups of people that it is no longer up to them, their insight or choice, to withdraw from the world.

(5) But it is true that in "dark times" the warmth which is the pariah's substitute for light exerts a great fascination upon all those who are so ashamed of the world as it is that they would like to take refuge in invisibility. And in invisibility, in that obscurity in which a man who is himself hidden need no longer see the visible world either, only the warmth and fraternity of closely packed human beings can compensate for the weird irreality that human relationships assume wherever they develop in absolute worldlessness, unrelated to a world common to all people.

(6) Wherever such a friendship succeeded at that time . . . a bit of humanness in a world become inhuman was achieved.

When people are expelled from or withdraw from politics, they settle into conditions of weird irreality. Without a place to be seen and to be heard and to act, pariahs and also those people who are fasci-nated with escaping from a polity they abhor, turn to fraternity, says Arendt, and forsake politics. In dark times what is wrong is the world, understood as that which is between people and allows for political action.

Ellison too engages the themes of the loss of reality and of the world, the turn to fraternity.[78]

Weird irreality and warmth are connected in Arendt, according to Allen. But what Allen wants to do, I think, is valorize neither warmth nor irreality, neither escape nor withdrawal; I think, instead, she wants to understand the crisis in Little Rock as an entrance into the public that is given as a mode of being public. This is to say that the planning and preparation of the ones who constitute the crisis are understood by Allen to be nothing other than a kind of becoming-public. It is of interest only insofar as it is a public preface to publicness, a political vestibularity, a set of events or instances in which the intent to go public can be discerned. It's not that the internal features of those events are unimportant; or that their internal qualities are unworthy of notice; but the heat or warmth that is generated there is relevant only insofar as it is to be contrasted with "real light" in Arendt's case or seen as prefatory to enlightenment in Allen's. But what if the refuge that is taken within invisibility constitutes the undercommonwealth of another kind of seeing, an audible improvisation of the unforeseeable? This possibility remains unattended for those who consider fraternity to be not so much delusional, but rather an effect of delusion, or, at least, of faulty vision and visibility. Weird irreality is our irresurrective haunt, our underground hold, our subterranean embrace. To resist returning to a metaphysics of ascent might itself be seen as a sacrifice more terrible than the one that is ascribed to Eckford in the interest of ascension. But what if the soloist who is not one is sent to tell us something about who and where we are?

The problem is that absence or incapacity for world that is attributed to the one who is called the pariah. Somehow, the one who is said to withhold the capacity for world, the one who enforces the pariah's worldlessness, thereby assuring that there is no world common to all people, is never himself understood to be incapable of world. So that we don't speak of the worldlessness or weird irreality of the Upper West Side. Nor do we speak of the surreality or hyperreality of Bronzeville's or Brownsville's social force. The world is conceived as the special reserve of the ones who render and enforce its general impossibility. The world is what belongs to the individual, which is to say, to the citizen, who comes into relief against the background of the exclusionarily incorporative state. The world surrounds or rises up between individuals, those whose inhabitation passes itself of as a kind of levitation whose support, in the form of backs called bridges, is universally claimed to be invisible. Again, this magical thinking of the public reveals an intractable problem. And what it feels like to be that problem turns out not to be discernible within the frame of interracial intersubjectivity.

We remain, rather, within this massive problematic of fallenness that Heidegger reveals, and which was already apparent in Kant as a kind of fearsome generativity to which the figure of the teleologically principled settler or surveyor can only respond as the agent of (black) thought's regulation. The trick, in Kant, is to get at the relation between fearsome generativity and the more or less general incapacity for individuals to escape minority. Perhaps it is this: that generativity is a kind of mass ungovernability; that the minor is the one who is un-self-governed. That un-self-governability is, in Kant's view, a function of isolation. He says, "It is difficult for the isolated individual to work himself out of the minority which has become almost natural for him."[79] This faux or second nature is a function of alien guidance, an external imposition, being held in hand by or under the protection of another, by way of a specific instrumentality: "Statutes and formulas, these mechanical tools of a serviceable use, or rather misuse, of his natural faculties, are the ankle-chains of a perpetual minority. Whoever threw it off would make an uncertain jump over the smallest trench because he is not accustomed to such free movement."[80] I have been thinking that the fearsomeness of ungoverned generativity is held, for Kant, in the fact that what is being generated is law; that, above all, it is what Cover calls "the fecundity of the jurisgenerative principle," which is manifest as endless mutation and differentiation, that freaks him out.[81] Kant is caught between the Heraclitean flux of the undercommon swarm's constant making and breaking of law and the individual's tendency to accede to the guidance of others that is administered through legal mechanism. The point of all this is that the image of an enlightened or illuminative public—where jurisgenerativity is kept in hand or held in check, where sociality's endless capacity for discrimination (for differentiation, for a kind of cellular mitosis, for runaway recombination) is given and put into play, precisely so that the individual can emerge out of isolation and into a rational polity within which he can be self-governing— reveals Arendt's Kantian inheritance. For Kant thinks that it is "more nearly possible for a public to enlighten itself"; that "this is even inescapable if only the public is given its freedom."[82] It's just that Arendt thinks this enlightened, illuminative public is no longer possible. The public can no longer split and thereby control the difference between undercommon sociality in all its jurisgenerativity and the isolated individual. Of course, Arendt posits the ontological priority of this stunted individual, the one who can only look out for his own personal liberty and vital interests, and does so precisely by way of an appeal to the legal mechanisms that are deployed by and in the name of alien guidance. She thinks the ineradicable tendency of the public to become obscure. What are public obscurity's roots? For Arendt, there is a trouble with the world, which no dialogue or independent thinking, no Kantian cultivation of mind, could ever remedy. At the same time, she implies that there is a capacity to illuminate that was part of the public's original nature. What if that trouble is nothing other than the impossible and illegitimate interplay between world and individual? What if this, too, is a problem that has to do with the difference between constitution and condition of possibility? What if the ongoing constitution of the public is flawed such that we can now speak of the exhaustion of an always already interdicted mutual manufacture? This always already gloomy and shrinking public is, in its impossibility, given the status of world, where frigidity and re-alness are intermittently conferred upon the citizen by the tepid image of an absent sun. We might, at some point, in our proximity to the earth's core, in the sacredness of our undercommon withdrawal, speak of the inauthenticity of natural light. For whom is seen and heard in and by the state in their op-timal condition? Address of this question demands an alternative that Piper attempts performatively and philosophically to provide.

Inadequately, I have tried to approach these matters before.[83] John Bowles corrects my imprecise suggestion that Piper denies the Kantian par-adox wherein the transcendental and the empirical are one another's condi-tion.[84] Certainly, as Bowles asserts, Piper does explain her work by way of it, thereby showing her attunement to some of its consequences. My concern is with an implication of that paradox that might be said to constitute data anomalous to Piper's conceptual scheme, which posits what Donald David-son calls "the very idea of a conceptual scheme" and a capacity to explain (her work) that such a scheme is supposed to ground. Inattention to this implication is imbricated not with Piper's having based her practice on a simplistic understanding of Kant's *Critique of the Power of Judgment* (which is what Bowles says I suggest) but, rather, with her relative inattention to that text, wherein Kant attempts to work around the remorseless working of a radical groundlessness.[85] This groundlessness, this (over)turned and aer-ated (under)ground, this open and nonparticulate gravitational field, is the surround in which the question of Piper's relation to her work comes into relief as a very large disarray wherein the entanglement of the empirical and the transcendental troubles the very ideas of Piper, her work, and their sepa-ration. In this regard, the conceptual scheme to which Piper is committed requires her to resist the implications of data anomalous to that scheme, which the entanglement of Piper and her work reveals and transmits. In general, the separation and relation of self and artwork is what's at stake here. The fullness of the identification of Piper with her work is not negated by the ambiguity of that identification. It is, however, the metaphysics that are supposed to ground identification that the differential entanglement of Piper in her work places in grave, playfully de/generative trouble. This trou-ble both induces and requires a kind of double vision, where clarity and blur are not incompatible. Separation, or detachment (of work from self, of self from soul), is unsustainable, rendering incomplete whatever would be sepa-rate. This concerns the capacity of (the very idea of) a conceptual scheme to sustain itself in the face of anomaly's tendency to collapse the distinction between inside and outside. More precisely, what's at stake is our capacity to study and practice the unavoidable trouble difference causes for distinction as well as for identification, both of which will have been grounded in the separation a conceptual scheme enacts and makes visible in that wildly pre-regulative turn the regulative imagination takes.

Piper's art, and her (dis)placement of herself in and by that art, is both exemplary of such study and practice and—insofar as it foregrounds the complex singularity of the autobiographical example—bound to their policing and foreclosure. She enacts and embodies, resists and reveals, the sameness of the work and the self that is given in and as their separation. The blur, or swarm, of entangled difference—the irregular irrealities of the senses, the wild unintelligibilities of the intelligence—violates the scheme, or frame, or home of xenophobic/egocentric particularity. Interiority's insistent fold and bend of itself, its tendency to go off in various twists and torques, is an essential topologisticality that will have been outside. Every last soliloquy is a resonant impersonation in search of care. It is as if the self and the work constitute one another's inadequate support in the face of the trouble they cause in and for one another in mutual dissolution. This simultaneity of condition and effect, this circularity, this possessive inextensiveness, must be open to the outside it voraciously and reductively takes in, like a white hole. The imperial absorptiveness of the self is an effect of self-absorption and self-assertion. What happens when it cannot bear not to take in what it cannot bear? Is it possible to show the absorption of selflessness from the inside out? Or to posit the interior as a conceptual scheme from which one observes one's own aggressive grasp as a kind of being-violated? If here I perform unintelligibility more fully than I describe it, perhaps it is because the laws of the self and the work break down when Piper walks the line—or, as Sarah Jane Cervenak might put it, wanders the nonlinearity—between (giving an account of her)self and (observing her) work.[86] The nearness of self and work is an unbridgeable distance and the movement between them, that oscillative nonarrival, can be touched, or tasted, if you look closely enough. If you look closely enough, it's a blur you can hear (as that olfactory funk-effect of black speech of and in which Baldwin speaks, in and out of wine- and urine-stained hallways, eternally dealing with his buddies) but here, the only way you can look that closely is if you're nowhere else but there, nothing but what the laws of observation say you cannot be. This autobiographical apposition, this view from nowhere, is black study's ubiquitous vestibule. Classical (meta)physics and neoclassical economics break down where we get down. I can't tell you about it but can't we talk it over? See how we might preserve this placelessness, where we suffer and enjoy? Let's call these Eckford's questions in admiration of the imprecision with which Piper all but silently recites them.

If the self is an artwork, if they are identical in the separation of artist, work, and observer—then art is the refusal of them and their identity-in-relation, their spectatorial or compositional rapprochement. Art consents not to be a single being. It is a matter of empathy, of transcendental and empirical availability, which performance produces and nonperformance discovers. You can't fight a regime of self-protection by means of self-protection. In consenting not to protect herself, Eckford is not an end but a means. If it's true, as Bowles suggests, that Piper's work constitutes a critique of the categorical imperative, it does so in Eckford's wake but against Eckford's grain given its recourse to self-protection and self-assertion. Such recursion is also at work in Mayfield, Forman, and Braxton, in Arendt and Allen, and in all the selves and works that you or I might misleadingly refer to as our own. Auto-protective auto-assertion is sometimes manifest in that giving of an account of oneself that takes the form of meta-artistic discourse. The meta-artistic impulse to "let you know what I'm doing" is, fortunately, unable to keep up with art's general embrace of the condition in which the left hand and the right hand elude one another's grasp or gaze. It is precisely because both Piper and her work are dark to themselves and one another—in mutual rendition of the inadequacy of the very idea of selves and others—that it becomes necessary and possible to see that what might be called a misreading of Piper might be better, if still imprecisely, described as a disagreement with Piper. To disagree with Piper's accounts of herself and her work is to depend upon the dehiscence of and within herself and her work, the gravity of which is a matter of the field they occupy rather than fiction of their particularity. In this dehiscence, this break, this differential inseparability, other motives emerge; what emerges is another motif of selflessness.

The condition in which the self is invented for its own protection—which is the antinomian essence of Kant's critical philosophy and the ge(n)ocidal modernity it codifies and constitutes—is, as anyone who studies American policing knows, manifest in seemingly endless quotidian disaster. There's a difference between a blindfold and some sunglasses. At stake is the quality of Eckford's vulnerability and the limits of Piper's invulnerabiity. Each is a kind of armature. It's a matter of position, or of apposition's apposition to opposition, that makes the difference. Where is Piper? In a counterxenophobic head in a xenophobic world. If she walks through Max's Kansas City as if on her way to the conceptual scheme from which her performance was launched, such circularity is unavailable to Eckford, sent from nowhere to nowhere else insofar as the depth of her outward descent admits of no return. Perhaps the difference can be characterized as that between counterxenophobia and xenogenerosity, possessive enclosure and dispossessive availability. To see what Piper sees you have to close your eyes in regular intellection, which keeps the sensuality that constitutes it at bay or, even, in chains, setting its conditions. To see what Eckford sees you have to see through her to what sent her, thereby sending Piper, too. Piper is committed to transferring a certain mythology of self-sending—the self-projected as its own end, to whose preservation it is devoted. In the interest of the self, Piper makes these excursions but they are infused with something other than her self-making, her intentions, her interests. There's an appositional volition when the senses become theoreticians in their practice, when rationality surrounds the sensual regulation that is supposed to instantiate an etiolated conception of theory. In that conception vision is given a kind of temporary hegemony before it, too, is shut down, before rationality will have been hamstrung by its own not so secret agent, its own intelligence, its own officers of (a narrow conception of) the law. Such anti-anti-rationality might have its own relation to the irrational but that's irrelevant. Neither Piper nor her work, nor their blurred, ambiguous entanglement with one another are reducible to or encapsulated by the accounts she gives of them. In seeking after what sends Eckford we seek after what sends Piper, too.

According to Piper, Kant conceptualizes personhood as rational agency and the self as rationally unified consciousness. Is the self, then, a derivative of personhood, which emerges from rationality's capacity to unify? If black study moves in and as self-denial it need not move in the denial of rationality but rather in rational refusal of rationality's capacity to unify and in resistance to the implied interplay of unity and separation. There's a question concerning reason's capacity for disunion that is at stake here. In the matter of the unity of Piper and her work, interestingly, Bowles accepts Piper's apparent assumption that she can simply resist or defy such unity insofar as the dehiscence of self and work resists the viewer's gaze while sharing the viewer's world. Where is this interstitiality that Piper walks, in which the resistance to the unity of self and work is an effect of that rational unification of consciousness that constitutes the self? Will it have been possible to remain where the self is protected from its work? If the work instantiates the mutual permeability of inside and outside as a general condition, then it constitutes not only its own deconstitution but that of the self who, in having made the work, is unmade by the work. Within a restrictive understanding of the theoretical, the figure of the philosopher will have been sustainable in this volatile artistic field only by way of an operation that seeks to shore up the walls of both self and work, subject and object. But the mechanics of this retrofit—given most emphatically and most rigorously in the phenomenological tradition Kant can be said to have refounded in his critical finding of it—sets the terms and conditions for the merger of subject and object. What if the problem of "Art Consciousness and Self-Consciousness about Art Consciousness," and its corollary, the problem of being "absorbed into the collective Art Self-Consciousness, either as object or as collaborator," is redoubled in the privatization of consciousness that Piper enacts in the "Untitled Performance at Max's Kansas City"? What if that redoubling is itself redoubled in performances of the Mythic Being and their simulation of shared vulnerability in a public bus or on a public street? When Bowles says I miss something in Piper's critique of the "Untitled Performance," perhaps this is it.[87] If I missed it perhaps it was because I was in search of something like an account of a rational resistance to unity that philosophy, or the philosopher, cannot bear. Perhaps black study relinquishes that search for the sake of another mode of pursuance altogether. The self that performs self-protection, and then offers an ongoing critique of that performance in subsequent performances and discursive meta-performances that pay special attention to the limits of privatization in the enactment and meta-enactment of self-dissolution, is still the projective artifact and guardian of a unified consciousness. In assuming a more than visual link between the complex of self and work called Adrian Piper and the ensemble of worked selflessness called Elizabeth Eckford I want to suggest that performances of unified consciousness, or political subjectivity, are (often righteously glorious) etiolations of the differential entanglement of blackness/sociality.

At stake is this practice of assuming the self (as rationality's object and defense). In the world and in the eyes of the white man, the unwelcome intruder is also the brutally desired prisoner—condition and danger given at once in the degraded figure of the unmade self. At the same time, the prisoner is xenophobic, too—necessarily so as the personhood thrust upon her in constant violation is, itself, constantly violated, its capacity for self-making thwarted in and by self-making's genocidal imposition. No one could deny her moral right to self-protection but the immoral, state-sanctioned, self-made self who denies her right to rights. Xenophobia is general in the world, given in the empirical situatedness of its citizens and non-citizens in their separation and relation. It is, at the same time, a transcendental condition that defies situation as the structure of an abstract and universal conceptual scheme that persons share across the divide that separates the possibility of unity from its impossibility. Both of these things are true. We can't proceed without dealing with this double truth, its double edges. Xenophobia is always accompanied by incorporative desire. To posit the self, to attempt to take up the self's position, is to accept, to submit to, this xenophobia, which is as ambivalent as it is absolute.

Piper encrypts her submission to it in her revelation of the essential xenophobia of the Kantian self. For her it is a matter of cognitive endowment—the very essence of the very possibility of a conceptual scheme—this disposition to resist anomalous data. Clipping the wings of the understanding, whether that data is exterior and sensory or a function of interior *Phantasie* or, more precisely and problematically, refusing the refusal of the inside outside distinction upon which the assumption and preservation of unity and integration are based, is mind's nature, given in the separability of every body, every brain. Piper's solo performances at the club, on the bus, or in the terrible suspension of an imaginary auction block/pedestal, mobilize disunity in the interest of projecting, and ultimately of protecting, unified consciousness. And yet, those performances are infused with a nonperformative atmosphere, animated by what one might call a de-segregative refusal of integration. It's not just the internal irresolution that happily won't allow Piper's aspects fully to align—first I see an artist, then I see a philosopher, then I see a yogi—it's that external anomalies abound. Corollary to her assertion that xenophobia is an irreducible part of our general cognitive endowment, Piper claims that it can be contained by proper, non-defective rationality. Does such rationality require the retrofitting of the conceptual scheme so that it allows for the anomalous? If so, how then are unity and integration preserved? What anomalous data fails to conform to this constant interplay of thwarted subjection and impossible predication that blackness, which is the unmaking of the imposition and denial of self-making, serially exposes through the nonperformances of black people? If such data cannot be experienced by a unified self what happens to it? Is it experienced at all? And by whom?

There is a securing of the border that unity, that completeness, requires. Is xenophobia itself a transcendental concept or is it something all but in transcendence of the transcendental given its implication in the subject-predicate relation. If the empirical initiates the transcendental then the concept of self and other already implies that somehow the empirical is, itself, (pre)conditioned. It's not just that this constant oscillation between the two cannot be stilled; it's also that given that oscillation the two are still no longer—their unity and the unity they would form having been irreparably shaken. That the body gives us the empirical, as it were, does not undermine that the idea of the body and its limits is a function of the transcendental aesthetic. To consider what might happen if we don't assume a self is also to consider all of the assumptions, and that constant movement back and forth between the empirical and the transcendental, that are required in order to assume the self.

The police, whether in state-issued uniform or arrayed in sundresses and short-sleeved shirts, are there to protect selves from anomaly. At the same time, they are selves who must be protected from anomaly. Against the grain of this delusion, and the very real murder it intends and carries out, how will anomaly serve and protect itself from the ranks of anti-anomalous force directed at it from and as its own most stunted possibility? If the repudiation of whiteness, which is earth's only hope, will have been given in anomaly's unrestricted openness to itself, how can anomaly resist autoxenophobia's powerful allure? How can we be protected from self-protection without being open to it? This is the paradoxical question that Piper performs. While the rupture of that paradox cannot be seen in Piper's performance, its collapse can be seen through Eckford's nonperformance, the jurisgenerative imperative of whose social situation in and as selflessness is to serve, not to protect.

Here, then, is the significance of Piper's Kantian distinction between self and personhood. Selves can be capable, as it were, in the mismanagement of their necessary xenophobia, "a cognitive failure to apply the transcendent concept of personhood consistently across all relevant cases."[88] But what is a relevant case? Is blackness a relevant case? Can black people provide or instantiate a relevant case? Is Betty's case relevant? Who determines relevance? Did Kant himself apply this transcendent concept of personhood? If so, then it is clear that it is not inconsistent with antiblackness. What if the problem is not personhood, bound up with a certain conception/assumption of humanness? What if the problem is the very idea of the self, its separateness, where the xenophobic comes inexorably online. Insofar as Piper assumes the self, she is consistent in her refusal to avoid some romantic fiction of selves overcoming xenophobia. For her, it's not about overcoming xenophobia; it's about living with it. But to say this is also to accept that, say, in his recognition of Sally Hemings's personhood, and in his predisposition to consider that she violated his conception of what and who (his) people were, Thomas Jefferson was, by way of his own internal rational resources as well as his worldly power, able (xenophilically and within the context of serial rape) to manage his xenophobia, to his own benefit and in the interest of preserving the honorific stereotype conforming to himself to which he subscribed. In this he was no different than the Little Rock citizen who would have had no problem forcing himself upon, or having her child cared for by, any member of the Little Rock Nine. The protection of privacy, or the restrictions of (anti-)sociality are not just compatible with but also structured by such integration, hence the de-segregative imperative and its refusal of genocidal desire. We might say that such management, such protection, such restriction—in whatever self-assertive form or deformation of liberality and in all of such liberality's historical refinements—are the constantly renewed privilege called "whiteness." Xenophobia is not simply managed but cultivated, in this regard, through the regulatory incorporative exclusion of anomaly, which implies no contradiction between racism and rationality.

Meanwhile, that which is separated, so that the difference they bear can be contained, can't be separate as a matter of law. The separated that won't be separate prove the ineluctable law of inseparability. They prove that law in passing through the sentence. That's the difference they keep making even when they can't believe in it, even when they are not there, or here, and now. The cost of this sufferance is all but as immeasurable as the benefit, which will have only been truly dispersed when the sufferance is truly disbursed. The social is the field of that dispersal and disbursal, the field of implication of the empirical and the transcendental. Blackness is both anomalous and anonymous, a range of complexity that makes of naming a form of prayer. Elizabeth Eckford, little rock air.

Jurisgenerative Grammar

Consider the difference and relation between knowing and making a language: What happens when the intersubjective validity of the moral or linguistic law within is displaced by the very generativity that law is said to constitute? Noam Chomsky has tried many times, in many different venues and contexts, to offer condensed but proper understandings of an intellectual project called "generative grammar" whose "central topic of concern is what John Huarte, in the sixteenth century, regarded as the essential property of human intelligence: the capacity of the human mind to 'engender within itself, by its own power, the principles on which knowledge rests.'"[89] Such a power must be what composer and historian George Lewis would describe as "stronger than itself," some thing, some totality, some singularity that *is* only insofar as it is in excess of itself and is, therefore, already cut and augmented by an irreducible exteriority to which it is constrained to refer *and to exhaust*, as the condition of its own seemingly impossible possibility.[90] Similarly, that which this power is said to generate exists only insofar as it, too, is open to and infused with the outside. However, Chomsky is circumspect in his delineation of this internal capacity to engender the internal. The outside, which we'll call historicity, but which must also be understood as form's degenerative and regenerative force, is, for Chomsky, not inadmissible. However, the inside, which we'll call essence, is rich in its discretion and therefore able to generate that for which external stimulus, in its poverty, is unaccountable. Exteriority, which we might also talk about under the rubric of alterity, is immaterial to the Chomskyan configuration of the problem of essence. For Chomsky, Wilhelm von Humboldt's reference to "the infinite use of language" is "quite a different matter from the unbounded scope of the finite means that characterizes language, where a finite set of elements yields a potentially infinite array of discrete expressions: discrete, because there are six-word sentences and seven-word sentences, but no 6.2 word sentences; infinite because there is no longest sentence ([insofar as one can] append 'I think that' to the start of any sentence)."[91] I'm interested in the difference between a wholly internally driven understanding of "discrete" infinity and that necessary and irreducible openness to the outside which will have been productive of an immeasurable range of linguistic indiscretion, because to be interested in art is to be concerned with the constant and irruptive aspiration, beyond the possible and the impossible, of the 6.2-word sentence. At stake, on the other side of the question of discretion (which is to say that for whatever singular grammar there is the nonsentence, the nonphrase, whose very elements and order can be made, by way of a certain capacity to engender, into a sentence), is the capacity for a certain refusal of sanctioned grammatical capacity, for rupture and augmentation that inheres in the word and the sentence as the continually circulated gift/power of the outside we take in and by which we are taken, in the ongoing history of our necessary dis/possession. The most interesting potential area of inquiry emerging from Huarte's insight into a seemingly self-generating power is our capacity to generate what shows up as the ungrammatical. How do we know and (re)produce the extragrammatical, the extralegal? How do we know (how to) escape when escape is the general name we give to the impulse by which we break law? Ultimately, I'd like to understand this question concerning what might be called grammar's general economy, its essential supplementarity, more precisely as that which concerns our general, criminal, illegitimately criminalized capacity to make law.

In the previous paragraph I offer a synthesized echo of a critical attitude toward Chomsky that is driven by the belief that historiography is, and should be, theoretical practice in linguistics and whose work might be characterized as a methodological extension of Fanon's sociogenic principle against the grain of a certain Kantian trace in Chomsky's ontophylogenic project.[92] At stake is not simply a historical account of the discipline, which a textbook would be obliged to provide, but also a recognition of the priority of the diachronic over the synchronic, the sociohistorical over the structural(ist), in any account of language. But even an account such as this is problematic for those critics since the genuinely sociohistorical account would, in the end, not really be of language at all. They would argue that a genuinely sociohistorical linguistics is one in which the question of the nature of language is displaced by pragmatic concerns regarding what it is to be a speaker of language, a mode of existence that is irreducibly sociohistorical in a way that the Chomskyan model of language as a fixed system is not. The key theoretical precursor in such a model would be Darwin, not Descartes. And languaging, the linguistic action that displaces whatever imaginary thing language is or has been thought to be, would be understood as a function of and subject to evolution. The question of whether or not a structure has a history, of how social history operates in and on, but without eradicating, structure (let's call this the poststructuralist question) is set aside as is its interesting corollary, the question of whether or not there can be a structure without a center. To ask such questions will have already been to veer into the underground that is called the humanities when these post-Chomskyan linguists would insist that linguistics must be not only open but also subject to the "latest findings from the social and natural sciences," while at the same time remaining insistently oblivious to the latest findings of the humanities and the arts.[93] Of course, the idea that a structure has a history, is subject to the transformative force of history, is, in the arts and humanities, not one of their latest findings but in fact old news. And while this is of little moment to those who are interested, finally, in the liquidation, rather than the historicization, of structure (or, at least, in the indefinite suspension of the necessarily and irremedi-ably structuralist question concerning the nature of language), it requires something that composer and instrumentalist Anthony Braxton might call a "restructuralist" approach to and rapprochement with the ongoing Chom-skyan revolution in structural linguistics.[94] By way of this engagement, the question "What is a language?" is not eclipsed but illumined by the question of what happens when we hear a sequence of sounds.

Without adhering to the anti-*mater*ial restrictions that derive from the Chomskyan model's demand that the utterance be both disembedded and disembodied, there is a certain black study of language (music) that is it-self derived from the inaugurative event of Afro-diasporic experience un-derstood precisely as an interplay of disembodiedness and disembeddedness from which the materialities of stolen life, its self-contextualizing, corpulent multiplicity, continually emerge. It's not that syntax just hovers out there, but that there is a serialization of the syntactic moment, at once obliterative and generative, that is materialized by flesh, in context, as if there were an (ongo-ing) event out of which language emerges that language sometimes tries to capture. If it is the case that even Chomsky's massive and massively genera-tive attempt remains incomplete, this is due to a certain refusal to think, and then to think through, the relation between structure and event that is endemic to a certain scientificity (and which Chomsky himself seems to have identified insofar as he has repeatedly asserted that it may well be that literature will have had the most to say about the question of the origin of language). Still, it is as if one remains in search of a contribution to the theory of human nature that cannot or doesn't want to deal with the trace of "the event of the thing" of human nature so as to open, uneventually, a super-natural refusal of the thing itself.[95] At stake, in other words, is the history of essence understood, precisely, as the animation—the making—of the thing, the materiality of its endowment in ruptural *poiesis*'s exhaustive capacity to make law in making language make music; at stake, in other words, is the history of essence understood precisely as the annihilation—the breaking—of the thing, the materiality of its endowment in ruptural poiesis's exhaustive capacity to break law when breaking language breaks music: degeneration and regeneration *de re* is our constant study.

Consider the relation between (extra)musical or (extra)legal behavior, on the one hand, and the internal cognitive systems that make (extra)mu-sicality or (extra)legality possible. This would entail taking interest in the generation of musicojuridical possibility and in the materiality of grammars that Cheryl Wall might characterize as "worrying the line" between inside and outside or between depth as biocognitive interior endowment or competence (which must at least be understood in relation both to universality and inalienability) and surface as the open set of performances in which the musicojuridical is instantiated improvisationally in relation to exteriority's anoriginal and irreducible differences, differentiation, and alienation.[96] What's at stake is the universality of grammatical generativity that is given in the instantiation of the universal capacity to break grammar. Can the principles on which knowledge of language rests (or knowledge of music moves) be improvised? Can principles, in their very composure, be improvised? Can there be commerce—beyond mere one-way transport, transformation, or loosening—between principle and anarchy? Can you perform your way into a singular and unprecedented competence, into an instant and unrepeatable composition? Addressing these questions requires some consideration of the soloist as a speaker, as more + less than one who languages, who acts linguistically even in and out of a brutally imposed languishing, but who is also an instrument through which others, or through which, deeper still, alterity, speaks; at the asymptotic confluence of these senses, the speaker is a bridge machine, a resonant connectivity, an articulate spacing, the transverse, untraversable distance by which we arrive at multiplicity. However, arrival, here, is a misnomer. Instead, we might speak, in echo of some Althusser-Brathwaite duet in our heads, of an ongoing, aleatory arrivance, that endless, vibratory aftereffect of departure, of being-sent or being-thrown (over or overboard), of which speech, or more generally and more generatively, sounding, always speaks.

Braxton imagines, composes, improvises multiplicity—in a thirty-year initiative he calls language music—by way of a new mode of structural planning that will eventually be manifest not only as sound but also as a kind of technical drawing that is that sound's and that sonic space's prefigurative condition. Braxton calls the initial maneuver of his practice "conceptual grafting," which maintains, through minute analysis and dissection, the differential/differentiated singularity—the cellular modularity—of musical elements. "I began," Braxton says, "to break down phrase construction variables with regard to material properties, functional properties, language properties; to use this as a basis to create improvised music and then rechannel that into the compositional process."[97] New compositional movement, the overturning of musical ground, emerges from the still, shedded posture of self-analytic listening, the hermetic, audiovisual attunement to the shape and color of sound and its internal relations.

We are required now to consider not only the relationship between the (open) cell and refuge but also the (grafted) cell's generativity. What is it to refuse, while seeking refuge in, the cell? This requires some immersion in the history of the crawlspace, which is also a sound booth, and a (temporarily preoccupied) corner, and a broken window. Such immersion is conducted publicly, in hiding, out in broken territory where one has been preventatively detained. (T)here, Braxton reinitializes the relation between the internal generativity of the outside and the enunciation of ensemble's already striated intention: he is the unit that is more than itself, greater than itself, stronger than itself, precisely insofar as he attends to the internal (and more than simply) phonic difference of phonic material. The soloist is a black study group, a monastery's modular calculus, whose innateness is a plain of abridged presences. Like an autoethnographic soundcatcher, driven and enabled by eccentric, hesitant, sociopoetic logic—a radical empiricism that avoids the spirit of empirical systems—Braxton collates and collects what is beyond category and reveals how solo performance is multiplicity's social study. Beyond the retrograde possibilities of artificial individuality there was always *Spaltung*, personal mitosis, the *retrait* of the unalone to the woodshed, the wilderness, the desert, the fjord, the north, in asylum, on Monk's or Magic Mountain, where solitude is broken, haunted, crowded with study. The soloist is unalone; the soloist is not (all) one. $1-n$, having been rendered less than one, but not simply because of that, she is and instantiates a power of $n+1$, because the one is not the one, this bridge, and therefore requires some *off* renewal of the question of the meaning of being, which will have again been achieved by way of an existential analytic of the instrument(alist) who is the nothing that is other than man, that public thing. This is Martin Heidegger:

38. Falling and Thrownness

Idle talk, curiosity and ambiguity characterize the way in which, in an everyday manner, Dasein is its "there"—the disclosedness of Being-in-the-world. As definite existential characteristics, these are not present-at-hand in Dasein, but help to make up its Being. In these, and in the way they are interconnected in their Being, there is revealed a basic kind of Being which belongs to everydayness; we call this the "falling" of Dasein. This term does not express any negative evaluation, but is used to signify that Dasein is proximally and for the most part *alongside* the "world" of its concern. This "absorption in . . ." has mostly the character of Being-lost in the publicness of the "they." Dasein has, in the first instance, fallen away [*abgefallen*] from itself as an authentic potentiality for Being its self, and has fallen into the "world." "Fallenness" into the world means an absorption in Being-with-one-another, in so far as the latter is guided by idle talk, curiosity and ambiguity. Through the Interpretation of falling, what we have called the "inauthenticity" of Dasein may now be defined more precisely. On no account however do the terms *inauthentic* and *non-authentic* signify "really not," as if in this mode of Being, Dasein were altogether to lose its Being. "Inauthenticity" does not mean anything like Being-no-longer-in-the-world, but amounts rather to quite a distinctive kind of Being-in-the-world—the kind which is completely fascinated by the "world" and by the Dasein-with of Others in the "they." Not-Being-its-self [*Das Nicht-es-selbst-sein*] functions as a positive possibility of that entity which, in its essential concern, is absorbed in a world. This kind of not-Being has to be conceived as that kind of Being which is closest to Dasein and in which Dasein maintains itself for the most part.

So neither must we take the fallenness of Dasein as a "fall" from a purer and higher "primal status." Not only do we lack any experience of this ontically, but ontologically we lack any possibilities or clues for Interpreting it.

In falling, Dasein *itself* as factical Being-in-the-world, is something *from* which it has already fallen away. And it has not fallen into some entity which it comes upon for the first time in the course of its Being, or even one which it has not come upon at all; it has fallen into the *world*, which itself belongs to its Being. Falling is a definite existential characteristic of *Dasein* itself. It makes no assertion about Dasein as something present-at-hand, or about present-at-hand relations to entities from which Dasein "is descended." Or with which Dasein has subsequently wound up in some sort of *commercium*.[98]

There's this other thing that happens when you dance so hard your hand flies across the room, or when you brush up against somebody and find that your leg is gone, that makes you also wonder about the relation between fallenness and thrownness. Improvisation is (in) that relation. But for Heidegger—and a certain tradition he both finds and founds, and which resounds in breaking away from him—improvisation bears and enacts an irremedial inauthenticity that is given in being given to what might be best imagined, though it is often merely and inadequately understood as base sociality where what is at stake, more than anything, is precisely this: to be fascinated by the world and by being with one another and to move in this fascination's undercommon concern with or engagement in idle talk, curiosity, and ambiguity, *but by way of a certain thickness of accent,* a counterscholastic accompaniment, that troubles the standard speech that is misunderstood to have been studied. A function of being-thrown into the history we are making, this sound must also be understood as having prefaced the fall from ourselves into the world we make and are that is often taken for that sound's origin. What's also at stake, then, is a certain valorization or "negative evaluation": not, as Heidegger says, of fallenness as "a definite existential characteristic of Dasein itself," but rather of "present-at-hand relations to [and, impossibly, between] entities. . . ." Now I cut it off here because I'm not making *that* kind of argument about Dasein's parentage, its line of descent, or even the specific direction of its fall. This is not some claim to what will have been relegated to a kind of primitivity (either as a kind of degraded prematurity or as opposed to some originary and higher purity [recognizing that these are two sides of the same coin, so to speak]). The issue, rather, is another exemplary possibility for misinterpretation that Heidegger offers: that Dasein, not itself being "something present-at-hand," has subsequently "wound up in some sort of *commercium*" with entities to which it has some kind of "present-at-hand relation." What is this commercium? Who are these entities, these things? What is their relation to world? What is the nature of their publicness, their "being-lost in the publicness of the 'they'"? What is their relation to fallenness and thrownness? What is their, and their descendants', relation to thinking and to being thought?

Perhaps "some sort of *commercium*" is like that which, according to Richard Pryor, the police have been known to call, in their very denial of its present materiality, "some kind of community sing." Maybe it's a singing prince kind of thing, a Heidelberg beer hall kind of thing, which is also a black thing cutting the understanding in the aftermath of serious lecture. The commercium is something like the symposium, replete or dangerously more than complete or rendering the academy incomplete with lyrical w(h)ine. It is a fall from, or luxuriant parody of, the *Sacrum Commercium,* St. Francis's exchange with Lady Poverty, his undercommon enrichment, the fantastic effect of study and prayer in small, public solitude. And insofar as commercium has been a term of business/law since the Romans, this valence is not entirely foreign to the motivation behind Heidegger's offhand devaluation of the present-at-hand. Yet again we are speaking of the sociality that attends being-subject to exchange, which befalls even those who are parties to exchange, thereby troubling a distinction so crucial to a current proliferation of anti- or pseudo-, rather than paraontological, descriptions of blackness. Heidegger's negative evaluation bears the materiality that undergirds an etymological descent he chooses not to trace. But it becomes clear that the problematic of fallenness into the world, which is an irreducible part of Dasein's being, is or can be given to a devolutionary intensification, an undercommon fall from fallenness, when *Dasein* gets "wound up" with "some sort of *commercium*." This fall$_2$ from the world to the (under)world, which is the subject of Heidegger's offhand dismissal, is, again, an object (and source) of constant study.

I am concerned with fallenness into the world of things. Theodor Adorno speaks of this, tellingly, with regard to jazz: "The improvisational immediacy which constitutes its partial success counts strictly among those attempts to break out of the fetishized commodity world which want to escape that world without ever changing it, thus moving ever deeper into its snare, . . . With jazz a disenfranchised subjectivity plunges from the commodity world into the commodity world; the system does not allow for a way out."[99] Improvisational immediacy, an effect Heidegger links to thrownness, becomes for Adorno a substitute for a certain mode of uprising that would at least reverse the fall from fallenness that itself substitutes escape from the world for changing the world, thereby displacing fight or honorable and manly resistance with ignoble flight. And this ignobility is necessarily maternal, which is to say that it is so deeply bound up with sustenance, maintenance, and a kind of otherworldly, underworldly care, that flight often turns out to be interinanimate with remaining in the path(ont)ological zone, as if the one who flees militantly remains for f(l)ight again. What emerges, as and by way of planning and study, is a certain problematic where what it is to fly, already wound up in tarrying, is now bound up with digging (which Amiri Baraka has already thought in its irreducible relation to the music that comes from it and reproduces it) so that the way out turns out, in fact, to be the way back into that continual reconstruction of the underground that is carried—out, as it were, in jazz, let's say—not by disenfranchised subjectivity but by the ones who refuse subjectivity's general disenfranchisement, the ones whose deep inhabitation of the snare instantiates the fall$_2$ from "the commodity world into the commodity world" as continually revalued commercium, continually revaluing community sing. Moreover, this social life in the collective head is the way back into the underground of metaphysics. The soloist not quite learning to read what she has written, the soloist unable to sight-read what he has composed, falls back into difference, into sociality, into generativity, and so ascends into the open secret of the coenobitic club where the anoriginal criminality of judgment, of legislation, is renewed. The gathering is tight aeration and subatomic access, the soft rupture of every custom in its enactment, the sharp cut of every law at the moment of its making.

So that solo performance is a kind of bloom! Autostriation in the open underground is where St. Anthony's head becomes a rose. If you keep humming it, if you keep trying to hear that anarrangement, if you practice all the time, you won't even have to count it off, you just set it off and thereby undertake and undergo harmonic mitosis—he splits, her cell splits, he splits himself in her cell. The trace of having been sold initializes this autoconjugal autodisruption, this self-divisive self-reproduction, as multiple seriality, expansive conservation. Folded into the commercium like a one-time would-be sovereign whose song and dance is, finally, irrevocable abdication of that regulative desire in the name of love, revolutionary suicide in the name of self-defense, the soloist is drenched, saturated in color like a slide, a chromatic transparency, through which other things show up as neither subject nor party to exchange however much they are indebted to it, which is to say indebted to one another, for their very lives. Already there was this juked, unruly monasticism. Jumpin', the joint was a chapel and a library. In considering music's relation to the jurisgenerative principle, one comes to think of a certain outlaw asceticism, the extravagant austerity of a certain criminal aestheticism, that is carried out in the vast history of various sojourns in the woodshed, of fallenness on a late night eremitic bridge become practice room or, after an abortive attempt at the self-generation of the inside, simply and falsely conceived as the simultaneously artificial and unpremeditated expression of a single being, in St. Anthony Braxton's fleeing temptation in Chicago, where cell and city keep on becoming one another in a range of ways, by joining the experimental band's disruptive, expansive, sensual intellection, its performed improvisation through common deformations of membership, where they celebrate what it is to be indebted to the outside for an inside song.

Consider how Braxton's long, cryptographic fascination with various modes of the switchable track, his practice and study of hiding information in plain sight, as a kind of riding of the blinds, instantiates, in *For Alto*, the methodological assertion of flight in and from a given order. "The 'diversion from' is what we put our attention on" in order to consider the relationship between fugitive inhabitation and generativity.[100] The performed and performative study is the intersection, the switching point, between nomos and logos—between self-destruktive, sociopoetic law and dispersively gathered, graphophonic word—but negatively. This is not *graphe paranomon*, a suspension of already given legislation that is instantiated by a solo irruption; nor is it speech uttered by a citizen in the legitimate (which is to say privatized) realm of public appearance—in which membership or an already given matriculation is assumed—that disrupts and suspends the ongoing legislative order. Rather, Braxton performs (by way of the difference he takes in and brings), the gnomic, paranomic writing of the noncitizen who refuses the citizenship that has been refused him. His musicked speech is encrypted. The solo performance of Braxton's essential, experimental dismemberment comes from deep outside, the open, the surround, which resists being enclosed or buried as much as it does being excluded.

This is part of what Braxton writes about in his notes on Composition No. 8F, which is dedicated to pianist Cecil Taylor, though its own particular autoexplosive reach for the outside is directed even more by and toward Trane's depths and heights.

> The second aspect of Composition 8F's material breakdown involves the use of long musical passages built from 32nd—and 64th note figures. Material constructions from this sensibility permeate the total canvas of the music and are used in many different ways (i.e., sound register and focus etc.) The instrumentalist in this context is asked to maintain a super-charged use of musical formings throughout the total presentation of the music. Given musical formings will then appear that utilize the entire spectrum of the instrument, and the construction nature of the work also calls for the use of isolated material and focus directives (as a basis to establish timbral focus and structural balance). The use of this operative can be viewed in the context of John Coltrane's "sheets of sound" language period because all of the language directives in Composition No. 8F are designed to provide a platform for continuous multiple phrase formations (invention). There is no slowing of the pulse continuum in this work, nor is there

any decreasing of its sound note input rate. What we have instead is a recipe for a dynamic unfolding music that calls for the rapid employment of material initiatives—throughout the whole of the improvisation (from beginning to end).[101]

Without losing the hearing of overabundant multiphonics' split singularity, the animation of Braxton's sound, it remains important to consider the tidal adventure that marks the ups and downs of his invention. In doing so remember that the slave ship is a language lab. The projects are a conservatory. The prison is a law school. Refusal to acknowledge this is not only an always already breached bulwark against the romantic flight of fancy that it denigrates but is also empiricist suppression of the empirical. While the material conditions always matter, because the sound will always change, in the end it doesn't matter if it's closed or open air: the fecundity of the jurisgenerative principle, as the open set of generative grammar's autoconstitutive autotransgressions, is irrepressible.

This sets the stage for the encounter between Braxton and Édouard Glissant, both of whom have already been in that kind of contact that deep aesthetic theorists have with the general problematic of problematized generality, generativity, and genius that Trane once called "a love supreme." Spookily, mutually inspirited, they are already in action at a distance in a brutal world, as a duo whose braided incommensurability sounds forth as mutually nonexclusive enunciations of poetic intention, manifest in the ecstatic asceticism, the remote coenobitic life they share as impossible movement in local space, electric slide as terse, monastic glide, tortuous flight from one pitch to another, accelerated ascent and descent of the scale, of the very apparatuses of measure. The undercommon gliss is rough, tossed, rolled by water, flung by waves and it might end up sounding, so to speak, like a choir at study in Faulkner, Mississippi, the night before he or she hopped a freight for Chitown. There's a kind of obscurity, even an always angular kind of madness, in Braxton's *glissement*, his glissando that allows us to recall Chomsky's assertion that "Huarte postulates a third kind of wit" beyond both a certain cognitive docility in which the mind is devoid of everything but sense data filtered through an internally imposed empirical system and the internally powered engendering of "the principles on which knowledge rests." This other ingenuity, "by means of which some, without art or study, speak such subtle and surprising things, yet true, that were never before seen, heard, or writ, no, nor ever so much as thought of" is understood by Chomsky to be Huarte's reference to "true creativity, an exercise of the creative imagination in ways that go beyond normal intelligence and may, he felt, involve "a mixture of madness."[102] Madness, here in conjunction with mixture, is one of the names that have been given to the more than internally driven power of the one who, insofar as he is more than mere interiority, is more than one. To have turned or taken the inside out is not only to have embraced, as it were, the dual enablement of both the poverty of stimulus and the poverty of internal volition. This potential is Braxton's constant, circular aspiration, bespeaking, against Huarte's grain, the supernatural movement of art and study. The language he generates is touched by an externally propelled submergence and surfacing that he bears as a kind of public property, as chorographic philosophy's gift of opacity, the blurred, serrated edge of thinking on the move, an exhaustive, imaginary mapping of an underworld and its baroque and broken planes. This ongoing, ruptural moment in the history of the philosophy of relation, "in which" as Glissant says, "we try to see how humanities transform themselves," is more and less than the same old story.[103] Its torqued seriality—bent, twisted, propelled off line—is occult, impossible articulation. The line is broken; the passage is overtaken, become detour; it is, again as Glissant says, unknown; it carries gentle, unavoidably violent overturning, a contrapuntal swerve of the underside; it performs a rhizomatic voluntarity, roots escaping from themselves without schedule into the outer depths. This involuntary consent of the volunteer is our descent, our inheritance, should we choose to accept it, claim it, assent to it: forced by ourselves, against force, to a paraontological attendance upon being-sent, we are given to discover how being-sent turns glide, *glissando*, into fractured and incomplete release of and from the scale, into the immeasurable. Braxton's music, its sharp-edged celebration, has a dying fall and rise. It descends and ascends us. It sends us and we are befallen by the fate of the one, which is to become many. Fallen into sociality, thrown into the history we make in having been thrown into it, we are given, in being given to this music, to flight away from a given syntax, from the linguistic law within, into a mode of autonomous autoregulation that will, itself, have been escaped.

The rough glide of Braxton's musical movement, the burred terrain of Glissant's words, sends us to find out more of what it means to have been sent to give yourself away. We are driven to resist this movement, where consent is now inseparable from a monstrous imposition, but we are also drawn, at the same time, against ourselves, to the rail, to the abyss, by the iterative, broken singularity it hides and holds, by the murmur of buried, impossible social life—that excluded middle passage into multiplicity, where pained, breathlessly overblown harmonic striation (*Sacrum Commercium*, sacred fragment; contramusical moment; catastrophe's counterstrophic movement), from way underneath some unfathomable and impossible to overcome violation, animates ecstasies driven down and out into the world as if risen into another: impossible assent, *consentement impossible, glissment impossible*, impossible Glissant, unimaginable axe, unheard of Braxton.

We study how to claim this sound that claims us, and that Glissant and Braxton amplify, in work that beautifully discovers, in the depths of our common impasse, our common flight, and our common habitation. They allow and require us to be interested in the unlikely emergence of the unlikely figure of the black soloist, whose irruptive speech occurs not only against the grain of a radical interdiction of individuality that is manifest both as an assumption of its impossibility as well as in a range of governmental dispositions designed to prevent the impossible, but also within the context of a refusal of what has been interdicted (admission to the zone of abstract equivalent citizenship and subjectivity, whose instantiations so far have been nothing but a set of pseudoindividuated aftereffects of conquest and conquest denial, a power trip to some fucked-up place in the burnt-out sun), a kind of free or freed "personality" that will have turned out to be impossible even for the ones who are convinced they have achieved it, even as they oversee its constant oscillation between incompleteness and repair, distress and fashion. That refusal is a kind of dissent that marks our descent, that moves in the terribly beautiful absence of patrimonial birthright or heritage and in the general, generative, maternally rotund and black Falstaffic recognition that necessarily masculinist honor is just a bunch of hot air. Such refusal, such dissent, takes the form of a common affirmation, an open consensus given in the improbable, more than im/possible, consent, in Glissant's words, "not to be a single being."[104] By what paradoxical means does the black soloist continue to give that consent, a regifting that not only instantiates but also redoubles just about all of the doubleness we come to associate with giving and the gift and the given? Here, the given is unfinished, as elastic composition, not (traditionally or sententiously) well formed.

Fear of the black soloist is a transcendental clue that tips us off to her importance. She is subject to beating and attack—whether by the state or its sanctioned, extragovernmental deputies—because her walking out alone is understood to be a threat to the order of things, a placement of that order under attack. But more often even than beating, the preferred institutional response to the (una)lone transgressor is her enforced isolation since solitary confinement is misunderstood to be a method for silencing what it only serves to amplify. This invasive irruption of fugued, fugitive singularity into the administered world both figures and performs an immanent rather than transcendent alterity—earthy, earthly, undercommon sociality in and under and surrounding the world, disruptive of its regulatory protocols, diversive of its executive grammar. My primary interest is in that range of explosive, melismatic voicing. I'm after a certain doo-wopped, post-bopped, aquado-olooped, da da da da da datted (un)broken circle of study—the general form of the development group, in some kind of community sing, a Child Development Group of Mississippi, say, where putatively motherless, always already endangered children move, not without moving but within movement, in specific, a capella instantiation of strain, of resistance to constraint, as instruments of deinstrumentalization, in the propelling and constraining force of the refrain, in that land of California, where Chicago is a city in Mississippi, where Mississippi is a refuge and a (fugue) state of mind—an ongoing digging, a continual digging, held, as if buried, underneath a little rock. Such voicing always moves, always in the wilderness, under regulatory duress and its own theory has it that that kind of trouble "really keeps us workin' our mind."[105] To set it off like that, to go off like that, to anarrange like that, is a kind of head start, but you have to have some sense of the value of playing, of being played with, of being played, of being-instrument, of being-endangered, of mere being, of having fallen, of doing the thing, of doing your thing, underwater, underground, out in the open secret, in public, exposed in the interest of safety—which is a kind of flower for refugees—and autonomy, when flown-away hands start clapping. All we have to do is find somebody that would love to sing. You want to sing? Well, somebody start singing . . . .

Generativity, our ongoing common growth in difference, is also escape in contemplative performance, reanimating the itinerant communal form of the city before as a study hall inside a dance hall. Black study is a mode of life whose initiatory figures are given as anarchic principles that are form-generating. Not just the proliferation of form, to which generativity would then submit itself, but proliferative, generative form. This is what Braxton is trying to produce, at the intersection of study, competence, composition, and performance (improvisation). There is a kind of anti-instrumental rationality that lends itself to a being-instrument. It moves by way of the instrument's disruptive extension. Again, this is instantiated, we might say, in the figure of the speaker, the bridge machine, through and across whom praises (voices, forces) flow. She consents not to be a single being. "Common alterity," he prays, "make me your instrument." It's the speaker's capacity to generate generative form, this fearsomeness of what the black soloist is and does, the one who, being so much more and less than one, so emphatically not but nothing other than human, discomposes for submerged choir (city), a song in flight that is sung while sunken. She moves in place, off the track he's on, for the love of the set it opens. There's an alto wind at your back, even if all you're trying to do is get out of the way of what you want to ride, so you can keep on generating these monkish dormitory chants, the archaeology of our potential, past, in the funereal birthplace, the venereal graveyard, which is a slave ship, a project, and a prison; a sound booth, a corner, and a broken window; a law school, a conservatory, and a language lab.

To imagine what we are waiting for everyone to imagine, one would have to have been able to really listen to this music; but, as Ellison once wrote, so few people really do. The inability to listen to Forman, Mayfield, and Braxton and the incapacity to claim and be claimed by the nearness and distance that mark their contrapuntal imagination expresses a more general self-imposition of sensory deprivation with regard to the black student and suspended intellection with regard to what is held in, and made possible by, black studies and the black arts. More specifically, in her sight unheard rejection of the resources that are given in that field of study and estrangement, Arendt relinquishes a certain magic—a kind of luxurious ability to conjure other worlds, another world—that impossibly emerges from a set of imperatives dictated by impoverishment in this one. This impossible emergence is a politico-aesthetic articulation that moves, as it were, notinbetween politics and aesthetics. At stake is an extra- or underpolitics given in and as the black arts of the impossible. Meanwhile, the ongoing administration of this world depends on the sharing of this attitude of rejection, even by those such as Arendt, who might be said to share it against her will and against her thought. Of course, many share this attitude without the slightest trace of internal conflict; it's just that it's particularly disappointing when the one who gives it expression and raises it to a level of philosophical rigor is also the one to whom many turn in order to understand and honor the absolute and singular possibilities that emerge when a stranger appears, and the ethical responsibilities that accrue to each of us insofar as we are strangers in a

world of strangers, refugees in search of refuge, refusing what has been refused, looking for and fleeing home. In expressing, by way of her nonencoun-
ter with the ensemble to which Forman disruptively belongs, the virulence
of that attitude toward the black study by which she is held captive, Arendt
samples her own recording of the near, and ongoing, miss. Sometimes, such
inattention brings something beautiful to our attention.

chapter 3

Chromatic
Saturation

The Case of Blackness

The cultural and political discourse on black pathology has been so pervasive that it could be said to constitute the background against which all representations of blacks or blackness or (the color) black take place. Its manifestations have changed over the years though it has always been poised between the realms of the pseudosocial scientific, the birth of new sciences, and the normative impulse that is at the heart of—but that strains against—the black radicalism that strains against it. From the origins of the critical philosophy in the assertion of its extrarational foundations in teleological principle; to the advent and solidification of empiricist human biology that moves out of the convergence of phrenology, criminology, and eugenics; to the maturation of (American) sociology in the oscillation between good- and bad-faith attendance to "the negro problem"; to the analysis of and discourse on psychopathology and the deployment of these in both colonial oppression and anticolonial resistance; to the regulatory metaphysics that undergirds interlocking notions of sound and color in aesthetic theory: blackness has been associated with a certain sense of decay, even when that decay is invoked in the name of a certain (fetishization of) vitality.

Black radical discourse has often taken up, and held itself within, the stance of the pathologist. Going back to David Walker, at least, black radicalism is animated by the question, What's wrong with black folk? The extent to which radicalism (here understood as the performance of a general critique of the proper) is a fundamental and enduring force in the black public sphere—so much so that even black "conservatives" are always constrained to begin by defining themselves in relation to it—is all but self-evident. Less self-evident is that normative striving against the grain of the very radicalism from which the desire for the norm is derived. Such striving is directed toward those lived experiences of blackness that are, on the one hand, aligned with what has been called radical and, on the other hand, aligned not so much with a kind of being-toward-death but with something that has been understood as a deathly or death-driven nonbeing. This strife between normativity and the deconstruction of norms is essential not only to contemporary black academic discourse but also to the discourses of the barbershop, the beauty shop, and the bookstore.

I'll begin with a thought from Frantz Fanon that doesn't come from any of these zones though it's felt in them, strangely, since it posits the being of, and being in, these zones as an ensemble of specific impossibilities:

> As long as the black man is among his own, he will have no occasion, except in minor internal conflicts, to experience his being through others. There is of course the moment of "being for others," of which Hegel speaks, but every ontology is made unattainable in a colonized and civilized society. It would seem that this fact has not been given enough attention by those who have discussed the question. In the *Weltanschauung* of a colonized people there is an impurity, a flaw, that outlaws [*interdit*] any ontological explanation. Someone may object that this is the case with every individual, but such an objection merely conceals a basic problem. Ontology—once it is finally admitted as leaving existence by the wayside—does not permit us to understand the being of the black man. For not only must the black man be black; he must be black in relation to the white man. Some critics will take it upon themselves to remind us that the proposition has a converse. I say that this is false. The black man has no ontological resistance in the eyes of the white man.[1]

This passage, and the ontological (absence of) drama it represents, leads us to a set of fundamental questions. How do we think the possibility and the law of outlawed, impossible things? And if, as Fanon suggests, the black cannot be an Other for another black, if the black can only be an Other for a white, then is there ever anything called black social life? Is the designation of this or that thing as lawless, and the assertion that such lawlessness is a function of an already extant flaw, something more than that trying, even neurotic, oscillation between the exposure and the replication of a regulatory maneuver whose force is held precisely in the assumption that it comes before what it would contain? What's the relation between explanation and resistance? Who bears the responsibility of discovering an ontology of, or of discovering *for* ontology, the ensemble of political, aesthetic, and philosophical derangements that compose the being that is neither for itself nor for the other? What form of life makes such discovery possible as well as necessary? Would we know it by its flaws, its impurities? What might an impurity in a worldview actually be? Impurity implies a kind of incompleteness, if not absence, of a worldview. Perhaps that incompleteness signals an originarily criminal refusal of the interplay of framing and grasping, taking and keeping—a certain reticence at the ongoing advent of the age of the world picture. Perhaps it is the reticence of the grasped, the enframed, the taken, the kept; or, more precisely, it is the reluctance that disrupts grasping and framing, taking and keeping, as epistemological stance as well as accumulative activity. Perhaps this is the flaw that attends essential, anoriginal impurity—the flaw that accompanies impossible origins and deviant translations.[2]

What's at stake is fugitive movement in and out of the frame, bar, or whatever externally imposed social logic—a movement of escape in and from pursuit, the stealth of the stolen that can be said, since it inheres in every closed circle, to break every enclosure. This fugitive movement is stolen life and its relation to law is reducible neither to simple interdiction nor bare transgression. Part of what can be attained in this zone of unattainability, to which the eminently attainable ones have been relegated, which they occupy but cannot (and refuse to) own, is some sense of the fugitive law of movement that makes black social life ungovernable, that demands a paraontological disruption of the supposed connection between explanation and resistance.[3] This exchange between matters juridical and matters sociological is given in the mixture of phenomenology and psychopathology that drives Fanon's work, his slow approach to an encounter with impossible black social life poised or posed in the break, in a certain intransitive evasion of crossing, in the wary mood or fugitive case that ensues between the fact of blackness and the lived experience of the black and as a slippage enacted by the meaning— or, perhaps too "trans-literally," the (plain[-sung]) sense—of things when subjects are engaged in the representation of objects.

"The Case of Blackness" is a spin on the title of the fifth chapter of Fanon's *Black Skin, White Masks*, infamously mistranslated as "the fact of blackness." "The lived experience of the black" is more literal—experience bears a German trace, translates *Erlebnis* rather than *Tatsache*, and thereby places Fanon within a group of postwar Francophone thinkers encountering phenomenology that includes Jean-Paul Sartre, Maurice Merleau-Ponty, Emmanuel Levinas, and Tran Duc Thao.[4] The more literal phrasing indicates Fanon's veering off from an analytic engagement with the world as a set of facts that are available to the natural scientific attitude, so it's possible to feel the vexation of certain commentators with what might be mistaken for a flirtation with positivism. However, I want to linger in, rather than quickly jump over, the gap between fact and lived experience in order to consider the word *case* as a kind of broken bridge or cut suspension between the two. I'm interested in how the troubled, illicit commerce between fact and lived experience is bound up with that between blackness and the black, a difference that is often concealed, one that plays itself out not by way of the question of accuracy or adequation but rather by way of the shadowed emergence of the ontological difference between being and beings. Attunement to that difference and its modalities must be fine. Perhaps certain recalibrations of Fanon—made possible by insights to which Fanon is both given and blind— will allow us to show the necessity and possibility of another understanding of the ontological difference. In such an understanding, the political phonochoreography of being's words bear a content that cannot be left by the wayside even if it is packaged in the pathologization of blacks and blackness in the discourse of the human and natural sciences and in the corollary emergence of expertise as the defining epistemological register of the modern subject who is in that he knows, regulates, but cannot be black. This might turn out to have much to do with the constitution of that locale in which "ontological explanation" *is* precisely insofar as it is against the law.

One way to investigate the lived experience of the black is to consider what it is to be the dangerous—because one is, because we are (Who? We? Who is this we? Who volunteers for this already given imposition? Who elects this imposed affinity? The one who is homelessly, hopefully, less and more?) the constitutive—supplement. What is it to be an irreducibly disordering, deformational force while at the same time being absolutely indispensable to normative order, normative form? This is not the same as, though it does probably follow from, the troubled realization that one is an object amid other objects, as Fanon would have it. In their introduction to a rich and important collection of articles that announce and enact a new deployment of Fanon in black studies' encounter with visual studies, Jared Sexton and Huey Copeland index Fanon's formulation in order to consider what it is to be "the thing against which all other subjects take their bearing."[5] But something is left unattended in their invocation of Fanon, in their move toward equating objecthood with "the domain of non-existence" or the interstitial space between life and death, something to be understood in its difference from and relation to what Giorgio Agamben calls naked life, something they call "raw life" that moves—or more precisely cannot move—in its forgetful nonrelation to that quickening, forgetive force that Agamben calls the form of life.[6]

Sexton and Copeland turn to the Fanon of *Black Skin, White Masks*, the phenomenologist of (the lived experience of) blackness, who provides for them the following epigraph:

> I came into the world imbued with the will to find a meaning in things, my spirit filled with the desire to attain to the source of the world, and then I found that I was an object in the midst of other objects.[7]

> J'arrivais dans le monde, soucieux de faire lever un sens aux choses, mon âme pleine du désir d'être à l'origine du monde, et voici que je me découvrais objet au milieu d'autres objets.[8]

Fanon writes of entering the world with a melodramatic imagination, as Peter Brooks would have it, one drawn toward the occult installation of the sacred in things and gestures (certain events, as opposed to actions, of muscularity), and in the subterranean field that is, paradoxically, signaled by the very cutaneous darkness of which Fanon speaks. That darkness turns the would-be melodramatic subject not only into an object but also into a sign, the hideous blackamoor at the entrance of the cave, that world underneath the world of light that Fanon will have entered, who guards and masks "our" hidden motives and desires.[9] There's a whole other economy of skins and masks to be addressed here. However, I'll defer that address in order to get at something (absent) in Sexton and Copeland. What I'm after is obscured by the fall from prospective subject to object that Fanon recites: namely, a transition from thing(s) (*choses*) to object (*objet*) that turns out to version a slippage or movement that animates the history of philosophy. What if we bracket the movement from (erstwhile) subject to object in order to investigate more adequately the change from object to thing (a change as strange as that from the possibility of intersubjectivity that attends majority to whatever is relegated to the plane or plain of the minor)? What if the thing whose meaning or value has never been found finds things, founds things? What if the thing will have founded something against the very possibility of foundation and against all anti- or postfoundational impossibilities? What if the thing sustains itself in that absence or eclipse of meaning that withholds from the thing the horrific honorific of "object"? At the same time, what if the value of that absence or excess is given to us only in and by way of a kind of failure or inadequacy—or, perhaps more precisely, by way of a history of exclusion, serial expulsion, presence's ongoing taking of leave, every time we say goodbye—so that the nonattainment of meaning or ontology, of source or origin, is the only way to approach the thing in its informal (enformed/enforming) (as opposed to formless), material totality? Perhaps this would be cause for black optimism or, at least, some black operations. Perhaps the thing, the black, is tantamount to another fugitive sublimity altogether. Some/thing escapes in or through the object's vestibule; the object vibrates against its frame like a resonator and troubled air gets out. The air of the thing that escapes enframing is what I'm interested in—an often unattended movement that accompanies largely unthought positions and appositions. To operate out of this interest might mispresent itself as a kind of refusal of Fanon.[10] But my reading is, rather, enabled by the way Fanon's texts continually demand that we read them—again or, deeper still, not or against again, but for the first time. I wish to engage a kind of pre-op(tical) optimism in Fanon that is tied to the commerce between the lived experience of the black and the fact of blackness and between the thing and the object—an optimism recoverable, one might say, only by way of mistranslation, that bridged but unbridgeable gap that Heidegger explores as both distance and nearness in his discourse on "The Thing."

Michael Inwood moves quickly in his explication of Heidegger's distinction between *Ding* and *Sache*: "*Ding*, 'thing,' is distinct from *Sache*, 'thing, (subject-)matter, affair.' *Sache*, like the Latin *res*, originally denoted a legal case or a matter of concern, while *Ding* was the 'court' or 'assembly' before which a case was discussed."[11] In Heidegger's essay "*Das Ding*," the speed of things is a bit more deliberate, perhaps so that the distinction between things and human affairs can be maintained against an explicatory velocity that threatens to abolish the distance between, which is also to say the nearness of, the two: "The Old High German word *thing* means a gathering, and specifically a gathering to deliberate on a matter under discussion, a contested matter. In consequence, the Old German words *thing* and *dinc* become the names for an affair or matter of pertinence. They denote anything that in any way bears upon men, concerns them, and that accordingly is a matter for discourse."[12] The descent from Old High German to Old German is held here and matters. Its trajectory is at issue such that we are to remain concerned with the detachment and proximity of "a gathering to deliberate" and "contested matter." It might even be worthwhile to think the gathering *as* contested matter, to linger in the break—the distance and nearness—between the thing and the case in the interest of the ones who are without interests but who are, nevertheless, a concern precisely because they gather, as they are gathered matter, the internally differentiated materiality of a collective head. The thing of it is the case of blackness.

For Heidegger, the jug is an exemplary thing. The jug is a vessel; it holds something else within it. It is also "self-supporting, or independent." But "does the vessel's self-support alone define the jug as a thing?"

> The potter makes the earthen jug out of earth that he has specially chosen and prepared for it. The jug consists of that earth. By virtue of what the jug consists of, it too can stand on the earth, either immediately or through the mediation of table and bench. What exists by such producing is what stands on in its own, is self-supporting. When we take the jug as a made vessel, then surely we are apprehending it—so it seems—as a thing and never as a mere object.
>
> Or do we even now still take the jug as an object? Indeed. It is, to be sure, no longer considered only an object of a mere act of representation, but in return it is an object which a process of making has set up before and against us. Its self-support seems to mark the jug as a thing. But in truth we are thinking of this self-support in terms of the making process. Self-support is what the making aims at. But even so, the self-support is still thought of in terms of objectness, even though the over-againstness of what has been put forth is no longer grounded in mere representation, in the mere putting it before our minds. But from the objectness of the object, and from the product's self-support, there is no way that leads to the thingness of the thing ("T," 167).

This is to say, importantly I think, that, the "jug remains a vessel whether we represent it in our minds or not" ("T," 167). (Later Heidegger says: "Man can represent, no matter how, only what has previously come to light of its own accord and has shown itself to him in the light it brought with it" ["T," 171].) Its thingliness does not inhere in its having been made or produced or represented. For Heidegger, the thingliness of the thing, the jug, is precisely that which prompts its making. For Plato—and the tradition of representational thinking he codifies, which incorporatively excludes Fanon—everything present is experienced as an object of making where object is understood, in what Heidegger calls its most precise expression, as "what stands forth" (rather than what stands before or opposite or against). In relation to Fanon, Kara Keeling calls on us to think that which stands forth as project and as problem. Accordingly, I am after a kind of shadow or trace in Fanon—the moment in which phenomenology strains against its own reification and ownership of experience, its own problematic commitment to what emerges from (a certain reductive regulation of) making, in order to get at "a meaning of things." Though decisive and disruptive in ways that remain to be thought, that strain is momentary in Fanon, is momentarily displaced precisely by that "representation of what is present, in the sense of what stands forth and of what stands over against as an object" that never, according to Heidegger, "reaches to the thing *qua* thing" ("T," 168–69).

For Heidegger, the jug's being, as vessel, is momentarily understood as being-in-its emptiness, the empty space that holds, the impalpable void brought forth by the potter as container. "And yet," Heidegger asks, "is the jug really empty?" ("T," 169). He argues that the jug's putative emptiness is a semipoetic misprision, that "the jug is filled with air and with everything that goes to make up the air's mixture" ("T," 169). Perhaps the jug, as thing, is better understood as filled with an always already mixed capacity for content that is not made. This is something other than either poetic emptiness or a strictly scientific fullness that understands the filling of the jug as simple displacement. As Heidegger puts it, "considered scientifically, to fill a jug means to exchange one filling for another." He adds,

These statements of physics are correct. By means of them, science represents something real, by which it is objectively controlled. But— is this reality the jug? No. Science always encounters only what *its* kind of representation has admitted beforehand as an object possible for science.

. . . Science makes the jug-thing into a nonentity in not permitting things to be the standard for what is real.

Science's knowledge, which is compelling within its own sphere, the sphere of objects, already had annihilated things as things long before the atom bomb exploded. The bomb's explosion is only the grossest of all gross confirmations of the long-since accomplished annihilation of the thing: the confirmation that the thing as a thing remains nil. The thingness of the thing remains concealed, forgotten. The nature of the thing never comes to light, that is, it never gets a hearing. This is the meaning of our talk about the annihilation of the thing ("T," 170).

"The Lived Experience of the Black" bears not only a lament over Fanon's own relegation to the status of object; it also contains a lament that it also suppresses over the general annihilation of the thing to which transcendental phenomenology contributes insofar as it is concerned with *Sachen*, not *Dinge*, in (what remains untranslatable as) its direction toward the things themselves. Insofar as blackness remains the object of a complex disavowing claim in Fanon, one bound up precisely with his understanding of blackness as an impure product—as a function of a making that is not its own, an intentionality that could never have been its own—it could be said that Fanon moves within an economy of annihilation even though, at the same time, he mourns his own intentional comportment toward a hermeneutics of thingliness. Is blackness brought to light in Fanon's ambivalence? Is blackness given a hearing—or, more precisely, does blackness give itself to a hearing—in his phenomenological description (which is not but nothing other than a representation) of it? Studying the case of blackness is inseparable from the case blackness makes for itself in spite and by way of every interdiction. In any case it will have been as if one has come down with a case of blackness.

Meanwhile, Heidegger remains with the question of the essential nature of the thing that "has never yet been able to appear" ("T," 171). He asks, What does the jug hold and how does it hold? "How does the jug's void hold?" ("T," 171). By taking and keeping what it holds but also, and most fundamentally, in a way that constitutes the unity, the belonging together, of taking and keeping, in the *outpouring* of what is held. "The holding of the vessel occurs in the giving of the outpouring. . . . We call the gathering of the twofold holding into the outpouring, which, as being together, first constitutes the full presence of giving: the poured gift. The jug's jug-character consists in the poured gift of the pouring out. Even the empty jug retains its nature by virtue of the poured gift, even though the empty jug does not admit of a giving out ("T," 172). What is it to speak of this outpouring, to speak of the thing, the vessel, in terms of what it gives, particularly when we take into account the horror of its being made to hold, the horror of its making that it holds or bears? This question is necessary and decisive precisely insofar as it insists upon a rough-hewn accompaniment to Heidegger's talk of gift and consecration. Sometimes what is given is refusal. How does refusal elevate celebration? Heidegger invokes the "gush" as strong outpouring, as sacrificial flow, but perhaps what accentuates the outpouring, what makes it more than "mere filling and decanting," is a withholding that is aligned with refusal, a canted secret ("T," 173). At any rate, in the outpouring that is the essence of the thing/vessel dwells the Heideggerian fourfold of earth, sky, divinity, and mortals that precedes everything that is present or that is represented. The fourfold, as staying and as appropriation is where thing approaches, if not becomes, event. This gathering, this event of gathering, is, for Heidegger, what is denoted in the Old High German word *thing*. By way of Meister Eckhart, Heidegger asserts that "*Thing* is . . . the cautious and abstemious name for something that is at all." He adds:

> Because the word *thing* as used in Western metaphysics denotes that which is at all and is something in some way or other, the meaning of the name "thing" varies with the interpretation of that which is—of entities. Kant talks about things in the same way as Meister Eckhart and means by this term something that is. But for Kant, that which is becomes the object of a representing that runs its course in the self-consciousness of the human ego. The thing-in-itself means for Kant: the object-in-itself. To Kant, the character of the "in-itself" signifies that the object is an object in itself without reference to the human act of representing it, that is, without the opposing "ob-" by which it is first of all put before the representing act. "Thing-in-itself," thought in a rigorously Kantian way, means an object that is no object for us, because it is supposed to stand, stay put, without a possible before: for the human representational act that encounters it ("T," 176–77).

Meanwhile, in contradistinction to Kant, Heidegger thinks being neither as idea nor as position/objectness (the transcendental character of being posed) but as thing. He might be best understood as speaking out of a clearing, or a flaw, that also constitutes a step back or away from the kind of thinking that produces worldviews or, at least, that particular worldview that accompanies what, for lack of a better turn, might be called intersubjection. Fanon offers, by way of retrospection, a reversal of that step back or away. In briefly narrating the history of his own becoming-object, the trajectory of his own being-positioned in and by representational thinking, Fanon fatefully participates in that thinking and fails to depart from the "sphere of mere attitudes" ("T," 181). At the same time, Fanon and the experience that he both carries and analyzes places the Heideggerian distinction between being (thing) and *Dasein*—the being to whom understandings of being are given; the not, but nothing other than, human being—in a kind of jeopardy that was already implicit, however much it is held within an interplay between being-overlooked and being-overseen.

So I'm interested in how the ones who inhabit the nearness and distance between Dasein and things (which is off to the side of what lies between subjects and objects), the ones who are attained or accumulated unto death even as they are always escaping the Hegelian positioning of the bondsman, are perhaps best understood as the extraontological, extrapolitical constant—a destructive, healing agent; a stolen, transplanted organ always eliciting rejection; a salve whose soothing lies in the corrosive penetration of the merely topical; an ensemble always operating in excess of that ancient juridical formulation of the thing (*Ding*), to which Kant subscribes, as that to which nothing can be imputed, the impure, degraded, manufactured (in)human who moves only in response to inclination, whose reflexes lose the name of action. At the same time, this dangerous supplement as the fact out of which everything else emerges, is constitutive. This special ontic-ontological fugitivity of and in the slave is what is revealed as the necessarily unaccounted for in Fanon. So that in contradistinction to Fanon's protest, the problem of the inadequacy of any ontology to blackness, to that mode of being for which escape or apposition and not the objectifying encounter with otherness is the prime modality, must be understood in its relation to the inadequacy of calculation to being in general. Moreover, the brutal history of criminalization in public policy, and at the intersection of biological, psychological, and sociological discourse, ought not obscure the already existing ontic-ontological criminality of/as blackness. Rather, blackness needs to be understood as operating at the nexus of the social and the ontological, the historical and the essential. Indeed, as the ontological is, as it were, moving within the corrosive increase that the ontic instantiates, it must be understood that what is now meant by ontological requires special elucidation. What is inadequate to blackness are already given ontologies. The lived experienced of blackness is, among other things, a constant demand for an ontology of disorder, an ontology of dehiscence, a paraontology whose comportment will have been (toward) the ontic or existential field of things and events. That ontology will have had to operate as a general critique of calculation even as it gathers diaspora as an open set—or as an openness disruptive of the very idea of set—of accumulative and unaccumulable differences, differings, departures without origin, leavings that continually defy the natal occasion in general even as they constantly bespeak the previous. This is a Nathaniel Mackey formulation whose full implications will have never been fully explorable.[13] What Fanon's pathontological refusal of blackness leaves unclaimed is an irremediable homelessness common to the colonized, the enslaved, and the enclosed. This is to say that what is claimed in the name of blackness is a disorder that has always been there, that is retrospectively and retroactively located there, that is embraced by the ones who stay there while living somewhere else. Some folks relish being a problem. Like Amiri Baraka and Nikhil Pal Singh (almost) say, "Black(ness) is a country" (and a sex) (that is not one).[14] Stolen life disorders positive value just as surely as it is not equivalent to social death or absolute dereliction.

So if we cannot simply give an account of things that, in the very fugitivity and impossibility that is the essence of their existence, resist accounting, how do we speak of the lived experience of the black? What limits are placed on such speaking when it comes from the position of the black, but also what constraints are placed on the very concept of lived experience, particularly in its relation to the black—when black social life is interdicted? Note that the interdiction exists not only as a function of what might be broadly understood as policy but also as a function of an epistemological consensus broad enough to include Fanon, on the one hand, and Daniel Patrick Moynihan, on the other—encompassing formulations that might be said not only to characterize but also to initiate and continually reinitialize the philosophy of the human sciences. In other words, the notion that there is no black social life is part of a set of variations on a theme that include assertions of the irreducible pathology of black social life as well as the implication that (nonpathological) social life is what emerges by way of the exclusion of the black or, more precisely, of blackness. But what are we to make of the pathological here? What are the implications of a social life that, on the one hand, is not what it is and, on the other hand, is irreducible to what it is used for? This discordant echo of one of Theodor Adorno's most infamous assertions about jazz implies that black social life reconstitutes the music that is its phonographic distillate.[15] That music, which Miles Davis calls "social music," to which Adorno and Fanon gave only severe and partial hearing, is of interdicted black social life operating on frequencies that are disavowed— though they are also amplified—in the interplay of sociopathological and phenomenological description. How can we fathom a social life that tends toward death, that enacts a kind of being-toward-death, and which, because of such tendency and such enactment, maintains a terribly beautiful vitality? Deeper still, what are we to make of the fact of a sociality that emerges when lived experience is distinguished from fact, in the fact of life that is implied in the very phenomenological gesture/analysis within which Fanon asserts black social life as, in all but the most minor ways, impossible? How is it that the off-harmony of life, sociality, and blackness is the condition of possibility of the claim that there is no black social life? Does black life, in its irreducible and impossible sociality and precisely in what might be understood as its refusal of the status of social life that is refused it, constitute a fundamental danger—an excluded but immanent disruption—to social life? What will it have meant to embrace this matrix of im/possibility, to have spoken of and out of this suspension? What would it mean to dwell on or in minor social life? Fanon imposes this set of questions on us. At the same time, and in a way that is articulated most clearly and famously by W. E. B. Du Bois, this set of questions is the position, which is also to say the problem, of blackness.

Musicologist and pianist Charles Rosen, in his monograph *Arnold Schoenberg*, speaks of the "strong . . . saturation of chromatic space" at the end of Schoenberg's epochal masterpiece, *Erwartung*:

> The last page of *Erwartung* has been so much imitated that it is hard to perceive its originality today, although it still makes an effect that is overpowering. "Oh, are you there," cries the woman about her dead lover, and then adds softly, "I searched," as the low woodwinds begin, triple *pianissimo*, a rising chromatic series of six-note chords. The other instruments enter with similar chords moving up or down the chromatic scale, each group moving at different rates of speed; the fastest speeds come in the last three beats with the dynamics remaining between triple and quadruple *pianissimo*.
>
> This massed chromatic movement at different speeds, both up and down and accelerating, is a saturation of the chromatic space in a few short seconds: and in a movement that gets ever faster, every note in the range of the orchestra is played in a kind of *glissando*. The saturation of musical space is Schoenberg's substitute for the tonic chord of the traditional musical language. The absolute consonance is a state of chromatic plenitude.[16]

Susan McClary might say that the feminine is profligate in this ending—that the woman, in the richness and poverty of her psychological and theatrical nonfullness, exerts a discomfiting force on musical rationality that is manifest in the aggressive taking up of space, a radical expropriation of the musical commons by elements whose exclusion (or, more precisely, whose highly regulated and exclusionary deployment) had been constitutive of a new understanding of musical reason in the age of the critical foundation of reason in general. But perhaps this is, in itself, a far too aggressive rendering of the situation. For, as Rosen argues, Schoenberg doesn't dispense with the concept of musical resolution as much as reconstruct it by way of the overload.

This concept of the saturation of chromatic space as a fixed point toward which the music moves, as a point of rest and resolution, lies behind not just *Erwartung* alone but much of the music of the period. Its importance for the future of music was fundamental. It can take two forms, strong and weak. The weak form is the more common, and became, indeed, canonical by the 1920s, although it was influential long before then: this is the filling out of chromatic space by playing all twelve notes of the chromatic scale in some individual order determined by the composer but without regard to the register, high or low. The strong form, found in *Erwartung* and in a very few other works, fills out the whole of the space in all the registers, or approaches this total saturation.[17]

For Rosen, the weak form of chromatic saturation acknowledges the tyranny of the octave, while the strong form, whenever it emerges, signals that resistance to such tyranny, that breaking of musical law understood as natural law, that accompanies the irruption of what Rosen might call new musical significance. Even in Schoenberg, as Rosen points out, the weak form of the saturation of chromatic space tends to dominate. However, it is on the last page of *Erwartung* that a certain strength asserts itself over weakness, as if the necessity of ending itself necessitates a reconstruction of musical ends. It is the end as if it had been thrown and Schoenberg throwing ends can feel just as stupendous as when, for a little while, Biggie Smalls was so inclined. This throwing or thrownness of the end, this propulsion of closely regulated elements into what had been enclosed musical space, reveals, indexes, and brings into relief and use a certain politicoethical rhetoric in the music that had been more or less submerged, as it were, since the age of baroque. At stake, here, is what Rosen recognizes as the necessity of (a) metaphor at the moment when the ontological and political question of musical (co)existence arises. He writes, "The metaphor of chromatic 'space' is necessary when one wishes to denote the theoretical coexistence of all possible notes that can be played. Our concept of music today is still that of fixed, determinate points called notes. These points are discontinuous: even a *glissando* or slide from one to the other cannot alter this, as only the end points have a true function of pitch.[18]

For Rosen it really is crucial to remember that for Schoenberg, "the filling out of the chromatic space is clearly a movement toward stability and resolution." As such it is, again, a recalibration rather than a disavowal of musical ends. But this attempt at what might be called a liberation of those musical ends, a bringing of them into the light of self-governance and self-regulation, precisely in the clarity of its essentially Kantian task—one that flirts with a certain unleashing of the unregulatable in the interest of a more perfect mode of regulation—is touched and troubled from the start by the audiovisual specter of broken containment. To release all the notes of the chromatic scale back into something like a musical free range is not just to denote but also to court, even if in the interest of a certain renewal of the regulative, both the theoretical and practical coexistence of all possible notes that can be played and, moreover, of all the impossible notes that can't be played. This flirtation with a certain inhabitation of and in a newly resaturated musical space in which the copresence of all the notes calls into existence new structures of regulative musical rationality precisely by announcing itself in and as a regime of uncut musical differences is not the kind of encounter that is easily gotten over.

Meanwhile, the language of strong and weak, masculine and feminine, begins to seem inadequate to this old-new sense and scene of chromatic saturation in which regulation and resolution are rendered spectral im/possibilities by the more than theoretical presence of what another pianist and musicologist, Cecil Taylor, might call, but with none of Rosen's reticence, "all the notes."[19] Neither strong nor weak, neither male nor female, let's call this other version of chromatic saturation *black/ness* so that we might consider more fully what it is for a normative musical matrix to be overrun by matrical promiscuity, by profligate madrigal, by accidental, unwritten, black notes. While keeping in mind that blackness is increasingly veiled and ever more securely overseen in the discourses of the (neo)classical age, we'll have to figure out a way to get to what remains buried, or unceremoniously unburied; what is left hidden below but also on and as the surface of certain serially uncited (black) sites; what will have been constantly taken by way of being given as the unwritten that you know you're supposed to read by sight. In the end, perhaps what remains to be read is that eternal, preternatural prenatality, that inveterate acting-out-in-groups, in which all the notes are commonly engaged as something on the order of a lawlessness of musical imagination calling the diatonic and even the chromatic into existence. So that what's at stake is not chromatic saturation so much as something on the other side of it (that theoreticopractical possibility of which Rosen speaks): the law of movement, the law of anoriginarily broken law, that takes up the local habitation and takes on the name of the homeless, nameless ones.

Improvisation, which is the dominant mode of black/ness, articulately moves in that break, that distance and dislocation, that *décalage*, that, as

Louis Althusser teaches us in his contribution to *Reading Capital,* exceeds reading at sight. Hence improvisation can always be seen as the enactment of a certain impatience with, or troubling of, the limits of notation. In collections of sixteenth-century madrigals, for instance—in music that is poised between the sacred and the profane, love and murder, mannerism and the baroque—chromatic saturation and notational fugitivity converge when *note nere* or black notes, signifying increased rhythmic complexity, give the page a blackened or colored (*chromatico*) appearance. What could be spoken of here, by way of a paranoiac history that props up racialization, as the saturation of sheet music by blackness, intimates that theoretical coexistence of all the notes that Rosen indexes. At the same time, the forces of musical regulation, in response to the unsettling vision that theoretical possibility imposes as the blackened, as chromatic saturation, will have pushed underground, between lines, into the marginal zones of the unwritten or the illegible, a range of musical differences that fall and are hidden under the rubrics of musica ficta or accidental notes, sounds given in performance but whose overpopular and overpopulated vulgarity must remain undocumented in spite of its necessity. Note that what is rendered illegible is the reductive force of regulation (which places musical material in the realm of the unwritten or unseen, however much it is heard) as well as the potentiality (whose presence is only in its absence) that calls such regulation into being in the first place—the not but nothing other than present theoretical and practical possibility of all the notes, all the shades, which is to say, all the differences. Implied here is that reading is seeing what is not/there beyond or beneath transparency. The irreducible problem of classical political economy, which Althusser's reading of Marx's reading of it reveals, "is not what it does not see, it is *what it sees*; it is not what it lacks, on the contrary, it is *what it does not lack*; it is not what it misses, on the contrary, it is *what it does not miss.*" This problematic of overlooking, and also of a regulative and disciplinary overseeing, of what one sees, is the visual field that blackness inhabits even when blackness irrupts into the discourse of music. As Althusser says, "the oversight no longer concerns the object, but *the sight* itself. The oversight is an oversight that concerns *vision:* non-vision is therefore inside vision, it is a form of vision and hence has a necessary relationship with vision."[20] In turning to this question of vision, and of an understanding of chromatic saturation (insofar as it is bracketed by the thing that comes before and after it) that will have been proper to the visual field, I'll be turning, again, to music.

In the literature of color vision, chromatic saturation refers to the relative amount of hue perceived in a colored stimulus. Black is generally understood as an unsaturated or achromatic color that, on the other hand, increases the apparent saturation or brightness of colors paired or juxtaposed with it. Now we might achieve some accurate sense of the differences between the uses of the terms *chromaticism* and *chromatic saturation* in music and the visual arts and sciences. In music the accent is on difference; in the visual the accent is on purity; in the visual, blackness is an absence or neutrality that brings chromatic saturation or purity into relief by way of contrast/proximity; in music, blackness indicates chromaticity as a potentially unregulated or profligate internal difference, an impurity derived from the mixture of modes (major/minor) or of scales (diatonic/chromatic); it can be situated between an unwritten but aurally performed abundance or improvisational excess derived from textual implication or a kind of visual overload of black marks on the page. At stake, perhaps, is the rediscovery of that other mode of reading that Althusser retrospectively announces. In this reading, which is not at sight, but which implies a certain insight, an impossible foresight that improvisation has often been misunderstood as opposing, blackness is im/properly held to be the monochromatic residence of all the notes, all the colors, all the shades. It is a commonness or common presence in absentia, in and on the run, *in cognito* or in cognegro, as the case may be. Sometimes heard, seldom seen, this heard scene is subject to constant overhearing and oversight. But sometimes, as in the example I'm about to consider, the scene emerges with that flash of black light that accompanies the encounter of the apparently incommensurable.

Now I want to place the problem of blackness, and the question of dwelling on or in minor social life in relation to the work of art, to the question of the artwork's thingliness, its madness, its lateness. This is to say that I'd like to bring the set of questions that is black social life into relief by way of, and by passing through, the notion of chromatic saturation, which is to say that misfire in or of the translation of that notion between the language of music and the language of vision. I'll do so by turning to an audiovisual ensemble composed of Ad Reinhardt and Cecil Taylor, Albert Ammons and Piet Mondrian. Something is unhinged in this set that might recalibrate in multiple ways our sense of the black/white encounter, particularly insofar as we acknowledge certain possibilities that emerge in and from impossible black social life when the city is about to be born and when minor conflict— its outlaw ontology, and its interdicted, criminal life—tends toward death but, escaping all ends, moves in relation to thrown ends, to a vast, stupendous range of throwing ends. I'll argue that Mondrian was deregulated by the urban underground he'd been dreaming of; that his great, final picture *Victory Boogie Woogie* is all black, is all of what had been absorbed in black, is the explication of a dissonant, chromatic saturation, the inhabitation of a break or border, the disruption embedded in the grid's boundaries. I want to amplify (Ammons, father of the Jug, in Mondrian and) Taylor in Reinhardt, where Taylor is severely threatened with submergence in Reinhardt's intractable misunderstanding of what is done through Reinhardt, by forces Reinhardt can neither understand nor assimilate due to his attempt to encompass what pierces and absorbs him. I'll try to illuminate Taylor's attempt to open things up in exchange with Reinhardt: embodying sound in a discourse of sight, making sound matter like an irruptive thing, enacting the victory of refusing to arrive, saying here we are never having got here, dancing an insistent aftereffect evading each and every fatal occasion, each minor occasion that is not one.

(There are other resonances that I know I won't get to: broken speeches of fugitive ontologues recorded in the texture of a black line; a boundary diffused into epiphenomenal swatches, later to become what seems to be unrecorded but showing up sounding everywhere; black differences, not only the collective heads in Reinhardt's unacknowledged black social thingliness, but also an unstable black cube named Gene Smith, mugging rupped-up proprieties like an other Tony Smith [Saginaw, Michigan] blowing up Michael Fried from way downtown, way outside. [I have gone off privately in public, in Fred Oakley's club, the *Neue Plastik*, just outside of Fordyce, Arkansas, in order to talk to somebody. Gone to curve angles. Bend and drop these notes right where you lost them, to get at what remains—unattainable, unrepresentable—of the thing. My flaw.])

In *Art as Art: The Selected Writings of Ad Reinhardt*, there is a text called "Black as Symbol and Concept."[21] Barbara Rose, the volume's editor, tells us that it's a transcript of Reinhardt's contribution to a discussion involving Taylor and five other artists based in New York or Toronto, Aldo Tambellini, Michael Snow, Arnold Rockman, Stu Broomer, and Harvey Cowan. I am particularly interested in the encounter between Taylor and Reinhardt that Rose's transcription erases. That encounter is, I think, part of a far larger structure of impossible erasures (of the impossible). This is to say that there seem to be some fundamental incommensurabilities that animate the encounter: one is black and the other white, which means not just different experiences that differently color their thinking about color but also Reinhardt's palpable inability to take Taylor seriously, a handicap that more often than not still structures interracial intellectual relations; the more important one, at least for my purposes today, has to do with the fact that one is a musician and the other a painter and this means they speak in those different, seemingly incommensurable languages about that for which the term *chromatic saturation* is only a beckoning gesture. Unfortunately, as we'll see, Reinhardt reads blackness at sight, as held merely within the play of absence and presence. He is blind to the articulated combination of absence and presence in black that is in his face, as his work, his own production, as well as in the particular form of Taylor. Mad, in a self-imposed absence of (his own) work, Reinhardt gets read a lecture he must never have forgotten, though, alas, he was only to survive so short a time that it's unclear how or whether it came to affect his work.

On August 16, 1967, with the cooperation of Bell Telephone Company and the Canadian Broadcasting Corporation, *Arts/Canada* magazine organized this "simultaneous conversation," devoting a full issue to this discourse on "black as a special concept, symbol, paint quality; the social-political implications of the black; black as stasis, negation, nothingness and black as change, impermanence and potentiality."[22] Reinhardt initiates things by saying black is interesting "not as a colour but as a non-colour and as the absence of colour." He adds, "I'd like then to talk about black in art—monochrome, monotone, and the art of painting versus the art of culture" ("B," 3). In the notion of blackness as absolute dereliction, as absence of color and antithetical to admixture, Reinhardt moves on a parallel track to Fanon or, at least, to a certain reading of Fanon. He proceeds by way of a bad or, at least, meaningless example: "Here is a quotation from [Japanese landscape painter Katsushika] Hokusai: 'there is a black which is old and a black which is fresh. Lustrous black and dull black, black in sunlight and black in shadow. For the old black one must use an admixture of blue, for the dull black an admixture of white, for the lustrous black, gum must be added. Black in sunlight must have grey reflections.' I want to read that because that doesn't have any meaning for us." ("B," 3). One wants to consider the relation between what Reinhardt understands to be meaningless—a small treatise on the relation between impurity and internal difference in the case of the color black—and what Fanon understands as rendering ontological explanation criminal. What does the color black do to the theory of color (as the manifestation of absence turned to the excessive, invaginative more-than-fullness of impurity)? What does the black or blackness do to ontological explanation (as fugal, centrifugal, fugitive ontological, and epistemological disruption)? For Reinhardt, the multiplicity of symbolic meanings that have been attached to the color black—sinfulness, evil, femininity, maternity, formlessness, and the "yearning for whiteness in the West that counters and accompanies these meanings"—are and must be detachable from the absence (of difference) that defines and is internal to the color black ("B," 3). This detachment is in the interest of "the negativeness of black" ("B," 3) which interests Reinhardt and which can, again, be understood in relation to something Fanon both desires and desires to appose.

A bit later in the conversation, Taylor intervenes.

> I think for my first statement I would like to say that the experience is two-fold and later, I think you'll see how the two really merge as one experience.
>
> "Whether its bare pale light, whitened eyes inside a lion's belly, cancelled by justice, my wish to be a hued mystic myopic region if you will, least shadow at our discretion, to disappear, or as sovereign, albeit intuitive, sense my charity, to dip and grind, fair-haired, swathed, edged to the bottom each and every second, minute, month: existence riding a cloud of diminutive will, cautioned to waiting eye in step to wild, unceasing energy, growth equaling spirit, the knowing, of black dignity."
>
> Silence may be infinite or a beginning, an end, white noise, purity, classical ballet; the question of black, its inability to reflect yet to absorb, I think these are some of the complexes that we will have to get into ("B," 4).

Taylor's musicopoetic intervention, which quotation marks mark as an intervention within an intervention, is a reinaugural rupture. Taylor interrupts himself and the conversation he joins by raising the question of black dignity in a discourse on black art. He moves differently to Reinhardt, whose opening of the discussion is followed and carried forth in a kind of uninterrupted seriality by other participants in the conversation—Arnold Rockman, Michael Snow, Harvey Cowan, and Stu Broomer before Taylor leaps, or breaks, in. Reinhardt will brook no interruption; this is confirmed in Rose's reproduction of "his" text. In interrupting and/or starting over, Taylor speaks, at the same time, in a kind of counterpoint to or with Reinhardt. Moreover his speaking is, immediately, of an experience of black/blackness that places his intervention in a Fanonian phenomenological mode. To speak of experience, and later of existence, is to move counter to Reinhardt's overly stringent essentialism. Deeper still, Taylor speaks by way of hue, mysticism, and myopia, all of which show up for Reinhardt as derangements. ("There is something wrong, irresponsible and mindless about colour" he says, "something impossible to control. Control and rationality are part of any morality" ("B," 6). Taylor moves against Reinhardt (in his best Kantian/Greenbergian aestheticoethical mode) in a set of lyric gestures that chart a trajectory to "spirit, the knowing, of black dignity" ("B," 4). In this sense he speaks not only out of but also of the lived experience of the black. This is to say that Taylor moves by way of but also through Fanon, in the wake of an experience, an aesthetic sociality that Fanon never can fully embrace insofar as he never comes really to believe in it, even though it is the object, for Fanon, of an ambivalent political desire as well as a thing (of darkness) he cannot acknowledge as his own. In other words, Taylor speaks of and out of the possibilities embedded in a social life from which Fanon speaks and of which he speaks but primarily as negation and impossibility. This simultaneous conversation becomes, by way of a kind of ghostly transversality, a dialogue between Taylor and Fanon in which Reinhardt serves as the medium.

Other remote participants might later emerge, in addition to the tentative, minimal address to the things Taylor says we'll have to get into. Taylor and Fanon are the underground of this conversation, all down up in wherever black/ness and color hang. It remains for Taylor to make his claim on black aestheticosocial life, on the "spirit, the knowing, of black dignity," more explicit in his next intervention:

> I think Richard Wright wrote a book . . . called *Black Power*. Unfortunately, newspapers must sell, and I think they give a meaning of the moment to something which has long been in existence. The black artists have been in existence. Black—the black way of life—is an integral part of the American experience—the dance, for instance, the slop, Lindy hop, applejack, Watusi. Or the language, the spirit of the black in the language—"hip," "Daddy," "crazy," and "what's happening," "dig." These are manifestations of black energy, of black power, if you will. Politically speaking, I think the most dynamic force in American political life since the mid-1950s has been the black surge for equal representation, equal opportunities and it's becoming an active ingredient in American life" ("B," 6).

It's a kind of Ralph Ellison formulation that might seem more characteristic of Wynton Marsalis than Taylor but for the fact that it waits on a Fanonian understanding of impurity as disruption even as it waits for Fanon to get to the related, nonexcluded, nonexclusive understanding of mixture, of color, as constitutive of blackness and of blackness or black as a constitutive social, political, and aesthetic power. It's a kind of Stokely Carmichael formulation.

Meanwhile, between Taylor's formulation and Reinhardt's next intervention, Rockman offers a kind of regulative mediation that displaces Taylor's invocation of the priority and inevitability of another mixture that black instantiates and is by calling on a certain discourse or structure of (black) feeling. He refers to the poem that erupts out of Taylor's first intervention as "a very moving experience" ("B," 6). He also invokes an earlier point in the discussion when Snow referred to his father's blindness. Blindness, according to Rockman, is an internal blackness that is opposed to the exterior or inessential blackness of which Taylor speaks in his invocation of black life, energy, and power. He adds, in a Fanonian vein, that "the whole negro bit is a creation of the white world" ("B," 7). This moment is important precisely insofar as it mediates between Taylor and Reinhardt, allows Reinhardt to avoid Taylor's intervention, his invocation of the social, even as it places Taylor between Rockman's feelings and Reinhardt's antisocial frigidity, both of which emerge against a black background. Reinhardt follows this apparent escape route, that moves by way of the assumed inessentiality of black life, in his objection to the introduction of blindness as sentimental. For Reinhardt, issues of blindness, space, and sexuality move away from what he calls "the highest possible discussion," which would be on "an aesthetic level" ("B," 7). Taylor's invocation of a necessarily social aesthetic, a black aesthetic and sociality whose essence is a politics of impure or impurifying facticity, is bypassed. Reinhardt is disturbed by Taylor's intervention. Though he never really addresses it, he is clearly unhappy with its power to make the discussion "go off into too many subjects" ("B," 7). Reinhardt adds:

> Well, of course, we have enough mixed media here. I just want to again stress the idea of black as intellectuality and conventionality. There is an expression "the dark of absolute freedom" and an idea of formality. There's something about darkness or blackness that has something to do with something that I don't want to pin down. But it's aesthetic. And it has *not* to do with outer space or the colour of skin or the colour

of matter. . . . And the exploitation of black as a kind of quality, as a material quality, is really objectionable. Again I'm talking on another level, on an intellectual level. ("B," 7)

One can feel Taylor fuming from an underground to which Reinhardt would have relegated him without mentioning him in his Friedian rejection of mixture-as-theatricality. And yet, Taylor's occupation of this underground, precisely in the richness of its black aesthetic and intellectual content, is inhabited by way of Taylor's refusal and not his being rendered or regulated. Rockman, duly chastened by the dismissal of his sentimentalism, meekly asks Reinhardt to explain his objection to glossy black. Interestingly, Reinhardt dislikes glossy black because it reflects and because it is "unstable" and "surreal" ("B," 7). The reflective quality of the color black—as well as the capacity of the black to reflect—have, of course, been introduced by Taylor. Only now, however, can these issues be addressed by Reinhardt on his own high level. Glossy black disturbs in its reflective quality: "It reflects all the [necessarily social] activity that's going on in a room" ("B," 7). But this is also to say that glossy black's reflection of the irreducibly social is problematic precisely insofar as it disrupts the solipsism of genuine intellectual reflection that painting is supposed to provide. This, in turn, is to say that glossy black denies the individual viewer's absorption into a painting that will have then begun to function also as a mirror but a mirror that serves to detach the viewer from the social and that characterizes that detachment as the very essence of intellectual and aesthetic experience. Reinhardt wants what he refers to as "less [*sic*] distractions and less [*sic*] intrusions tha[n] colour or light or other things might make" ("B," 8). Taylor, having spoken of and from blackness as aesthetic sociality, of and from the eternal, internal, and subterranean alien/nation of black things in their unregulatable chromaticism, must have been fuming.

The discussion moves again along the lines and laws that Reinhardt lays down. Objection to him is held within an old discourse that combines primitivism, futurism, and blackness as the disavowal of physicality. I'm speaking of Tambellini's invocation of the Soviet cosmonaut who, upon experiencing outer space, says, "Before me—blackness, an inky-black sky studded with stars that glowed but did not twinkle; they seemed immobilized." Tambellini continues,

Here again is a primitive man, a caveman, but he's the caveman of the space era. I see him as the most important man. It's immaterial who he is; it's even immaterial what his name is. But that's what our children are going to be, that's what the future is going to be, and this is what the extension of man has got to. He's got to get rid of this whole concept of black pictures or of black anything as a physical object. He's got to realize that he is black right now ("B," 12).

Against the grain of Tambellini's enthusiasm for whatever transcends the material, out of his own particular and exclusionary intellectualism, and taking up the question of sentiment or emotion again, Reinhardt responds, "The reason for the involvement of darkness and blackness is, as I've said, an aesthetic-intellectual one, certainly among artists. And it's because of its non-colour. Colour is always trapped in some kind of physical activity or assertiveness of its own; and colour has to do with life. In that sense it may be vulgarity or folk art or something like that. But you'd better make sure what you mean by emotion, that's what I would say" ("B," 12–13). And now the encounter between Taylor and Reinhardt can really begin, interrupted only by a couple of brief but telling interjections by Tambellini (though it should be noted that for Reinhardt the encounter brings into play other ghostly eminences for whom Taylor is a medium: Marcel Duchamp, whose theatrical excess, which Taylor might be said to embody, is an object of Reinhardt's particular antitheatrical prejudice; and Mondrian, whose dramatic politics, which Taylor might be said to embody, Reinhardt mistakes for asceticism).[23]

Taylor: Would you give us a definition?
Reinhardt: Well, Clive Bell made it clear that there was an aesthetic
        emotion that was *not* any other kind of emotion. And prob-
        ably you could only define that negatively. Art is always made
        by craftsmen—it's never a spontaneous expression. Artists
        always come from artists and art forms come from art forms.
        At any rate, art is involved in a certain kind of perfection. Ex-
        pression is an impossible world. If you want to use it I think
        you have to explain it further.
Taylor: In pursuit of that perfection, once it is attained, what then?
        What is your reaction to that perfection?
Reinhardt: Well, I suppose there's a general reaction. I suppose in the
        visual arts good works usually end up in museums where they
        can be protected.
Taylor: Don't you understand that every culture has its own mores, its
        way of doing things, and that's why different art forms exist?

People paint differently, people sing differently. What else does it express but my way of living—the way I eat, the way I walk, the way I talk, the way I think, what I have access to?

Reinhardt: Cultures in time begin to represent what artists did. It isn't the other way around.

Taylor: Don't you understand that what artists do depends on the time they have to do it in, and the time they have to do it in depends upon the amount of economic sustenance which allows them to do it? You have to come down to the reality. Artists just don't work, you know, just like that—the kind of work, the nature of their involvement is not separate from the nature of their existence, and you have to come down to the nature of their existence. For instance, if they decide to go into the realm of fine art, there are certain prerequisites that they must have.

Tambellini: This guy floating in space has more to do with the reality that I'm living in than some idiotic place with walls and pictures in it. This man made one of the most poetic statements I've heard in my life. And furthermore I recognize the act he performs out there; he's destroying every possible square idea I've ever known, every possible notion that man can any longer be up and down. In the tradition of Mondrian you have the floor and the top; the tradition of Egyptian and western man is in the horizontal and the vertical. I don't work with that concept. It is the concept of nature. But he's telling me what's going on there. When the black man breaks out of his tradition, he's telling me what he's feeling, he's telling me what western man has done. He's telling me about segregation, he's telling me directly "see what your museums are, preservation of your own culture," "see what the radio is, the propaganda for your own culture," "see what this newspaper is, the propagation of your own . . ." and this space guy says to me, "see what the universe is up there, something which has no ups and downs," "see what space is, total darkness." He's telling me something I have to deal with. I have to create some kind of images ("B," 13–14).

The distinction between what Tambellini has and doesn't have to deal with, along with Tambellini's off-translation of Taylor's formulations, given in a manner that is foreshadowed by Rockman's, serves to sanction Reinhardt's dismissal, and provides another context for the relegation of Taylor's appeal. It is, after all, Reinhardt who makes judgments, who speaks with a kind of juridical authority. But Reinhardt is not trying to hear the case Taylor makes for (another understanding of) blackness. Reinhardt continues, in response now to Tambellini (and setting up Taylor's final disruption, an invocation to something like a phenomenological description of the artist's routine):

> Reinhardt: This hasn't anything to do with your day-to-day problems.
> Taylor: Day-to-day problems? What do you mean by day-to-day problems?
> Reinhardt: The artist has a day-to-day routine.
> Taylor: What is that routine specifically?
> Reinhardt: It is boring, drudging . . .
> Taylor: My work gives me pleasure. But the minute I walk outside there is enough that is evil and ugly and full of that which I call drudgery and boredom for me not to want it in my work and around me. Poverty is not a very satisfying thing.

Aldo said it very clearly, western art is involved and has been involved with one perspective, one idea, one representation of one social-racial entity and aesthetic; and I'm saying that I must be aware of that, in what that has meant to black men or to the Indians. I have to be aware of the social dynamics of my society in order to function. I don't only have a responsibility to myself, I have a responsibility to my community.

> Reinhardt: As a human being, not as an artist.
> Taylor: Now look, you are not the one, you are positively not the one to talk about human beings, since you rule out the human element in your art. That kind of dichotomy is very common in the west, and it has resulted in paranoia.
> And so, therefore, I'm involved in making people aware of the black aesthetic. That fine art which you talk about is an exclusive art, and it excludes not according to ability, but according to wealth.
> Tambellini: I don't even go to the god damn museums any more. I get the creeps, god damn it, I get depressed for months—it reminds me what the fucking black man must feel when he

walks in the damn upper class of this society. I see the god damn slums in this country. I know how it feels to be black and walking the streets of a white society and as a white man, I feel what this damn ruling class is doing to anybody creative. They are set up there to destroy, because I can not go along with this intellectualization of protecting this particular class, this particular structure.

Reinhardt: There was an achievement in separating Fine Art from other art.

Taylor: The Russian ballet masters took the peasants and made them fine dancers; but the spirit of the ballet comes from the peasant.

Reinhardt: Tambellini suggested that we may abandon the historical approach to art, and get into a kind of simultaneity in which you have all twenty-five thousand years of art and you have to think about it. Quoting an astronaut isn't meaningful.

Tambellini: To me it's essential and meaningful.

Reinhardt: Not you as an artist, but maybe as a human being. It is certainly interesting to me as a human being.

Taylor: It is interesting to me as a musician, because it has to do with space, and space automatically implies time. Like I'm involved with rhythm, and rhythm is like the marginal division of time. Of course Reinhardt visualizes blackness as some kind of technical problem. I visualize it as the quality that shapes my life, in terms of the quality of the acceptance that my work gets or does not get based on the fact that it is from the Afro-American community.

Reinhardt: But your art should be free from the community ("B," 14–16).

As their encounter and their general contribution to the discussion concludes, it becomes clear that Reinhardt operates within a strict antipathy to thingliness—which Reinhardt mistakes, perhaps after Michael Fried, for objecthood—in or as artworks which, in turn, require the freedom (which, for Reinhardt, is associated in its absoluteness with darkness and an idea of formality) of art and the artist from the community, from politicotheatricality, from the city or *polis* as world stage.[24] That antipathy is anticipated in the art criticism of Clement Greenberg and, even more stringently, in that of Greenberg's protégé, Fried, both of whom move within what Yve-Alain Bois, in an essay on Reinhardt, describes as "a clear demarcation between picto-riality and objecthood."[25] Reinhardt believes intensely in the legitimacy of the demarcations between art/ists and community, pictoriality, and (object-hood-as-)thingliness, but those demarcations are irreparably blurred by his most important work, his celebrated series of black paintings. This blurring is a source of anxiety for Reinhardt, whose allergy to mixture is, as it were, an allergy to thingliness. That intolerance of the blurring of art and life, in the words of Marcel Duchamp and Allen Kaprow, is famously formulated by Fried as a disavowal of theater, which is associated with the thingly in art, with what Bois intimates that Greenberg might have called "the passage of the picture into the realm of things."[26] Painting becomes something like a new kind of sculpture, according to Greenberg, and Bois describes this logic as that which led Frank Stella's black paintings, and presumably Re-inhardt's, to look almost like objects. Reinhardt's formulations on black are meant to stave off the slide into thingliness, the complete fall into the world of things. He wants his works to represent (which is to say to present them-selves as)—as Mondrian's paintings do, according to Greenberg, and in spite of their over-allness, their sculpturality—"the scene of forms rather than . . . one single, indivisible piece of texture."[27] To insist on the distinction between the canvas as scene and the canvas as thing is to detach oneself from the scene as much as it is also to represent the scene. It is to establish something like a freedom *from the community* in the most highly determined, regula-tive, *legal* sense of that word, in the sharpest sense of its constituting a field in which the human and the (disorderly) thing are precisely, pathologically, theatrically indistinct. Let's call this community the black community, the community that is defined by a certain history of blackness, a history of pri-vation (as Taylor points out) and plenitude, pain and (as Taylor points out) pleasure. It is from and as a sensual commune, from and as an irruptive ad-vent, at once focused and arrayed against the political aesthetics of enclosed common sense, that Taylor's music emerges.

Interestingly, Mondrian is invoked by both Greenberg and Reinhardt in the interest of, on the one hand, establishing the difference between easel painting's representational essence and minimalist, literalist, thingliness and, on the other hand, maintaining the separation of art and life that Duchamp and his minimalist descendants desired. At the same time, there is a syntac-tic, compositional "equivalence"—a social life of forms within the painting—that animates Mondrian's work. It is not merely an accident that this social life—of which Mondrian writes a great deal in his extended meditation on neoplastic art production's relation to the city, to the bar, to jazz—is spoken of in theatrical terms as "the scene of forms" by Greenberg who recognizes (or at least reveals) more clearly than Reinhardt or Fried an *irreducible* theatricality.[28]

That theatricality or social life has a politics, as well, which Taylor constantly recognizes and invokes but to deaf ears. And it's important to note that deafness places the severest limitations on the visual imagination. Reinhardt cannot, or refuses to, hear, if you will, a certain chromatic saturation that inhabits black as that color's internal, social life. The many colors that are absorbed and reflected in the color black, and in and as black social life, on the other hand, flow with an extraordinary theatrical intensity in *Victory Boogie Woogie*. It is as if they were poured out of (the father of) the jug, which is and is more than its "absence"; as if Ammons's rhythms inhabit and animate the painting, thereby challenging formulations regarding either its emptiness or its flatness, vivifying it as a scene in the form of tactile and visual translation and rearticulation of sound. But this is not all. The intensity of Mondrian's last work, as Harry Cooper argues, constitutes something like a critique of neoplasticism's insistence on the dualistic equivalence—which is necessarily a reduction—of differences within the paintings by way of the unleashing of a certain occult instability to which I shall return.[29] Such mixture, in which painting becomes phonotopography, would seem profoundly against the grain of Reinhardt, who claims Mondrian as an ancestor. However, the texture and landscape of black social life, of black social music, are given in *Victory Boogie Woogie*, making visible and audible a difference that exists not so much between Reinhardt's and Mondrian's paintings but between the way they deal with what might be understood as the social chromaticism of the color black and of blackness-in-color in their paintings. Taylor is more attuned, in the end, to what he might call the "sliding quadrants" that demarcate Mondrian's late New York rhythms, rhythms that don't blur so much as restage the encounter between art and life.[30] *Victory Boogie Woogie* is a scene of forms as well as a thing within the black community of things.

This becomes clearer by way of Bois, who concludes his essay "Piet Mondrian, *New York City*" in this way: "When . . . asked . . . why he kept repainting *Victory Boogie Woogie* instead of making several paintings of the different solutions that had been superimposed on this canvas, Mondrian answered, 'I don't want pictures. I just want to find things out.'"[31] Cooper thinks the recollection of this exchange comes through the filter of the post-Pollock mythology of the action painter, as Bois calls it, but no one is more vigilant regarding that mythology than Bois, who places Reinhardt against it. Cooper himself takes note of Mondrian's increasing obsession with revision, which we might think not only as repetition but also as a kind of pianistic repercussion.[32] If action painter–style expression is understood as a sort of choreographically induced interior voyage, this seems not at all what Mondrian had in mind. The question, of course, concerns finding things out precisely in its relation to obsessional revision, and perhaps Mondrian knew what Taylor knew and Reinhardt did not: that repercussive revision and a certain inventive discovery are fundamental protocols of black socioaesthetic activity. This is a question concerning sound and movement or, more precisely, a kind of audiotheatricality that is the essence of political consciousness.

And Mondrian's paintings are political if Bois is correct when he says that "an 'optical' interpretation of Mondrian, conceived in the assurance of immediate perception, cannot account for his New York paintings."[33] This is to say that the political in Mondrian is initialized as an excess, though not an erasure, of the optical; as an interplay of the sensual and social ensembles in the constant cutting and augmentation of their fullness. Cooper moves us more firmly in the direction of a mediated, more than visual perception and interpretation of Mondrian's work not only by attending carefully to the structural trace of boogie-woogie piano in Mondrian's improvisatory, revisionary compositional practice but by offering a brief history of the color black's career in Mondrian's late phase. He notes, along with Bois, that the black lines that instantiated dualistic equilibrium by "bounding color planes" proliferate and are made glossier, more reflective before Mondrian, in exile and at the unfinished end of a twenty-year project, under the influence of boogie-woogie, "burst[s] the pod of painting and disseminated its elements across a broken border."[34] This is to say not only that the border is crossed, that something moves through it; it is also to say, or at least to imply, that the border is (already) broken, that what it had contained within itself pours out. Any accounting of what the limit contains must also be an accounting of the contents of the limit. This is a matter of touch—of painterly and pianistic feel. Color pours from as well as across the border records and, as it were, reverses, the sound, the social music, that had been poured into the painting. The rhythmic story of left hand, right hand explodes into every note that can and can't be played, in every possible shade and shading of that note. Implicature erupts from the primary and the tonic as if the painting were one of Taylor's cluster bombs, his detonated rainbows, his inside figures played outside. Mondrian all but discovers certain ochres and blues in his strange, estranged homecoming, in appositional placements of the primary that allow for the secondary, for the minor that had been repressed, to emerge. He could be said to interpret, from the standpoint of a radical social aesthetic, the rhythmic images of his country. He joins Ammons in joining what we will see Fanon come to recognize as "that fluctuating movement which [the] people are just giving shape to, and which, as soon as it has started, will be the signal for everything to be called in question."[35] That country, that broken body, is black. That crossed, broken border is also a broken vessel. Crossing borders and oceans in serial exile, crossing over into the dead zone, involves staging the appositional encounter, which has always already started, of blackness and color for Mondrian. The native returns to places he's never been to get ready for one last trip. We're always crossing this frontier we carry. The smuggler who crosses is the border, its contents pouring out. Invasion out from the outside continues. Black explodes violently, victoriously in Mondrian's last painting, his careful, painstaking ode to proliferation, impurity, and incompleteness. It is the victory of the unfinished, the lonesome fugitive; the victory of finding things out, of questioning; the victorious rhythm of the broken system. Black(ness), which is to say black social life, is an undiscovered country.

Du Bois might say that it is the evident incalculability in human action that infuses *Victory Boogie Woogie*. He might claim, more pointedly, that Mondrian brings to certain fields of attention and inattention the evident incalculability of black life that corresponds to black life's evident rhythms in spite of how those rhythms might seem to lend themselves to the easy arithmetic of so many births and deaths or so many heavy beats to the bar.[36] In fact, it is the evidently incalculable rhythm of the life of things that Mondrian had been finding out in New York City, that he had been after for a long time if his meditations on the relationship between jazz and neoplastic are any indication. In the end, what remains is Mondrian's insistence on his late paintings as a mode of "finding things out," as things bodying forth a self-activated, autoexcessive inquiry into the possibility of a politics of the melodramatic social imagination. In Mondrian's city things making and finding one another out actively disrupt the grids by which activities would be known, organized, and apportioned. Mondrian's late paintings show the true colors with which blackness is infused. The paintings are an open, textured, mobile, animated, content-laden border, a sculptural, audiotheatrical outskirts, whose chromatic saturation indicates that Mondrian's late, exilic, catastrophic work was given over to a case of blackness.

Like the more than mindless, more than visceral events and things whose meaning is unattained even as their political force is ascertained, for Fanon, chromatic saturation has repercussions:

> If we study the repercussions of the awakening of national conscious-
> ness in the domains of ceramics and pottery-making, the same obser-
> vations [regarding the artist's forging of an invitation to participate in
> organized movement] may be drawn. Jugs, jars, and trays are modi-
> fied, at first imperceptible, then almost savagely. The colors, of which
> formerly there were but few and which obeyed the traditional rules
> of harmony, increase in number and are influenced by the repercus-
> sion of the rising revolution. Certain ochres and blues, which seemed
> forbidden to all eternity in a given cultural area now assert themselves
> without giving rise to scandal.[37]

Fanon speaks of repercussions that we might take to be the rhythmic accompaniment to this new harmonic disruption of the traditional, of the very
idea of the authentic and any simple recourse to it. Yet repercussion implies
a repetition, however different and differentiating, of a beat which, when it
is understood as resistance in the broadest sense, lies radically and anoriginally before us. Moreover, while the repercussive chromaticism of which
Fanon speaks is no simple analogue to the primary rhythms of Mondrian
in New York, one cannot help but hear in his paintings a striving for what is
underground and anoriginal in the city, for what is held in and escapes the
city's limits, the interiority of its black border or bottom, the bottom in which
its unwelcome bo(a)rders dwell politically as well as poetically.

Fanon shares Du Bois's Kantian ambivalence toward the tumultuous derangements that emerge from imagination and that are inseparable from the
imaginative constitution of reason and reality. The ambiguity is shown in
what elsewhere appears as a kind of valorization of the depths that are held
and articulated in the surface of actual events, as the call for intellectuals
to linger in the necessarily rhythmic and muscular music of the *"lieu de dé-
séquilibre occulte"* (which Farrington translates as "zone of occult instability"
and Philcox translates as "zone of hidden fluctuation") wherein *"son âme et
que s'illuminent sa perception et sa respiration"* (Farrington: "our lives are
transfused with light"/Philcox: "their perception and respiration [is] trans-
figured."[38] Note, in the choice of translations, a return to one of the problems with which we started, crystallized here in the distinction between our
lives and their perception and respiration. The difference between "our" and

"their" does not displace, by way of a politico-intellectual detachment, nearness with absolute distance. Rather, it attends the claim—which is to say that
imaginative flight, that descent into the underground—that finding (the)
people and things requires. On the other hand it most certainly can be said
to recover a gap, a border of black color, that, in the end, Fanon demands
we inhabit alongside the ones who have always been escaping the absolute
dereliction of the reality to which they have been yoked.

Meanwhile, Reinhardt sees black as a kind of negation even of Mondrianic color, of a certain Mondrianic urban victory. Like all the most profound
negations, his is appositional. This is to say that, in the end, the black paintings stand alongside Mondrian's late work and stand as late work in the private and social senses of lateness. Insofar as blackness is understood as the
absence and negation of color, of a kind of social color and social music,
Reinhardt will have had no music playing or played as he painted or as you
behold—neither Ammons's strong, or Taylor's exploded and exploding, left
hand. But blackness is not the absence of color. So far is black art also always
late work, correspondent to the victory of escape. The blackness of Mondrian's late work is given in Reinhardt's black negation of it, just as Taylor
amplifies as well as instantiates a black sociality hidden and almost unre-
producible in Reinhardt and his paintings that overwhelms or displaces the
antisociality of a black-and-white exchange that never really comes off either
as instrumentalist dismissal or objectifying encounter. We could call such instantiation, such violence, the accomplishment of the unfinished, the incomplete, the flawed. It is a victory given in left-out left hands and their excluded
handiwork, in impossible recordings on tape, on taped-over re-recordings,
on broken flutes and fluted wash stands in which makers wash their right
hands and their left-out left hands. It is the unfinished accomplishment of a
victory that finished accomplishment takes away. Mondrian's victory is Harriet Jacobs's—it occurs in a cramped, capacious room, a crawlspace defined
by interdicted, impossible but existent seeing and overhearing. It's a victory
that only comes fully into relief when it is taken by way of the gift of one's
freedom. What one desires, instead, is the unfinished victory of things who
cannot be bought and sold especially when they are bought and sold. Left
hands stroll in the city, fly off the handle like left eyes, burn playhouses down,
fly away, crash and burn sometimes, then come out again next year on tape
and fade away.

Meanwhile, Reinhardt's dream of a painting freed from the city would
return whatever animates what Cooper calls the "riot of blocks" that animate

Victory Boogie Woogie to its cell.[39] Reinhardt might have said, might be one of the inspirations for, what Adorno writes in "Black as an Ideal": "To survive reality at its most extreme and grim, artworks that do not want to sell themselves as consolation must equate themselves with that reality. Radical art today is synonymous with dark art; its primary color is black. Much contemporary art is irrelevant because it takes no note of this and childishly delights in color."[40] For Adorno, "The ideal of blackness with regard to content is one of the deepest impulses of abstraction." Moreover, "there is an impoverishment entailed by the idea of black," according to Adorno, to which "trifling with sound and color effects" is a mere reaction.[41] It is, however, precisely through a consideration of the unstable zone between the lived experience of the black and the fact of blackness, between the color black and what it absorbs and reflects, what it takes in and pours out, that we can begin to see how it is possible to mistake impossibility or impoverishment for absence or eradication. That zone, made available to us by the broken bridge of mistranslation, is where one lives a kind of oscillation between virtual solitude and fantastic multitude (which could be said to be the very theme of Mondrian's late work that Reinhardt takes it upon himself to negate and therefore inadvertently confirms, or of a certain lateness in Fanon's work that a certain earliness in his work seeks to negate but inadvertently confirms). This canted zone or curved span moves between a fact and an experience that, in themselves and in the commerce between them, remain inaccessible to all concepts of and desires for the racial object and unavailable to the protocols of dematerializing representation.

Finding things out, getting at the meaning of things, turns out to mean and to demand an investigation of instability, a courting of tumult, of riot, of derangement, of the constitutive disorder of the polis, its black market, border and bottom, the field of minor internal conflict, of the minor occasion or event through which the essence of an interminable struggle takes form. It means settling down in the uninhabitable, where one is constrained to re-initialize what has been dismissed as the pathontological in the discourse of the militant ontopathologist. It means producing mad works—prematurely, preternaturally late works—that register the thingly encounter; works that are both all black and in which black is conspicuous in its absence, between blackness and chromatic saturation.

Fanon understands, in the attention he pays in his late work to mental disorder and/as anticolonial refusal, that such blackness as Mondrian is infused with and performs shows up in color, that it is more than merely mindless and irresponsible, as Reinhardt believed. Now the interplay between blackness, color, madness, and late work that I have been trying to consider demands a turn to this important and familiar passage from "On National Culture," *Wretched of the Earth*:

> The colonized intellectual frequently lapses into heated arguments and develops a psychology dominated by an exaggerated sensibility, sensitivity, and susceptibility. This movement of withdrawal, which first of all comes from a petitio principi in his psychological mechanism and physiognomy, above all calls to mind a muscular reflex, a muscular contraction.
>
> The foregoing is sufficient to explain the style of the colonized intellectuals who make up their mind to assert this phase of liberating consciousness. A jagged style, full of imagery, for the image is the drawbridge that lets out the unconscious forces into the surrounding meadows. An energetic style, alive with rhythms bursting with life. A colorful style, too, bronzed, bathed in sunlight and harsh. This style, which Westerners once found jarring, is not, as some would have it, a racial feature, but above all reflects a single-handed combat and reveals how necessary it is for the intellectual to inflict injury on himself, to actually bleed red blood and free himself from that part of his being already contaminated by the germs of decay. A swift, painful combat where inevitably the muscle had to replace the concept.
>
> Although this approach may take him to unusual heights in the sphere of poetry, at an existential level it has often proved a dead end (*W/P*, 157).

Fanon's reading of the staging that launches the colonized intellectual's reflexive grasp at authenticity must itself be read in its relation to his analysis of the particular psychosomatic disorders colonialism fosters and resistance to colonialism demands. This is to say that the muscle's problematic replacement of the concept needs also to be understood as psychosomatic disorder. The problem of the colonized intellectual as the condition of im/possibility of emergent national culture shows up with a certain clarity in Fanon's attention to mental disorders under colonialism even when the limits of psychopathology are exposed. "The increasing occurrence of mental illness and the rampant development of specific pathological conditions are not the only legacy of the colonial war in Algeria. Apart from the pathology of torture, the pathology of the tortured and that of the perpetrator, there is a pathology of the entire atmosphere in Algeria, a condition that leads the attending physician to say when confronted with a case they cannot understand: "This will all be cleared up once the damned war is over" (*W/P*, 216). Whose case is it? Who's on the case? Are we to consider the pathological fantasy that "this will all be cleared up"; or the decayed orbit of diagnosis that leads from the failure to understand down to that fantasy; or must we be concerned with the one big case of an entire pathological public atmo/sphere? In any case, the cases with which Fanon is concerned here are instances of psychosomatic pathology, "the general body of organic disorders developed in response to a situation of conflict" (*W/P*, 216). In a note, Fanon characterizes the tradition of Soviet psychological theorization of these disorders as "putting the brain back in its place" as "the matrix where precisely the psyche is elaborated." That tradition operates by way of a terminological shift from "psychosomatic" to "cortico-visual" (*W/P*, 216n35). Such disorders are both symptom and cure insofar as they constitute an avoidance of complete breakdown by way of an incomplete outwitting, in Fanon's terms, of the originary conflict.

Fanon continues by turning to a disorder seemingly unique to the Algerian atmosphere:

> g. Systemic contraction, muscular stiffness
> These are male patients who slowly have difficulty making certain movements such as climbing stairs, walking quickly, or running (in two cases it is very sudden). The cause of this difficulty lies in a characteristic rigidity which inevitably suggests an attack on certain areas of the brain (central gray matter). Walking becomes contracted and turns into a shuffle. Passive bending of the lower limbs is practically impossible. No relaxation can be achieved. Immediately rigid and incapable of relaxing of his own free will, the patient seems to be made in one piece. The face is set, but expresses a marked degree of bewilderment.
> The patient does not seem to be able to "demobilize his nerves." He is constantly tense, on hold, between life and death. As one of them told us: "You see, I'm as stiff as a corpse" (*W/P*, 218–19).

Fanon offers an anticipatory explication:

> Like any war, the war in Algeria has created its contingent of cortico-visceral illnesses. . . . This particular form of pathology (systemic muscular contraction) already caught our attention before the revolution

began. But the doctors who described it turned it into a congenital stigma of the "native," an original feature of his nervous system, manifest proof of a predominant extrapyramidal system in the colonized. This contraction, in fact, is quite simply a postural concurrence and evidence in the colonized's muscles of their rigidity, their reticence and refusal in the face of the colonial authorities. (*W/P*, 217)

Perhaps these contractions create a staging area for questions. What's the relation between the body seeming to be all of one piece and the uncountable set of minor internal conflicts that Fanon overlooks in his assertion of the absence of black interiority or black difference? Is jaggedness an effect or an expression of rigidity, reticence, refusal? Is such gestural disorder a disruptive choreography that opens onto the meaning of things? At the same time, would it not be fair to think in terms of a gestural critique (of reason, of judgment)? Muscular contraction is not just a sign of external conflict but an expression of internal conflict as well. Perhaps such gesture, such dance, is the body's resistance to the psyche and to itself the thing's immanent transcendence, the fissured singularity of a political scene?

But is this anything other than to say that dance such as this moves in a pathological atmosphere? It is fantastic and its rigor is supposed to be that of the mortis, the socially dead, of a dead or impossible socius. The point, however, is that disorder has a set of double edges in the case (studies) of Fanon. Such disorder is, more generally, both symptom and cure—a symptom of oppression and a staging area for political criminality. And such disorder is deeply problematic if the onto-epistemological field of blackness is posited as impossible or unexplainable; if the social situation of blackness is a void, or a voided fantasy or simply devoid of value; if resistance itself is, finally, at least in this case, a function of the displacement of personality. Fanon seeks to address this complex in the transition from his description of muscular contraction to his understanding of the relation between what has been understood to be a natural propensity to "criminal impulsiveness" and the war of national liberation. Now the relation between the colonized intellectual and his impossible authenticity is to be thought in its relation to that between "the militant" and "his people" whom the militant believes he must drag "up from the pit and out of the cave" (*W/P*, 219). At stake is the transition from romantic identification with the pathological to the detached concern of the psychopathologist who ventures into the dead space of the unexplainable in the interest of a general resuscitation. Fanon is interested in a kind of rehabilitation and reintegration that the militant psychopathologist is called upon to perform in the interest of procuring "substance, coherence, and homogeneity" and reversing the depersonalization of "the very structure of society" on the collective as well as individual levels (W/P, 219). For Fanon, the militant corticovisceral psychopathologist, the people have been reduced "to a collection of individuals who owe their very existence to the presence of the colonizer" (W/P, 220). A set of impossible questions ought to ensue from what may well be Fanon's pathological insistence on the pathological: Can resistance come from such a location? Or, perhaps more precisely and more to the point, can there be an escape from that location, can the personhood that defines that location also escape that position? What survives the kind of escape that ought never leave the survivor intact? If and when some thing emerges from such a place, can it be anything other than pathological? But how can the struggle for liberation of the pathological be aligned with the eradication of the pathological? This set of questions will have been symptoms of the psychopathology of the psychopathologist—in them the case of the one who studies cases will have been given in its essence. It is crucial, however, that this set of questions that Fanon ought to have asked are never really posed. Instead, in his text Fanon insistently stages the encounter between anticolonial political criminality and colonially induced psychopathology. In so doing he discovers a certain nearness and a certain distance between explanation and resistance as well.

Fanon is embedded in a discourse that holds the pathological in close proximity to the criminal. At stake, in this particular nearness, is the relation between psychic and legal adjustment. In either case, the case *is* precisely in relation to the norm. But the case of a specifically colonial psychopathology, in its relation to the case of a specifically anticolonial criminality, has no access to the norm. Moreover, if, in either case, there were access to the norm, that access would be refused and such refusal would be folded into the description of criminal, pathological anticolonialism. In such cases, what would be the meaning of adjustment or "reintegration"? What does or should the liberation struggle have to do, in the broadest sense, with the "rehabilitation of man"? The flipside of this question has to do, precisely, with what might be called the liberatory value of ensemblic depersonalization. This is Fanon's question. He achieves it, in the course of his career, by way of an actual engagement with what is, in *Black Skin, White Masks*, dismissed as the "minor internal conflicts" that show up only in contradistinction to authentic intraracial intersubjectivity but which is, in *The Wretched of the Earth*, taken up with all of the militant psychopathologist's ambivalence, under the rubrics of "cortico-visceral disorder" (muscular contraction) and "criminal impulsiveness" in its irreducible relation to "national liberation."

While Fanon would consider the zealous worker in a colonial regime a quintessentially pathological case, remember that it is in resistance to colonial oppression that the cases of psychopathology with which Fanon is concerned in *The Wretched of the Earth*—in particular, those psychosomatic or corticovisceral disorders—emerge. What's at stake is Fanon's ongoing ambivalence toward the supposedly pathological. At the same time, ambivalence is, itself, the mark of the pathological. Watch Fanon prefiguratively describe and diagnose the pathological ambivalence that he performs:

> The combat waged by a people for their liberation leads them, depending on the circumstances, either to reject or to explode the so-called truths sown in their consciousness by the colonial regime, military occupation, and economic exploitation. And only the armed struggle can effectively exorcise these lies about man that subordinate and literally mutilate the more conscious-minded among us.
>
> How many times in Paris or Aix, in Algiers or Basse-Terre have we seen the colonized vehemently protest the so-called indolence of the black, the Algerian, the Vietnamese. And yet in a colonial regime if a fellah were a zealous worker or a black were to refuse a break from work, they would be quite simply considered pathological cases. The colonized's indolence is a conscious way of sabotaging the colonial machine; on the biological level it is a remarkable system of self-preservation and, if nothing else, is a positive curb on the occupier's stranglehold over the entire country (*W*/P, 220).

Is it fair to say that one detects in this text a certain indolence sown or sewn into it? Perhaps, on the other hand, its flaws are more accurately described as pathological. To be conscious-minded is to be aligned with subordination, even mutilation; the self-consciousness of the colonized is figured as a kind of wound at the same time that it is also aligned with wounding, with armed struggle that is somehow predicated on that which it makes possible, namely the explosion of so-called truths planted or, as it were, woven into the consciousness of the conscious-minded ones. They are the ones who are given the task of repairing (the truth) of man; they are the ones who would heal by way of explosion, excision, or exorcism. This moment of self-conscious self-description is sewn into Fanon's text like a depth charge. However, authentic upheaval is figured, in the end, not as an eruption of the unconscious in the conscious-minded but as that conscious mode of sabotage carried out every day—in and as what had been relegated, by the conscious-minded, to the status of impossible, pathological sociality—by the ones who are not, or are not yet, conscious. Healing wounds are inflicted, in other words, by the ones who are not conscious of their wounds and whose wounds are not redoubled by such consciousness. Healing wounds are inflicted appositionally, in small, quotidian refusals to act that make them subject to charges of pathological indolence. Often the conscious ones, who have taken it upon themselves to defend the colonized against such charges, levy those charges with the greatest vehemence. If Fanon fails to take great pains to chart the tortured career of rehabilitative injury, it is perhaps a conscious decision to sabotage his own text insofar as it has been sown with those so-called truths that obscure the truth of man.

This black operation that Fanon performs on his own text gives the lie to his own formulations. So that when Fanon claims that "the duty of the colonized subject, who has not yet arrived at a political consciousness or a decision to reject the oppressor, is to have the slightest effort literally dragged out of him," the question that emerges is why one who is supposed yet to have arrived at political consciousness, one who must be dragged up out of the pit, would have such a duty (W/P, 220). This in turn raises the more fundamental issue, embedded in this very assertion of duty, of the impossibility of such nonarrival; this is to say that the failure to arrive at a political consciousness is a general pathology suffered by the ones who take their political consciousness with them on whatever fugitive, aleatory journey they are making. They will have already arrived; they will have already been there. They will have carried something with them before whatever violent manufacture, whatever constitutive shattering is supposed to have called them into being. While noncooperation is figured by Fanon as a kind of staging area for or a preliminary version of a more authentic "objectifying encounter" with colonial oppression (a kind of counterrepresentational response to power's interpellative call), his own formulations regarding that response point to the requirement of a kind of thingly quickening that makes opposition possible while appositionally displacing it. Noncooperation is a duty that must be carried out by the ones who exist in the nearness and distance between political consciousness and absolute pathology. But this duty, imposed by an erstwhile subject who clearly is supposed to know, overlooks (or, perhaps more precisely, looks away from) that vast range of nonreactive disruptions of rule that are, in early and late Fanon, both indexed and disqualified. Such disruptions, often manifest as minor internal conflicts (within the closed circle, say, of Algerian criminality, in which the colonized "tend to use each other as a screen") or muscular contractions, however much they are captured, enveloped, imitated, or traded, remain inassimilable (W/P, 231). These disruptions trouble the rehabilitation of the human even as they are evidence of the capacity to enact such rehabilitation. Moreover, it is at this point, in passages that culminate with the apposition of what Fanon refers to as "the reality of the 'towelhead'" with "the reality of the 'nigger,'" that the fact, the case, and the lived experience of blackness—which might be understood, here, as the troubling of and the capacity for the rehabilitation of the human—converge as a duty to appose the oppressor, to refrain from a certain performance of the labor of the negative, to avoid his economy of objectification and standing against, to run away from the snares of recognition (W/P, 220). This refusal is a black thing, is that which Fanon carries with(in) himself, and in how he carries himself, from Martinique to France to Algeria. He is an anticolonial smuggler whose wares are constituted by and as the dislocation of black social life that he carries, almost unaware. In Fanon, blackness is transversality between things, escaping (by way of) distant, spooky actions; it is translational effect and affect, transmission between cases, and could be understood, in terms Brent Hayes Edwards establishes, as diasporic practice.[12] This is what he carries with him, as the imagining thing that he cannot quite imagine and cannot quite control, in his pathologizing description of it that it—that he—defies. A fugitive cant moves through Fanon, erupting out of regulatory disavowal. His claim on this criminality was interdicted. But perhaps only the dead can strive for the quickening power that animates what has been relegated to the pathological. Perhaps the dead are alive and escaping. Perhaps ontology is best understood as the imagination of this escape as a kind of social gathering; as undercommon plainsong and dance; as the fugitive, centrifugal word; as the word's autointerruptive, autoilluminative shade/s. Seen in this light, black(ness) is, in the dispossessive richness of its colors, beautiful.

I must emphasize that what's at stake here is not some puritanically monochromatic denunciation of an irreducible humanism in Fanon. Nor is one after some simple disavowal of the law as if the criminality at stake here had some stake in such a reaction. Rather, what one wants to amplify is a certain Fanonian elaboration of the law of motion that Adorno will come to speak of in Fanon's wake. Fanon writes, "Here we find the old law stating that anything alive cannot afford to remain still while the nation is set in motion, while man both demands and claims his infinite humanity" (*W/P*, 221). A few years later, in different contexts, Adorno will write,

> The inner consistency through which artworks participate in truth always involves their untruth; in its most unguarded manifestations art has always revolted against this, and today this revolt has become art's own law of movement [*Bewegungsgesetz*].[43]

and

> Artworks' paradoxical nature, stasis, negates itself. The movement of artworks must be at a standstill and thereby become visible. Their immanent processual character—the legal process that they undertake against the merely existing world that is external to them—is objective prior to their alliance with any party.[44]

In the border between *Black Skin, White Masks* and *The Wretched of the Earth*, the body that questions is a truth that bears untruth. It is a heavy burden to be made to stand as the racial-sexual embodiment of the imagination in its lawless freedom, and the knowledge it produces exclusively, particularly when such standing is a function of having one's wings clipped by the understanding.[45] However, the burden of such exemplarity, the burden of being the problem or the case, is disavowed at a far greater cost. So that what is important about Fanon is his own minor internal conflict, the viciously constrained movement between these burdens. On the one hand, the one who does not engage in a certain criminal disruption of colonial rule is pathological, unnatural; on the other hand, one wants to resist a certain understanding of Algerians as "born idlers, born liars, born thieves, and born criminals" (*W/P*, 221). Insofar as Fanon seems to think that the colonized subject is, as it were, born into a kind of preconscious duty to resist, that the absence of the capacity to perform or to recognize this duty is a kind of birth defect that retards the development of political consciousness, Fanon is caught between a rock and a crawlspace. Against the grain of a colonial psychological discourse that essentially claims "that the North African in a certain way is deprived of a cortex" and therefore relegated to a "vegetative" and purely "instinctual" life, a life of involuntary muscular contractions, Fanon must somehow still find a way to claim, or to hold in reserve, those very contractions insofar as they are a mobilization against colonial stasis (*W/P*, 225). Against the grain of racist notions of "the criminal impulsiveness of the North African" as "the transcription of a certain configuration of the nervous system into his pattern of behavior" or as "a neurologically comprehensible reaction, written into the nature of things, of the thing which is biologically organized," Fanon must valorize the assertion of a kind of political criminality written into the nature of things while also severely clipping the wings of an imaginative tendency to naturalize and pathologize the behavior of the colonized (W/P, 228). Insofar as crime marks the Algerian condition within which "each prevents his neighbor from seeing the national enemy" and thereby arriving at a political consciousness, Fanon must move within an almost general refusal to look at the way the colonized look at themselves, a denial or pathologization or policing of the very sociality that such looking implies (W/P, 231). Here Fanon seems to move within an unarticulated Kantian distinction between criminality as the teleological principle of anticolonial resistance and crime as the unbound, uncountable set of illusory facts that obscure, or defer the advent of, postcolonial reason. This distinction is an ontological distinction; it, too, raises the question concerning the irreducible trace of beings that being bears.[46]

This is all to say that Fanon had very little time to glance at or glance off the immense and immensely beautiful poetry of (race) war, the rich music of a certain underground social aid, a certain cheap and dangerous socialism, that composes the viciously criminalized and richly differentiated interiority of black cooperation that will, in turn, have constituted the very ground of externally directed noncooperation. It turns out, then, that the pathological is (the) black, which has been figured both as the absence of color and as the excessively, criminally, pathologically colorful (which implies that black's relation to color is a rich, active interinanimation of reflection and absorption); as the corticovisceral muscular contraction or the simultaneously voluntary and impulsive hiccupped "jazz lament" that, in spite of Fanon's formulations, must be understood in relation to the acceptable jaggedness, legitimate muscularity, and husky theoretical lyricism of the bop and post-bop interventions that are supposed to have replaced it (W/P, 176). Because finally, the question isn't whether or not the disorderly behavior of the anticolonialist is pathological or natural, whether or not he is born to that behavior, whether or not the performance of this or that variation on such behavior is "authentic"; the question, rather, concerns what the vast range of black authenticities and black pathologies does. Or, put another way, what is the efficacy of that range of natural born disorders that have been relegated to what is theorized as the void of blackness or black social life but which might be more properly understood as the fugitive being of "infinite humanity," or as that which Marx calls wealth?

> Now, wealth is on one side a thing, realized in things, material products, which a human being confronts as subject; on the other side, as value, wealth is merely command over alien labour not with the aim of ruling, but with the aim of private consumption, etc. It appears in all forms in the shape of a thing, be it an object or be it a relation mediated through the object, which is external and accidental to the individual. Thus the old view, in which the human being appears as the aim of production, regardless of his limited national, religious, political character, seems to be very lofty when contrasted to the modern world, where production appears as the aim of mankind and wealth as the aim of production. In fact, however, when the limited bourgeois form is stripped away, what is wealth other than the universality of individual needs, capacities, pleasures, productive forces, etc., created through universal exchange? The full development of human mastery over the forces of nature, those of so-called nature as well as of humanity's own nature? The absolute working-out of his creative potentialities, with no presupposition other than the previous historic development, which makes this totality of development, i.e. the development of all human powers as such the end in itself, not as measured on a *predetermined* yardstick? Where he does not reproduce himself in one specificity, but produces his totality? Strives not to remain something he has become, but is in the absolute movement of becoming?[47]

While Fanon is justifiably wary of anything that is presented as if it were written into the nature of things and of the thing, this notion of wealth as the finite being of a kind of infinite humanity, especially when that in/finitude is understood (improperly, against Marx's grain) as constituting a critique of any human mastery whatever, must be welcomed. Marx's invocation of the thing leads us past his own limitations such that it becomes necessary and possible to consider the thing's relation to human capacity independent of the limitations of bourgeois form.

Like the (colonial) states of emergency that are its effects, like the enclosures that are its epiphenomena; like the civil war that was black reconstruction's aftershock, like the proletariat's anticipation of abolition; it turns out that the war of "national liberation" has always been going on, anoriginally, as it were. Fanon writes of "a lot of things [that] can be committed for a few pounds of semolina," saying, "You need to use your imagination to understand these things" (*W/P*, 231). This is to say that there is a counterpoint in Fanon, fugitive to Fanon's own self-regulative powers, that refuses his refusal to imagine those imagining things whose political commitment makes them subject to being committed, those biologically organized things who really have to use their imaginations to keep on keeping on, those things whose constant escape of their own rehabilitation as men seems to be written into their nature. In such contrapuntal fields or fugue states, one finds (it possible to extend) their stealing, their stealing away, their lives that remain, fugitively, even when the case of blackness is dismissed.

Preoccupied Breathing

These notes on Fanon resume with a disagreement with Fanon that is enabled by Fanon. Contrary to his formulations, the white man did not create the black man and the black man did not create blackness.[48] These negative axioms are indispensable for investigating the etiology of revolution's transformative power, which must itself come from, which is to say through, somewhere, which may turn out to be nowhere reimagined, a rhythmic feel or field where creature and creator are generatively undone in/by preservation. If revolution is and has a condition of possibility that need not and must not itself be originary, then revolution and preservation are inseparable. So let me proceed by beginning, again, with a question: How do we resist the ridiculously overwhelming armature of the settler, through which his weakness is serially revealed? This weakness must be articulated in as well as seen through preservative, revolutionary resistance to the settler's reaction. Malcolm X's most aggressive and vicious pronouncement to the members of his Harlem mosque is "You're dealing with a silly man!" And Hannah Arendt is prescient when she ruefully speaks of "the impotence of power" in her *On Violence*, a text that otherwise, and unfortunately, illuminates and exemplifies that interplay of silliness and weakness that emerges in response to black radicalism.[49] To reread *Les damnés de la terre* against the grain of Arendt's nonreading of it is to consider that we don't and can't either know or fight the murderous brutality of the settler's weakness with our own; rather, we think and struggle from and with our potency.[50] But this means that not only must we recalibrate our sense of, our senses with regard to, what it is to think and fight, and what both of these activities have to do with what it is to be violent; we also have to resound that strength in rigorous attendance upon the lived experience *and the facticity* of the black, the colonized, the Antillean, the Algerian, the Afro-American, the damned. This facticity is given in the thing and force that is called blackness. This is what Fanon was always preparing himself to do. Such resonance would also begin to emerge in a question: Is there a sense, the beginning of an analysis, of an open set of forms of life or modes of aspiration, a kind of preoccupied breathing, that is given not in the interplay of the precolonial and the postcolonial but rather in the ongoing force of the anticolonial, when one abides in and with the everyday life and experimental practices of those to whom Gilles Deleuze refers as "the exhausted"?[51]

I'd like to begin by working in the space between Frank Wilderson's call to "attend to our wretchedness" and Miguel Mellino's exhortation to retranslate and retransmit the (no)thingly materiality of the damned.[52] A conceptualization of that materiality that can approach its richness is something Fanon constantly produces but less frequently discovers. And yet his work is part of the great tradition that makes such discovery possible if we continue to read him by way of the militant protocols that he and others have established. What if damnation is (also) a mode of voluntarity, the common social fashioning of the poor (in spirit), the interplay of mutual aid and mutual indebtedness? The damned, the dispossessed, are, in this sense, not "created" by the ones who claim and attempt to establish their own cultural and economic superiority; rather, they are, as E. P. Thompson says of the English working class, present at their own making.[53] The damned are also the black, which is to say that what they have or claim in common, in their dispossession, is something called blackness. If this is so, the idea of the inevitable disappearance of the black around which "*Sur la culture nationale*" is organized, and the placement of black culture within the systemic opposition of possibility and impossibility, require further thought.[54] While, as Fanon asserts, there is an imposition onto the figure of the black that would signify the confluence of racial identity and racial inferiority, there is also, in a way that is prior to the regulative force of that imposition and calls it into question, a resource working through the epidermalization of a fantasmatic inferiority as the anti-epidermalization of the radical alternative, to which the peoples who are called black have a kind of (under)privileged relation in and as the very history of that imposition. One might speak, then, of the blackening of the common, which would imply neither that any and every person who is called black claims or defends the sociopoetic force of that fantasy nor that persons who are not called black are disqualified from making such claims and enacting such defense.

This force shows up only insofar as we develop a kind of paraontological comportment toward it. This is the thing that interdicts ontological explanation. Psychopathologically informed phenomenological analysis of the black's lived experience comes into its own only in relation to a paraontological approach to the facticity of blackness. Mistranslation in *Peau noir, masques blancs* has, in this case, a kind of illuminative value, alerting us to a certain irruption at the end of *Les damnés de la terre* where anticolonial struggle—the common assertion of the dispossessed—is the field in which what is relegated to the status of mental disorder turns out to be interarticulate with the program of "total disorder" for which Fanon calls.[55] This suggests that the forms of anticolonial struggle are already in place as a radical force of undercommon autonomization in ecstatic choreography and minor internecine struggle. So it is necessary to consider, along with Fanon, how program and informality, organization and spontaneity, go together. In the end, the total disorder of revolutionary confrontation is better imagined not as derivative shocks enclosed by an already given regulatory order, but as the obscurity of a disorder out of which order emerges. Colonial power does not initiate; it responds. In appositional, anticipatory counterpoint to the disappearance of the black that colonial power turns out to have rendered both possible and impossible through revolutionary consciousness and action, something emerges, in doubly redoubled aspect, mistaken first as the splitting then as loss, seen only in relation to the illusion of the single and the full. That choired voluntarity, affirmative refusal given in and as remote compact and dispersed interiority, exhausts the proper and, in so doing, brings revolution online as disruptive, invaginative preservation of the paraontological totality. This is what it is to take up and take on the black mask, to engage in the retroactively named and interdicted black act, to applaud (on) the uncountable beat of the black fact, to enter and extend the hard social life of black facticity.

Perhaps I can further elaborate this by reciting some directives I hear in two long passages from work Fanon collected in *L'an V de la Révolution Algerienne*. If that work can be considered as anticipatory to *Les damnés de la terre*, then I hope that what I can record here contributes to a more devoted, because heretical, reading of and in and with *les damnés*.

As for the Algerian woman, she is "inaccessible, ambivalent, with a masochistic component." Specific behaviors are described which illustrate these different characteristics. The truth is that the study of an occupied people, militarily subject to an implacable domination, requires documentation and checking difficult to combine. It is not the soil that is occupied. It is not the ports or the airdromes. French colonialism has settled itself in the very center of the Algerian individual and has undertaken a sustained work of cleanup, of expulsion of self, of rationally pursued mutilation.

There is not occupation of territory, on the one hand, and independence of persons on the other. It is the country as a whole, its history, its daily pulsation that are contested, disfigured, in the hope of a final destruction. Under these conditions, the individual's breathing is an observed, an occupied breathing. It is a combat breathing.

From this point on, the real values of the occupied quickly tend to acquire a clandestine form of existence. In the present of the occupier, the occupied learns to dissemble, to resort to trickery. To the scandal of military occupation, he opposes a scandal of contact. Every contact between the occupied and the occupier is a falsehood.[56]

It is now time for reason to make itself heard. If the French Government now hopes to revive the conditions that existed before 1954 or even 1958, it is well that it should know that this is now impossible. If on the other hand, it is willing to take account of the changes that have occurred in the consciousness of Algerian man in the last five years, if it is willing to lend an ear to the insistent and fraternal voices that give impetus to the Revolution and that are to be heard in the struggle of a people who spare neither their blood nor their suffering for the triumph of freedom, then we say that everything is still possible.

The crushing of the Algerian Revolution, its isolation, its asphyxiation, its death through exhaustion—these are mad dreams.

The Revolution in depth, the true one, precisely because it changes man and renews society, has reached an advanced stage. This oxygen which creates and shapes a new humanity—this, too, is the Algerian Revolution.[57]

1. Consider this problematic of oxygen, which seems to have been in the conceptual air that Fanon and Althusser share, as bound up not only with a certain alchemy of social revolution but also with the structure of scientific revolution insofar as what is given in its invocation is the question of the concept of the object, the distinction between the production and the discovery of the object. Althusser (after Friedrich Engels) regards the concept of oxygen as the accidental effect of a deliberate and occult experimental protocol.[58] Such

an effect is, in turn, known by way of *its* effect: oxygen comes into relief by way of fire, explosion, a destructiveness whose creative substance must be discovered, conceptualized, after the fact, as something more than repressed aggressivity toward whatever happens to have been burned. Obviously, the burning of the colonizer, the overturning of his order, will have never been understood as mere accident. However, it will also never have been understood merely as an effect of the colonizer. As a matter of fact, it will simply never have been understood. After the collision of every particle, the essential question will remain. One necessarily preliminary form of it might be: What's the relation between production and discovery on the one hand and im/possibility and exhaustion on the other?

2. Consider that the massive field of information that we call anticolonial struggle is best understood as a range of sociopoetic preoccupation in which the interplay of imaginative study and self-defense begins in excess of the Manicheism—in particular the stark opposition of old and new, the same and change—that Fanon describes and inscribes. What Bertolt Brecht says of refugees (that they "are the keenest dialecticians"; that they "are refugees as a result of changes and their sole object of study is change") is true of the damned more generally.[59] What if the last becoming first is nothing other than the wedge that exists within, while calling forth the systemic relation of, the possible and the impossible, which we both surround and continually escape? Manicheism's (thread)bare life/slow death, otherwise known as the postcolonial, is now often and rightly figured as another, which is to say an extended, colonial imposition. This is already theorized in Fanon, in and against and under his own breath. It brings occupied breathing into relief as enabling respiratory disability. When, moreover, without valorization, Fanon invokes labored breath, clandestine form, trickery, and the scandal of contact, his primary focus on the encounter between the occupier and the occupied more than merely threatens to eclipse contact within and between the preoccupied, in which these modes of interactivity might be more precisely understood as ways of worldmaking. The question of how to get at the "deeper, outside thing" of this other contact, this other breathing, that is preoccupied with change, and which must be understood not simply as the antagonism between colonizer and colonized but as the general antagonism of and in the undercommon, is crucial and difficult, located as it is up where the relation between observing and being observed is connected to the discernment, transformation, and encoding of values. Here's where cryptanalysis and cryptography sort of go together, where study opens out

into what surrounds the limits, the colonial enclosure, of the possible and the impossible, particularly when that enclosure is misunderstood to have itself held the fantasmatic infinity that Fanon calls "the circle of the dance."

3. Consider that the circle is unlimited and unbounded, too. That it is the surround, that it surrounds the interplay of politics and war, the possible and the impossible, that marks the horizon of Fanon's thought. Let's call this prior resistance of the exhibit, this anexemplary force of the dis/possessed, who have been inspirited and inhabited, a sociopoetics of exhabitation. At stake is observation of and in, preoccupation with form's emergence in and from, the informal. Speaking almost always of what it is to be in the presence of the occupier, Fanon can only give us glimpses—as a matter of epistemological course, as an effect of a necessary obscurity that he is both sworn and therefore constrained to uphold—of what surrounds that presence, in and as the open, in and as the secret. When observation is given in and by the accompaniment of a claim that is both disruptive and exhaustive, one claims observation as studious *materiel*, the weapon of theory, its glancing blow. Real values, which are serially given in the revaluation of all value, come into and out to play in a low-down plane of regard. This ordinary plain is more than just that. Welcome to the shit that is not what it is in the universal drama between the clandestine existence of real values and the performativity of every contact.

4. Consider Fanon's calculus of the im/possible in relation to Deleuze's analytic of "The Exhausted": "Being exhausted is much more than being tired. 'It's not just tiredness, I'm not just tired, in spite of the climb.' The tired person no longer has any subjective possibility at his disposal; he therefore cannot realize the slightest (objective) possibility. But the latter remains, because one can never realize the whole of the possible; in fact, one even creates the possible to the extent that one realizes it. The tired person has merely exhausted the realization, whereas the exhausted person exhausts the whole of the possible. The tired person can no longer realize, but the exhausted person can no longer possibilize."[60] Deleuzean exhaustion is inseparable from the massive discourse of muscularity, the muscular tension of the native, that all but structures Fanon's texts and organizes his thoughts on violence and his sense of the relation between what Huey P. Newton calls revolutionary suicide and what Fanon denigrates under the rubrics of myth, magic, dance, and emotional sensitivity.[61] Both are involved with Albert Camus's invocation of exhaustion, which goes back to Pindar, whom he invokes in the famous epigraph to *The Myth of Sisyphus*: "O my soul, do not aspire

to immortal life, but exhaust the limits of the possible."[62] Deleuze addresses this tension between aspiration and exhaustion with regard to Samuel Beckett's late work which emphatically stages the interplay of drama and dance, a choreography of surrepetitious order, and against the backdrop of the theme and the fact of exhaustion in Deleuze's late work and life, in which the problem of suicide is raised and materially addressed. Exhaustion is a condition that expresses, once again by repudiation, the necessity and necessary relation of preservation and revolution. Deleuze is interested in the exhaustion of possibility, not its compromise. Or, after the fact of the realization that possibility is necessarily compromised, that it moves wholly within the zero-sum calculus of political reversal that Fanon puts forward, and is surrounded by the incalculable that Fanon holds in reserve, the exhausted situate themselves elsewhere. It's not enough to question one's comfort or discomfort with inequality, one's love or hatred of domination; instead, one must question one's comfort or discomfort with life itself when life is held to be the occupied territory of necessarily interdicted personality, of the citizen/ subject mired in colonial abstraction and political enclosure. Making visible the reciprocal nonexistence of the white man and the black man, dwelling in and on the im/possibility of proper self-possession, shies away from the general theory or the general question of endurance and from the general ecology and economy of things, as Mellino suggests. There is work that submits itself to the im/possible and then there is work that exhausts it. This is what Deleuze says about Beckett. It could also be said of John Coltrane, Fanon's contemporary, whom I invoke precisely because of his own insistence on his lack of the anger that accompanies thwarted subjectivity but whose work at every instance bears the trace of violent transubstantiation in complex personhood.[63] Such work, in Deleuze's terms, is "pervaded by exhaustive series, that is, exhausting series."[64] He adds, "The combinatorial [which I would oppose to the political] is the art or science of exhausting the possible through inclusive disjunctions. But only an exhausted person can exhaust the possible, because he has renounced all need, preference, goal, or signification. Only the exhausted person is sufficiently disinterested, sufficiently scrupulous."[65] Fanon speaks of and for the exhausted; Trane plays that field of difference, therein exhausting the instrument, thereby becoming the instrument, a meditative medium, a conduit, a means to the long history of exhaustion's still extant capacity to catapult us into and as the old-new thing: that whole extended combination of exhausted feet and rested souls that moves within the zone of the relegated, where the informal and the maternal converge, and which, for Fanon, will have always been waiting for the revolutionary unveiling that it will have always been carrying out.

5. Consider the relation between preoccupation (which is also to say, in a double sense, what lies before our present state of occupation, our imposed and pseudovoluntary labors, our own flirtations with and surrenders to, as well as our having been brutalized by, settling and settlement, all of which can be considered being-occupied) and revolution by way of the relations between prehistory and historicity, the informal (not the formless) and form. I do so as a dissident from within the dissident protocols of black studies, glancingly by way of the music that is called jazz, because there is a certain question of jazz as prehistory that is Fanonian, inaugurated by a formulation in "*Sur la culture nationale*" regarding the jazz howl of the misfortunate negro that will have been upheld by whites (as well as various models of what are supposed to be their black intellectual creations) as an expression of inert authenticity.[66] Everything depends on how one accounts for the sociopoetics of the howl (*jazz-cri*) (perhaps Allen Ginsberg's fetishistic attempt at such an account is not only what Fanon seeks to critique but also what remains for us actually to read, by way of an analytic of thingly exhaustion, of being beat, of the beat, of beating one's chest in the wake of the exhaustion of the instrument, as Trane is reported once to have done, Trane, servant of the exhaustive series, who might be said to have been constantly playing both Fanon's critique and the critique of Fanon). In the meantime, a bunch of stuff that is cognate with the howl's irreducible relation to a certain sociality, a certain hard-ass labor—scream, sweat, strain—is also put in suspension, awaiting a more or less permanent kind of space-time separation. This might be seen as occurring, if it can or should occur, by way of machines, supposedly new methodological operations and, most immediately, by way of a terminological shift.

6. Consider a kind of social buzz or hum as electric historicity. This would require regrounding, as Guyanese revolutionary intellectual Walter Rodney might now have said, in ways that disrupt Fanon's understanding of and adherence to the "phases of development" of the colonized intellectual.[67] "Because," as Rodney explains, "that is black power, that is one of the elements, a sitting down together to reason, to 'ground' as the Brothers say. We have to 'ground together.'"[68] In a gully, in a dungle, in the jungle, on an oil drum, this grounding or undergrounding is the historicity of form, the lumpen residue and experimental exercise of black social life that, most famously and influentially, Orlando Patterson means to dismiss under the

rubric of the informal and which Fanon relegates to a zone of impotence, the etiolated field of minor internal struggle, even as he requires us to consider the relation between total disorder and mental disorder or to imagine the revolutionary and preservative force of a certain dance of the veil. The question of how jazz could have im/possibly happened accompanies Rodney's question concerning how a functioning proletariat emerges so soon, without having been roused, in Guyana, after the emancipation of slavery. The only answer—which Rodney develops by way of C. L. R. James, his predecessor in pan-African and Caribbean social and intellectual insurgency—is that they were already there in the subsoil, underground, in exhaustion, as elemental aspiration and projectivity, as ongoing, improper approach, something already given in a necessarily open internal structure that is only insofar as it takes the outside in. All this has to do with how fugitivity surrounds enclosure, how anticolonialism surrounds the settlement, which is manned with subjects whose aggression is the magnified reflection of their weakness and im/possibility. The first responsibility is to see the settler's incapacity as clearly as his brutality, to realize that there is no *poesis* of the settler. Paradoxically, fruitfully, thankfully, it is Fanon's poetics of the settler, his account of what he understands to be colonialism's sociogenic power, that moves us to the threshold of knowing not only the impotence of that power but our own *prior* sociopoetic resistance to it. Fighting from there is a new experiment in nonbeginning and an endless assertion of means against ends, a violence of absolute overturning in which no one ever takes either the first breath or the last.

Mysticism in the Flesh

Black study refreshes lines of rigorously antidisciplinary invention, effecting intellectual renewal against academic sterility. When wardens of established disciplines and advocates of interdisciplinary reform fight to secure depleted sovereignty in and over the same depleted real estate—whose value increases as its desertification progresses; whose value is set by the new masters of another form of what Thomas Jefferson called silent profit—and when note of this false alternative is taken by those who offer nothing but a critique of the very idea of a true one, the degenerative, which is to say deconstructive, condition that is black study, expressing its own general, generative economy, keeps on pushing over the edge of refusal, driven by a visionary impetus their work requires and allows us to try to see and hear and feel, out of love for the undercommon project, out of love for the immanence and effervescence of its own unowned differences, out of love for black people, out of love for blackness.

I have thought long and hard, in the wake of the remarkable work of Frank B. Wilderson III and Jared Sexton, in a kind of echo of Bob Marley's question, about whether blackness could be loved; there seems to be a growing consensus that analytic precision does not allow for such romance but I remain devoted to the impression that analytic precision is, in fact, a function of such romance. And this, perhaps, is where the tension comes, where it is and will remain, not in spite of the love but in it, embedded in its difficulty and violence, not in the impossibility of its performance or declaration but out of the evasion of, the evasion that is, its open natality. More precisely, if Afropessimism is the study of this impossibility, the thinking I have to offer moves not in that impossibility's transcendence but rather in its exhaustion. Moreover, I want to consider exhaustion as a mode or form or way of life, which is to say sociality, thereby marking a relation whose implications constitute, in my view, a fundamental theoretical reason not to believe, as it were, in social death. Like Curtis Mayfield, however, I do plan to stay a believer. This is to say, again like Mayfield, that I plan to stay a black motherfucker.

Over the course of this essay, we'll have occasion to consider what that means, by way of a discussion of my preference for the terms *life* and *optimism* over *death* and *pessimism* and in light of Wilderson's and Sexton's brilliant insistence not only on the preferential option for blackness but also on the requirement of the most painstaking and painful attention to our damnation, a term I prefer to *wretchedness*, after the example of Miguel Mellino, not simply because it is a more literal translation of Fanon (though often, with regard to Fanon, I prefer the particular kinds of precision that follow from what some might dismiss as mistranslation) but also because wretchedness emerges from a standpoint that is not only not ours, that is not only one we cannot have and ought not want, but that is, in general, held within the logic of im/possibility that delineates the administered world of the subject/citizen.[69] But this is to say, from the outset, not that I will advocate the construction of a necessarily fictive standpoint of our own but that I will seek out not just the absence but the refusal of standpoint, to actually explore and to inhabit and to think what Bryan Wagner calls "existence without standing" from no standpoint because this is what it would truly mean to stay in the hold of the ship (when the hold is thought with properly critical, and improperly celebratory, clarity).[70] What would it be, deeper still, what is it, to think from no standpoint; to think outside the desire for a standpoint? What emerges in the desire that constitutes a certain proximity to that thought is not (just) that blackness is ontologically prior to the logistic and regulative power that is supposed to have brought it into existence but that blackness is prior to ontology; or, in a slight variation on what Nahum Dimitri Chandler might say, blackness is the anoriginal displacement of ontology, that it is ontology's anti- and antefoundation, ontology's underground, the irreparable disturbance of ontology's time and space. This is to say that what I do assert, not against, I think, but certainly in apposition to Afro-pessimism, as it is, at least at one point, distilled in Sexton's work, is not what he calls one of that project's most polemical dimensions, "namely, that black life is not social, or rather that black life is lived in social death."[71] What I assert is this: that black life—which is as surely to say *life* as black thought is to say *thought*—is irreducibly social; that, moreover, black life is lived in *political* death or that it is lived, if you will, in the burial ground of the subject by those who, insofar as they are not subjects, are also not, in the interminable (as opposed to the last) analysis, "death-bound," as Abdul JanMohamed would say.[72] In this, however, I also agree with Sexton insofar as I am inclined to call this burial ground "the (administered) world" and to conceive of it and the desire for it as pathological. At stake, now, will be what the difference is between the pathological and the pathogenic, a difference that will have been instantiated by what we might think of as the view, as well as the point of view, of the pathologist. Against the grain of the enervating effects of the analytic assumption of black sociality as pathological—which need not be derived from the idea that black life is lived in and as a set of complex, errant proximities to the sovereign's crypt—I believe that blackness, in its necessarily pathogenic, irreducibly aesthetic sociality, bears the potential to end this funereal reign with an animative breath.

The question concerning the point of view, or standpoint, of the pathologist is crucial, but so is the question of what it is that the pathologist examines. What, precisely, is the morbid body upon which Fanon, the pathologist, trains his eye? What is the object of his "complete lysis?"[73] And if it is more proper, because more literal, to speak of a lysis of universe, rather than body, how do we think the relation between transcendental frame and the body, or nobody, that occupies, or is banished from, its confines and powers of orientation? What I offer here as a clarification of Sexton's understanding of my relation to Afro-pessimism emerges from my sense of a kind of terminological dehiscence in Patterson's work that emerges in what I take to be his deep but unacknowledged affinity with and indebtedness to the work of Hannah Arendt, namely, with a distinction crucial to her work between the social and the political. The "secular excommunication" that describes slavery for Patterson is more precisely understood as the radical exclusion from a political order, which is tantamount, in Arendt's formulation, to something on the order of a radical relegation *to* the social.[74] The problem with slavery, for Patterson, is that it is political death, not social death; the problem is that slavery confers the paradoxically stateless status of the merely, barely living; it delineates the inhuman as unaccommodated *bios*. At stake is the transvaluation or, better yet, the invaluation or antivaluation, the extraction from the sciences of value (and from the very possibility of that necessarily fictional, but materially brutal, standpoint that Wagner calls "being a party to exchange").[75] Such extraction will, in turn, be the very mark and inscription (rather than absence or eradication) of the sociality of a life, given in common, instantiated in exchange. What I am trying to get to, by way of this terminological slide in Patterson, is the consideration of a radical disjunction between sociality and the state-sanctioned, state-sponsored terror of power-laden intersubjectivity, which is, or would be, the structural foundation of Patterson's epiphenomenology of spirit. To have honor, which is, of necessity, to be a *man* of honor, for Patterson, is to become a combatant in transcendental subjectivity's perpetual civil war. To refuse the induction that Patterson desires is to enact or perform the recognition of the constitution of civil society as civil butchery. It is, moreover, to consider, by way of Sexton, that the unspoken violence of political friendship constitutes a capacity for alignment and coalition that is constituted and continually enhanced by the unspeakable violence that is done to what and whom the political excludes. This is to say that, yes, I am in total agreement with the Afro-pessimistic understanding of blackness as exterior to civil society and, moreover, as unmappable within the cosmological grid of the transcendental subject. However, I understand civil society and the coordinates of the transcendental aesthetic—cognate as they are with the brutal indistinctness in which failed and successful states and citizens, sovereigns and subjects, mix it up—to be the fundamentally and essentially antisocial nursery for a necessarily necropolitical imitation of life. So that if Afro-pessimists were to say that social death is not the condition of black life but is, rather, the political field that would surround it, then that's a formulation with which I would agree. Social death is not imposed upon blackness by or from the standpoint or positionality of the political; rather, it is the field of the political, from which blackness is relegated to the supposedly undifferentiated mass or blob of the social, which is, in any case, where and what blackness chooses to stay.

This question of the location and position of social death is, as Sexton has shown far more rigorously than I could ever hope to do, crucial. It raises again that massive problematic of inside and outside that animates thought since before its beginning as the endless end to which thought always seeks to return. Such mappability of the space-time or state of social death would, in turn, help us better understand the positionalities that could be said, figuratively, to inhabit it. This mass is understood to be undifferentiated precisely because from the imaginary perspective of the political subject—who is also the transcendental subject of knowledge, grasp, ownership, and self-possession—difference can only be manifest as the discrete individuality that holds or occupies a standpoint. From that standpoint, from the artificial, officially assumed position, blackness is nothing, that is, the relative nothingness of the impossible, pathological subject and his fellows. I believe it is from that standpoint that Afro-pessimism identifies and articulates the imperative to embrace that nothingness which is, of necessity, relative. It is from this standpoint, which Wilderson defines precisely by his inability to occupy it, that he, in a painfully and painstakingly lyrical tour de force of autobiographico-analytic writing, declares himself to be nothing and proclaims his decision, which in any case he cannot make, to remain as nothing, in genealogical and sociological isolation even from every other nothing.

> Now, all that remains are unspoken scraps scattered on the floor like Lisa's grievance. I am nothing, Naima, and you are nothing: the unspeakable answer to your question within your question. This is why I could not—would not—answer your question that night. Would I ever be with a Black woman again? It was earnest, not accusatory—I know. And nothing terrifies me more than such a question asked in earnest. It is a question that goes to the heart of desire, to the heart of our *black capacity to desire*. But if we take out the nouns that you used (nouns of habit that get us through the day), your question to me would sound like this: Would nothing ever be with nothing again?[76]

When one reads the severity and intensity of Wilderson's words—his assertion of his own nothingness and the implications of that nothingness for his reader—one is all but overwhelmed by the need for a kind of affirmative negation of his formulation. It's not that one wants to say no, Professor Wilderson, you are, or I am, somebody; rather, one wants to assert the presence of something between the subjectivity that is refused and that one refuses and nothing, whatever that is. But it is the beauty—the fantastic, celebratory force of Wilderson's and Sexton's work, which study has allowed me to begin more closely to approach—of Afro-pessimism that allows and compels one to move past that contradictory impulse to affirm in the interest of negation and to begin to consider *what nothing is*, not from its own standpoint or from any standpoint but from the absoluteness of its generative dispersion of a general antagonism that blackness holds and protects in and as critical celebration and degenerative and regenerative preservation. That's the mobility of place, the fugitive field of unowning, in and from which we ask, paraontologically, by way of but also against and underneath the ontological terms at our disposal: What is nothingness? What is thingliness? What is blackness? What's the relationship between blackness, thingliness, nothingness, and the (de/re)generative operations of what Deleuze might call *a life* in common? Where do we go, by what means do we begin, to study blackness? Can there be an aesthetic sociology or a social poetics of nothingness? Can we perform an anatomy of the thing or produce a theory of the universal machine? Our aim, even in the face of the brutally imposed difficulties of black life, is cause for celebration. This is not because celebration is supposed to make us feel good or make us feel better, though there would be nothing wrong with that. It is, rather, because the cause for celebration turns out to be the condition of possibility of black thought, which animates the black operations that will produce the absolute overturning, the absolute turning of this motherfucker out. Celebration is the essence of black thought, the animation of black operations, which are, in the first instance, our undercommon, underground, submarine sociality.

In the end, though *life* and *optimism* are the terms under which I speak, I agree with Sexton—by way of the slightest, most immeasurable reversal of emphasis—that Afro-pessimism and black optimism are not but nothing other than one another. I will continue to prefer the black optimism of his work just as, I am sure, he will continue to prefer the Afro-pessimism of mine. We will have been interarticulate, I believe, in the field where annihilative seeing, generative sounding, and rigorous touching and feeling require an improvisation of and on friendship, a sociality of friendship that will have been, at once, both intramural and evangelical. I'll try to approach that field, its expansive concentration, by way of Don Cherry and Ed Blackwell's extended meditation on nothingness; by way of Fanon's and Peter Linebaugh's accounts of language in and as vehicularity; by way of Michel Foucault's meditations on the ship of fools and Deleuze's consideration of the boat as interior of the exterior when they are both thoroughly solicited by the uncharted voices that we carry; by way, even, of Lysis and Socrates; but also, and in the first instance, by way of Hawk and Newk, just friends, trading fours. Perhaps I'm simply deluding myself, but such celebratory performance of thought, in thought, is as much about the insurgency of immanence as it is about what Wagner calls the "consolation of transcendence."[77] But, as I said earlier, I plan to stay a believer in blackness, even as thingliness, even as (absolute) nothingness, even as imprisonment in passage on the most open road of all, even as—to use and abuse a terribly beautiful phrase of Wilderson's—fantasy in the hold.[78]

Where we were, not—withstanding, wasn't there . . .

Where we
were was the hold of a ship we were
caught
in. Soaked wood kept us afloat. . . . It
wasn't limbo we were in albeit we
limbo'd our way there. Where we
were was what we meant by "mu."[79]

There are flights of fantasy in the hold of the ship: the ordinary fugue and fugitive run of the language lab, black phonographies' brutally experimental venue. Paraontological totality is still in the making. Present and unmade in presence, blackness is an instrument in the making. *Quasi una fantasia* in its paralegal swerve, its mad-worked braid, the imagination produces nothing but exsense in the hold. Do you remember the days of slavery? Nathaniel Mackey rightly says, "The world was ever after, / elsewhere. / . . . no / way where we were / was there."[80] Do you remember where we are? No way where we are is here. Where we were, where we are, is what we meant by *mu*, which Wilderson rightly calls the void of our subjectivity, which we extend, in consent beyond all voluntary, in our avoidance of subjectivity.[81] And so it is that we remain in the hold, in the break, as if entering again and again the broken world, to trace the visionary company and join it. This antiphonal island, where we are marooned in search of marronage, where we linger in stateless emergency, is our mobile, constant study, our lysed cell and held dislocation, our blown standpoint and lyred chapel. We study our seaborne variance, sent by its prehistory into arrivance without arrival, as a poetics of lore, of abnormal articulation, where the relation between joint and flesh is the pleated distance of a musical moment that is emphatically, palpably imperceptible and therefore exhausts description. Having defied degradation, the moment becomes a theory of the moment, of the feeling of a presence that is ungraspable in the way that it touches. Such musical moments—of advent, of nativity in all its terrible beauty, of the alienation that is always already born in and as *parousia*, of the disruption in duration of the very idea of the moment—are rigorous performances of the theory of the social life of the shipped, given in the terror of enjoyment and its endlessly redoubled folds. If you take up the hopelessly imprecise tools of standard navigation, the deathly reckoning of difference engines, maritime clocks, and tables of damned assurance, you might stumble on such a moment about two and a half minutes into another Cherry and Blackwell's duet called "Mutron."[82] You'll know the moment by how it requires you to think the relation between fantasy and nothingness: what is mistaken for silence is, all of a sudden, transubstantial.

It's terrible to have come from nothing but the sea, which is nowhere, navigable only in its constant autodislocation. The absence of solidity seems to demand some other ceremony of hailing that will have been carried out on some more exalted frequency. This is exacerbated by the venal refusal of a general acknowledgment of the crime, which is, in any case, impossible, raising the question of whether the only way adequately to account for the horror of slavery and the brutality of the slaver, the only way to be (in Sexton's words) a witness rather than a spectator, is to begin by positing the absolute degradation of the enslaved. This is not a trick question; it's not merely rhetorical. If the slave is, in the end and in essence, nothing, what remains is the necessity of an investigation of that nothingness. What is the nothingness, which is to say the blackness, of the slave that it is not reducible to what they did, though what they did is irreducible in it? This is a question concerning the undercommon inheritance of earth and air, which is given in and as submarine fantasy in the hold. Those who are called into being by the desire for another call relinquish the fantastic when they make, or even when they bear, the choice to leave the hold behind. In resistance to such departure we linger in the brutal interplay of advent and enclosure. Marcus Rediker offers us a scene of that interplay:

They resumed paddling and soon began to sing. After a while she could hear, at first faintly, then with increasing clarity, other sounds—the waves slapping the hull of the big ship, its timbers creaking. Then came muffled screaming in a strange language.

The ship grew larger and more terrifying with every vigorous stroke of the paddles. The smells grew stronger and the sounds louder—crying and wailing from one quarter and low, plaintive singing from another; the anarchic noise of children given an underbeat by hands drumming on wood; the odd comprehensible word or two wafting through: someone asking for *menney*, water, another laying a curse, appealing to *myabeca*, spirits. As the canoemen maneuvered their vessel up alongside, she saw dark faces, framed by small holes in the side of the ship above the waterline, staring intently. Above her, dozens of black women and children and a few red-faced men peered over the rail. They had seen the attempted escape on the sandbar. The men had cutlasses and barked orders in harsh, raspy voices. She had arrived at the slave ship.[83]

Her name is Hortense. Her name is NourbeSe. Her name is B. The black chant she hears is old and new to her. She is unmoored. She is ungendered. Her mother is lost. Exhausted, exhaustive maternity is her pedagogical imperative.

What's required is some attempt to think the relation between fantasy and nothingness: emptiness, dispossession in the hold; an intimacy given most emphatically, and erotically, in a moment of something that, for lack of a better word, we call "silence," a suboceanic feeling of preterition—borne by a common particle in the double expanse—that makes vessels run over or overturn. The temporal coordinates 2'29" and 2'30" mark the not-in-betweenness and mobile location of the span, so we can consider that what is mistaken for silence can also be given in and as nothingness in its full transubstantiality, but also the compression and dispersion, the condensation and displacement, of caged duration, the marking more emphatically of its beginning and end, and, especially, the concentrated air of its propulsion that shows up as waiting, *Erwartung*, embarrassment in our expectation, Blackwell's antic, anticipatory pulse. This moment of nothingness. "Unhoused vacuity," paroikic, metoikic, vernacular, the rich materiality of the hold's, the jug's, emptiness, its contents having fled in their remaining, fled as the remainder, the danger, the supplement, votive and unelect.[84]

Blackwell offers what is held in mu as the impossible-to-understand black thing, the Cherry thing as a seriality of openings, a vestibular chain, a kind of spillway, as Hortense Spillers might say.

I am concerned with the mu in "Mutron"—by way of an approach through Rediker that describes his attempt to describe what might be called a birth into death, or an entrance into bare life or raw life, but which I will insist, not despite but precisely because of its being the blood-stain'd gate through which the radically nonanalagous enters, is the impure immanence of the undercommons' (an)originary refrain—because the task of continually instigating this flown, recursive imagining demands the inhabitation of an architecture and its acoustic, an inhabitation given as if in an approach from outside. What is required—and this is recited with such terrible beauty in the work of Wilderson and Sexton, in echo of Lewis Gordon—is not only *to reside* in an unlivability, an exhaustion that is always already given as foreshadowing afterlife, as a life in some absolutely proximate and unbridgeable distance from the living death of subjection, but also *to discover and to enter* it. Mackey, in the fantastic sear and burned, spurred overhearing of his preface to *Splay Anthem*, outlining the provenance and relationship between the book's serial halves ("Each was given its impetus by a piece of recorded music from which it takes its title, the Dogon 'Song of the Andoumboulou' in one case, Don Cherry's *'Mu' First Part* and *'Mu' Second Part* in the other"), speaks of mu in relation to a circling or spiraling or ringing, this roundness or rondo linking beginning and end; the wailing that accompanies entrance into and expulsion from sociality; that makes you wonder if music, which is not only music, is mobilized in the service of an eccentricity, a centrifugal force, whose intimation Mackey also approaches, that marks sociality's ecstatic existence beyond beginning and end, ends and means.[85] Forgive this long series of long quotations from that preface, to passages of which I remain imprisoned insofar as the range of phonemic, historical, and parageographic resonance in mu get me to the elsewhere and elsewhen that I already inhabit but which I have to keep learning to desire. Actually, if you forgive me, there will be no need to thank me.

> Multi-instrumentalist Don Cherry, best known as a trumpeter, includes voice among the instruments used on the "*Mu*" albums and resorts to a sort of dove-coo baby talk on one piece, "Teo-Teo-Can," emitting sounds that might accompany the tickling of a baby's chin if not be made by the baby itself. It recalls Amiri Baraka's comment on hearing

a John Coltrane solo that consisted of playing the head of "Confirmation" again and again, twenty times or so: "like watching a grown man
learning to speak." In both cases, as with the Dogon trumpet burst and
as it's put in "Song of the Andoumboulou: 58," one is "back / at / some
beginning," some extremity taking one back to animating constraint.
The antelope-horn trumpet's blast and bleat, Cherry's ludic warble
and Trane's recursive quandary are variations on music as gnostic announcement, ancient rhyme, that of end and beginning, gnostic accent
or note that cuts both ways.

But not only music. "Mu" (in quotes to underscore its whatsaid-
ness) is also lingual and imaginal effect and affect, myth and mouth
in the Greek form *muthos* that Jane Harrison, as Charles Olson was
fond of noting, calls "a re-utterance or pre-utterance, . . . a focus of
emotion," surmising the first *muthos* to have been "simply the interjec-
tional utterance *mu*." "Mu" is also lingual and erotic allure, mouth and
muse, mouth not only noun but verb and muse likewise, lingual and
imaginal process, prod and process. It promises verbal and romantic
enhancement, graduation to an altered state, momentary thrall translated into myth. Proffered from time immemorial, poetry's perennial
boon, it thrives on quixotic persistence, the increment or enablement
language affords, promise and impossibility rolled into one (Anuncia/
Nunca). "Mu" carries a theme of utopic reverie, a theme of lost ground
and elegiac allure recalling the Atlantis-like continent Mu, thought by
some during the late nineteenth century and early twentieth century to
have existed long ago in the Pacific. The places named in the song of the
Andoumboulou, set foot on by the deceased while alive but lost or taken
away by death, could be called "Mu." Any longingly imagined, mourned
or remembered place, time, state, or condition can be called "Mu." . . .

Serial form lends itself to andoumboulouous liminality, the draft
unassured extension knows itself to be. Provisional, ongoing, the serial poem moves forward and backward both, repeatedly "back / at /
some beginning," repeatedly circling or cycling back, doing so with
such adamance as to call forward and back into question and suggest an eccentric step to the side—as though, driven to distraction
by short-circuiting options, it can only be itself beside itself. So it is
that "*Mu*" is also *Song of the Andoumboulou*, and *Song of the Andoumboulou* also "*Mu*." H.D.'s crazed geese, circling above the spot that was
once Atlantis or the Hesperides or the Islands of the Blest, come to

mind, as do John Coltrane's wheeling, spiraling runs as if around or in pursuit of some lost or last note, lost or last amenity: a tangential, verging movement out (outlantish). The ring shout comes to mind, as do the rings of Saturn, the planet adopted by Sun Ra, one of whose albums, *Atlantis*, opens with a piece called "Mu."[86]

Now I want us to try to think about the relation between Mackey's and Wilderson's dialectics of held fantasy. Wilderson's register is more explicitly philosophical, so our registers might have to shift as well. Entrance into the philosophy of the subject is also perilous, but it seems as if our belatedness makes such peril necessary if the goal is to approach the ship and its hold. Wilderson says:

> To put it bluntly, the imaginative labor of cinema, political action, and cultural studies are all afflicted with the same theoretical aphasia. They are speechless in the face of gratuitous violence.
>
> This theoretical aphasia is symptomatic of a debilitated ensemble of questions regarding political ontology. At its heart are two registers of imaginative labor. The first register is that of description, the rhetorical labor aimed at explaining the way relations of power are named, categorized, and explored. The second register can be characterized as prescription, the rhetorical labor predicated on the notion that everyone can be emancipated through some form of discursive, or symbolic, intervention.
>
> But emancipation through some form of discursive or symbolic intervention is wanting in the face of a subject position that is not a subject position—what Marx calls "a speaking implement" or what Ronald Judy calls "an interdiction against subjectivity." In other words, the Black has sentient capacity but no relational capacity. As an accumulated and fungible object, rather than an exploited and alienated subject, the Black is openly vulnerable to the whims of the world and so is his or her cultural "production." What does it mean— what are the stakes—when the world can whimsically transpose one's cultural gestures, the stuff of symbolic intervention, onto another worldly good, a commodity of style?[87]

He continues:

> The Afro-pessimists are theorists of Black positionality who share Fanon's insistence that, though Blacks are . . . sentient beings, the

structure of the entire world's semantic field . . . is sutured by anti-Black solidarity. . . . Afro-pessimism explores the meaning of Blackness not—in the first instance—as a variously and unconsciously interpellated identity or as a conscious social actor, but as a structural position of noncommunicability in the face of all other positions; this meaning is noncommunicable because, again, as a position, Blackness is predicated on modalities of accumulation and fungibility, not exploitation and alienation.[88]

A certain kind of sociological desire is announced in this utterance, in echo not only of Fanon, not only of Patterson, but of an anticipatory counterutterance in Du Bois as well. What is our methodological comportment in the face of the question concerning the strange meaning of being black when the ontological attitude is already under a kind of interdiction with regard to such being? A sociology of relations that would somehow account for the radically nonrelational—but this only insofar as relationality is understood to be an expression of power, structured by the givenness of a transcendental subjectivity that the black cannot have but by which the black can be had; a structural position that he or she cannot take but by which he or she can be taken. The givenness and substantiveness of transcendental subjectivity is assured by a relative nothingness. In a relationality that can only be manifest as a general absence of relations, by way of a theoretically established noncommunicability that is, itself, somehow given for thought by way of some kind of spooky action at a distance (How else would we know this noncommunicability? How else would it show up as the nonrelationality that structures all relationality?).

Within this framework blackness and antiblackness remain in brutally antisocial structural support of one another like the stanchions of an absent bridge of lost desire over which flows the commerce and under which flows the current, the logistics and energy of exclusion and incorporation, that characterizes the political world. Though it might seem paradoxical, the bridge between blackness and antiblackness *is* "the unbridgeable gap between Black being and Human life."[89] What remains is the necessity of an attempt to index black existence by way of what Chandler would call paraontological, rather than politico-ontological, means.[90] The relative nothingness of black life, which shows up for political ontology as a relation of nonrelation or counterrelation precisely in the impossibility of political intersubjectivity, can be said both to obscure and to indicate the social animation of the bridge's underside, where the im/possibilities of political intersubjectivity are exhausted. Political ontology backs away from the experimental declivity that Fanon and Du Bois were at least able to blaze, each in his own way forging a sociological path that would move against the limiting force, held in the ontological traces, of positivism, on the one hand, and phenomenology, on the other, as each would serve as the foundation of a theory of relations posing the nothingness of blackness in its (negative) relation to the substance of subjectivity-as-nonblackness (enacted in antiblackness). On the one hand, blackness and ontology are unavailable for one another; on the other hand, blackness must free itself from ontological expectation, must refuse subjection to ontology's sanction against the very idea of black subjectivity. This imperative is not something up ahead, to which blackness aspires; it is the labor, which must not be mistaken for Sisyphean, that blackness serially commits. The paraontological distinction between blackness and blacks allows us no longer to be enthralled by the notion that blackness is a property that belongs to blacks (thereby placing certain formulations regarding non/relationality and non/communicability on a different footing and under a certain pressure) but also because ultimately it allows us to detach blackness from the question of (the meaning of) being. The infinitesimal difference between pessimism and optimism lies not in the belief or disbelief in descriptions of power relations or emancipatory projects; the difference is given in the space between an assertion of the relative nothingness of blackness and black people in the face, literally, of substantive (antiblack) subjectivity and an inhabitation of appositionality, its internal social relations, which remain unstructured by the protocols of subjectivity insofar as mu—which has been variously translated from the Japanese translation of the Chinese *wu* as no, not, nought, nonbeing, emptiness, nothingness, nothing, no thing, but which also bears the semantic trace of dance, therefore of measure given in walking/falling, that sustenance of asymmetry, difference's appositional mobility—also signifies an absolute nothingness whose antirelative and antithetical philosophical content is approached by way of Nishida Kitarō's enactment of the affinities between structures and affects of mysticism that undergird and trouble metaphysics in the "East" and the "West." Indeed, the content that is approached is approach, itself, and for the absolute beginner, who is at once pilgrim and penitent, mu signals that which is most emphatically and lyrically marked and indicated in Wilderson's and Mackey's gestures toward "fantasy in the hold," the radical unsettlement that is where and what we are. Unsettlement is the displacement of sovereignty by initiation, so that what's at stake—here, in displacement—is a certain black incapacity to desire sovereignty and ontological relationality whether they are recast in the terms and forms of a Levinasian ethics or an Arendtian politics, a Fanonian resistance or a Pattersonian test of honor.

Unenabled by or in this incapacity, Nishida's philosophy folds sovereignty in the delay that has always given it significance, putting it on hold, but not in the hold, where to be on hold is to have been committed to a kind of staging, a gathering of and for the self in which negation is supposed to foster true emergence in "a self-determination of that concrete place of the contradictory identity of objectivity and subjectivity."[91] What I term, here, a *delay* is understood by Nishida as "the moment [that] can be said to be eternal . . . [wherein] consciously active individuals, encounter the absolute as its inverse polarity, its mirror opposite, at each and every step of our lives."[92] It is in echoing a traditional Buddhist teaching, which asserts the *nonself* even against what are considered foolish declarations of the *nonexistence of self*, that Nishida restages a standard ontotheological skit in which sovereignty—whether in the form of the consciously active individual or in that individual's abstract and equivalent dispersion in the nation, "the mirror image of the Pure Land in this world"—takes and holds the space-time, the paradoxically transcendental ground, of the everyday unreality of "the real world," where the sovereign's endless show carries a brutally material imposition.[93] What remains to be seen is what (the thinking and the study of) blackness can bring to bear on the relation between the un/real world and its other(s). What if blackness is the refusal to defer to, given in the withdrawal from the eternal delay of, sovereignty? What if Nishida's preparatory vestibule for a general and infinite self-determination is pierced, rather than structurally supported, by (the very intimation of) the no-place to which it is opposed in his own work? When Nishida argues that "the human, consciously active volitional world makes its appearance from the standpoint of the paradoxical logic of the *Prajnaparamita Sutra* literature," which offers us the phrase "Having No Place wherein it abides, this Mind arises," he means to assert the legitimacy of an idea or image of the whole that takes "the form of the contradictory identity of the consciously active self and the world, of the volitional individual and the absolute."[94] What if (the thinking and the study of) blackness is an inhabitation of the hold that disrupts the whole in which the absolute, or absolute nothingness, is structured by its relation to its relative Other? What if the nothing that is in question here moves through to the other side of negation, in "the real presence" of blackness, in and as another idea of nothingness altogether that is given in and as and to things?

Both against the grain and by way of Fanon's negation of the condition of relative nothingness, which is instantiated in what he takes to be the white man's manufacture of the black, black study is attunement of and toward blackness as the place where something akin to the absolute nothingness that Nishida elaborates and a radical immanence of things that is not disavowed so much as it is unimagined in that same elaboration converge. This is to say that what remains unimagined by Nishida—not simply radical thingliness but its convergence with nothingness—is nevertheless made open to us by and in his thinking. Nishida helps prepare us to consider, even in the nationalist divagation of his own engagement with the heart of a teaching that has no center, that blackness is the place that has no place. "Having no place where it abides, this Mind [of the Little Negro Steelworker] arises."[95] Things are in, but they do not have, a world, a place, but it is precisely both the specificity of having neither world nor place and the generality of not having that we explore at the nexus of openness and confinement, internment and flight. Having no place wherein they abide, in the radically dispossessive no-place of the hold, in "Mutron," Cherry and Blackwell touch intimacy from the walls. In that break, the architectonic intent of the hold as sovereign expression and recuperation breaks down. Feel the complete lysis of this morbid body/universe. Touch is not where subjectivity and objectivity come together in some kind of self-determining dialectical reality; beyond that, in the hold, in the *basho* (the place of nothingness, that underground, undercommon recess), is the social life of black things, which passeth (the) understanding. In the hold, blackness and imagination, in and as consent not to be a single being, are (more and less than) one.

We are prepared for this generative incapacity by Wilderson's work, where what distinguishes the sovereign, the settler, and even the savage from the slave is precisely that they share "a capacity for time and space coherence. At every scale—the soul, the body, the group, the land, and the universe—they can both practice cartography, and although at every scale their maps are radically incompatible, their respective 'mapness' is never in question. This capacity for cartographic coherence is the thing itself, that which secures subjectivity for both the Settler and the 'Savage' and articulates them to one another in a network of connections, transfers, and displacements."[96] Absent the "cartographic coherence [that] is the thing itself," we must become interested in things, in a certain relationship between thingliness and nothingness and blackness that plays itself out—outside and against the grain of the very idea of self-determination—in the unmapped and unmappable immanence of undercommon sociality. This is fantasy in the hold, and Wilderson's access to it is in the knowledge that he can have nothing and in the specific incapacity of a certain desire that this knowledge indexes. It remains for us to structure an accurate sense of what nothing is and what it constitutes in the exhaustion of home, intersubjectivity, and what Sexton calls "ontological reach."[97] The truth of the formulation that the black cannot *be* among or in relation to his or her own is given in terminological failure. What's at stake is how to improvise the declension from what is perceived as a failure to be together to the unmappable zone of paraontological consent. The promise of another world, or of the end of this one, is given in the general critique of world. In the meantime, what remains to be inhabited is nothing itself in its fullness, which is, in the absence of intersubjective relationality, high fantastical or, more precisely, given in the fugal, contrapuntal intrication that we can now call, by way of Mackey and Wilderson, fantasy in the hold, where the interplay of blackness and nothingness is given in an ongoing drama of force and entry.

In a tradition of Buddhist teaching that goes back to the opening of *The Gateless Gate*, a thirteenth-century gathering of *koans* (case studies that take the form of stories, dialogues, or questions meant to induce in the initiate dual intensities of doubt and concentration), that drama emerges as a deconstructive and deconstructed question, as exemplified in conventional presentations and interpretation of "Jōshū's Dog." The koan reads: "A monk asked [Zen master] Jōshū in all earnestness, 'Does a dog have Buddha nature or not?' Jōshū said, 'Mu!'"[98] Even when we take into account Steven Heine's warnings regarding the legitimacy of traditional attributions and interpretations of the Mu Koan—which require us to consider both that it was not Jōshū who responded to the question or that Jōshū's response was the opposite of mu and that, therefore, the negative way that response is understood to open ought now to be closed—we are left with an ontotheological possibility that blackness may well exhaust.[99] There is an appositional response, which this phantom query cannot properly be said to have called, that persists in and as an echoepistemology of passage, a sociotheology of the *aneschaton*, the instrumental interruption of telos by the universal (drum) machine, Blackwell's prompt out to the study of the last things, the study carried out by the things that are last, by the least of these, whose movement constitutes a critique of the general and necessary relation between politics and death, a critique of the critique of judgment, a deconstruction of the opposition of heaven and hell. Cherry brings the noise of the end of the world in the invention of the earth. Though eschatology is understood to be a department, as it were, of theology, it has been both displaced by an administrative desire for the teleological and appropriated by a retributive desire for a kind of finality of and in sentencing, each in its commitment to sovereignty and the already existing structures that depend on the very idea. But it's not that I want to enclose things in the dialectical movement between beginning and end. Invention and passage denote an already existing alternative for which we are not constrained to wait. We are already down here on and under the ground, the water, as worked, unwrought nothingness working fleshly releasement in a privation of feasting, a fragility of healing. Mu is a practice of mysticism in the flesh; "Mutron," the ritual Blackwell and Cherry perform, is their concentration meditation. It indexes the specific and material history of the drowned and burned, the shipped and held, as the condition for the release not just of the prevailing worldview but of the very idea of worldview, of transcendental standpoint and Pure Land. Cherry and Blackwell are initiates, who in turn initiate us, in what it is to abide in the social materiality of no place, of Having No Place, as a place for study. This shows up as a radical displacement of binary logic, moving through negation, because the way of the hold is no *via negativa*. Rather, the hold is distressed circuitry, an impedance or impediment of current, a placement of the self's or the settler's or the sovereign's dyadic currency in kenotic abandon. "Mutron" is a way out of no way given in and as the exhaustion of what it is to abide, where the first and the last are neither first nor last.

To remain in the hold is to remain in that set of practices of living together where antikinetic theorizing is both bracketed and mobilized by performative contemplation, as in the monastic sociality of Minton's, where the hermetic absence of and from home is given in and as a playhouse, a funnyhouse, a madhouse. The club, our subcenobitic thing, our block chapel, is a hard row of constant improvisational contact, a dispossessive intimacy of rubbing, whose mystic rehearsal is against the rules or, more precisely, is apposed to rule, and is, therefore, a concrete social logic often (mis)understood as nothing but foolishness, which is, on the other hand, exactly and absolutely what it is. Foucault's meditations point precisely in this direction:

> The ship of fools was heavily loaded with meaning, and clearly carried a great social force. . . . The madman on his crazy boat sets sail

for the other world, and it is from the other world that he comes when he disembarks. This enforced navigation is both rigorous division and absolute Passage, serving to underline in real and imaginary terms the *liminal* situation of the mad in medieval society. It was a highly symbolic role, made clear by the mental geography involved, where the madman was *confined at the gates of the cities*. His exclusion was his confinement, and if he had no *prison* other than the *threshold* itself he was still detained at this place of passage. . . .

A prisoner in the midst of the ultimate freedom, . . . he is the Passenger *par excellence*, the prisoner of the passage. It is not known where he will land, and when he lands, he knows not whence he came. His truth and his home are the barren wasteland between two lands that can never be his own. . . . The link between water and madness is deeply rooted in the dream of the Western man.[100]

Deleuze has seized on this dimension of Foucault's thought to probe how for him "the inside [functions] as an operation of the outside." Indeed, he notes, "in all his work Foucault seems haunted by this theme of an inside which is merely the fold of the outside, as if the ship were a folding of the sea. . . . Thought has no other being than this madman himself. As Blanchot says of Foucault: 'He encloses the outside, that is, constitutes it in an interiority of expectation or exception.'"[101] Deleuze continues:

Forces always come from the outside, from an outside that is farther away than any form of exteriority. So there are not only particular features taken up by the relations between forces, but particular features of resistance that are apt to modify and overturn these relations and to change the unstable diagram. . . . [This is] "where one can live and in fact where Life exists *par excellence*." . . . [This is] *life within the folds*. This is the central chamber, which one need no longer fear is empty since one fills it with oneself. Here one becomes a master of one's speed and, relatively speaking, a master of one's molecules and particular features, in this zone of subjectivation: the boat as interior of the exterior.[102]

Passage, which is to say this passage, which is to say the passage between these passages of Foucault and Deleuze, the passage between these and those of Wilderson and Mackey, is given in the hold that Cherry and Blackwell deconstructively reconstruct just so you'll know that the music and its performance was never about transcendence unless transcendence is understood as immanence's fugitive impurity. How would you recognize the antiphonal accompaniment to gratuitous violence—the sound that can be heard as if in response to that violence, the sound that must be heard as that to which such violence responds? Wilderson asks the question again so that it can be unasked; so that we can hear Cherry and Blackwell unask it in and as intimacy in dislocation. Unasking takes the form of a caesura, an arrhythmia of the iron system, that Blackwell presses into the interruptive, already interrupted New Orleans continuum of his roll whose distended rearticulation stretches out so you can go down in it enough to think about what it means to be somewhere you're only supposed to be going through, to be contained in the atopic atemporality that propels you, as the immanence of the transcendental hallway of our endless preparation, our experimental trial, given as our ongoing study of how to speak, the terrible beauty of our imprisonment in the passage, our life in the folds. Blackwell asks a question that Cherry anticipates, but by which Cherry is driven and to which Cherry responds in the bent, appositional reflection that unasks it. This drama is revived in Wilderson's questioning; the question is a seizure that moves us to unask it. That unasking is mu not because the question's terms and assumptions are incorrect; not because the implied opposition of nothing and something—where nothingness is too simply understood to veil (as if it were some epidermal livery) (some higher) being and is therefore relative as opposed to absolute—doesn't signify; but because nothing (this paraontological interplay of blackness and nothingness, this aesthetic sociality) remains to be explored; because we don't know what we mean by it even when we recite or record its multiphonic swerve; because blackness is not a category for ontology or for phenomenological analysis. Wilderson's question—"Would nothing ever be with nothing again?"—precisely in its irreducible necessity, cannot be answered but can only be unasked in the lyricism of that ill logic that black monks incessantly, thelonially, perform, as difference without opposition, in "a black hole," as Jay Wright, "germ and terminal, expansive/in its nothingness."[103]

What would it be for this drama to be understood in its own terms, from its own standpoint, on its own ground? This is not simply a question of perspective awaiting its unasking, since what we speak of is this radical being beside itself of blackness, its appositionality. The standpoint, the home territory, *chez lui*—Charles Lam Markmann's insightful mistranslation of Fanon, *among his own*, illuminates something that Richard Philcox obscures by way of correction—signifies a relationality that displaces the already displaced impossibility of home and the modes of relationality that home is supposed to afford.[104] Can this sharing of a life in homelessness, this interplay of the refusal of what has been refused and consent, this undercommon appositionality, be a place from which to know, a place out of which emerges neither self-consciousness nor knowledge of the other but an improvisation that proceeds from somewhere on the other side of an unasked question? But not simply to be among one's own; rather, also, to live among one's own in dispossession, to live among the ones who cannot own, the ones who have nothing and who, in having nothing, have everything. To live, in other words, within the general commonness and openness of *a life* in Deleuze's sense (hence the necessity of a philosophy of life; hence the necessity but also the rigor of a disbelief in social death, where social death is precisely understood as the imposition of the subject's necessity rather than the refusal of the subject's possibility, which, in any case, the imposition founds and enforces). At stake is the curve, the suppleness and subtlety, not only of contemplation on social life but of contemplative social life; at stake is the force of an extraphenomenological poetics of social life. And so we arrive, again and again, at a profound impulse in Fanon that—as Chandler indicates in his reading, which is the initial reading, of Du Bois—constitutes Du Bois's horizon and which appears in the various forms of that question whose necessity is so fundamental that it must be unasked—the question of the meaning of (black) being, the question of the meaning of (black) things. We study in the sound of an unasked question. Our study is the sound of an unasked question. We study the sound of an unasked question. In the absence of the amenity (some pleasantness or pleasantry of welcome or material comfort), what is borne in the emptiness or nothingness of the amenity (of which love or soul is born, in exhaustion, as a society of friends), what are the other elements of mu? Chant and koan and moan and *Sprechgesang*, and babble and gobbledygook, *le petit nègre*, the little nigger, pidgin, baby talk, bird talk, Bird's talk, bard talk, bar talk, our locomotive bar walk and black chant, our pallet cries and shipped whispers, our black notes and black cant, the tenor's irruptive habitation of the vehicle, the monastic preparation of a more than three-dimensional transcript, an imaginal manuscript we touch upon the walls and one another, so we can enter into the hold we're in, where there is no way we were or are.

Let's try to come at the central, centrifugal chamber of the open/ing again, this time by way of Linebaugh and Fanon.

"The most magnificent drama of the last thousand years of human history" was not enacted with its strophes and prosody ready-made. It created a new speech. A combination of, first, nautical English; second, the "sabir" of the Mediterranean; third, the hermetic-like cant talk of the "underworld"; and fourth, West African grammatical construction, produced the "pidgin English" that became in the tumultuous years of the slave trade the language of the African coast.

Linguists describe pidgin as a "go-between" language, the product of a "multiple-language situation," characterized by "radical simplification." "Il est meme né pour permettre une communication josque-là impossible," Calvet has written. . . . Where people had to understand each other, pidgin English was the lingua franca of the sea and the frontier. Inasmuch as all who came to the New World did so after months at sea, pidgin or its maritime and popular cognates became the medium of transmission for expressing the new social realities. . . . Pidgin became an instrument, like the drum or the fiddle, of communication among the oppressed: scorned and not easily understood by polite society.[105]

In the interest of a radical restaging of what Linebaugh calls, after Du Bois, this "magnificent drama," Fanon initiates a complex critical disavowal of the "new speech" it produces, beginning—but not paradoxically—with an assertion of language's irreducibly dramatic character. "We attach," Fanon writes, "a fundamental importance to the phenomenon of language and consequently consider the study of language essential for providing us with one element in understanding the black man's dimension of being-for-others, it being understood that to speak is to exist absolutely for the other" (*BSWM*, 1). In a philosophical register cognate with that of Nishida, Fanon posits an "[existence] absolutely for the other," in speech, that is given in and as "absolutely nothing."

> Our only hope of getting out of the situation is to pose the problem correctly, for all these findings and all this research have a single aim: to get man to admit he is nothing, absolutely nothing—and get him to eradicate this narcissism whereby he thinks he is different from the other "animals."
>
> This is nothing more nor less than the *capitulation of man.*
>
> All in all, I grasp my narcissism with both hands and I reject the vileness of those who want to turn man into a machine. If the debate cannot be opened up on a philosophical level—i.e., the fundamental demands of human reality—I agree to place it on a psychological

level: in other words, the "misfires," just as we talk about an engine misfiring.[106]

But what if the situation we ought to hope to get out of is "that concrete place of the contradictory identity of objectivity and subjectivity" of which both Nishida and Fanon speak? What if the emergence of man is best understood as the obsessive restaging not of the magnificent drama that Linebaugh indexes but of an epiphenomenal burlesque in which self-determination is enacted with murderous indirection? In a way that is, again, similar to that of Nishida, Fanon's gesture toward nothingness prepares our approach to these questions. It can be said, then, that Fanon moves to distinguish the language of farce from the language of tragedy; it remains for us both to learn from and to augment his analysis, which continues by way of (the) man's casual and uninformed commentary on the social situation of the new speech.

> It is said that the black man likes to palaver, and whenever I pronounce the word "palaver" I see a group of boisterous children raucously and blandly calling out to the world: children at play insofar as play can be seen as an initiation to life. The black man likes to palaver, and it is only a short step to a new theory that the black man is just a child. Psychoanalysts have a field day, and the word "orality" is soon pronounced. . . . [In this] we are interested in the black man confronted by the French language. We would like to understand why the Antillean is so fond of speaking good French.[107]

When Fanon proceeds to isolate the new speech from its disavowal it is because it is the disavowal in which he is interested. This is to say that the new speech doesn't yet show up for Fanon as an object of analysis; more precisely, the new speech doesn't show up as speech. After all, "To speak means being able to use a certain syntax and possessing the morphology of such and such a language but it means above all assuming a culture and bearing the weight of a civilization" (BSWM, 1–2). And what's at stake, in the very newness of pidgin, is precisely its improvisatory refusal, rather than use, of "a certain syntax" so that the given is given over to its poetic alternative; its construction, rather than assumption, of a culture; its burial under the weight of civilization and the unlikely, paradoxically animative, exhaustion of such inter(n)ment. But while it can be said of Fanon that in this point in his text he neglects the new speech he offers a profound understanding of (the provenance of) a certain desire for the standard.

Monsieur Achille, a teacher at the Lycée du Parc in Lyon, cited a personal experience during his lecture. . . . As a Roman Catholic, he took part in a pilgrimage. Seeing a black face among his flock, the priest asked him: "Why have you left big savanna and why you come with us?" Achille answered most politely. . . . Everyone laughed at the exchange. . . . But if we stop to reflect, we realize that the priest's usage of pidgin calls for several remarks.

1. . . . A white man talking to a person of color behaves exactly like a grown-up with a kid, simpering, murmuring, fussing, and coddling. . . . Speaking to black people in this way is an attempt to reach down to them, to make them feel at ease, to make oneself understood and reassure them. . . .

2. To speak gobbledygook to a black man is insulting, for it means he is the gook. . . .

If the person who speaks to a man of color or an Arab in pidgin does not see that there is a flaw or a defect in his behavior, then he has never paused to reflect.[108]

The violence of insincere and unflattering imitation that materializes such absence of reflection is vividly portrayed in Fanon's text. However, infantilization of the ones who utter the speech that, according to Fanon, cannot be spoken, does not mean that the new speech is merely infantile. The implication, here, that the new speech is also old is not a function of anything that it retains other than an essential and irreducible vehicularity. Fanon's concern with the pathological desire to speak good French, seen in its relation to the normal desire to be spoken to in good faith, understands the speaker's being absolutely for the Other to imply reciprocity within the shared possession of a language. Speech in bad faith moves in the wake of not listening, of neither acknowledging nor recognizing the speaker's capacity to be for or with the one to whom he or she speaks. Such being for can be spoken of in terms of contemporaneity—implying not only joint ownership of a language but also a shared spatiotemporal frame, transcendental aesthetic, body schema, or home—but might be better elaborated in terms of the differentiation of any given spatiotemporal frame, the shared and social construction of an immanent aesthetic, within the constantly shifting schemata of a fleshly historicity in which language moves to connect a vast, differential range of unmoored unowning.

(This is why it's important to note that this tragic [or tragi-comic] homelessness of the new speech is something Fanon approaches in his analysis of an exhaustion of return in Aimé Césaire's poetry—return is exhausted in descent, plunge, fall; a propulsive transport through the crush and density of an absolute singularity, in the interest of avoiding "this absurd drama that others have staged around me" [BSWM, 174]. What Fanon celebrates in Césaire, however, are instances of language whose emphasis on rising he sees implicitly to assert the necessity of a departure from undercommon linguistic sociality that traverses the distance between pidgin and poetry. "*Césaire went down. He agreed to see what was happening at the very bottom, and now he can come back up. He is ripe for the dawn. But he does not leave the black man down below. He carries him on his shoulders and lifts him up to the skies*" [BSWM, 172]. Return, which had been reconfigured as descent, is now surrogate to an elevation in and of language that enacts the rediscovery of the meaning of the poet's identity.[109] But there is profound ambivalence in Fanon with regard to the mechanisms of uplift that he reads in Césaire. *Lysis* is meant to stave off the interplay—which lyric often induces—of narcissism and alienation that produces, and is grotesquely reproduced in, the black man. Fanon alerts us to a breaking brokenness in Césaire's work that moves against the grain of the lyrical, upwardly mobile self-determination that carries it. This is the ordinance and disorder that the new speech affords. Paralyric sociality has no place in the sun. The night holds fantasy, not identity. The new speech, which animates Césaire's poetry as well as Fanon's invocation of Césaire in the interest of disavowing the new speech, is where we discover, again and again, the various and unrecoverable natality that we share. Fanon recognizes that what can't be recovered becomes [sur]real in not being itself. This corrosive insistence on and in the new is where lyric and lysis converge in mutual submergence, but Fanon is constrained to avow the disavowal that is encrypted in the desire to speak good French. Later, I will return to the fallen poetics of return, its high and dissident fidelity; now it remains necessary to concentrate on Fanon's analytic of speech in bad faith, which begins with his concern with the white usage of pidgin, its effects on "privileged" blacks interpellated by such speech, and, then, the ensuing commitment of those blacks to "speaking good French.")

Fanon takes great care to emphasize not just that the fact that there are whites who don't talk down to blacks is irrelevant for the study of the effects produced by whites who do but that the purpose of his study of the Negro and language is to "eliminate a number of realities" that occur as a function of pathological behavior indexed to an inhuman psychology. He's interested, finally, in how pathological white behavior breeds or fabricates a kind of pathological black behavior. Fanon is interested in acknowledging, isolating, studying, and eradicating what Frederick Douglass calls our "plantation peculiarities."[110] Moreover, while this process may be initiated by way of a psychological or psychoanalytic discourse predicated on the notion of the inferiority complex, a discourse that might also be discussed as a kind of misfire, in language that anticipates that of J. L. Austin—an infelicitous speech act, one that fails, ultimately, to achieve an intention—ultimately, Fanon appeals to a different metaphorics, a different language, the language of the biochemistry and alchemy of nothingness, a language of and on the experiment's double edge. What if we conceive of the sold, old-souled child who utters the new speech as having been submitted to the most brutal forms of violent investigation: placed on a kind of endless trial, given over to an interminable testing, the brutality of the biological market in which the self-possession of a body is interdicted by fleshly dispossession, marking that condition where to be grasped/held/owned is also to be studied? But what if we simultaneously conceive of the child as a scientist, one engaged in experiments, and in a metaexperimental undertaking of and in research predicated on the embrace of precisely that dispossessive fleshliness that corresponds to the *fullest possible understanding* of what Fanon refers to as "absolutely nothing"—a nothingness without reserve, independent of the desire to show up in and for the conventional optics wherein somebody is delineated and identified? Then palaver would best be understood as the language of the playground if the playground is more accurately understood as a laboratory. This means considering "palaver" or "gobbledygook" not as degraded forms of the standard but rather as modes of linguistic experimentation, modes of linguistic theory given in experimental linguistic practice that have at least two possible effects: the calling into existence of a kind of carceral standard that will have been fabricated in the instance of a whole range of administrative, normative, and regulatory modes and desires and the equally problematic calling forth of certain acts of tone-deaf imitation, equal parts condescension and brutality, the production of a sound meant to accompany an image/livery of subordination in the interest of self-determination's dumbshow.

What's at stake here is the priority of anoriginally insubordinate, jurisgenerative, as opposed to juridically systemic, linguistic experimentation. Speaking "gobbledygook" to a black man is insulting if it takes pidgin for gobbledygook, if such a sclerotic understanding, and the imprecision that follows from it, imagines pidgin to be something other than a language of study. Fanon bristles at the casualness of such a form of speech, the easy way in which the informal is understood to be the occasion for a kind of brutal informality on the part of the one who arrogantly deigns to understand it. The absence of any intention to give offense is no defense, in his estimation, for the absence of any intention not to give offense. One takes no care to avoid the incidental or accidental suffering of the thing. And this is, finally, evidence of a flaw, a moral defect; such lack of concern is rightly understood to be pathological. But what must be clearly understood is that it is not pidgin or *le petit nègre* that instantiates imprisonment at an uncivilized and primitive level: it is, rather, the inaccurate, imprecise, and, for all intents and purposes, absent reflection—wholly outside of any protocol of study, wholly outside of the experimental social, aesthetic, and intellectual modalities that determine the making of the language in the first place—of pidgin that constitutes this particular prison house of language. This means that we must then discuss the no less carceral effects that attend the disavowal of pidgin that often attends the righteous refusal of its less than vulgar imitation. Some might say that such imitation is merely an extension of pidgin's experimental force, but I would argue that it is more precisely understood as always in service, always enacting the exaltation, of the standard. In this instance imitation is the sincerest form of brutality. What remains is to consider what it is for Fanon to have felt himself lapsing.

> When I meet a German or a Russian speaking bad French I try to indicate through gestures the information he is asking for, but in doing so I am careful not to forget that he has a language of his own, a country, and that perhaps he is a lawyer or an engineer back home. Whatever the case, he is a foreigner with different standards.
>
> There is nothing comparable when it comes to the black man. He has no culture, no civilization, and no "long historical past." . . .
>
> Whether he likes it or not, the black man has to wear the livery the white man has fabricated for him.[111]

Fanon elaborates:

> The fact is that the European has a set idea of the black man, and there is nothing more exasperating than to hear: "How long have you lived in France? You speak such good French."
>
> It could be argued that this is due to the fact that a lot of black people speak pidgin. But that would be too easy. . . .

After everything that has . . . been said, it is easy to understand why the first reaction of the black man is to say *no* to those who endeavor to define him. It is understandable that the black man's first action is a *reaction*, and since he is assessed with regard to his degree of assimilation, it is understandable too why the returning Antillean speaks only French: because he is striving to underscore the rift that has occurred. He embodies a new type of man whom he imposes on his colleagues and family. His old mother no longer understands when he speaks of her pj's, her ramshackle dump, and her lousy joint. All that embellished with the proper accent.[112]

What's problematic in Fanon is the belief in the priority of the standard except for the special case of the black for whom there is no standard, where standard, in its priority, corresponds to *patria* and patrimony. This will re-emerge in Patterson's discourse as the assertion of the absence of a heritage (wherein a past is detached from or deprived of long historical duration) and natal alienation. At stake, in a way that must be understood with more precision than the phrase "black civilization" and whatever its impossibility might signify, is the relation, or in Wilderson's more precise formulation, the antagonism between blackness and civilization. The famously mistranslated title of Foucault's opus *L'histoire de la folie a l'âge classique* has a kind of relevance here in part because the ongoing and irrepressible event of the nonstandard, the antestandard, given now in the language of the standard as madness, as social psychosis, has blackness, also, for another name. We might consider, here, the structural relation between name and livery, designation and uniform, precisely in order to think about what historical task their interinanimative imposition, which takes the form of a sumptuary law, confers upon the ones who have been so burdened. At stake is the givenness of the given's constant disruption, which is prior to its naming; the gift of a project whose conferral is prior to its venal imposition. This is a massive, immeasurable problematic of responsibility.

Meanwhile, the phonics of pidgin is an epiphenomenon, not only in that it is an effect of, but also in that it indicates, fabrication. Moreover, it entraps what it indicates. In this view, it's not just that pidgin is prison language but that being made to speak it imprisons. Imprisonment in pidgin, the imprisonment that is enacted in being made to speak pidgin, is, itself, an epiphenomenon of epidermalization, nothing more than its verbal accompaniment. Implicit here, again, is the assumed priority of the standard.

One is made to speak pidgin in response to an imposition, in response to speech uttered in bad faith. The standard rises as a kind of background that pidgin fails pitiably and pitifully to represent. That failed representation is then burlesqued and parodied by the white whose utterance—whether in condescension or in a more direct kind of cruelty—is meant to do nothing other than impose the subordination and incarceration that is instantiated in the black man–as–good nigger's speech.

In outlining a certain problematic of return, the problem of why upon his return to the Antilles the privileged one desires to speak good French, describes one who sees himself as moving within a condition in which suspicion of the black student's erudite and standard speech is confined only to the periphery of the university where "an army of fools" resides (*BSWM*, 18). But the point isn't that life in the university undermines any such faith in the wisdom of its inhabitants; the point is that a set of assumptions about class now edges into clarity. That the capacity for standard speech, whether of another tongue or of one's own, is aligned with the achievement of a certain interconnection of class status and educational accomplishment. One who recognizes that alignment, upon meeting the German who speaks bad French, politely assumes that he is an engineer or a lawyer, that he has a language, that he has standards, that he has a home. The black man is the living embodiment and visualization of the absence of the standard, however, and no such assumption can be made about him. But this lived experience of the nonstandard, of the standard's absence, does not mean that one is unable either to see or to revere the standard and its idealized locale. The army (as opposed to the ship) of fools that surrounds and protects the inner sanctum of the metropole, the holy of holies, need neither know nor embody the standard that it protects. It is, in fact, nearest and clearest to the one who recognizes it as the site of "equal footing," where the weak assertion of one's capacity for feeling and reason is replaced by emphatically proper linguistic performance (*BSWM*, 19).

Again, Fanon is concerned with the narcissism of the new returnee, the social climber, as he or she links up with Arendt's own stringent analysis of the parvenu. That narcissism disallows a rigorous and requisite full inhabitation of the zone of nonbeing, an "extraordinarily sterile and arid region, an incline stripped bare of every essential from which a genuine new departure can emerge" (*BSWM*, xii). This incline, or declivity, or ramp, bespeaks, again, the bio(al)chemical laboratory in which the black is made. What remains in question is whether or not he or she is present at his or her own making. How do we speak of that presence, of a real transubstantial presence, in the same breath with which we describe sterility and aridity? What if we choose—while also choosing not to assume the barrenness of—the paraontic field? This incline, where experimentation in the interest of securing the normal requires the production and imposition of the pathological, where investigation in the interest of freedom demands incarceration, is, or ought to be, a site of study. To speak of pidgin, then, as the language of nothingness or of nonbeing, the language whose shadow delineates the territory of the inexistent, is not to utter a decree that legitimizes skipping the question concerning the constitution of that language or paralanguage and moving straight to its reduction to the subordination it is supposed to indicate. Four questions emerge: What is pidgin? Who makes it? What pressure does it place on the very idea of the standard? Isn't such pressure, in fact, the making of the standard? These questions open us onto another understanding of the experiment, which Fanon takes up both literally and figuratively: "We have just used the word 'narcissism.' We believe, in fact, that only a psychoanalytic interpretation of the black problem can reveal the affective disorders responsible for this network of complexes. We are aiming for a complete lysis of this morbid universe" (*BSWM*, xiv).

In a paragraph that begins by asserting the necessity of psychoanalytic interpretation for revealing the black man's affective disorders/anomalies, we note this movement between consciousness and the unconscious, cut and augmented by commitment to the trajectory of self-consciousness, wherein "an individual must endeavor to assume the universalism inherent in the human condition" (*BSWM*, xiv). Edmund Husserl, G. W. F. Hegel, and Sigmund Freud are present—but in a kind of Sartrean light, or frame—beginning with that fateful, fatal interplay between the miraculously self-positing individual and the uncut givenness of the standard. But analysis is then cut by something, a natural process if not attitude: corrosion, compromise of the cell's integrity. "*Nous travaillons à une lyse totale de cet univers morbide.*"[113] "We are aiming for a complete lysis of this morbid universe" (*BSWM*, xiv). "I shall attempt a complete lysis of this morbid body."[114] The two translations, one in its literalness, the other in its avoidance of the literal in the interest of greater idiomatic precision, allow us to linger in and consider the relation between the universe and the body, between the transcendental aesthetic and the body that it makes possible and that makes it possible. It is as if both are, in their morbidity, to be submitted to a radical breakdown.

The language of biochemistry permeates Fanon's text, as it should. It's all bound up with the language of friendship, the massive corollary problematic of like and unlike, rending the distinction between friend and enemy that Plato gets to in "Lysis." *Lysis* indicates separation and the breaking down of walls; refutation as well as redemption. The pursuit of the meaning of friendship moves by way of bondage: "By the road which skirts the outside of the wall," thinking on or over the edge of the city, there is "a palaestra that has lately been erected."[115] We made a space, we formed a pit, here, here, "there where," in the very place of resistance (says Jacques Derrida).[116] There's all this lunatic noise Hippothales is constantly emitting; Lysis is his means and his end, which is interminable. *Lysis* defies *ana*, according to Derrida. Madness is the condition within which the question of friendship arises. Madness will have been the method—a resistance without meaning, lysis without origin or end—no friend, neither first nor last. Is "Lysis" the invisible bridge between *Politics of Friendship* and *Resistances of Psychoanalysis*? Between *Black Skin, White Masks* and *The Wretched of the Earth*? The body that questions, because it is a body that is in question, is an experiment. This de/generative materiality, this unending differentiation, bears Hippothales's self-referential moan. Socrates autotunes it but always in the interest of this interplay of questioning and unasking that is his sociodramatic method. The matter for thought, here, is the matter of thought, which is to say the madness of thought, fantasy in the hold, as Wilderson almost has it, the witch's flight, as Deleuze and Guattari offer it for Kara Keeling's rigorous rematerialization.[117]

> For myself, I was rejoicing, with all a hunter's delight, at just grasping the prey I had been so long in chase of, when presently there came into my mind, from what quarter I cannot tell, the strangest sort of suspicion.[118]

> Can we possibly help, then, being weary of going on in this manner, and is it not necessary that we advance at once to a beginning which will not again refer us to friend upon friend, but arrive at that to which we are in the first instance friends, and for the sake of which we say we are friends to all the rest?[119]

Trane says that he plays multiple lines in the same head, plays the same head multiple times, because he doesn't know the one path to the essential. Trane's questioning and unasking, his experimental method—is it Socrates's method, too? Trane's fantasy. He dreamed his treasure. Maybe he knew there was no single way. Maybe he didn't want there to be one way. He didn't want it to be one way; there were the other ways. Trane's mysticism, the polyvalent collectivity of his constant worrying of beginning, instantiates the problem of ana-lysis, of improvisation as self-ana-lysis.[120] Derrida speaks of this nonpresence, which is insofar as it is copresence, the real presence, interdicted and interpenetrative, of archetropic return and philolytic nonarrival, where means and end, object and aim, converge, Tao-like, in their mutual incompleteness within a social field, as ensemblic consent, where the first is displaced by the last, by what is supposed to have been relegated to the presupposed, already posited emptiness of a vessel filled with nothing. A jug or a cup of earthenware or Lorenzo, their otherworldly interventions, the otherworldly intervention of servants and bearers, their thought of the outside, their disruption of closure, their suspension of pursuit is dismissed, in common, as already (de)valued commonness's underside, which is animated by that whose form it takes: "mere idle talk put together after the fashion of a lengthy poem."[121] Phenomenology's variously public and private debts to the transcendental subject and to transcendental intersubjectivity are often manifest as impatience with idle talk, idle chatter, even when such chatter is understood to be the subhuman insignificance of those who are relegated to the fullest possible employment, which evokes not only the wordlessness of the work song but also the expropriated linguistic underlabor, expropriated within the general project of exclusionary, self-possessive subjectivation, that is given in the form of an implied response to the bad faith speech of antiblackness. This is to say—and I think this is what Fanon is most pissed off about, and righteously so—that the doctor's impertinent questions to his black patients already imply an answer that would be given in the gestures that accompany mute, impossible positionality. And so Fanon performs, in thought, such questioning's appositional unasking. This is the character of his complete lysis. It is complete, but, as Wallace Stevens would say, in an unexplained completion. This is the interminable as opposed to the last analysis, the interminable analysis of the last, the anaeschatalogical sounding of the unfathomable alternative. We still have to discover, we have to keep discovering, what that sounding sounds like, in the ongoing refusal of a standpoint, of a jurisdiction, for such hearing, in the ongoing critique of the critique of a certain notion of judgment. The absence and refusal of the standpoint is given in the sound of that sounding, which Fanon leads us to but to which he didn't always listen. Here's where the problematic of lyric disturbs and augments lysis. Here's where whatever it is that the pathologist means to examine, in its own degenerative and regenerative differentiation, moves in disruption of the pathologist's standpoint. This is to say that the tools and protocols and methods of the pathologist, however much they have made possible an approach, cannot, shall we say, manage entrance into the zone of nonbeing. From outside that zone, from the ruins of a standpoint, from one of the numberless husks of an inhabitable possibility, lysis morphs into autopsy so that nonbeing's generativity—as it is manifest in noise, chatter, gobbledygook, pidgin's social refusal of imposed and impossible intersubjectivity—is taken for sterility, its flow taken for aridity. But we will note the beauty and insistence of Fanon's animating claim, his animated *clameur*. He writes, "There is a zone of nonbeing, an extraordinarily sterile and arid region, an incline stripped bare of every essential from which a genuine new departure can emerge. In most cases, the black man cannot take advantage of this descent into a veritable hell" (*BSWM*, xii).

Naked declivity? Gradient centrifugation, as Mackey would have it. The zone of nonbeing is experimental, is a kind of experiment, this double edge of the experiment, this theater of like and unlike in which friendship's sociality overflows its political regulation. Destination down and out, whence springs the difference that earthly beauty brings. *Lysis, lyse, lycée*—Socrates and Lysis, Césaire and Fanon, somewhere between the lyceum and the academy, a recitation of unrequited love.

> Society, unlike biochemical processes, does not escape human influence. Man is what brings society into being. The prognosis is in the hands of those who are prepared to shake the worm-eaten foundations of the edifice.[122]

> It is considered appropriate to preface a work on psychology with a methodology. We shall break with tradition. We leave methods to the botanists and mathematicians. There is a point where methods are resorbed.[123]

To absorb again, to dissolve and assimilate. "That is where we would like to position ourselves" (*BSWM*, xvi). This appeal to resorption, another biochemical term/process that is free of human influence. Fanon deploys biochemical metaphors for the ana/lysis of sociogenic products by way of sociogenic means. And here's the crux, making explicit what would emerge from this overlay of social and biochemical processes, sociopsychoanalytic and experimental practices. Is the laboratory, the encounter, the experimental zone of nonbeing, the paraontic or anontic zone? The otherwise-than-being-ness of the experiment, which turns out to be ante-ethical as well if ethics is even, as Emmanuel Levinas understands it, neither illness nor death. This internal sociality of the experiment, a sociality and sociology of the anontic, a social biopoetics of and in the experiment, is given in the on-going disturbance of language that is language's anoriginal condition. The experiment is poetic; pidgin is a poetics.

Consider the constraint of black poetry—of fantasy in the hole or whole or hold or over the side. If it's a constraint, how is it a constraint? It is, first of all, a conceptual field, as Spillers would allow. A field in which, more precisely, the concept of the object is a kind of imperative at the level of both study and performance, in zones where neither the presumption nor the disavowal of self—each in its own obsessive self-regard—are the limits of poetic pos-sibility, which is, itself, animated by both lyric and lysis, continually driven toward new fields of exhaustion. We have to continually work—where arid-ity is only insofar as it is inseparable from hyperhydration; where thirst and submergence converge; in the hold on the open sea—through this interplay of the establishment and the breakdown of the cell if we are ever to attend the birth of an insurgency that Fanon prophesies and enacts. The splitting of the cell is inseparable from the splitting of the ego that could be said to impose narcissism while also constituting narcissism's closure. There is a hydroptique phono-optics of the general balm and it's the general bomb!

It is as if Fanon is providing commentary on the unpublished notebook of his own return, precisely in order to tell slant the experimental slant. This powerful sociolinguistic self-analysis is a kind of jumping-off point, but what I want to do is slow down and linger, for a little while, over the question of the little Negro, which is a monument to the mind of the little Negro dock-workers and fieldworkers, and work shirkers, and so on. The black man's relegation to pidgin understood as prison, as imprisonment in passage, or as naked, experimental incline, or both, begs the question of the relationship between blackness and the black man, the paraontological distinction that is everywhere implicit in Fanon's text, precisely at or as the point in which self-analysis becomes possible, that space Sexton talks about in which we discern the distinction between vantage and view. But in neither Fanon nor Sexton nor Wilderson, even in texts that we are constrained to call autobiographical, and, moreover, nowhere in the cramped and capacious nowhere from which the vast ante- and anti-autobiographical field from and within which black thought and black literature plots its escape and fantasizes its flight, can the brutally unauthorized author be said simply to be talking about him- or herself.

He or she's talking about *the* self, precisely in the service of a complete lysis of that morbid body and/in its morbid universe. Fanon says, "We are aiming at nothing less than to liberate the black man from himself," which is to say the self that he cannot have and cannot be, but against which he is posed as the occupant of no position (*BSWM*, xii). Is this liberation complete in Fanon? Can self-analysis, which is the name Cecil Taylor gives to improvisation, liberate us from the self, or does it only further secure our incarceration? Again, this is a question that emerges not only in relation to Fanon but also in relation to Olaudah Equiano and Mary Prince, Douglass and Harriet Jacobs, Du Bois and Anna Julia Cooper, Wilderson and Saidiya Hartman, permeating through and in an autobiographical trace that continues to animate the black radical tradition. On the other hand, the new black music is this: find the self, then kill it, as M. NourbeSe Philip's work instantiates. But, to echo Ralph Ellison again and again, so few people really listen to this music. It is, moreover, seldom that even the ones who make this music listen to it, hence the ongoing challenge, the ongoing construction of the intramural.

I'm not sure that Fanon really listens or that, more generally, he really senses the symposium he prepares for us. This preparation could be said to take the form of a sacrifice in which he takes on the unpleasant task of rigorously describing what's so hateful in the way antiblackness mishears what it overhears. Faulty recordings can't help but trigger violent disavowal. The distance between "I don't sound like that" and "I'm not like that" is infinitesimal in its immeasurable vastness. Does black speech, does the little Negro, assume a culture or bear a civilization? If not, then how could it be speech? What does it mean to consider that black speech is the sound of natal alienation, the sound of being without a heritage, without a patrimony? It means, first of all, that all these terms must be revalued, precisely from the already exhausted perspective of the ones who are both (de)valued and invaluable. When Fanon speaks of "local cultural originality," who or what is speaking? (*BSWM*, 2). Who speaks the possession of a language, of a culture, of (a) civilization? Who speaks the necessity of a heritage such that its absence is understood as relative nothingness? Fanon moves by way of a model of the subject that is evacuated even as he writes. This is a James Snead formulation in a sense; a Gordon formulation in another. Derrida speaks, too, out of Algeria, of a problematic of accent, correspondent in its way to the Martinican swallowing of *r*'s of which Fanon speaks. The dispossessive force of black speech confirms, in one sense, and obliterates, in another, the "monolingualism of the Other."[124] My language is not mine, also, because its undercommonness cuts me and mine. The trouble is that Fanon leaps from an analysis of the social situation of pidgin in France, its force as a verbal adjunct, to a visual imposition, without investigating the social situation of the making of pidgin and without raising the question of its structure, its syntax, its logic. It is simply assumed to be both subsequent and subordinate to the standard in its givenness. Is it possible for the new returnee actually to think about pidgin? Another way to put it is that Fanon prepares us for Glissant in his lysis of the morbid body, which begins with an attention to language that is then carried through in his investigation of the structure of epidermalization, of which the supposed imposition of pidgin and the imposition of the desire for French, in their interinanimation, form a kind of verbal supplement and servant.

> "Dirty nigger!" or simply "Look! A Negro!"
> I came into this world anxious to uncover the meaning of things, my soul desirous to be at the origin of the world, and here I am an object among other objects.
> Locked in this suffocating reification, I appealed to the Other so that his liberating gaze . . . would give me back the lightness of being I thought I had lost. . . . Nothing doing. I explode. Here are the fragments put together by another me. . . .
> We were given the occasion to confront the white gaze. An unusual weight descended on us. The real world robbed us of our share. In the white world, the man of color encounters difficulties in elaborating his body schema. The image of one's body is solely negating. . . .
> "Look! A Negro!" . . .
> "Look! A Negro!" . . .
> "Look! A Negro! . . .
> "*Maman*, look, a Negro; I'm scared!" Scared! Scared! Now they were beginning to be scared of me. I wanted to kill myself laughing, but laughter had become out of the question.[125]

Fanon investigates what it is to be eager to grasp, to uncover, while having been robbed of the capacity to have a share. No past, no future, nonexistent, "my originality had been snatched from me" (BSWM, 108). The failed natality of the fabricated explodes so that the mechanism (the instrument, the toy) can, at the very least, piece itself together. This is the itinerary of Fanon's black deconstruction, which ends in an image of inquisitive reassembly, *as if* the futurial project of blackness that he forecloses was always meant to live on only in and through him. The reification he decries suffocates in the absence of other aspirations. This attends the bodily schema's collapse into an epidermal-racial schema. In the aftermath of this interplay of implosion and explosion, Fanon's lesson takes the form of a postmortem reconstruction. This is forensic phenomenology: autopsy, eyewitness, unflinching determination of the cause of our sociality, which is taken for our death, given in or initiated by a metaphorics of biochemistry and supplemented by figures of text and textile. The pigmentation alluded to at the beginning will now be applied to newly woven cloth so that livery can be made in the service of a strict visual determination. Fanon sees it all so clearly, now, and the irony, of course, is that the eyes he sees with are not his. One sees only from the Other's perspective, with the other's instruments, that which is of the Other's fabrication. How do we account for this forced borrowing of normative sense, normative senses, and the forms they take? Moreover, what remains silent in this ocular field? Does Fanon step out of the brutal structural adjustment this regime of credit enforces? The forensic knowledge that underwrites this postmortem is an imposition/gift conferred on "the occasion to confront the white gaze." What if consciousness of double consciousness is an effect of paraontological considerations? What if this auspicious Du Boisian beginning is thrown off-track in Fanon, but precisely in the service of its placement in and on multiple tracks? Here, I think, is how the distinction between sociology and sociogeny turns toward a sociopoetic cognizance of the real presence of the people in and at their making, where that retrospective ascription of absence that Fanon's inhabitation of the problematic of damnation, which is activated in his return to his native land, is given in and to a lyrical, analytic poetics of the process of revolutionary transubstantiation that begins with the experience of the nonnative's nonreturn to the village and to the consensual exsense of its social speech, where and by way of which we study what it is to live in what is called dispossession. This is a problematic that shows up in relation to mu, to nothingness, as well as in relation to the question of being, its unasking, (and the unmasking of the one who frames it).

John Donne says, "If I an ordinary nothing were, / As shadow, a light, and body must be here. // But I am none; nor will my sun renew."[126] In the absence of what is taken for light, in the absence of the thought, the scheme, that is called a body, how do we describe extraordinary, or absolute, nothing? Is this certain uncertainty, an inability to distinguish oneself from one's things that implies, more precisely and more urgently, that disruption of the distinction between self and thing that makes possession possible? The body schema manifests itself as (a breakdown in) the relay between (knowledge of) the necessity of grasping and the capacity to grasp where necessity and capacity each denote, in turn, a relay between knowing and acting. No ontological reach, no epistemological grasp. Meanwhile, it is precisely this implicit knowledge (of the difference between self and thing) that enfleshes questions. Linebaugh speaks of this nonsense, the extrasensorial assertion, which must have emerged in the ship's hold, which was a language lab, a zone of experimental, audiovisual intonation but also—and it is Omise'eke Natasha Tinsley who approaches this almost complete unapproachability—a scene, an erotic vestibule, a prison house of violent pleasure, where flesh is rendered in the absolute exposure of a terrible open secret.[127] Linebaugh's critics, some in their best old-fashioned Marxist ways, anticipatory of Patterson's dismissive relegation of lore in the interest of data, say no, nothing could ever come of such formal deprivation (other than the poverty of the informal, which they have neither the capacity nor the desire to think in its incalculable rhythm). To which I would answer yes. Only nothing. Only that less and more than subjective and subjected sociality. Fantasy in the hold. And this is to say, basically, at the level of Sexton's real intellectual and social aims, if not at the level of the specific critical objects of our work, I am totally with him in locating my optimism in appositional proximity to his pessimism even if I would tend not to talk about the inside/outside relationality of social death and social life while speaking in terms of apposition and permeation rather than in terms of opposition and surrounding. Perhaps this difference turns out to bear and make some greater difference if it is accompanied by another kind of attunement to some other, broader notions of enjoyment and abandonment; perhaps the difference can be made clearer by way of the brilliance of Sexton's interpellation of Gordon's brilliance.

> And yet, this is precisely what Gordon argues is the value and insight of Fanon: he [Fanon] fully accepts the definition of himself as pathological as it is imposed by a world that knows *itself* through that imposition, rather than remaining in a reactive stance that insists on the . . . heterogeneity [or difference] between a self and an imago originating in culture. Though it may appear counterintuitive, or rather because it is counterintuitive, this . . . affirmation [of the pathological] is active; it is a willing or willingness, in other words, to pay whatever social costs accrue to being black, to inhabiting blackness, to living a black social life under the shadow of social death. This is not an accommodation to the dictates of the antiblack world. The affirmation

of blackness, which is to say an affirmation of pathological being, is a refusal to distance oneself from blackness in a valorization of minor differences that bring one closer to health, to life, or to sociality.[128]

A complete, which is to say a lyric, lysis of our living flesh and earthly sociality, which is often taken for a morbid body or a morbid universe, requires us to recognize that blackness is not reducible to its social costs; it is also manifest in a set of benefits and responsibilities. And if I said that the serially epigraphic positing of our wretchedness doesn't come close to getting at how bad it has been and how bad it is, thereby extending, rather than foreclosing, the overseeing and overlooking of slavery and its afterlife, I would do so by indexing not only the imposition of cost but the interdiction of benefit. Paying implies capacities to have and to relinquish that are irreducible to expropriation. Choosing to be black implies paying the cost; it is a kind of ethical gesture to claim this dispossession, this nothingness, this radical poverty-in-spirit. This is what Afro-pessimism performs, in and as theory—an affirmative gesture toward nothingness, an affirmation of negation and its destructive force. It implies and demands a negative political ontology that is manifest as a kind of affirmative nihilism.

Nevertheless, my first impulse in reading Wilderson's long, Trane-like recitation in *Incognegro* of his exchange with his friend and colleague Naima was to ask, in a kind of Quinean rebuttal, why are we something rather than nothing? But the real task, and I follow in the footsteps of Sexton in taking it up, is to think about the relation between something and nothing or, if you'd rather, life and death. Is life surrounded by death, or does each move in and as the constant permeation of the other? But this is not even precise enough. The question is, Where would one go or how would one go about studying nothing's real presence, the thingly presence, the facticity, of the nothing that is? What stance, what attitude, what comportment? If pessimism allows us to discern that we are nothing, then optimism is the condition of possibility of the study of nothing as well as what derives from that study. We are the ones who engage in and derive from that study: blackness as black study as black radicalism. In the end, precisely as the end of an analysis, the payment of a set of social costs will have coalesced into the inability properly to assess the nothingness that one claims. Blackness is more than exacted cost. Nothing is not absence. Blackness is more and less than one in nothing. This informal, informing, insolvent insovereignty is the real presence of the nothing we come from, and bear, and make.

Consider the relation between nothingness and exhaustion as Deleuze describes it (by way of Samuel Beckett): the real presence, the presence of the thing in exhaustion, its differential ecology, its "echo-muse-ecology," to quote Stephen Feld, its clamor, its *clameur*, its claim, its demand, its plaint, its complaint, its working and layering and folding, as in Jacques Coursil's an(a)themic inclination, which also trumpets a movement from the subject of politics to the subject of life.[129] To be subject to life might be understood as a kind of being enthralled by generativity. What the biopolitical continuum (the trajectory of sovereignty's illegitimate, speculative dissemination) attempts to regulate, suppress, and consume is the social poetics, the aesthetic sociality of this generativity. The care of the self, which can be figured as a kind of dissident member of the set of the self's various technologies, is part of the history of sovereignty as surely as the biopolitical deconstruction of sovereignty is an extension of that history. Another way to put it might be that biopolitics is already given in the figure of the political animal; that the move from natural history to biology is a held trajectory; that the regulation of generativity is already given in the idea of a natural kind. Teleological principle, which is meant to disrupt and disable the catology that accompanies biopolitics, reestablishes its ground and impetus, which is sovereignty. This asserts something that has to be worked through: the relationship between teleological principle and sovereignty, which will be established not by way of recourse to God as sovereign creator but by way of an appeal to transcendental subjectivity as a kind of manager (of anoriginal creativity or generativity). What's interesting and implicit here, what Kant is always working toward and through, is the political subject as a natural kind, the political subject as the subject of natural history, natural history as a field that is presided over by the political animal. The mobile hold and block chapel of pidgin, the little Negro's church and logos and gathering, this gathering in and against the word, alongside and through the word and the world as hold, manger, wilderness, tomb, upper room, and cell: there is fantasy in all of these, which makes you wonder what happens when you put your fantasy on hold, when what is seen and sung of being-unheld is, at once, not held on to and not passed on.

Insofar as I am concerned, by way of a certain example to which Sexton appeals in order to explain (away) the difference that lies between us, with what surrounds, with what the nature is of surrounding and enclosure, I am also, of necessity, concerned with the relation between the inside and the outside, the intramural and the world. The difference that is not one is, for

Sexton, a matter of "ontological reach." Perhaps he thinks of that difference as set-theoretic, a matter of calculating over infinities with the understanding that the infinity of social death is larger, as it were, than that of social life; that the world is bigger than the other (than) world, the underworld, the outer world of the inside song, the radical extension and exteriority that animates the enclosed, imprisoned inner world of the ones, shall we say, who are not poor in world but who are, to be more precise, poor-in-the-world. Black people are poor in the world. We are deprived in, and somehow both more and less than deprived of, the world. The question is how to attend to that poverty, that damnation, that wretchedness. I invoke Martin Heidegger's formulation regarding the animal, that it is poor in world, up against the buried contour of his question concerning the way that technology tends toward the displacement of world with a world-picture, in order to make the distinction between the animal's status and our own, which some might call even more distressing. What is it to be poor in the world? What is this worldly poverty, and what is its relation to the otherworldliness that we desire and enact, precisely insofar as it is present to us and present in us? Sexton characterizes this worldly poverty as attenuated ontological reach, knowing that to say this is tricky and requires care. What if poverty in this world is manifest in a kind of poetic access to what it is of the other world that remains unheard, unnoted, unrecognized in this one? Whether you call those resources tremendous life or social life in social death or fatal life or raw life, it remains to consider precisely what it is that the ones who have nothing have. What is this nothing that they have or to which they have access? What comes from it? And how does having it operate in relation to poverty?

At the same time, for Sexton, recognition of this attenuation (which marks the fact that the tone world is, as it were, surrounded by the deaf world) is already understood to indicate possession, as it were, of ontological reach. Maybe there's another implicit distinction between ontic extension and ontological grasp. But who but the transcendental subject can have that grasp or attain the position and perspective that corresponds to it? Husserl, at the end of his career, when his own attainment of it is radically called into question, speaks of this exalted hand-eye coordination as the phenomenological attitude; a few years earlier, when his career was much nearer to its fullest height and he could claim to be master of all he surveyed—modestly, on the outer edges of his work, under the breath of his work in a way that demands a more general attunement to the phenomenological whisper—Husserl spoke of it in these terms: "I can see spread out before me the endlessly open plains of true philosophy, the 'promised land,' though its thorough cultivation will come after me."[130] Marianne Sawicki is especially helpful here because she so precisely teases out the implications of his imagery: "By means of this spatial, geographical metaphor of crossing over into the 'new land,' Husserl conveys something of the adventure and pioneer courage that should accompany phenomenological work. This science is related to 'a new field of experience, exclusively its own, the field of "transcendental subjectivity,"' and it offers 'a method of access to the transcendental-phenomenological sphere.' Husserl is the 'first explorer' of this marvelous place."[131]

We should be no less forthright in recognizing that such positionality is the desire that Fanon admits, if only perhaps to disavow, when he conducts his philosophical investigations of the lived experience of the black. Two questions arise: Does he disavow it? Or is it, in its necessity, the very essence of what Wilderson calls "our black capacity to desire"? Certain things about the first few paragraphs of Fanon's phenomenological analysis seem clearer to me now than when I was composing "The Case of Blackness."[132] The desire to attain transcendental subjectivity's self-regard is emphatic even if it is there primarily to mark an interdiction, an antagonism, a declivity, a fall into the deadly experiment that will have been productive of "a genuine new departure," the end of the world and the start of the general dispossession that will have been understood as cost and benefit (*BSWM*, xii). But that desire returns, as something like the residual self-image of the phenomenologist that he wants to but cannot be, to enunciate the (political) ontology he says is outlawed, in what he would characterize as the abnormal language of the demand, called, as he is, to be a witness in a court in which he has no standing, thereby requiring us to reconsider, by way of and beyond a certain Boalian turn, what it is to be a specta(c)tor. Earlier, I assert that Fanon is saying that there is no and can be no black social life. What if he's saying that is all there can be? The antephenomenology of spirit that constitutes *Black Skin, White Masks* prepares our approach to sociological or, more precisely, sociopoetic grounding, as Du Bois, say, or later Walter Rodney would have it, by way of the description of the impossibility of *political* life, which is, nevertheless, at this moment and for much of his career, Fanon's chief concern. The social life of the black, or of the colonized, is, to be sure, given to us in or through Fanon, often in his case studies, sometimes in verse, or in his narrative of the career of the revolutionary cadre. It is as if Fanon is there to remind us that the lunatic, the (revolutionary) lover, and the poet are of imagination all compact. They occupy and are preoccupied with a zone of the alternative, the zone of nonbeing (antic disposition's tendency to cut and displace organic position) that asks and requires us to consider whether it is possible to differentiate a place in the sun, a promised land, a home—or merely a place and time—in this world, from the position of the settler. Is it possible to desire the something-other-than-transcendental subjectivity that is called nothing? What if blackness is the name that has been given to the social field and social life of an illicit alternative capacity to desire? Basically, that is precisely what I think blackness is. I want it to be my constant study. I listen for it everywhere. Or, at least, I try to. If I read Sexton correctly, after trying to get underneath the generous severity of his lesson, he objects, rightly and legitimately, to the fact that in the texts he cites I have not sufficiently looked for blackness in the Afro-pessimistic texts toward which I have sometimes gestured. In the gestures I have made here I hope I have shown what it is that I have been so happy to find, that projection or relay or amplification carried out by the paraontological imagination that animates and agitates Afro-pessimism's antiregulatory force.

Black optimism and Afro-pessimism are asymptotic. Which one is the curve and which one is the line? Which is the kernel and which is the shell? Which one is rational, which one is mystical? It doesn't matter. Let's just say that their nonmeeting is part of an ongoing manic depressive episode called black radicalism/black social life. Is it just a minor internal conflict, this intimate nonmeeting, this impossibility of touching in mutual radiation and permeation? Can pessimists and optimists be friends? I hope so. Maybe that's what friendship is, this bipolarity, which is to say, more precisely, the commitment to it. To say that we are friends is to say that we want to be friends. I want to try to talk about the nature and importance of the friendship I want, that I would like us to have, that we are about to have, that in the deepest sense we already more than have, which is grounded in and enabled by that commitment even as it is continually rethought and replayed by way of our differences from one another, which is held within and holds together our commonness. The difference has to do with the proper calibration of this bipolarity. Sexton is right to suggest that the far too simple opposition between pessimism and optimism is off, and that I was off in forwarding it, or off in forwarding an imprecision that made it seem as if I were, having been seduced by a certain heuristic and its sound, thereby perhaps inadvertently seducing others into mistaking an alternating current for a direct one. The bipolarity in question is, at every instance, way too complicated for that, and I really want you to hear what we've been working on, this under-riff we've been trying to play, to study, to improvise, to compose in the hyperreal time of our thinking and that thinking's desire. There is an ethics of the cut, of contestation, that I have tried to honor and illuminate because it instantiates and articulates another way of living in the world, a black way of living together in the other world we are constantly making in and out of this world, in the alternative planetarity that the intramural, internally differentiated presence—the (sur)real presence—of blackness serially brings online as persistent aeration, the incessant turning over of the ground beneath our feet that is the indispensable preparation for the radical overturning of the ground that we are under.

The Subprime and the Beautiful

In his review of Fredric Jameson's *Valences of the Dialectic*, Benjamin Kunkel writes:

> It's tempting to propose a period . . . stretching from about 1983 (when Thatcher, having won a war, and Reagan, having survived a recession, consolidated their popularity) to 2008 (when the neoliberal programme launched by Reagan and Thatcher was set back by the worst economic crisis since the Depression). During this period of neoliberal ascendancy—an era of deregulation, financialization, industrial decline, demoralization of the working class, the collapse of Communism and so on—it often seemed easier to spot the contradictions of Marxism than the more famous contradictions of capitalism.[133]

The year that marks the beginning of the period Kunkel proposes—which is characterized by "the peculiar condition of an economic theory that had turned out to flourish above all as a mode of cultural analysis, a mass movement that had become the province of an academic 'elite,' and an intellectual tradition that had arrived at some sort of culmination right at the point of apparent extinction"—is also the year of the publication of Cedric Robinson's *Black Marxism: The Making of the Black Radical Tradition*, a book that could be said to have announced the impasse Kunkel describes precisely in its fugitive refusal of it.[134] If the culmination of the Marxian intellectual tradition coincides with the moment in which Jameson begins magisterially to gather and direct all of its resources toward the description and theorization of what most clear-eyed folks agree is the deflated, defeated spirit of the present age, Robinson's project has been to alert us to the radical resources that lie before that tradition, where "before" indicates both what precedes and what awaits, animating our times with fierce urgency.

One of the fundamental contradictions of capitalism is that it establishes conditions for its own critique (which anticipates a collapse whose increasing imminence increasingly seems to take the form of endless deferral); that those very conditions seem to render that critique incomplete insofar as it will have always failed to consider capitalism's racial determination is, in turn, a contradiction fundamental to Marxism. While *Black Marxism* emphatically exposes these contradictions, it is not reducible to such exposure. Rather, in elucidating an already given investigation of the specificities of Marxism's founding, antifoundational embarrassment, which bears the massive internal threat of critique becoming an end in itself while operating in the service of the renovation, rather than the overturning, of already existing social and intellectual structures, Robinson understands the Marxian tradition as part of the ongoing history of racial capitalism. This is not dismissal; indeed it echoes the deepest and richest sounds of Marx's own blackness. It does, however, sanction the question in which I am interested today: What made Robinson's critique—and, more importantly, that which, in Robinson's work (and in Marx's), exceeds critique—possible? The answer, or at least the possibility for a more precise rendering of the question, is also to be found in *Black Marxism*, where critique is interrupted by its own eruptive condition of possibility roughly at the book's rich, dense, but simultaneously open and capacious center, a chapter called "The Nature of the Black Radical Tradition."

Robinson's critical discovery of racial capitalism depends on and extends the preservation of what he calls "the ontological totality." In describing this integrated totality's character, Robinson notes how preservation impossibly proceeds within the confines of "a metaphysical system that had never allowed for property in either the physical, philosophical, temporal, legal, social or psychic senses." Its motive force is "the renunciation of actual being for historical being," out of which emerges a "revolutionary consciousness" that is structured by but underived from "the social formations of capitalist slavery, or the relations of production of colonialism."[135] It is not just that absolutist formulations of a kind of being-fabricated are here understood themselves to be fabrications; it is also that renunciation will have ultimately become intelligible only as a general disruption of ownership and of the proper when the ontological totality that black people claim and preserve is understood to be given only in this more general giving. The emergence and preservation of blackness, as the ontological totality, the revolutionary consciousness that black people hold and pass, is possible only by way of the renunciation of actual being *and* the ongoing conferral of historical being—the gift of historicity as claimed, performed, dispossession. Blackness, which is to say black radicalism, is not the property of black people. All that we have (and are) is what we hold in our outstretched hands. This open collective being is blackness—(racial) difference mobilized against the racist determination it calls into existence in every moment of the ongoing endangerment of "actual being," of subjects who are supposed to know and own. It makes a claim on us even as it is that upon which we all can make a claim, precisely because it—and its origins—are not originary. That claim, which is not just one among others because it is also just one + more among others, however much it is made under the most extreme modes of duress, in an enabling exhaustion that is, in Stanley Cavell's word, *unowned*, takes the form, in Glissant's word, of *consent*.[136] Consent not to be a single being, which is the anoriginal, anoriginary constitution of blackness as radical force—as historical, paraontological totality—is for Robinson the existential and logical necessity that turns the history of racial capitalism, which is also to say the Marxist tradition, inside out. What cannot be understood within, or as a function of, the deprivation that is the context of its genesis can only be understood as the ongoing present of a common refusal. This old-new kind of transcendental aesthetic, off and out in its immanence as the scientific productivity such immanence projects, is the unowned, differential, and differentiated thing itself that we hold out to one another, in the bottom, under our skin, for the general kin, at the rendezvous of victory.

To say that we have something (only insofar as we relinquish it) is to say that we come from somewhere (only insofar as we leave that place behind). Genesis is dispersion; somewhere is everywhere and nowhere as the radical dislocation we enact, where we stay and keep on going, before the beginning, before every beginning and all belonging, in undercommon variance, in arrivance and propulsion, in the flexed load of an evangelical bridge, passed on this surrepetitious vamp, *here*. Where? There, in our hyperspacious presencing. If you need some, come on, get some. We come from nothing, which is something misunderstood. It's not that blackness is not statelessness; it's just that statelessness is an open set of social lives whose ani*mater*ialized exhaustion remains as irreducible chance. Statelessness is our terribly beautiful open secret, the unnatural habitat and *habitus* of analytic engines with synthetic capacities. Preservation is conditional branching, undone computation (tuned, forked, tongued), improvisation and what it forges, digital speculation beyond the analogical or representational or calculative reserve. Critique—for example, the deciphering of the fundamental discursive structures that (de)form Western civilization—is part of its repertoire but it must always be kept in mind that cryptanalytic assertion has a cryptographic condition of possibility.

Robinson's movement within and elucidation of the open secret has been a kind of open secret all its own. For a long time before its republication in 2000, *Black Marxism* circulated underground, as a recurrent seismic event on the edge or over the edge of the university, for those who valorized being on or over that edge even if they had been relegated to it. There at least we could get together and talk about the bomb that had gone off in our heads. Otherwise we carry around its out, dispersive *potenza* as contraband, buried under the goods that legitimate parties to exchange can value, until we can get it to the black market, where (the) license has no weight, and hand it around out of a suitcase or over a kitchen table or from behind a makeshift counter. Like Richard Pryor said, "I got some shit, too, nigger; now you respect my shit and I'll respect yours."[137] Maybe there's some more shit in the back of our cars that we don't even know about. Certainly this smuggled cargo would be cause for optimism, even against the grain of the unflinching ones who also carry it, even against the general interdiction—the intellectual state of emergency—enforced by the emphysemic ones who authorize themselves to speak of the spirit of the age. That spirit marks the scene in which the etiolation of black study in the name of critique is carried out by those who serially forget their own animation, the collective being that is more precisely understood as being-in-collection insofar as the latter term denotes a debt that is not only incalculable but subprime.

Therefore, by way of the brilliant black light in Frank B. Wilderson III's Afro-pessimistic sound—which materializes, in an investigation of black being, another way to forget it—I'd like to consider what it is (again and again) to lose a home. This is Wilderson:

> Slavery is the great leveler of the black subject's positionality. The black American subject does not generate historical categories of entitlement, sovereignty, and immigration for the record. We are "off the map" with respect to the cartography that charts civil society's semiotics; we have a past but not a heritage. To the data-generating demands of the Historical Axis, we present a virtual blank, much like that which the Khosian presented to the Anthropological Axis. This places us in a

structurally impossible position, one that is outside the articulations of hegemony. However, it also places hegemony in a structurally impossible position because—and this is key—our presence works back on the grammar of hegemony and threatens it with incoherence. If every subject—even the most massacred among them, Indians—is required to have analogs within the nation's structuring narrative, and the experience of one subject on whom the nation's order of wealth was built is without analog, then that subject's presence destabilizes all other analogs.

Fanon writes, "Decolonization, which sets out to change the order of the world, is, obviously, a program of complete disorder." If we take him at his word, then we must accept that no other body functions in the Imaginary, the Symbolic, or the Real so completely as a repository of complete disorder as the black body. Blackness is the site of absolute dereliction at the level of the Real, for in its magnetizing of bullets the black body functions as the map of gratuitous violence through which civil society is possible—namely those bodies for which violence is, or can be, contingent. Blackness is the site of absolute dereliction at the level of the Symbolic, for blackness in America generates no categories for the chromosome of history and no data for the categories of immigration or sovereignty. It is an experience without analog—a past without a heritage. Blackness is the site of absolute dereliction at the level of the Imaginary, for "whoever says 'rape' says Black" (Fanon), whoever says "prison" says black (Sexton), and whoever says "AIDS" says black—the "negro is a phobogenic object."[138]

In the United States, whoever says "subprime debtor" says black as well, a fact that leads, without much turning, to the question of what a *program* of complete disorder would be. In any case it is difficult to see how, in the impossibility that marks its "positionality," the negation that is always already negated would carry out such a program. In conversation with Saidiya Hartman, Wilderson takes care to point out that "obviously I'm not saying that in this space of negation, which is blackness, there is no life. We have tremendous life. But this life is not analogous to those touchstones of cohesion that hold civil society together."[139] What remains is some exploration of the nature of this anti-analog, which is more accurately characterized as an ante-analog, an anticipatory project pessimism is always about to disavow as celebration. Of course, the celebration of what exceeds any analogy with the antisocial hostilities that constitute civil society is, by definition, antithetical to any agenda seeking integration in a civil society that, in any case, will have never survived such integration. On the other hand, precisely in the on-going, undercommon instantiation of an already given, already integrated totality, celebration is an ontological claim, an ontological affiliation, a social and historical paraontology theorized in performance; it gives criticism breath while also being that to which criticism aspires. If "the tremendous life" we have is nothing other than intermittent respite in what Hartman accurately calls the ravages and brutality of the last centuries, then feeling good about ourselves might very well be obscene. But what if there is something other than the phantasmatic object-home of assimilationist desire—which is rightly seen by Hartman simply to be the extension of those ravages and that brutality—to which we can appeal, to which we have always been appealing, in flight or, deeper still, in movement? Again, the question concerns the open secret, the kinetic refuge, of the ones who consent not to be a single being. The corollary question is how to see it and how to enjoy it. This is a question concerning resistance, which is not only prior to power but, like power, is everywhere—as the mutual constitution of a double ubiquity that places the question of hegemony somewhere beside the point. The dark, mobile materiality of this ruptural, execonomic generality is a violence in the archive that only shows up by way of violence to the archive. Because I don't want to kill anybody, because I want us to enjoy ourselves past the point of excess, I am violent in the archive. Because I am a thing seeing things I am violence in the archive.

Perhaps what is required is an acknowledgment of the fact that the discourse of social development, of the ongoing advent of the Earth that is both in and out of this world, has always been subprime. What we want is always already unaffordable and, moreover, the financialization of everyday life was a plantation imposition. Consider, then, a certain underground speculation. What if the subprime crisis is best understood as a kind of collateral agency (something Lauren Berlant approaches in the faces and bodies of the ones who are preoccupied in subprime Chicago, in the invasive form of a seemingly undifferentiated mass of fat, black maternity acting out as adjuncts in the general neighborhood of the neighborhood)?[140] Then it is also the disruption and resocialization of an already given crisis. For a minute, by way of policy that accompanied another of those periodic attempts to deconcentrate that mass and its ongoing project(s), home ownership became a kind of carnival, a country-ass hoedown, an embarrassing barbecue. It was a kind of squatting, sanctioned by the presiding public-private partnership so that it could continue in its brutal habit of enclosing our common capacity, insofar as we are one another's means, to live beyond our means. The dispersed remnants of the motley crew (which was, in the first place, composed of remnants) was engaged in a kind of general taking—an expropriation, however temporary—of refuge, a serial postponement of externally imposed contingency whose supposed intermittence is better understood as a whole other timeline's broken circle. It's not that people don't hate to lose the home they were holding, the home they didn't have; it's just that they had no moral scruples about engaging it, about claiming it, about moving in together (out from) under the virtual auspices of authority. Driven by manmade catastrophes of high water and boll weevils, drought and cotton, by scientific management and fucked-up customary spontaneities, the subprime debtor is bedu in the bayou, in the desert, in the cell, in school, still the itinerant researcher. Stopped for a juked-up minute, this bookish, monkish, Thelonial, disobediently Jeromeboyish homegirl at study, learning dark arts on the Octavian highway of Loseiana, in the indebtedness of mutual aid, for which she remains without credit, also remains to be (im)properly thought, which is to say, celebrated.

This is an ode to the subprime debtor. What is owed to the subprime debtor? Think of her as a poacher in that black-lit river of the mind where the water remembers; consider the double edge of the black act, the relation between the black act and the black arts. Poaching in black(ened) face and strange habit is the jurisgenerative, extralegal, contemplative performance of the ones who were and continue to be present at their own making (onstage, under enclosure, hard row, long road), the transgenerational sharing of a mobile deixis marking there in here so we can get there from here. We bear an interinanimation of displacement and location that cannot be borne, as the speculative and material foundation of another world. What Daphne Brooks calls the Afro-alienation act is an irruption of this bearing, this gestic, jestural natality.[141] Consider the evasiveness of the natal occasion, the moving, ludic refuge of the big mama, the play mama, and the auntie. Consider the relation between leaving and claiming, lost and found, which means thinking before the concept of fabrication. If it is true that the colonist fabricates the colonized subject, or that the master fabricates the slave, it is also true that the irrepressible making and unmaking of the ones who are made and unmade makes them more and less than that. The lack is terminally conceived in isolation from its excessive double and must of necessity show a kind of critical hostility to what it clearly sees as certain fantasies of fullness. On the one hand, what's implied in this fantasy is loss, violated owner-ship; on the other hand what's implied in the clear-eyed, unflinching iden-tification of colonized or enslaved, which is to say interdicted, subjectivity is a being-fabricated that laments the ontology its evacuated, evacuating positionality serves to orient. Moreover, loss and fabrication are cognate if we are only made in dispossession. The remainder is ownership, but can it remain? Can the fabricated bear a trace of what lies before their fabrication? Think about Fanon's rejection of negritude's proffering of a kind of memory of ownership. The nothing that remains in or as that rejection is borne in an assumption and analytic of abandonment or "absolute dereliction." Think-ing (through) this interinanimation of fabrication and abandonment more or less demands the meditation of and on ubiquitous and unexplained incompletion—something that is both more and less. But Fanon's work is brutally cut off when he begins to consider an irreducible presence at its own making as a mode of abandon (a certain choreographic permissiveness that recurs in revolution's punctuation of the impossible social life that is its condition of possibility). Whoever chooses not to acknowledge Fanon's approach to this question leaves that question behind, thereby abandoning himself to the empty positionality of an eternal preface to something s/he can neither sense nor want. Meanwhile, what lies before being-fabricated needs neither to be remembered nor romanticized when it is being lived.

This is all to say that the paraontological distinction between blackness and black people is forgotten in the discursive assemblage of Afro-pessimism. So, therefore, is the black thing that assemblage seeks to understand or to constitute as the impossible aim of an analysis that turns out to be nothing other than a prologue to the disavowal that Afro-pessimists, to their credit—which is, of necessity, bad—attempt to disavow. Insofar as it is always behind a kind of theoretical red line, the sociality that Afro-pessimism does not and cannot want, however much they are willing to claim it as its own impossi-bility, is shadowed by another impossibility that a certain disability enables the Afro-pessimist to desire—the very citizenship and civic obligation that evades him, whose unavailability for him he has taken great pains to prove, whose destruction he believes his *empty* positionality to foster. His desire is, of course (and this is contrary to his analysis as well as his own affec-tive relation to that desiring subject), not unrequited. He is trapped within a brutal and obsessive codependence that he cannot, and cannot want to, refuse. For to refuse what has been refused to you is only possible from the perspective of having had something (beyond the constant imposition of a lack or barrier or impossibility). But having had, in this case, is not the description of some previous, violated ownership; it is, instead, a prophecy of having given everything away (in having consented *not* to be a single being, in having been continually acting out and enacting the massive theoretical implications of holding and being held, against ownership, in dispossessive enjoyment of the undercommon underprivilege). Everything I love is an effect of an already given dispossession and of another dispossession to come. Everything I love survives dispossession, is therefore before dispossession. Can we own or claim dispossession while resisting it? Can we resist it while embracing it? We make new life, we make our refuge, on the run. We protect the old thing by leaving it for the new thing. Refusal is only possible for the ones who have something, who have a form, to give away—the ones who ain't got no home anymore in this world except a moving boxcar full of the sound and scent of animate pillows, strangers, readers; except a built clearing in a common word they break and scar to rest and lay to rest; except Aunt Kine's house which ain't hers, which is hers to hold and hand when we got no place to stay, and then they take it away, but she already gave it away.

Meanwhile, some folks, whose situational commitment to revolution is a function of the high regard in which they hold their own violated sense of personal dignity, are too subject to being-situated; they justify their own misapprehension of revolution as the violent response to a given transgression, a given gratuitousness; they step to black history as if it were nothing other than a serial injury inflicted upon them; as if every injury were their private property, which they legitimately claim, insofar as they have a kind of consciousness of it that is unavailable to the ones who are just up from Tupelo or still hustling on the streets of Accra. It seems, sometimes, that a consciousness of personal injury that moves in excess or in a kind of eclipse of any awareness of personal loss. Though there is a constant discourse of (social) death, the precipitating event is always trauma, which accompanies one's own living death rather than the loss or death of something other or more than oneself. Or, if there is something lost it is oneself, which is to say one's standing, which is to say one's patrimony, which is to say one's delusionally self-made single being. Having lost one's father, one also mourns the loss of one's heteronormatively derived dignity. That loss often takes the representational form of a mother who just won't do or just won't do right. Memoir is a privileged mode here but, as Albert Ayler used to say, "It's not about you." The memoirist, who declares himself, more or less simply, to be nothing, and who claims the right to speak for nothing everywhere, misses everything, with a brilliant, blinding insight. But on the city's edge, where everything is fucked up, everything is everything. Something is held out in somebody's hand because, as Billy Preston used to say, "nothing from nothing leaves nothing; you gotta have something if you wanna be with me." But this is just to say that even in the enactment of Afro-pessimistic purity something shines through, and therefore remains necessary, in its prodigiously indefinite extension of the political analysis of the unalloyed *ex nihilo*. Meanwhile, the nothing we are is alloyed in sharing.

The crisis is given—in a kind of acceleration-in-equilibrium—as our quintessence. You have to be more than critical about some shit like that. The subprime debtor, clothed in and tainted by the sin/garment of pathological black maternity, actively instantiates her own paralogic, like a paratrooper (dropped behind lines), like a hermetic meaning or a hermitic tenor (John Gilmore, between the lines, playing studies in ignorance). The awareness of nakedness is immediately manifest as something ready to wear. Is there knowledge in the service of not knowing, of study as unowning knowledge? The ones who are in the know say not. They speak, instead, of the postblack, emphatically disclosing their own prematurity in the insistence with which they unify black criticism and black misery. People speak, too, of the post–civil rights era, or the post–soul movement. However, these things don't die, they multiply, in whatever mixture of what is to some the unlikely and the embarrassing. They are the derivative's material precursor and disruption, as returned externality, the excluded bringing the sound and fury of outsourced risk like a redirected storm surge, derelict content, absolute volume, sowing utopian disaster on the run like a bunch of heretical prophets of shock, reverberating a noisy backbeat of doubt that even Alan Greenspan couldn't pretend not to hear. It keeps happening like that; that other history of working with and in catastrophe; the parastrophic poetics of emergency is still good—not as destruction but as out inhabitation, total disorder as the carnival alternative. Meanwhile, the half-life of antagonism, as Wilderson would have it, is what Marxists used to call, when they were talking about something other than themselves and the incapacity they are glad to be unhappy to claim as their own, contradiction. Again, it's not that we're not that; it's just that we're all that and then some.

The pathologizing discourse within which blackness's insurgent *materiality* has long been framed takes a couple of reactionary forms in relation and with reference to the subprime crisis. One, which proudly claims the mantle of reaction, criminalizes. But black maternal criminality is also irresponsible, in this view. The tendency to lie, to overreach by way of somebody else's swindle, in the wake of their interested unasked question, is a function of always already disabled self-possession, a fundamental incapacity for personal responsibility, an inability to mature, an endless developmental delay, a reckless childishness that demands instant gratification after hundreds of years. Here's where criminality and abnormality converge and it is the meeting place of the two modes of reaction, the other of which rejects that name in the name of a kind of recycled progress, a certain old-new liberality. In this other mode, the subprime debtor is a victim of predatory lenders and a long history of residential and financial segregation and exclusion while also remaining, most fundamentally, a victim of her own impulses, which could be coded as her own desire to climb socially, into a neighborhood where she doesn't belong and is not wanted—the general neighborhood of home ownership, wherein the normative conception, embodiment, and enactment of wealth, personhood, and citizenship reside.

The distinction between pathologic and paralogic, upon which our entire history turns, emerges here as well. Consider the subprime debtor as guerilla, establishing pockets of insurgent refuge and marronage, carrying revaluation and disruptively familial extensions into supposedly sanitized zones. Deployed by the imposition of severalty, demobilized from the general project, she infiltrates domesticity, restages race war's theater of operations under the anarchic principles of poor theater. In this, she extends and remodels the freedom movement's strategies of nonexclusion, where courts of law were turned into jurisgenerative battlefields, where public schools and public accommodations became black study halls, greyhounds-contra-hellhounds where fugitive spirits, sometimes misconstrued as evil even by themselves, take freedom rides on occasions that parallel the radical commensality of the counter-lunch. The subprime debtor, in the black radical tradition of making a way out of no way (out), is also a freedom fighter, a community disorganizer, a sub-urban planner.

But where does this transsexual revolutionary come from? (She is revolutionary in that old extra way; he violently brings their ordinary culture to bear in a kind of nonviolent overturning and eschews the clotted, marmish imperatives of "exposure" or "psychological warfare" that compose the half-measures of the ones who think they have nothing beyond their fantasies of patrimonial honor either to lose or defend.) Where do we get these Tiresian audiovisions of broken home ownership? Where are we coming from and what is the time of our irruption? Having considered the relation between impossible maternity, on the one hand, and the inalienable natality that evades each and every natal occasion, one is given to believe that what is given is that the given cuts the given. Fanon's phenomenology is inadequate to this broken, breaking givenness, though it infuses—though it is, as it were, regifted in—his work, as the thingly contragrain and mechanical counter-time that his disciples seem sometimes to be trying too hard not to hear. In refusing to pay—or in enacting a constitutional inability to pay—the debt we have contracted, we pay the debt we never promised, the one they say should never have been promised, the one that can't be calculated, and thereby extend another mode of speculation altogether.

Melinda Cooper and Angela Mitropoulos argue that the moralistic denunciation of usury that neoliberalism cranked out in the aftermath of its latest episode of recognizing, which is to say policing, the crisis is really an attempt to eliminate all forms of incalculable debt, particularly insofar as those forms constantly bear the capacity to induce "the liquefaction of securitized investment" in the mixture of surprise and precedent that every day composes the new *commercium* as the stolen life traditionally led in common projects on brilliant corners.[142] What's cool is that in their very language—which I can't help but think bears the echo of an old reference to the sweetly flowing liquefaction of Julia's clothes, that brave vibration each way free, the fugitive desire she walks around with, in that housecoat, always threatening to blow up whatever outpost on "the household frontier"—Cooper and Mitropoulos move with Robinson in the line he studies and extends, beyond the critique of *them*, and what *they* think, and what *they* try to do, toward the life *we* (dis)locate and imagine when the materiality of the subprime cuts the sublime by grounding its excess in the anarchic materiality of social flesh in history. What we say must seem stupid to the regulators; the unbroken code of our enchanted, inkantatory refreshment of the paraontological totality—theorizing what it is to hold some land or what it is to be let to hold twenty dollars—is so much undercomputational nonsense to the ones who cannot see the con/sensual, contrarational beauty of blackness, the universal machine.

NOTES

Preface

1 See Nahum Dimitri Chandler, *X: The Problem of the Negro as a Problem for Thought* (New York: Fordham University Press, 2013).

2 George Lewis, "Toneburst (Piece for 3 Trombones Simultaneously)," *The Solo Trombone Record*, SKCD2–3012, Sackville, 2001.

3 Hortense Spillers, "Mama's Baby, Papa's Maybe: An American Grammar Book," in *Black and White and in Color: Essays on American Literature and Culture* (Chicago: University of Chicago Press, 2003), 228.

4 Such toppling is a fundamental concern, leading to fundamental insight, in the work of André Lepecki. See his *Exhausting Dance: Performance and the Politics of Movement* (New York: Routledge, 2006).

5 Immanuel Kant, "Answer to the Question: What Is Enlightenment?," trans. Thomas K. Abbott, in *Basic Writings of Kant*, ed. Allen K. Wood (New York: Modern Library, 2001), 135.

6 Nathaniel Mackey, *Atet A.D.* (San Francisco: City Lights Books, 2001), 119.

7 Jan Patočka, *Body, Community, Language, World*, trans. Erazim Kohák (Chicago: Open Court, 1998), 178.

8 For the most beautiful elaboration of this principle of incompleteness see Cedric J. Robinson, *The Terms of Order: Political Science and the Myth of Leadership*, 2nd ed. (Chapel Hill: University of North Carolina Press, 2016), 196–97.

Chapter 1: There Is No Racism Intended

Epigraph: Emmanuel Levinas, "Intention, Event, and the Other," trans. Andrew Schmitz, in *Is It Righteous to Be? Interviews with Emmanuel Levinas*, ed. Jill Robbins (Stanford, CA: Stanford University Press, 2001), 149.

1 Franz Rosenzweig, *Franz Rosenzweig: His Life and Thought*, ed. Nahum Glazer (New York: Schocken Books, 1961), 62–63. This passage is the epigraph for Annette Aronowicz's introduction to her translation of Levinas, *Nine Talmudic Readings* (Bloomington: Indiana University Press, 1990), ix.

2 Emmanuel Levinas, "Reflections on the Philosophy of Hitlerism," trans. Seán Hand, *Critical Inquiry* 17, no. 1 (1990): 70–71; emphasis in the original.

3 Emmanuel Levinas, "Interview with Francis Poiré," trans. Jill Robbins and Marcus Coelen with Thomas Loebel, in *Is It Righteous to Be?*, ed. Jill Robbins, 64–65.

4 Levinas, "Interview with Francis Poiré," 79.

5 Andrew McGettigan, "The Philosopher's Fear of Alterity: Levinas, Europe, and Humanities 'Without Sacred History,'" *Radical Philosophy* 140 (2006): 15.

6 McGettigan, "The Philosopher's Fear," 15.

7 McGettigan, "The Philosopher's Fear," 16.

8 McGettigan, "The Philosopher's Fear," 19.

9 McGettigan, "The Philosopher's Fear," 17.

10 Emmanuel Levinas, *Totality and Infinity: An Essay on Exteriority*, trans. Alphonso Lingis (Pittsburgh: Duquesne University Press, 1969), 29. Quoted in McGettigan, "The Philosopher's Fear," 20. The emphasis is Levinas's.

11 McGettigan, "The Philosopher's Fear," 19. Here is the passage he reads: "The 'communication' of ideas, the reciprocity of dialogue, already hide the profound essence of language. It resides in the irreversibility of the relation between me and the other, in the Mastery of the Master coinciding with his position as other and as exterior. For language can be spoken only if the interlocutor is the commencement of his discourse, if, consequently, he remains beyond the system, if he is not *on the same plane* as myself. The interlocutor is not a Thou [*Toi*], he is a You [*Vous*]; he reveals himself in his lordship. The exteriority coincides with a mastery. My freedom is thus challenged by a master who can invest it. Truth, the sovereign exercise of freedom, becomes henceforth possible" (Levinas, *Totality and Infinity*, 101).

12 McGettigan, "The Philosopher's Fear," 20.

13 McGettigan, "The Philosopher's Fear," 20. McGettigan quotes Levinas, *Totality and Infinity*, 99.

14 McGettigan, "The Philosopher's Fear," 23.

15 Paul Gilroy, *Darker than Blue: On the Moral Economies of Black Atlantic Culture* (Cambridge, MA: Harvard University Press, 2010), 73.

16 Gilroy, *Darker than Blue*, 189n29. One wonders, in particular, by way of the general suggestion that animates Gilroy's recent work, about Arendt, Levinas, and Fanon, and their postphenomenological, antiontological notions of transcendence, whether explicitly or implicitly advanced. Fanon, too, is interested in what exceeds ontological explanation but this transcendence occurs in the intrahuman world, as the degraded immanence of its infrahuman residue. It is as if, on the one hand, the intrahuman relation that a certain Fanon theorizes and desires actually constitutes much of the ethicopolitical substance that is mistakenly attributed to Levinas; it is as if his relegation of the racially/culturally/spiritually human Other did not constitute an unmistakable motif throughout the body of his work. At the same time, this intrahuman relation is understood by a certain Fanon to be an impossibility in the social life of blacks or of the colonized, in the secret life of things, as it were, those who live under that range of interdictions that attend the shame/rage of encountering a master who, in Levinas's words, "brings me more than I contain" (McGettigan, "The Philosopher's Fear, 25n33). To be more precise, black social life is understood as an impossibility that attends

the absence of content, of an originary, constitutive, unintended dispossession. Blackness is a fatal facticity that is or bears the absence of social life, where being with or for or in another is experienced. It is a zone of radical incapacitation, the crippling immanence of the ones without (sacred) history; meanwhile, the promised land of nonraciality can only be entered by way of interraciality. But here, where blackness is theorized as conviviality's impossible presence and present, given in the impossible consent and impossible intent not to be a single being, not to represent Single Being, as if personhood is now the potential image of radical instrumentality, radical givenness, radical difference, and the radical differentiation of inside and out, is where Glissant walked in, sat in, stood up, as I have attempted briefly to suggest.

17 This is to say that the thing and its disavowal are animating forces in the tradition of philosophy.

18 Emmanuel Levinas, "Is Ontology Fundamental?," trans. Richard Atterton and revised by Simon Critchley and Adriaan T. Peperzak, in *Emmanuel Levinas: Basic Philosophical Writings*, ed. Adriaan T. Peperzak, Simon Critchley, and Robert Bernasconi (Bloomington: Indiana University Press, 1996), 9.

19 Félix Guattari, *Chaosmosis: An Ethico-Aesthetic Paradigm*, trans. Paul Baines and Julian Pefanis (Bloomington: Indiana University Press, 1995), 4–5.

20 See Michael Inwood, *A Heidegger Dictionary* (London: Blackwell, 1999), 215.

21 Edmund Husserl, *Ideas Pertaining to a Pure Phenomenology and to a Phenomenological Philosophy—First Book: General Introduction to a Pure Phenomenology*, trans. Fred Kersten (The Hague: Martinus Nijhoff, 1982), 166.

22 David Carr, translator's introduction to Edmund Husserl, *The Crisis of European Sciences and Transcendental Phenomenology* (Evanston, IL: Northwestern University Press, 1970), xxxiii.

23 Edmund Husserl, "Philosophy and the Crisis of European Humanity," in *The Crisis of European Sciences and Transcendental Phenomenology*, ed. E. H. Carr (Evanston, IL: Northwestern University Press, 1970), 282, 287.

24 Emmanuel Levinas, "Freiburg, Husserl, and Phenomenology," in *Discovering Existence with Husserl*, trans. Richard A. Cohen and Michael B. Smith (Evanston, IL: Northwestern University Press, 1998), 34–36.

25 Levinas, "Freiburg, Husserl, and Phenomenology," 34.

26 See Emmanuel Levinas, *Existence and Existents*, trans. Alphonso Lingis (Pittsburgh: Duquesne University Press, 2001), 45–60; and "Interview with Francis Poiré," 45–48.

27 Emmanuel Levinas, "Martin Heidegger and Ontology," trans. Committee of Public Safety, *Diacritics* 26, no. 1 (1996): 26–27; emphasis in the original.

28 Levinas, "Is Ontology Fundamental?," 3.

29 Tom Sheehan, personal interview, May 3, 1997. See also Reiner Schürmann, *Heidegger on Being and Acting: From Principles to Anarchy*, trans. Christine-Marie Gros and Reiner Schürmann (Bloomington: Indiana University Press, 1990).

30 Levinas, "On the Usefulness of Insomnia," in *Is It Righteous to Be?*, ed. Jill Robbins, 234.

31 Levinas, "Insomnia," 235.

32 The subtitle of "Fecundity of the Caress"—"A Reading of Levinas, *Totality and Infinity*, section IV, B, 'The Phenomenology of Eros'"—is Irigaray's announcement of an engagement with Levinas that her writing disavows. The engagement is announced because the disavowal comes both in the form and after the fact of an ecstatic and fleshly touch, a fecundity borne in the birth of a third writing, another language that is neither hers nor his, that is both hers and his. A third is borne in their coming together that is disavowed in the announcement of a reading of Levinas that never mentions him, that cites him only once, but joins him and, in so doing, escapes him. The escape is in the touch, the coming together of flesh. The touch enacts a separation from the one for whom separation is made imperative precisely in the refusal of separation. Can this refusal be anything other than a comprehension, comprehension in the form of a reading that is not a reading, that is more than a reading or other than a reading in a juncture that is also an eclipse, an immanence that is also a transcendence? Is Irigaray's fleshly comprehension of Levinas, her invaginative envelopment of him, justified in the formation of a third before procreation whose irruption denies the very comprehension that it justifies? Irigaray says that Levinas "knows nothing of communion in pleasure." Is there a communion in pleasure initiated by Irigaray with and, therefore, against Levinas? A communion in pleasure where she seeks the qualities of the other's—Levinas's—flesh and of her own? And is this communion not broken off, or disrupted, precisely in the renewal of its engagement? There is a way in which the "Questions to Emmanuel Levinas" break off the communion in pleasure that "The Fecundity of the Caress" enacts. At the same time, the fleshly touch that animates and determines "The Fecundity of the Caress" becomes, in the enactment of separation that animates the "Questions to Emmanuel Levinas," precisely that which Irigaray disavows in her questions: the "caress [that] consists . . . not in approaching the other in its most vital dimension, the touch, but in the reduction of that vital dimension of the other's body to the elaboration of a future for [one]self." The trouble is that this dialectic of communion and divorce in Irigaray's engagement with Levinas replicates a similar dialectic in Levinas's relation to being, to Heidegger, to philosophy, to Europe—a dialectic that Levinas inhabits as a kind of inevitability, an inevitability that Irigaray joins precisely in her disavowal of it, thereby seeming to confirm it. What is the source of this virtual inevitability? What is the source of that failure of escape that is initiated by touch and aborted by the caress (of questioning, of reading)? The source is the drive for comprehension and the fantasmatic subjectivity that drive affirms. The source, put another way, is the ongoing disavowal, and the attendant misunderstanding, of the thing and of existence in the world of things. This misunderstanding of the thing, of existence in the world of things, of constitution of the world by the thing and the inherence of the world in the thing, is a function of a failure to think the thing as thinking, to think the thinking, in other words, of the other (Descartes's delineation of man as *res cogitans*, as thinking thing, is the severest reinitialization of the perennial relegation of the *thing-as-everything-else*, as *everything-other-than-man*, to the field of the nonthinking). This failure to think the Other is a failure to think as the Other, to think, as it were, from the

Other, out of the place of the Other, from a place that had been assumed to be beyond the borders of thinking, a place that had, in fact, determined, in its very exteriority, the borders of thinking, which is to say, in a Levinasian parlance that only makes explicit the very interiority of his tradition, of Europe. This failure, or its recognition, prompts three more questions: 1. From where, from what position or locale, does one think the other, the thing? 2. What about the other's internal differentiation, the difference to and from itself of the thing's place? (This is a question that must immediately be directed toward the same. But this is only to say that the other already is precisely that question and that direction.) 3. Is there a thinking that is of or from the Other? These questions lead quickly to another: How might another understanding of the thing, an understanding of the thing from the position of the thing, of the radically Other, a position heretofore conceived as beyond thinking's frontier, serve to rehabilitate—which is to say, to bridge—separation and the touch in all of their interinanimate necessity? In and as the very cut of communion, of the commune, of the (under)commons, given in the disruptive re*mater*ialization of the caress and of the abstract equivalence of its exchanges and of the persistence of its pure but fantasmatic interiors, is there another gathering of gathering—a bridge, a circle, a sphere; a black market and a black city of things? As Irigaray says, by way of Derrida, in parallel to Delany, this is a phonogrammatic question. It is also a choreographic question—of separation and touch (or feel, or grain); it's a question of contact (and) improvisation; a question of cant. The fugitivity of the thing is a question of song and dance, of the general problematic of flavor. See Luce Irigaray, "Questions to Emmanuel Levinas," in *The Irigaray Reader*, ed. Margaret Whitford (London: Blackwell, 1991), 179, 180.

33 Eric L. Santner, *On Creaturely Life: Rilke, Benjamin, Sebald* (Chicago: University of Chicago Press, 2006), 1; hereafter abbreviated *OCL*.

34 Santner, *OCL*, 2–3.

35 Immanuel Kant, *Critique of the Power of Judgment*, trans. Paul Guyer and Eric Matthews (Cambridge: Cambridge University Press, 2000), 19.

36 Santner, *OCL*, 5–7; emphasis in the original.

37 See Adrian Piper, "Cultural Hegemony and Aesthetic Acculturation," *Noûs* 19, no. 1 (1985): 29–40; and Santner, *OCL*, 7.

38 Santner, *OCL*, 11–12; emphasis in the original. Santner quotes Giorgio Agamben, *The Open: Man and Animal*, trans. Kevin Attell (Stanford, CA: Stanford University Press, 2002), 65.

39 This is a respectful but deviant echo of Achille Mbembe. See his "Necropolitics," trans. Libby Meintjes, *Public Culture* 15, no. 1 (2003): 11–40.

40 Cedric J. Robinson, *Black Marxism: The Making of the Black Radical Tradition*, 2nd ed. (Chapel Hill: University of North Carolina Press, 2002), 182.

41 Santner, *OCL*, 15.

42 Judith Butler, *The Psychic Life of Power: Theories in Subjection* (Stanford, CA: Stanford University Press, 1997), 6–10; emphasis in the original.

43 Santner, *OCL*, 16–17.

44 Kant, "On the Use of Teleological Principles in Philosophy," trans. Jon Mark Mikkelsen, in *Race*, ed. Robert Bernasconi (London: Blackwell, 2001), 38.

45 Santner, *OCL*, 17–18.

46 Kant, "Teleological Principles," 38.

47 Kant, "Teleological Principles," 40.

48 Kant, "Teleological Principles," 43.

49 Santner, *OCL*, 20–22; emphasis in the original.

50 Jacques Lacan, "The Mirror Stage as Formative of the *I* Function as Revealed in Psychoanalytic Experience," in *Écrits: The First Complete Edition in English*, trans. Bruce Fink in collaboration with Héloïse Fink and Russell Grigg (New York: W. W. Norton, 2006), 78.

51 Santner, *OCL*, 27–28. Santner quotes Julia Lupton, "Creature Caliban," *Shakespeare Quarterly*, 51, no. 1 (spring 2000), 1 (hereafter abbreviated cc).

52 Santner, *OCL*, 29.

53 Denis Diderot, "In Praise of Richardson," *Selected Writings on Art and Literature*, trans. Geoffrey Bremner (New York: Penguin, 1994), 84.

54 Santner, *OCL*, 36n56.

55 Santner, *OCL*, 39–40.

56 William Kentridge, quoted in Stacy Boris, "The Process of Change: Landscape, Memory, Animation, and *Felix in Exile*," in *William Kentridge*, ed. Neal Benezra, Staci Boris, and Dan Cameron (New York: Harry N. Abrams, 2001), 32. See also Kentridge, "'Fortuna': Neither Programme nor Chance in the Making of Images," in *William Kentridge*, ed. Dan Cameron et al. (London: Phaidon, 1999), 114.

57 William Kentridge, "Art in a State of Grace, Art in a State of Hope, Art in a State of Siege (extract)," in *William Kentridge*, ed. Dan Cameron et al. (London: Phaidon, 1999), 104.

58 See Rosalind Krauss, "'The Rock': William Kentridge's Drawings for Projection," *October* 92 (2000): 3–35.

59 William Kentridge, excerpts from "Dear Diary: Suburban Allegories and Other Infections," in *William Kentridge*, ed. Carolyn Christov-Bakargiev (Brussels: Société des Expositions du Palais des Beaux-Arts/Vereniging voor Tentoonstellingen van het Paleis voor Schone Kunsten Brussel, 1998), 75. Cited in Krauss, "'The Rock,'" 4.

60 See Kant, *Critique*, 197.

61 Dan Cameron speaks of Kentridge's work in terms that I would move with, in and off step. See Cameron, "A Procession of the Dispossessed," in *William Kentridge*, ed. Dan Cameron et al., 38–81.

62 The artist speaks of the emergence of images that come about neither "through a plan, a programme, a story-board," nor "through sheer chance." He adds: "'Fortuna' is the general term I use for this range of agencies—something other than cold statistical chance, and something too outside the range of rational control." See Kentridge, "Fortuna," 116. See also Krauss, "'The Rock,'" (5–10) for her discussion of "fortuna" as the interstitial, ambulatory modality of form that allows Kentridge to escape the headlong force of the rock of South African history. Krauss assumes, by way of a selective understanding of the manifold meanings of "The Rock" in Kentridge's discourse, the necessity of a simplified detour around what Santner might call "postcolonial historicization." I am moving toward the suggestion that the ideas of escape and of what is to be escaped that are propa-

gated through Kentridge are somewhat more complex than Krauss's reading, however astute, allows. My suggestion is animated by the thinking of Laura Harris who speaks, in an unpublished manuscript called "Undocuments of US Imperialism: Hélio Oiticica's *Newyorkaises*," of resistances in the work to the very idea of the work that compose an appositional historiography in artistic practice.

63 I am referring, here, to Krauss's reference to Stanley Cavell's analysis of what might be called the improvisational imperative in twentieth-century music. Krauss links this musical imperative to Kentridge's notion of *fortuna*. Neither Krauss nor Cavell consider the Afro-diasporic irruption that breaks the oppositional framing of twentieth-century music between the rock of chance operations and the hard place of electronic programming. Kentridge's improvisations must, it seems to me, be understood as part of that irruption. See Krauss, "'The Rock,'" 10–12; and Cavell, "Music Discomposed," in *Must We Mean What We Say?* (Cambridge: Cambridge University Press, 2002), 180–212.

64 William Kentridge, "*Felix in Exile*: Geography of Memory (extract)," in *William Kentridge*, ed. Dan Cameron et al. (London: Phaidon, 1999), 123.

65 Kentridge, "Art in a State of Grace," 102.

66 Kentridge, "*Felix in Exile*," 123.

67 Antonio Negri, *Negri on Negri: In Conversation with Anne Dufourmantelle*, trans. M. B. DeBevvoise (New York: Routledge, 2004), 65.

Chapter 2: Refuse, Refuge, Refrain

1 Of course, as we'll see, the restaging I propose is already of a revival, where legitimate political theater tries to suppress that long arc of refreshment wherein the scene of instruction is understood only as the dissemination of the seeds of destruction. The explicit body, in such performance, is always demure, always well-dressed (more often complete with wire rims or wireless, though sometimes in shades that bespeak how she is always in shadow). Even in the instant of her always assumed nakedness, which is the liberal accompaniment to reactionary attack, she's sharp as a tack.

2 Hannah Arendt, *On Violence* (New York: Harcourt, Brace, and World, 1970), 95.

3 In partially replaying once again the resonant phrase Arendt composed to describe her relation to the Jewish people—"I merely belong to them"—I risk confusion. I am neither asserting nor implying that Arendt's belonging to the Jewish people is equivalent or necessarily bound to antiblack racism. Rather, what I am trying to index is Arendt's belonging to—her having been given to or conscripted by—a modernity, and more specifically, a modern intelligence (not, or not simply a historicophilosophical trajectory, but rather something on the order of a Weltanschauung flawed by [the desire for] purity) for which the antiblack racism to which it is not reducible is, nevertheless, constitutive. I approach this belonging by way of Arendt's phrase and Judith Butler's reading of that phrase, which is marked by its attunement to a general problematic of belonging in Arendt whose analysis will have demanded attendance to the question of race and the force of racism in her work. See Arendt, "The Eichmann Controversy: A Letter to Gershom

Scholem," in *The Jewish Writings*, ed. Jerome Kohn and Ron H. Feldman (New York: Schocken Books, 2007), 465–71; and Judith Butler's review of *The Jewish Writings*, "'I Merely Belong to Them,'" *London Review of Books*, May 10, 2007, www.lrb.co.uk/v29/n09/but102_.html.

4   Columbia University is where the moral obligation to be intelligent was first and most emphatically asserted by John Erskine, professor of English and originator of the General Honors Course, a two-year undergraduate seminar that would ultimately become the second component of Columbia College's core curriculum. Such a curriculum, while always predicated on some sense of the intrinsic worth of its content, is, finally, most accurately understood militarily, as an aggression figured as a kind of bulwark, an interminably one-sided exchange of fire. Such a curriculum's framers often produce elegantly aggressive defenses of such aggressively expansionist culturalism, which imagines itself to be under assault from the ones who are denied access to what is forcefully imposed on them. Erskine's 1915 essay, "The Moral Obligation to Be Intelligent" is exemplary in this regard—so much so that its title is taken as the heading of a selection of essays by Erskine's most important and influential student, Lionel Trilling. That selection, recently edited by Trilling's student Leon Wieseltier, reveals, if nothing else, the endurance of a particular mode of New York intellectuality into which Arendt was welcomed and smoothly naturalized not only as its embodiment but also as the broken, displaced object of its Europhilic desire. That object's b-side (its breaking side; its already given brokenness) is, of necessity, a thing of darkness whose constant, negrophobic disavowal is also a hallmark of this particular New York state of mind, linking it to an elite American intellectual common sense that another of Trilling's students, Louis Menand, has recently outlined. Think of what I'm beginning to try to do here as a consideration of the relation between Arendt's antiblack racism, her particular brand of intelligence, and a natural(ized) pragmatism that might someday be better understood in its relation to an originary interplay (in Kant) of race and phenomenology. See John Erskine, *The Moral Obligation to Be Intelligent* (New York: Duffield, 1915); Lionel Trilling, *The Moral Obligation to Be Intelligent: Selected Essays*, ed. Leon Wieseltier (Evanston, IL: Northwestern University Press, 2008); and Louis Menand, *The Metaphysical Club: A Story of Ideas in America* (New York: Farrar, Straus and Giroux, 2001).

5   See Arendt, *On Violence*, Appendix XVI, 100–101.

6   Perhaps the current critical devotion to Arendt, which is manifest in readings that are unfaithful to her work precisely by echoing its overlordly tone and silencing its interinanimate movements of opening and foreclosure, is most precisely understood as the sterility of what remains of thought for those who believe in nothing other than their own intelligence, narrowly and imperiously conceived, and the moral irresponsibility of the unintelligent, broadly and imperiously conceived. Within these interlaced conceptions, what is it to have failed in one's moral obligation to be intelligent? Who are the ones who have abdicated their responsibility? Ralph Ellison spoke of the "Olympian authority" with which Arendt expressed her "Reflections on Little Rock." This must be aligned with some

sense of her willingness to choose authority over equality insofar as its opposition to equality, and not freedom's, is, for her, the perennial problem of politics. She speaks as one who has authority and, in so doing, chooses authority, which is to say her own authority. Arendt matters and so, therefore, do her disciples who, in declaring openly her importance and surreptitiously their own, imply the nonimportance, the not mattering, of many. The unintelligent do not stand out from the multitude. They have not authorized themselves. They don't have a story. They are not moral beings. They have failed their moral obligation insofar as they are unable to recognize that they (might) have one. What is entailed in such recognition? To what does one's recognition of one's moral obligation to be intelligent—which is the instantiation of being intelligent—commit one? Consider that to be committed to one's own authority is to be committed to the state, the corporate authority of the subjects who are supposed to be intelligent.

7 Here is the relevant passage, from *On Violence* (Appendix VIII, 95): "Bayard Rustin, the Negro civil-rights leader, has said all that needed to be said on the matter: 'College officials should "stop capitulating to the stupid demands of Negro students"; it is wrong if one group's "sense of guilt and masochism permits another segment of society to hold guns in the name of justice"; black students were "suffering from the shock of integration" and looking for "an easy way out of their problems"; what Negro students need is "remedial training" so that they "can do mathematics and write a correct sentence," not "soul courses."' (Quoted from the *Daily News*, April 28, 1969.) 'What a reflection on the moral and intellectual state of society that much courage was required to talk common sense in these matters! Even more frightening is the all too likely prospect that in about five or ten years this "education" in Swahili (a nineteenth century kind of no-language spoken by the Arab ivory and slave caravans, a hybrid mixture of a Bantu dialect with an enormous vocabulary of Arab borrowings; see the *Encyclopaedia Britannica*, 1961), African literature, and other non-existent subjects will be interpreted as another trap of the white man to prevent Negroes from acquiring an adequate education.'"

8 Jon Landau, "Review of *Curtis/Live!*" *Rolling Stone*, June 24, 1971, www.rollingstone .com/music/albumreviews/curtis-live-19710624.

9 Frederick Douglass, "Letter to His Former Master," in *The Narrative and Selected Writings*, ed. Michael Meyer (New York: Modern Library, 1984), 286.

10 "I Plan to Stay a Believer," in *Curtis/Live*, LP, Curtom Records, CRS 8008, 1971.

11 Hear The Impressions, "Choice of Colors," on *The Young Mods' Forgotten Story*, LP, Curtom Records, CRS 8003, 1969.

12 Arendt, *On Violence*, 99.

13 Paul Guyer, *Kant and the Claims of Taste*, 2nd ed. (Cambridge: Cambridge University Press, 1997), 3.

14 Arendt, *On Violence*, 8. Also see 42, where Arendt asserts: "The extreme form of power is All against One, the extreme form of violence is One against All." This formulation is at the heart of a hermeneutic phenomenological description (insofar as Arendt persists in declaring if she has a method it is phenomenology) of violence. Something like an ontological distinction—between violence and violent acts—is implied that allows Arendt to disavow any insurgence against acts of

violence perpetrated by whatever entity is supposed to represent and protect all. The ones who are neither represented nor protected by power are reduced to a single intoxicating voice by the ones who do not hear (other) voices. We are left, after reading Arendt's essay, to ponder what it is to do violence nonviolently and to repress the repressive acts of violence done by the entity that is supposed to be incapable of violence.

15 The Black National Economic Conference, "A Black Manifesto," *New York Review of Books*, July 10, 1969, www.nybooks.com/articles/11267.

16 Arendt, *On Violence*, 8. See Kara Keeling, *The Witch's Flight: The Cinematic, the Black Femme, and the Image of Common Sense* (Durham, NC: Duke University Press, 2007); and Wahneema Lubiano, ed., "Black Nationalism and Black Common Sense: Policing Ourselves and Others," in *The House That Race Built: Original Essays by Toni Morrison, Angela Y. Davis, Cornel West, and Others on Black Americans and Politics in America Today* (New York: Vintage, 1998), 232–52.

17 Hannah Arendt to Mary McCarthy, December 21, 1968; quoted in Elizabeth Young-Bruehl, *Hannah Arendt: For Love of the World*, 2nd ed. (New Haven, CT: Yale University Press, 2004), 418.

18 Hannah Arendt, "Reflections on Little Rock," in *Responsibility and Judgment*, ed. Jerome Kohn (New York: Schocken, 2003), 193–213.

19 Arendt, "Reflections on Little Rock," 193.

20 See Laura Harris, *Experiments in Exile: C. L. R. James, Hélio Oiticica, and the Aesthetic Sociality of Blackness* (New York: Fordham University Press, 2018).

21 This brief engagement with the problem of Arendt's precarious empathy is indebted to Saidiya Hartman, *Scenes of Subjection: Slavery, Terror and Self-Making in Nineteenth-Century America* (Oxford: Oxford University Press, 1997).

22 Judith Butler, "Is Kinship Always Already Heterosexual?," in *Undoing Gender* (New York: Routledge, 2004), 110.

23 Butler, "Kinship," 111; emphasis in the original.

24 In this formulation, and much else, I echo Lindon Barrett, "Captivity, Desire, Trade: The Forging of National Form," in *Racial Blackness and the Discontinuity of Western Modernity*, ed. Justin A. Joyce, Dwight A. McBride, and John Carlos Rowe (Urbana: University of Illinois Press, 2014), 72–136.

25 In my head, I'm charting a little survey of late twentieth-century literature and cultural theory in Arkansas. It includes the sound of the still unsounded depths of Henry Dumas's classic tale, "Will the Circle Be Unbroken?" (in *Echo Tree: The Collected Short Fiction of Henry Dumas* [Minneapolis: Coffee House Press, 2003], 105–10), while relinquishing recourse to the recursive, restricted origin that Dumas was brutally stopped from beginning more fully to work through with the lawless imagination that he shared with Eckford, his neighbor. He also had that open secret seeing that still remains to be seen in his double-edged fades-to-black. I am also thinking of another reading of one of the series of photographs taken of Eckford on her way to school that is worthy of note. In honor of the Little Rock Nine, Bill Clinton has remarked: "Forty years ago, a single image first seared the heart and stirred the conscience of our nation, so powerful most of us who saw it then recall it still. A fifteen-year-old girl wear-

ing a crisp black and white dress, carrying only a notebook, surrounded by large crowds of boys and girls, men and women, soldiers and police officers, her head held high, her eyes fixed straight ahead. And she is utterly alone." Like Arendt, Clinton performs, with the increased sympathy that hindsight affords, the inattention that insufficient attention to the problematic of intention seems to impose even on those who have the best intentions. It is plain to see that the soloist is never unaccompanied. Clinton's speech is excerpted in *Freedom: A Photographic History of the African American Struggle*, ed. Manning Marable, Leith Mullings, and Sophie Spencer-Wood (New York: Phaidon, 2005), 271. See also the photograph of Eckford's experimental band, at study, on the following page.

26 But note that restaging prompts a degenerative as well as regenerative condition. Perhaps the description of a performance, say Piper's, more fully gestures toward something that (the) performance itself can't even approach. This might be that problem that emerges at the intersection of portraiture and the concept. That intersection is loneliness. But Elizabeth Eckford was not alone, a fact that can neither be restaged nor recited by anyone, least of all me. In accord with Piper's performative echo, and, later, Danielle Allen's politicotheoretical interpretation, perhaps it will be possible to think Elizabeth Eckford as a field and festival of ethical accompaniment. This is to say, by way of Sora Han, that Eckford's nonperformance is itself a restaging, or reopening, of *Betty's Case*. See Han, "Slavery as Contract: *Betty's Case* and the Question of Freedom," *Law and Literature* 27, no. 3 (2015): 395–416.

27 Adrian Piper, "Untitled Performance for Max's Kansas City," in *Out of Order, Out of Sight—Volume I: Selected Writings in Meta-Art, 1968-1992* (Cambridge, MA: MIT Press, 1996), 27.

28 See Piper, "Talking to Myself: The Ongoing Autobiography of an Art Object," in *Out of Order, Out of Sight*, 51; see the passage, around seven minutes into the film *Dreams Are Colder Than Death*, dir. Arthur Jafa, ZDF, 2014, in which Hortense Spillers elaborates on empathy's entanglement with vulnerability (as opposed to something like Arendt's unfeeling self-projective self-protection); see Spillers, "Interstices: A Small Drama of Words," in *Black and White and in Color: Essays on American Literature and Culture* (Chicago: University of Chicago Press, 2003), 152–75; and see the poem which Spillers echoes and elucidates in that essay, Audre Lorde, "Who Said It Was Simple," in *The Collected Poems of Audre Lorde* (New York: W. W. Norton, 2003), 92.

29 Piper, "Talking to Myself," 51. "One World in Relation: Édouard Glissant in Conversation with Manthia Diawara," trans. by Christopher Winks, *Journal of Contemporary African Art* 28 (2011): 5.

30 Frantz Fanon, *Black Skin, White Masks*, trans. Charles Lam Markmann (New York: Grove Press, 1967), 109.

31 James Baldwin, "Down at the Cross: Letter from a Region in My Mind," in *Collected Essays*, ed. Toni Morrison (New York: Library of America, 1998), 346–47.

32 Hannah Arendt "The Meaning of Love in Politics: A Letter by Hannah Arendt to James Baldwin, November 21, 1962." *HannahArendt.net*, www.hannaharendt.net/index.php/han/article/view/95/156.

33 James Baldwin, *The Fire Next Time*, in *James Baldwin: Collected Essays*, ed. Toni Morrison (New York: Library of America, 1998), 310.

34 "Letter 169: Hannah Arendt to Karl Jaspers, August 6, 1955," in Hannah Arendt and Karl Jaspers, *Correspondence 1926-1967*, ed. Lotte Kohler and Hans Saner, trans. Robert and Rita Kimber (New York: Harcourt Brace, 1992), 264. Quoted in Young-Bruehl, *Hannah Arendt*, xxiv.

35 Young-Bruehl, *Hannah Arendt*, xxiv.

36 Arendt and Jaspers, *Correspondence*, 264. Quoted in Young-Bruehl, *Hannah Arendt*, xxiv.

37 Baldwin, "Autobiographical Notes," in *James Baldwin: Collected Essays*, 6.

38 Baldwin, *The Fire Next Time*, in *James Baldwin: Collected Essays*, 311.

39 Baldwin, *No Name in the Street*, in *James Baldwin: Collected Essays*, 366.

40 Baldwin, *No Name in the Street*, in *James Baldwin: Collected Essays*, 366.

41 Karl Marx, "Private Property and Communism," in *Early Writings*, trans. Rodney Livingstone and Gregor Benton (New York: Vintage, 1975), 352.

42 Baldwin, *No Name in the Street*, in *James Baldwin: Collected Essays*, 366.

43 For a different take on Arendt's take on the photograph and what it shows us of natality's exposure, see Vicky Lebeau, "The Unwelcome Child: Elizabeth Eckford and Hannah Arendt," *Journal of Visual Culture* 3, no. 1 (2004): 51–62. For an excellent account of the relation between what might be called the social intentionality of blackness and photography during the Civil Rights Movement, see Leigh Raiford, "'Come Let Us Build a New World Together': SNCC and Photography of the Civil Rights Movement," *American Quarterly* 59, no. 4 (2007): 1129–57. For more on Piper's performance see my *In the Break: The Aesthetics of the Black Radical Tradition* (Minneapolis: University of Minnesota Press, 2003), 233–54. For the definitive word on all that is given and made when maternity—against a history of being taken—impossibly takes flight, see Hortense J. Spillers, "Mama's Baby, Papa's Maybe: An American Grammar Book," in *Black and White and in Color: Essays on American Literature and Culture* (Chicago: University of Chicago Press, 2003), 203–29.

44 Arendt, "Civil Disobedience," in *Crises of the Republic* (New York: Harcourt Brace, 1972), 89.

45 Arendt, *On Violence*, 18–19.

46 See Louis Menand, *The Metaphysical Club: A Story of Ideas in America* (New York: Farrar, Straus and Giroux, 2001).

47 See Arendt, "Civil Disobedience," 90; and Stanley M. Elkins, *Slavery: A Problem in American Institutional and Intellectual Life* (New York: Grosset and Dunlap, 1963), 140–93.

48 Arendt, "Civil Disobedience," 92.

49 Arendt, *The Origins of Totalitarianism* (New York: Harcourt, Brace, 1975), 297.

50 See Robert Bernasconi, "Who Invented the Concept of Race? Kant's Role in the Enlightenment Construction of Race," in *Race*, ed. Robert Bernasconi, 11–36 (London: Blackwell, 2001).

51 All quotations in this paragraph are from Arendt, *Lectures on Kant's Political Philosophy*, ed. Ronald Beiner (Chicago: University of Chicago Press, 1982), 75.

52 Hear two versions of "We're a Winner" on The Impressions, *We're a Winner*, ABC Records, ABCS-635, LP, 1968 and on *Curtis/Live!*

53 Danielle Allen, "Law's Necessary Forcefulness: Ralph Ellison vs. Hannah Arendt on the Battle of Little Rock," in *Multiculturalism and Political Theory*, ed. Anthony Simon Laden and David Owen (Cambridge: Cambridge University Press, 2007), 323.

54 Allen, "Law's Necessary Forcefulness," 316–17.

55 See George Lipsitz, *The Possessive Investment in Whiteness* (Philadelphia: Temple University Press, 1998).

56 Baldwin, "Autobiographical Notes," in *Collected Essays*, 6.

57 Allen, "Law's Necessary Forcefulness," 319.

58 Allen, "Law's Necessary Forcefulness," 320.

59 I want to acknowledge, here, that in trying to go against the grain of Arendt's political theory, and Allen's anti-exclusionary correction of it, I am also challenging, in a direct and all but sacrilegious way, the tenets and interpretations of those who are rightly regarded as heroes, as well as theoreticians, of the movement. Even my reverent recognition that my capacity to show such audacity is a function of (their) movement doesn't really justify this presumption. Perhaps it is unjustifiable, this hearing through someone's speech. I remember very vividly the first time I saw and heard C. T. Vivian, a hero of (the) movement, say these words in *Eyes on the Prize*: "it was a clear engagement between the forces of the movement and the forces of the structure that would destroy the movement. It was a clear engagement between those who wished the fullness of their personalities to be met, and those that would destroy us physically and psychologically. You do not walk away from that. This is what movement meant. Movement meant that finally we were encountering, on a mass scale, the evil that had been destroying us on a mass scale. You do not walk away from that, you continue to answer it. Uh, it does not matter whether you are beaten, that's a secondary matter. The only important thing is that you reach the conscience of those who are with you and of anyone watching—both the so-called enemy, and those who are preparing the battle, and anyone else who may be watching." What struck me then, now thirty years ago, was a shift for which I am still trying to account, when the definite article no longer precedes the word *movement*. At that moment, when a hero began to explain the general heroism, understood as a desire to confront but also to encounter and be encountered in the fullness of personality, movement asserts itself as something profoundly impersonal by way of the smallest of signals, the most barely noticeable of omissions, a silence that enacts a profound bending of speech. If I argue that what is given in that dehiscence is barely noticeable but emphatic notice of the non-fullness of personality, asserted through a profound impersonation we have to see and hear through to who and what we are, it is, again, with reverence for the ones, like Vivian, who are more and less than that and who preserved us in their demonstration of us. If politics, where subject/citizens speak and act in public, is the mechanism through which personalities are encountered in their fullness, it is also the geocidal frame in which the necessary nonfullness of personality is denied, in murderous intent and possessive obsession. I want to say, in trying to illuminate Vivian's anti-political

impersonation, that it remains the window through which I see Elizabeth Eckford's passion as the window through which I see black social life. All I'm trying to do is be a window, too. See "Interview with C. T. Vivian," conducted by Blackside, Inc. on January 23, 1986, for *Eyes on the Prize: America's Civil Rights Years (1954–1965)*, Washington University Libraries, Film and Media Archive, Henry Hampton Collection, http://digital.wustl.edu/cgi/t/text/text-idx?c=eop;cc=eop;rgn=main;view=text;idno=viv0015.0233.104.

60 See Allen, "Anonymous: On Silence and the Public Sphere," in *Speech and Silence in American Law*, ed. Austin Sarat (Cambridge: Cambridge University Press, 2010), 121–26.

61 See Erica Edwards, *Charisma and the Fictions of Black Leadership* (Minneapolis: University of Minnesota Press, 2012), 107–13.

62 Edwards, *Charisma*, 113. See also, Daisy Bates, *The Long Shadow of Little Rock* (Fayetteville: University of Arkansas Press, 1986).

63 Edwards, *Charisma*, 113.

64 Allen, "Law's Necessary Forcefulness," 323.

65 Allen, "Law's Necessary Forcefulness," 324.

66 See Hartman, *Scenes of Subjection*, 17–112.

67 Natalie Depraz, "When Transcendental Genesis Encounters the Naturalization Project," in *Naturalizing Phenomenology: Issues in Contemporary Phenomenology and Cognitive Science*, ed. Jean Petitot, Francisco J. Varela, Bernard Pachoud, and Jean-Michel Roy (Stanford, CA: Stanford University Press, 1999), 464–65.

68 Allen, "Law's Necessary Forcefulness," 325.

69 Allen, "Law's Necessary Forcefulness," 325.

70 Allen, "Law's Necessary Forcefulness," 325.

71 See Robert M. Cover, "The Supreme Court, 1982 Term—Foreword: *Nomos* and Narrative," *Harvard Law Review* 97, no. 1 (1983): 4–65.

72 See Wendy Brown, *States of Injury: Power and Freedom in Late Modernity* (Princeton, NJ: Princeton University Press, 1995).

73 Edmund Husserl, *Cartesian Meditations: An Introduction to Phenomenology*, trans. Dorion Cairns (The Hague: Martinus Nijhoff, 1960), 49. Quoted in Jean-Michel Salanskis, "Sense and Continuum in Husserl," trans. George Collins, in *Naturalizing Phenomenology*, ed. Petitot et al., 491.

74 Salanskis, "Sense and Continuum in Husserl," 491.

75 Allen, "Law's Necessary Forcefulness," 326.

76 Allen, "Law's Necessary Forcefulness," 328.

77 See Ursula K. Le Guin, "The Ones Who Walk Away from Omelas," in *The Wind's Twelve Quarters* (New York: Perennial), 275–84; Elizabeth A. Povinelli, "The Child in the Broom Closet: States of Living and Letting Die," *South Atlantic Quarterly* 107, no. 3 (2008): 509–30; and Povinelli, *Economies of Abandonment: Social Belonging and Endurance in Late Liberalism* (Durham, NC: Duke University Press, 2011), 1–46.

78 Allen, "Law's Necessary Forcefulness," 332–33. Allen is quoting from Arendt, "On Humanity in Dark Times," trans. Clara and Richard Winston, in *Men in Dark Times* (New York: Harcourt, 1968), 4, 10, 11, 12–13, 16, 23.

79 Immanuel Kant, "Answer to the Question: What is Enlightenment?" trans. Thomas K. Abbot, in *Basic Writings of Kant*, ed. Allen W. Wood (New York: Modern Library, 2001), 135.

80 Kant, "Answer to the Question: What Is the Enlightenment?," 136.

81 Cover, "The Supreme Court, 1982 Term—Foreword," 40.

82 Kant, "Answer to the Question: What Is the Enlightenment?," 136.

83 See Fred Moten, *In the Break: The Aesthetics of the Black Radical Tradition* (Minneapolis: University of Minnesota Press, 2003), 233–54.

84 John P. Bowles, *Adrian Piper: Race, Gender, and Embodiment* (Durham, NC: Duke University Press, 2011), 285–86n81.

85 Donald Davidson, "On the Very Idea of a Conceptual Scheme," in *Inquiries into Truth and Interpretation*, 2nd ed. (Oxford: Oxford University Press, 2001), 183–98.

86 See Sarah Jane Cervenak, *Wandering: Philosophical Performances of Racial and Sexual Freedom* (Durham, NC: Duke University Press, 2014), 145–72.

87 Bowles, *Adrian Piper*, 278n41.

88 Piper, "Xenophobia and Kantian Rationalism," in *Feminist Interpretations of Immanuel Kant*, ed. Robin May Schott (University Park: Penn State University Press, 1997), 24.

89 Noam Chomsky, *Language and Mind*, 3rd ed. (Cambridge: Cambridge University Press, 2006), viii.

90 See George E. Lewis, *A Power Stronger Than Itself: The AACM and American Experimental Music* (Chicago: University of Chicago Press, 2008).

91 Chomsky, "What We Know: On the Universals of Language and Rights," *Boston Review* (summer 2005). bostonreview.net/archives/BR30.3/chomsky.php.

92 I have been the grateful recipient of extended tutelage on the matter of a historicist critique of Chomsky by my colleague Julie Tetel Andresen.

93 Julie Tetel Andresen, "Historiography's Contribution to Theoretical Linguistics," in *Chomskyan Evolutions and Revolutions: Essays in Honor of E. F. K. Koerner*, ed. Douglas Kibbee (Amsterdam: John Benjamins, 2010), 443–69.

94 Anthony Braxton, *Composition Notes: Book A* (Lebanon, NH: Frog Peak Music/Synthesis Music, 1988), 91.

95 See Michael Marder, *The Event of the Thing: Derrida's Post-deconstructive Realism* (Toronto: University of Toronto Press, 2009).

96 Cheryl A. Wall, *Worrying the Line: Black Women Writers, Lineage, and Literary Tradition* (Chapel Hill: University of North Carolina Press, 2005).

97 Graham Lock, *Forces in Motion: The Music and Thoughts of Anthony Braxton* (New York: Da Capo, 1988), 167.

98 Martin Heidegger, *Being and Time*, trans. John Macquarrie and Edward Robinson (New York: Harper, 1962), 219–20.

99 Theodor W. Adorno, "On Jazz," trans. Jamie Owen Daniel and Richard Leppert, in *Essays on Music*, ed. Richard Leppert (Berkeley: University of California Press, 2002), 492.

100 Braxton, liner notes, *Donna Lee*, CD 05 067 863–2, Free America, 2005.

101 Braxton, *Composition Notes: Book A*, 139–40.

102 Chomsky, *Language and Mind*, 9.

103 "One World in Relation: Édouard Glissant in Conversation with Manthia Diawara," trans. Christopher Winks, *Journal of Contemporary African Art* 28 (2011): 15.

104 "One World in Relation," 5.

105 See Polly Greenberg, *The Devil Has Slippery Shoes* (London: Macmillan, 1969). Hear Greenberg's *Head Start: With the Child Development Group of Mississippi*, CD FW02690, Smithsonian Folkways Recordings, 2004.

Chapter 3: Chromatic Saturation

1 Frantz Fanon, *Black Skin, White Masks*, trans. Charles Lam Markmann (London: Paladin, 1970), 77–78.

2 For more on translation and its relation to his concept of "anoriginal difference," see Andrew Benjamin, *Translation and the Nature of Philosophy: A New Theory of Words* (London: Routledge, 1989).

3 I am invoking, and also deviating from, Nahum Dimitri Chandler's notion of *paraontology*, a term derived from his engagement with Du Bois's long anticipation of Fanon's concern with the deformative or transformative pressure blackness puts on philosophical concepts, categories, and methods. For a full account and elaboration of paraontology see Chandler, *X: The Problem of the Negro as a Problem for Thought* (New York: Fordham University Press, 2013).

4 For more on Fanon's relation to phenomenology see David Macey, *Frantz Fanon* (New York: Picador, 2001), 162–68.

5 Jared Sexton and Huey Copeland, "Raw Life: An Introduction," *Qui Parle* 13, no. 2 (2003): 53.

6 There is a certain American reception of Agamben that fetishizes the bareness of it all without recognizing the severity of the critique he levels at movements of power/ knowledge that would separate life from its form(s). The critical obsession with bare life, seen in its own vexed relation with the possibility of another translation that substitutes naked for bare and perhaps has some implications, is tantamount to a kind of sumptuary law. The constant repetition of bare life bears the annoying, grating tone that one imagines must have been the most prominent feature of the voice of that kid who said the emperor has no clothes. It's not that one wants to devalue in any way the efficacy of such truth telling, such revelation; on the other hand, one must always be careful that a certain being-positive, if not positivism, doesn't liquidate the possibility of political fantasy in its regulation of political delusion. There's more to be said on this question of what clothes life, of how life is apparell'd (as John Donne might put it); this, it seems to me, is Agamben's question, the question of another commonness. So why is it repressed in the straight-ahead discourse of the clear-eyed? This question is ultimately parallel to that concerning why Foucault's constant and unconcealed assumptions of life's fugitivity are overlooked by that generation of American academic overseers—the nonseers who can't see because they see so clearly—who constitute the prison guards of a certain understanding of the carceral. Judith Butler might say that

they see too clearly to see what lies before them. See her analytic of the "before" in the second chapter of *Gender Trouble: Feminism and the Subversion of Identity* (New York: Routledge, 1989). See also Giorgio Agamben, *Homo Sacer: Sovereign Power and Bare Life*, trans. Daniel Heller-Roazen (Stanford, CA: Stanford University Press, 1998) and *Means without Ends: Notes on Politics*, trans. Vincenzo Binetti and Cesare Casarino (Minneapolis: University of Minnesota Press, 2000).

7 Fanon, *Black Skin, White Masks* (1970), 77.

8 Fanon, *Peau noire, masques blancs* (Paris: Editions du Seuil, 1952), 88.

9 This is an image—taken from Diderot's reading of Samuel Richardson—that Brooks deploys in his analysis of melodrama. See Peter Brooks, *The Melodramatic Imagination: Balzac, Henry James, Melodrama, and the Mode of Excess* (New Haven, CT: Yale University Press, 1995), 19.

10 Or it might show up as a refusal of the resonance of Fanon in Sexton and Copeland, or in Achille Mbembe and David Marriott, or in important work by Kara Keeling and Frank Wilderson. See Kara Keeling, "'In the Interval': Frantz Fanon and the 'Problems' of Visual Representation," *Qui Parle* 13, no. 2 (2003): 91–117 (wherein she takes up that passage in Fanon with which I began, thereby both authorizing and directing the course of my own reading; wherever I might diverge from her understanding, I do so only as a function of her thinking, in kinship and respect). See also Kara Keeling, *The Witch's Flight: The Cinematic, the Black Femme, and the Image of Common Sense* (Durham, NC: Duke University Press, 2007); David Marriott, *On Black Men* (New York: Columbia University Press, 2000); Achille Mbembe, *On the Postcolony*, trans. A. M. Berrett et al. (Berkeley: University of California Press, 2001); and Frank Wilderson III, *Red, White, and Black: Cinema and the Structure of U.S. Antagonisms* (Durham, NC: Duke University Press, 2010).

11 Michael Inwood, *A Heidegger Dictionary* (London: Blackwell, 1999), 214.

12 Martin Heidegger, "The Thing," in *Poetry, Language, Thought*, trans. Albert Hofstadter (New York: Harper and Row, 1971), 174; hereafter abbreviated "T."

13 For more on the relation between evasive previousness and unavailable natality, consult Nathaniel Mackey's multivolume epic *From a Broken Bottle Traces of Perfume Still Emanate*, especially the first installment, *Bedouin Hornbook*, Callaloo Fiction Series, Volume 2 (Lexington: University Press of Kentucky, 1986).

14 See Amiri Baraka (LeRoi Jones), "Black Is a Country," in *Home: Social Essays* (New York: Morrow, 1966), 82–86; and Nikhil Pal Singh, *Black Is a Country: Race and the Unfinished Struggle for Democracy* (Cambridge: Cambridge University Press, 2004).

15 See Theodor W. Adorno, "On Jazz," trans. Jaime Owen Daniel, modified by Richard Leppert, in *Essays on Music*, ed. Richard Leppert (Berkeley: University of California Press, 2002), 472.

16 Charles Rosen, *Arnold Schoenberg* (Chicago: The University of Chicago Press, 1996), 57–58.

17 Rosen, *Arnold Schoenberg*, 58.

18 Rosen, *Arnold Schoenberg*, 59n14.

19 Hear Cecil Taylor, *All the Notes*, Cadence Jazz Records CJR 1169 CD, 2004.

20 Louis Althusser, "From *Capital* to Marx's Philosophy." In Althusser et al., *Reading Capital: The Complete Edition*, trans. Ben Brewster and David Fernbach (New York: Verso, 2015), 21.

21 "Black as Symbol and Concept," in *Art as Art: The Selected Writings of Ad Reinhardt*, ed. Barbara Rose (Berkeley: University of California Press, 1975), 86–88.

22 Stu Broomer et al., "Black," *Arts/Canada* 113 (1967): 3–19; hereafter abbreviated "B."

23 Yve-Alain Bois cites the following statement by Reinhardt: "I've never approved or liked anything about Marcel Duchamp. You have to choose between Duchamp and Mondrian." See Bois, "The Limit of Almost," in *Ad Reinhardt*, ed. William Rubin and Richard Koshalek (New York: Rizzoli, 1991), 13.

24 Bois wonders if the nonsentence Reinhardt pronounces on theater ("Theater, acting, 'lowest of the arts'") alludes to Fried's in/famous essay on what he took to be the degrading force of theatricality in minimalist art, "Art and Objecthood." The essay originally appeared in *Artforum* a couple of months before Reinhardt's death on August 31, 1967, a couple of weeks after his encounter with Taylor. See Bois, "Limit of Almost," 13, 30n21. Also see Reinhardt's unpublished notes from 1966–67, collected by Rose under the title "Art-as-Art," in *Art as Art*, 74; and Fried, "Art and Objecthood," in *Art and Objecthood* (Chicago: University of Chicago Press, 1998), 148–72.

I would like to acknowledge the influence of Paul Kottman's ideas regarding what he calls "the politics of the scene" on my attempt to think through this interplay of politics and theatricality.

25 Bois, "Limit of Almost," 15.

26 Bois, "Limit of Almost," 16.

27 Clement Greenberg, "The Crisis of the Easel Picture," in *The Collected Essays and Criticism: Arrogant Purpose, 1945–1949*, ed. John O'Brian (Chicago: University of Chicago Press, 1986), 223, quoted in Bois, "Limit of Almost," 17.

28 See, for instance, Mondrian's 1927 essay "Jazz and Neo-Plastic," in *The New Art—The New Life: The Collected Writings of Piet Mondrian*, ed. and trans. Harry Holtzman and Martin S. James (Boston: Da Capo, 1993), 217–22.

29 See Harry Cooper, "Mondrian, Hegel, Boogie," *October* 84 (1998): 136.

30 See/hear Cecil Taylor, "Cecil Taylor Segments II (Orchestra of Two Continents)," *Winged Serpent (Sliding Quadrants)*, LP Soul Note SN 1089, Soul Note, 1985.

31 Bois, "Piet Mondrian, New York City," in *Painting as Model* (Cambridge, MA: MIT Press, 1990), 183.

32 Cooper, "Mondrian, Hegel, Boogie," 134.

33 Bois, "Piet Mondrian," 182.

34 Cooper, "Mondrian, Hegel, Boogie," 136, 142.

35 Fanon, *The Wretched of the Earth*, trans. Constance Farrington (New York: Grove, 1968), 227.

36 See W. E. B. Du Bois, "Sociology Hesitant," *boundary 2* 27, no. 3 (2000): 41.

37 Fanon, *Wretched of the Earth* (1968), 242.

38 Fanon, *Les damnés de la terre* (Paris: Éditions Gallimard, 1991), 273. See also Fanon, *Wretched of the Earth* (1968), 227, and Fanon, *The Wretched of the Earth*,

trans. Richard Philcox (New York: Grove, 2004), 163; hereafter abbreviated *W/P*. Forgive my oscillation—undertaken, primarily, due to considerations of style (which is not only eternal, as Mackey says, but fundamental)—between the poles of these translations.

39 Cooper, "Mondrian, Hegel, Boogie," 140.

40 Theodor Adorno, *Aesthetic Theory*, trans. Robert Hullot-Kentor (Minneapolis: University of Minnesota Press, 1997), 39.

41 Adorno, *Aesthetic Theory*, 39.

42 See Brent Hayes Edwards, *The Practice of Diaspora: Literature, Translation, and the Rise of Black Internationalism* (Cambridge, MA: Harvard University Press, 2003).

43 Adorno, *Aesthetic Theory*, 168–69.

44 Adorno, *Aesthetic Theory*, 176–77.

45 This is a Kantian formulation that I have elsewhere tried to explicate by way of the work of Winfried Meninghaus. See my "Knowledge of Freedom," *CR: The New Centennial Review* 4, no. 2 (2004): 269–310. See also Winfried Menninghaus, *In Praise of Nonsense: Kant and Bluebeard*, trans. Henry Pickford (Stanford, CA: Stanford University Press, 1999); and Immanuel Kant, "On the Combination of Taste with Genius in Products of Beautiful Art," in *Critique of the Power of Judgment*, trans. Paul Guyer and Eric Matthews (Cambridge: Cambridge University Press, 2000), 196–97.

46 Perhaps this paradox—wherein the colonized intellectual must deconstruct and disavow what the anticolonial revolutionary has to claim, in a double operation on and from the same questioning, questionable body; wherein national consciousness and mental disorder are interinanimate—is proximate to what Gayatri Chakravorty Spivak thinks under the rubric of the "'native informant' as a name for that mark of expulsion from the name of Man." Perhaps Fanon's late work operates as something on the order of a refusal of that expulsion and of that name, even in his invocation of it. See Spivak, *A Critique of Postcolonial Reason: Toward a History of the Vanishing Present* (Cambridge, MA: Harvard University Press, 1999), 6.

47 Karl Marx, *Grundrisse: Foundations of the Critique of Political Economy*, trans. Martin Nicolaus (New York: Penguin, 1973), 487.

48 See Frantz Fanon, "Algeria Unveiled," in *A Dying Colonialism*, trans. Haakon Chevalier (New York: Grove, 1967), 47.

49 See Hannah Arendt, *On Violence* (New York: Harcourt, Brace, and Jovanovich, 1970), 85–87.

50 Imagine potency, here, as a translation of *potenza* (as opposed to *potere*) or *puissance* (as opposed to *pouvoir*) and, therefore, as moving within the specificity of a conceptual distinction that the unaccompanied utterance of the word *power* fails to mark. If I could arrange the typographical equivalent of a certain gesture, a certain inflection, the raising of a hand or voice, I would, just to let you know that what I'm after is a vivrant thing, an undercommon public thing, a social thing. This is to say that it is not, contra Arendt, a political thing; that her relegation of the social in favor of a regulated and specifically political publicness

is, in fact, inseparable from her commitment to an already given structure of power in which both acknowledged and unacknowledged constituents subsist in a shadow they cast but cannot control. That submissive subsistence is manifest as ritual dramas that fail to perform, ritualized distinctions (within strict enclosures of conceptual diversity) that fail to differentiate. With regard to the former, each election is more fully exemplary than the last. At the same time, Arendt's distinction between (necessarily collective) *power* and (fatefully individual) *strength*, and between these and the "natural" *force* (of "energy released by physical or social movements") as opposed to the *authority* that is vested in persons by institutions, exemplifies a certain impotence of theoretical power that is derived from commitment to a closed structure of political power that aggressively fosters and protects the privatization of the public thing, such that its birth and continuity are both best understood as crisis. See Arendt, *On Violence*, 44–46.

51 See Gilles Deleuze, "The Exhausted," in *Essays Critical and Clinical*, trans. Daniel W. Smith and Michael A. Greco (Minneapolis: University of Minnesota Press, 1997), 152–74. I thank Peter Pál Pelbart for bringing this essay to my attention.

52 My thinking is enabled by and indebted to that of Wilderson and Miguel Mellino. Wilderson's call to attention came on May 20, 2006, during his invocation for a conference he organized at the University of California, Irvine, titled "Black Thought in the Age of Terror." Mellino's insistence on a new analytic of the damned that places Fanon in the tradition of revolutionary modernism is given in "Notes from the Underground: Fanon, Africa, and the Poetics of the Real" (unpublished manuscript). Mellino's amplication of *il dannito* brilliantly echoes an earlier recovery of the term given in the work of Walter D. Mignolo. See his "On Subalterns and Other Agencies," *Postcolonial Studies* 8, no. 4 (2005): 381–407. I thank David Lloyd for alerting me to Mignolo's essay and for every other incalculable thing. This essay is dedicated to him.

53 See E. P. Thompson, *The Making of the English Working Class* (New York: Pantheon, 1964), 9.

54 See Fanon, *Wretched of the Earth* (2004), 169.

55 Fanon, *Wretched of the Earth* (2004), 2.

56 Fanon, "Appendix," in *A Dying Colonialism*, 64–65.

57 Fanon, "Conclusion," in *A Dying Colonialism*, 180–81.

58 See Althusser, "From *Capital* to Marx's Philosophy," 22–29.

59 Bertolt Brecht, quoted in Martin Jay, *Permanent Exiles: Essays on the Intellectual Migration from Germany to America* (New York: Columbia University Press, 1986), 28.

60 Deleuze, "The Exhausted," 152.

61 See Huey P. Newton, *Revolutionary Suicide* (New York: Writers and Readers, 1995), 3–7.

62 Albert Camus, *The Myth of Sisyphus and Other Essays*, trans. Justin O'Brien (New York: Vintage, 1991), 2.

63 For more on complex personhood see Avery F. Gordon, *Ghostly Matters: Haunting and the Sociological Imagination* (Minneapolis: University of Minnesota Press, 1997), 4–5.

64 Deleuze, "The Exhausted," 154.

65 Deleuze, "The Exhausted," 154. Elsewhere it may be possible to think of exhausted, exhaustive seriality as glissando or, at the same time, as Glicentin consent.

66 Fanon, *Wretched of the Earth* (2004), 176. In his translation, Philcox substitutes "lament" for Constance Farrington's "howl." I have allowed myself to follow a series of suggestions more fully given in the "uncorrected" version. See Fanon, *Wretched of the Earth* (1968), 243.

67 See Fanon, *Wretched of the Earth* (2004), 157–59.

68 Walter Rodney, *The Groundings with My Brothers* (London: Bogle-L'Ouverture, 1975), 63–64.

69 Miguel Mellino, "The *Langue* of the Damned: Fanon and the Remnants of Europe," *South Atlantic Quarterly* 112, no. 1 (2013): 79–89.

70 Bryan Wagner, *Disturbing the Peace: Black Culture and the Police Power after Slavery* (Cambridge, MA: Harvard University Press, 2009), 1.

71 Jared Sexton, "The Social Life of Social Death: On Afro-Pessimism and Black Optimism," *InTensions* 5 (2011): 28. www.yorku.ca/intent/issue5/articles/jaredsexton.php.

72 See Abdul R. JanMohamed, *The Death-Bound Subject: Richard Wright's Archaeology of Death* (Durham, NC: Duke University Press, 2005).

73 Frantz Fanon, *Black Skin, White Masks*, trans. Richard Philcox (New York: Grove Press, 2008), xiv; hereafter abbreviated *bswm*.

74 Orlando Patterson, *Slavery and Social Death: A Comparative Study* (Cambridge, MA: Harvard University Press, 1982), 5.

75 Wagner, *Disturbing the Peace*, 1.

76 Frank B. Wilderson III, *Incognegro: A Memoir of Exile and Apartheid* (Cambridge, MA: South End Press, 2008), 265.

77 Wagner, *Disturbing the Peace*, 2.

78 See Wilderson's "Acknowledgments" in his *Red, White, and Black: Cinema and the Structure of U.S. Antagonisms* (Durham, NC: Duke University Press, 2010, xi). There he thanks, among others, Saidiya Hartman (to whom anyone who is trying to think about anything is indebted), for requiring him "to stay in the hold of the ship, despite [his] fantasies of flight."

79 Nathaniel Mackey, "On Antiphon Island," in *Splay Anthem* (New York: New Directions, 2006), 64.

80 Mackey, "On Antiphon Island," 65.

81 Wilderson, *Red, White, and Black*, xi.

82 Don Cherry and Ed Blackwell, *El Corazón*, ECM 1 1230, LP, ECM Records, 1982.

83 Marcus Rediker, *The Slave Ship: A Human History* (New York: Viking, 2007), 2.

84 Nathaniel Mackey, *Atet A. D.* (San Francisco: City Lights Books, 2001), 118.

85 Mackey, *Splay Anthem*, ix.

86 Mackey, *Splay Anthem*, ix–xii.

87 Wilderson, *Red, White, and Black*, 56.

88 Wilderson, *Red, White, and Black*, 58–59.

89 Wilderson, *Red, White, and Black*, 57.

90 Nahum Dimitri Chandler, "The Problem of the Centuries: A Contemporary Elaboration of 'The Present Outlook for the Dark Races of Mankind' circa the 27th of December, 1899," unpublished manuscript, 2007, 41.

91 Nishida Kitarō, "The Logic of the Place of Nothingness and the Religious Worldview," in *Last Writings: Nothingness and the Religious Worldview*, trans. David W. Dilworth (Honolulu: University of Hawai'i Press, 1987), 96.

92 Nishida, "Logic of the Place of Nothingness," 96.

93 Nishida, "Logic of the Place of Nothingness," 123.

94 Nishida, "Logic of the Place of Nothingness," 95–96.

95 This sentence gestures toward a convergence I keep imagining between Fanon's analysis of *Le petit Nègre* and Thornton Dial's sculptural *Monument to the Minds of the Little Negro Steelworkers*. At stake is the possibility of another reinitialization of the interplay of critique and celebration in black life and thought.

96 Wilderson, *Red, White, and Black*, 181.

97 Jared Sexton, "People-of-Color-Blindness," YouTube video, 1:23:31, posted by UC Berkeley Events, October 27, 2011, www.youtube.com/watch?v=qNVMI3oiDaI.

98 Yamada Kōun, *The Gateless Gate: The Classic Book of Zen Kōans* (Somerville, MA: Wisdom Publications, 2004), 11.

99 Steven Heine, "Four Myths about Zen Buddhism's *Mu Koan*," blog.oup.com /2012/04/four-myths-about-zen-buddhisms-mu-koan/ (accessed May 18, 2013).

100 Michel Foucault, *History of Madness*, ed. Jean Khalfa, trans. Jonathan Murphy and Jean Khalfa (New York: Routledge, 2006), 10–11.

101 Gilles Deleuze, *Foucault*, ed. and trans. Seán Hand (New York: Continuum, 1988), 81.

102 Deleuze, *Foucault*, 100–101.

103 Jay Wright, *Disorientations: Groundings* (Chicago: Flood Editions, 2013), 56.

104 See Fanon, *Black Skin, White Masks*, trans. Charles Lam Markmann (New York: Grove Press, 1967).

105 Peter Linebaugh, "All the Atlantic Mountains Shook," *Labour/Le Travail* 10 (1982): 110–11.

106 Fanon, *Black Skin, White Masks* (2008), 6–7.

107 Fanon, *Black Skin, White Masks* (2008), 10.

108 Fanon, *Black Skin, White Masks* (2008), 14–15.

109 See Fanon, *Black Skin White Masks* (2008), 175.

110 Frederick Douglass, "To Thomas Auld, September 3, 1848," in *Frederick Douglass: Selected Writings and Speeches*, ed. Philip S. Foner (Chicago: Chicago Review Press, 2000), 115.

111 Fanon, *Black Skin, White Masks* (2008), 17.

112 Fanon, *Black Skin, White Masks* (2008), 18–19.

113 Fanon, *Peau noire, masques blancs* (1952), 8.

114 Fanon, *Black Skin, White Masks* (1967), 10.

115 Plato, "Lysis," trans. J. Wright, in *The Collected Dialogues*, ed. Edith Hamilton and Huntington Cairns (Princeton, NJ: Princeton University Press, 1961), 146.

116 Jacques Derrida, *Resistances of Psychoanalysis*, trans. Peggy Kamuf, Pascale-Anne Brault, and Michael Naas (Stanford, CA: Stanford University Press, 1998), 24.

117 Gilles Deleuze and Félix Guattari, *What Is Philosophy?*, trans. Graham Burchell and Hugh Tomlinson (New York: Columbia University Press, 1996), 41.

118 Plato, "Lysis," 162.

119 Plato, "Lysis," 163.

120 Derrida, *Resistances of Psychoanalysis*, 19–20.

121 Plato, "Lysis," 166.

122 Fanon, *Black Skin, White Masks* (2008), xv.

123 Fanon, *Black Skin, White Masks* (2008), xvi.

124 See Derrida, *Monolingualism of the Other; or, The Prosthetics of Origin*, trans. Patrick Mensah (Stanford, CA: Stanford University Press, 1998).

125 Fanon, *Black Skin, White Masks* (2008), 89–91.

126 John Donne, "A Nocturnal upon S. Lucy's Day," in *The Complete English Poems*, ed. A. J. Smith (New York: Penguin, 1977), 73.

127 Omise'eke Natasha Tinsley, "Black Atlantic, Queer Atlantic," *GLQ: A Journal of Gay and Lesbian Studies* 14, nos. 2–3 (2008): 191–215.

128 Sexton, "The Social Life of Social Death," 27.

129 See Deleuze, "The Exhausted"; Steven Feld, "From Ethnomusicology to Echo-Muse-Ecology: Reading R. Murray Schafer in the Papua New Guinea Rainforest," *Soundscape Newsletter*, no. 8 (1994); and hear Jacques Coursil, *Clameurs*, Universal Music (France) 984 748 2, 2007.

130 Edmund Husserl, *Ideas Pertaining to a Pure Phenomenology and to a Phenomenological Philosophy—First Book: General Introduction to a Pure Phenomenology*, trans. Fred Kersten (The Hague: Martinus Nijhoff, 1982), 429.

131 Marianne Sawicki, "Edmund Husserl (1859–1938)," *Internet Encyclopedia of Philosophy: A Peer-Reviewed Academic Resource* (accessed March 24, 2013), www.iep.utm.edu/husserl.

132 Fred Moten, "The Case of Blackness," *Criticism* 50, no. 2 (2007): 177–218. A slight revision is printed in this volume.

133 Benjamin Kunkel, "Into the Big Tent," *London Review of Books*, April 22, 2010, 12.

134 Kunkel, "Into the Big Tent," 12. See also Cedric J. Robinson, *Black Marxism: The Making of the Black Radical Tradition*, 2nd ed. (Chapel Hill: University of North Carolina Press, 2000).

135 Robinson, *Black Marxism*, 246, 243, 243–44.

136 See Stanley Cavell, *Philosophical Passages: Wittgenstein, Emerson, Austin, Derrida* (Cambridge, MA: Blackwell, 1995), 101; and "One World in Relation: Édouard Glissant in Conversation with Manthia Diawara," trans. Christopher Winks, *Journal of Contemporary African Art*, no. 28 (2011): 5.

137 Richard Pryor, *Craps*, Umgd B000001ECF, Umgd, CD, 1994.

138 Frank B. Wilderson III, "The Prison Slave as Hegemony's (Silent) Scandal," in *Warfare in the American Homeland: Policing and Prison in a Penal Democracy*, ed. Joy James (Durham, NC: Duke University Press, 2007), 31–32.

139 "The Position of the Unthought: An Interview with Saidiya V. Hartman. Conducted by Frank B. Wilderson III," *Qui Parle* 13, no. 2 (2003): 187.

140 Lauren Berlant, "Slow Death (Sovereignty, Obesity, Lateral Agency)," *Critical Inquiry* 33, no. 4 (2007): 754–80.

141 Daphne A. Brooks, *Bodies in Dissent: Spectacular Performances of Race and Freedom, 1850–1910* (Durham, NC: Duke University Press, 2006), 3–9.

142 Melinda Cooper and Angela Mitropoulos, "In Praise of Usura," *Mute* 2, no. 13 (2009), www.metamute.org/editorial/articles/praise-usura.

WORKS CITED

Adorno, Theodor. *Aesthetic Theory*. Translated by Robert Hullot-Kentor. Minneapolis: University of Minnesota Press, 1997.

———. "On Jazz." In *Essays on Music*, edited by Richard Leppert, 470–95. Translated by Jamie Owen Daniel and Richard Leppert. Berkeley: University of California Press, 2002.

Agamben, Giorgio. *Homo Sacer: Sovereign Power and Bare Life*. Translated by Daniel Heller-Roazen. Stanford, CA: Stanford University Press, 1998.

———. *Means without Ends: Notes on Politics*. Translated by Vincenzo Binetti and Cesare Casarino. Minneapolis: University of Minnesota Press, 2000.

———. *The Open: Man and Animal*. Translated by Kevin Attell. Stanford, CA: Stanford University Press, 2002.

Allen, Danielle. "Law's Necessary Forcefulness: Ralph Ellison vs. Hannah Arendt on the Battle of Little Rock." In *Multiculturalism and Political Theory*, edited by Anthony Simon Laden and David Owen, 315–49. Cambridge: Cambridge University Press, 2007.

Althusser, Louis. "From *Capital* to Marx's Philosophy." In Louis Althusser, Étienne Balibar, Roger Establet, Pierre Macherey, and Jacques Rancière, *Reading Capital: The Complete Edition*, 9–72. Translated by Ben Brewster and David Fernbach. New York: Verso, 2015.

Andresen, Julie Tetel. "Historiography's Contribution to Theoretical Linguistics." In *Chomskyan Evolutions and Revolutions: Essays in Honor of E. F. K. Koerner*, edited by Douglas Kibbee, 443–69. Amsterdam: John Benjamins, 2010.

Arendt, Hannah. "Civil Disobedience." In Arendt, *Crises of the Republic*, 49–102. New York: Harcourt Brace, 1972.

———. "The Eichmann Controversy: A Letter to Gershom Scholem." In *The Jewish Writings*, edited by Jerome Kohn and Ron H. Feldman, 465–71. New York: Schocken Books, 2007.

———. *Lectures on Kant's Political Philosophy*. Edited by Ronald Beiner. Chicago: University of Chicago Press, 1982.

———. "The Meaning of Love in Politics: A Letter by Hannah Arendt to James Baldwin, November 21, 1962." *HannahArendt.net*. www.hannaharendt.net/index.php /han/article/view/95/156.

———. *On Violence*. New York: Harcourt, Brace, Jovanovich, 1970.

———. *The Origins of Totalitarianism*. New York: Harcourt, Brace, 1975.

———. "Reflections on Little Rock." In *Responsibility and Judgment*, edited by Jerome Kohn, 193–213. New York: Schocken, 2003.

Arendt, Hannah, and Karl Jaspers. *Correspondence 1926–1967*. Edited by Lotte Kohler and Hans Saner. Translated by Robert and Rita Kimber. New York: Harcourt Brace, 1992.

Aronowicz, Annette. "Introduction." In Emmanuel Levinas, *Nine Talmudic Readings*. Bloomington: Indiana University Press, 1990.

Baldwin, James. "Autobiographical Notes." In *Notes of A Native Son*. In *James Baldwin: Collected Essays*, edited by Toni Morrison, 3–9. New York: Library of America, 1998.

———. *James Baldwin: Collected Essays*, edited by Toni Morrison. New York: Library of America, 1998.

Baraka, Amiri. (LeRoi Jones). "Black Is a Country." In Amiri Baraka, *Home: Social Essays*. New York: Morrow, 1966.

Barrett, Lindon. "Captivity, Desire, Trade: The Forging of National Form." In *Racial Blackness and the Discontinuity of Western Modernity*. Edited by Justin A. Joyce, Dwight A. McBride, and John Carlos Rowe, 72–136. Urbana: University of Illinois Press, 2014.

Bates, Daisy. *The Long Shadow of Little Rock*. Fayetteville: University of Arkansas Press, 1986.

Black National Economic Conference. "A Black Manifesto." *New York Review of Books*, July 10, 1969. www.nybooks.com/articles/11267.

Benjamin, Andrew. *Translation and the Nature of Philosophy: A New Theory of Words*. London: Routledge, 1989.

Berlant, Lauren. "Slow Death: Sovereignty, Obesity, Lateral Agency." *Critical Inquiry* 33, no. 4 (2007): 754–80.

Bois, Yve-Alain. "The Limit of Almost." In *Ad Reinhardt*, edited by William Rubin and Richard Koshalek, 11–33. New York: Rizzoli, 1991.

———. "Piet Mondrian, New York City." In *Painting as Model*, 157–83. Cambridge, MA: MIT Press, 1990.

Boris, Staci. "The Process of Change: Landscape, Memory, Animation, and *Felix in Exile*." In *William Kentridge*, edited by Neal Benezra, Staci Boris, and Dan Cameron, 29–37. New York: Harry N. Abrams, 2001.

Braxton, Anthony. *Composition Notes: Book A*. Lebanon, NH: Frog Peak Music/ Synthesis Music, 1988.

———. Liner notes, *Donna Lee*. CD 05 067 863–2, Free America, 2005.

Brooks, Daphne A. *Bodies in Dissent: Spectacular Performances of Race and Freedom, 1850–1910*. Durham, NC: Duke University Press, 2006.

Brooks, Peter. *The Melodramatic Imagination: Balzac, Henry James, Melodrama, and the Mode of Excess*. New Haven, CT: Yale University Press, 1995.

Broomer, Stu, Harvey Cowan, Ad Reinhardt, Arnold Rockman, Michael Snow, Aldo Tambellini, and Cecil Taylor. "Black." *Arts/Canada* 113 (1967): 3–19.

Butler, Judith. *Gender Trouble: Feminism and the Subversion of Identity*. New York: Routledge, 1989.

————. "'I Merely Belong to Them.'" Review of *The Jewish Writings*, edited by Jerome Kohn and Ron H. Feldman. *London Review of Books*, May 10, 2007. www.lrb.co .uk/v29/n09/but102_.html.

————. "Is Kinship Always Already Heterosexual?" In Butler, *Undoing Gender*, 102–30. New York: Routledge, 2004.

————. *The Psychic Life of Power: Theories in Subjection*. Stanford, CA: Stanford University Press, 1997.

Cameron, Dan. "A Procession of the Dispossessed." In *William Kentridge*, edited by Dan Cameron et al., 38–81. London: Phaidon, 1999.

Camus, Albert. *The Myth of Sisyphus and Other Essays*. Translated by Justin O'Brien. New York: Vintage, 1991.

Carr, David. Translator's introduction to Edmund Husserl, *The Crisis of European Sciences and Transcendental Phenomenology*, xv–xxxvii. Evanston, IL: Northwestern University Press, 1970.

Cavell, Stanley. "Music Discomposed." In *Must We Mean What We Say?*, 180–212. Cambridge: Cambridge University Press, 2002.

————. *Philosophical Passages: Wittgenstein, Emerson, Austin, Derrida*. Cambridge: Blackwell, 1995.

Cecil Taylor Segments II (Orchestra of Two Continents). *Winged Serpent (Sliding Quadrants)*. Line 17: LP. Soul Note SN 1089. Soul Note, 1985.

Chandler, Nahum Dimitiri. "The Problem of the Centuries: A Contemporary Elaboration of 'The Present Outlook for the Dark Races of Mankind' circa the 27th of December, 1899." Unpublished manuscript. 2007.

————. *X: The Problem of the Negro as a Problem for Thought*. New York: Fordham University Press, 2013.

Chomsky, Noam. *Language and Mind*. 3rd ed. Cambridge: Cambridge University Press, 2006.

————. "What We Know: On the Universals of Language and Rights." *Boston Review* (summer 2005). bostonreview.net/chomsky-what-we-know.

Cooper, Harry. "Mondrian, Hegel, Boogie." *October* 84 (1998): 118–42.

Cooper, Melinda, and Angela Mitropoulos. "In Praise of Usura." *Mute* 2, no. 13 (2009). Accessed October 6, 2009. www.metamute.org/editorial/articles/praise-usura.

Coursil, Jacques. *Clameurs*. Universal Music (France). 2007.

Cover, Robert M. "The Supreme Court, 1982 Term—Foreword: *Nomos* and Narrative." *Harvard Law Review* 97, no. 1 (1983): 4–65.

Deleuze, Gilles. "The Exhausted." In *Essays Critical and Clinical*, 152–74. Translated by Daniel W. Smith and Michael A. Greco. Minneapolis: University of Minnesota Press, 1997.

————. *Foucault*. Edited and translated by Seán Hand. New York: Continuum, 1988.

Deleuze, Gilles, and Félix Guattari. *What Is Philosophy?* Translated by Graham Burchell and Hugh Tomlinson. New York: Columbia University Press, 1996.

Derrida, Jacques. *Monolingualism of the Other; or, The Prosthetics of Origin*. Translated by Patrick Mensah. Stanford, CA: Stanford University Press, 1998.

————. *Resistances of Psychoanalysis*. Translated by Peggy Kamuf, Pascale-Anne Brault, and Michael Naas. Stanford, CA: Stanford University Press, 1998.

Diderot, Denis. "In Praise of Richardson." In *Selected Writings on Art and Literature*, translated by Geoffrey Bremner, 82–97. New York: Penguin, 1994.

Donne, John. "A Nocturnal upon S. Lucy's Day." In *The Complete English Poems*, edited by A. J. Smith, 73. New York: Penguin, 1977.

Douglass, Frederick. "Letter to His Former Master." In *The Narrative and Selected Writings*, edited by Michael Meyer, 280–90. New York: Modern Library, 1984.

———. "To Thomas Auld, September 3, 1848." In *Frederick Douglass: Selected Writings and Speeches*, ed. Philip S. Foner, 115. Chicago: Chicago Review Press, 2000.

Du Bois, W. E. B. "Sociology Hesitant." *boundary 2* 27, no. 3 (2000): 37–44.

Dumas, Henry. "Will the Circle Be Unbroken?" In *Echo Tree: The Collected Short Fiction of Henry Dumas*, 105–10. Minneapolis: Coffee House Press, 2003.

Edwards, Brent Hayes. *The Practice of Diaspora: Literature, Translation and the Rise of Black Internationalism*. Cambridge, MA: Harvard University Press, 2003.

Elkins, Stanley M. *Slavery: A Problem in American Institutional and Intellectual Life*. New York: Grosset and Dunlap, 1963.

Erskine, John. *The Moral Obligation to Be Intelligent*. New York: Duffield, 1915.

Fanon, Frantz. *Black Skin, White Masks*. Translated by Charles Lam Markmann. New York: Grove Press, 1967.

———. *Black Skin, White Masks*. Translated by Charles Lam Markmann. London: Paladin, 1970.

———. *Black Skin, White Masks*. Translated by Richard Philcox. New York: Grove Press, 2008.

———. *A Dying Colonialism*. Translated by Haakon Chevalier. New York: Grove Press, 1967.

———. *Les damnés de la terre*. Paris: Gallimard, 1991.

———. *Peau noire, masques blancs*. Paris: Editions du Seuil, 1952.

———. *The Wretched of the Earth*. Translated by Constance Farrington. New York: Grove, 1968.

———. *The Wretched of the Earth*. Translated by Richard Philcox. New York: Grove, 2004.

Feld, Steven. "From Ethnomusicology to Echo-Muse-Ecology: Reading R. Murray Schafer in the Papua New Guinea Rainforest." *Soundscape Newsletter*, no. 8 (June 1994).

Foucault, Michel. *History of Madness*. Edited by Jean Khalfa. Translated by Jonathan Murphy and Jean Khalfa. New York: Routledge, 2006.

Fried, Michael. "Art and Objecthood." In *Art and Objecthood*, 148–72. Chicago: University of Chicago Press, 1998.

Gilroy, Paul. *Darker than Blue: On the Moral Economies of Black Atlantic Culture*. Cambridge, MA: Harvard University Press, 2010.

Gordon, Avery F. *Ghostly Matters: Haunting and the Sociological Imagination*. Minneapolis: University of Minnesota Press, 1997.

Greenberg, Clement. "The Crisis of the Easel Picture." In *The Collected Essays and Criticism: Arrogant Purpose, 1945–1949*, edited by John O'Brian, 221–25. Chicago: University of Chicago Press, 1986.

Greenberg, Polly. *The Devil Has Slippery Shoes*. London: Macmillan, 1969.

———, ed. *Head Start: With the Child Development Group of Mississippi*. CD. Smithsonian Folkways Recordings, 2004/Folkways Records, 1967.

Guattari, Félix. *Chaosmosis: An Ethico-Aesthetic Paradigm*. Translated by Paul Baines and Julian Pefanis. Bloomington: Indiana University Press, 1995.

Guyer, Paul. *Kant and the Claims of Taste*, 2nd ed. Cambridge: Cambridge University Press, 1997.

Han, Sora. "Slavery as Contract: *Betty's Case* and the Question of Freedom." *Law and Literature* 27, no. 3 (2015): 395–416.

Harris, Laura. *Experiments in Exile: C. L. R. James, Hélio Oiticica, and the Aesthetic Sociality of Blackness*. New York: Fordham University Press, 2018.

Hartman, Saidiya. *Scenes of Subjection: Slavery, Terror and Self-Making in Nineteenth-Century America*. Oxford: Oxford University Press, 1997.

Heidegger, Martin. *Being and Time*. Translated by John Macquarrie and Edward Robinson. New York: Harper, 1962.

———. "The Thing." In Martin Heidegger, *Poetry, Language, Thought*, 163–86. Translated by Albert Hofstadter. New York: Harper and Row, 1971.

Heine, Steven. "Four Myths about Zen Buddhism's *Mu Kōan*." Accessed May 18, 2013. blog.oup.com/2012/04/four-myths-about-zen-buddhisms-mu-koan.

Husserl, Edmund. *The Crisis of European Sciences and Transcendental Phenomenology: An Introduction to Phenomenological Philosophy*. Translated by David Carr. Evanston, IL: Northwestern University Press, 1970.

———. *Ideas Pertaining to a Pure Phenomenology and to a Phenomenological Philosophy—First Book: General Introduction to a Pure Phenomenology*. Translated by Fred Kersten. The Hague: Martinus Nijhoff, 1982.

———. "Philosophy and the Crisis of European Humanity." In *The Crisis of European Sciences and Transcendental Phenomenology*, 269–99. Translated by David Carr. Evanston, IL: Northwestern University Press, 1970.

The Impressions. "Choice of Colors." On *The Young Mods' Forgotten Story*. CD. Chicago: Curtom Records, 1969, 2006.

"Interview with C. T. Vivian." Conducted by Blackside, Inc., on January 23, 1986, for *Eyes on the Prize: America's Civil Rights Years (1954–1965)*. Washington University Libraries, Film and Media Archive, Henry Hampton Collection. http://digital.wustl.edu/cgi/t/text/text-idx?c=eop;cc=eop;rgn=main;view=text;idno=viv0015.0233.104.

Inwood, Michael. *A Heidegger Dictionary*. London: Blackwell, 1999.

Irigaray, Luce. "The Fecundity of the Caress: A Reading of Levinas, *Totality and Infinity* section IV, B, 'The Phenomenology of Eros.'" In *Face to Face with Levinas*, edited by Richard A. Cohen, 231–56. Albany: State University of New York, 1986.

———. "Questions to Emmanuel Levinas." In *The Irigaray Reader*, edited by Margaret Whitford, 178–89. London: Blackwell, 1991.

JanMohamed, Abdul R. *The Death-Bound Subject: Richard Wright's Archaeology of Death*. Durham, NC: Duke University Press, 2005.

Jay, Martin. *Permanent Exiles: Essays on the Intellectual Migration from Germany to America*. New York: Columbia University Press, 1986.

Kant, Immanuel. "Answer to the Question: What Is Enlightenment?" Translated by Thomas K. Abbott. In *Basic Writings of Kant*, edited by Allen K. Wood, 133–41. New York: Modern Library, 2001.

———. *Critique of the Power of Judgment*. Translated by Paul Guyer and Eric Matthews. Cambridge: Cambridge University Press, 2000.

———. "On the Use of Teleological Principles in Philosophy." In *Race*, edited by Robert Bernasconi, 37–56. Translated by Jon Mark Mikkelsen. London: Blackwell, 2001.

———. *Critique of the Power of Judgment*. Translated by Paul Guyer and Eric Matthews. Cambridge: Cambridge University Press, 2000.

Keeling, Kara. "'In the Interval': Frantz Fanon and the 'Problems' of Visual Representation." *Qui Parle* 13, no. 2 (2003): 91–117.

———. *The Witch's Flight: The Cinematic, the Black Femme, and the Image of Common Sense*. Durham, NC: Duke University Press, 2007.

Kentridge, William. "Art in a State of Grace, Art in a State of Hope, Art in a State of Siege (extract)." In *William Kentridge*, edited by Dan Cameron et al., 102–5. London: Phaidon, 1999.

———. "*Felix in Exile:* Geography of Memory (extract)." In *William Kentridge*, edited by Dan Cameron et al., 122–27. London: Phaidon, 1999.

———. "'Fortuna': Neither Programme nor Chance in the Making of Images." In *William Kentridge*, edited by Dan Cameron et al., 114–19. London: Phaidon, 1999.

———. Excerpts from "Dear Diary: Suburban Allegories and Other Infections." In *William Kentridge*, edited by Carolyn Christov-Bakargiev, 74–77. Brussels: Société des Expositions du Palais des Beaux-Arts/Vereniging voor Tentoonstellingen van het Paleis voor Schone Kunsten Brussel, 1998.

Kōun, Yamada. *The Gateless Gate: The Classic Book of Zen Kōans*. Somerville, MA: Wisdom Publications, 2004.

Krauss, Rosalind. "'The Rock': William Kentridge's Drawings for Projection." *October* 92 (2000): 3–35.

Kunkel, Benjamin. "Into the Big Tent." *London Review of Books*, April 22, 2010, 12–16.

Lacan, Jacques. "The Mirror Stage as Formative of the *I* Function as Revealed in Psychoanalytic Experience." In *Écrits: The First Complete Edition in English*. Translated by Bruce Fink in collaboration with Héloïse Fink and Russell Grigg. New York: W. W. Norton, 2006.

Landau, Jon. Review of *Curtis/Live! Rolling Stone*, June 24, 1971. Accessed January 29, 2017. www.rollingstone.com/music/albumreviews/curtis-live-19710624.

Lebeau, Vicky. "The Unwelcome Child: Elizabeth Eckford and Hannah Arendt." *Journal of Visual Culture* 3, no. 1 (2004): 51–62.

Lepecki, André. *Exhausting Dance: Performance and the Politics of Movement*. New York: Routledge, 2006.

Levinas, Emmanuel. *Existence and Existents*. Translated by Alphonso Lingis. Pittsburgh: Duquesne University Press, 2001.

———. "Freiburg, Husserl, and Phenomenology." In *Discovering Existence with Husserl*. Translated by Richard A. Cohen and Michael B. Smith, 32–38. Evanston, IL: Northwestern University Press, 1998.

———. "Intention, Event, and the Other." Translated by Andrew Schmitz. In *Is It Righteous to Be? Interviews with Emmanuel Levinas*, edited by Jill Robbins, 000–000. Stanford, CA: Stanford University Press, 2001.

———. "Interview with Francis Poiré." Translated by Jill Robbins and Marcus Coelen with Thomas Loebel. In *Is It Righteous to Be? Interviews with Emmanuel Levinas*, edited by Jill Robbins. Stanford, CA: Stanford University Press, 2001.

———. *Is It Righteous to Be? Interviews with Emmanuel Levinas*, edited by Jill Robbins. Stanford, CA: Stanford University Press, 2001.

———. "Martin Heidegger and Ontology." Translated by the Committee of Public Safety. *Diacritics* 26, no. 1 (1996): 11–32.

———. "Is Ontology Fundamental?" Translated by Richard Atterton and revised by Simon Critchley and Adriaan T. Peperzak. In *Emmanuel Levinas: Basic Philosophical Writings*, edited by Adriaan T. Peperzak, Simon Critchley, and Robert Bernasconi, 1–10. Bloomington: Indiana University Press, 1996.

———. "On the Usefulness of Insomnia." In *Is It Righteous to Be? Interviews with Emmanuel Levinas*, edited by Jill Robbins. Stanford, CA: Stanford University Press, 2001.

———. "On the Use of Teleological Principles in Philosophy." Translated by Jon Mark Mikkelsen. In *Race*, edited by Robert Bernasconi, 37–56. London: Blackwell, 2001.

———. "Reflections on the Philosophy of Hitlerism." Translated by Seán Hand. *Critical Inquiry* 17, no. 1 (1990): 62–71.

———. *Totality and Infinity: An Essay on Exteriority*. Translated by Alphonso Lingis. Pittsburgh: Duquesne University Press, 1969.

Lewis, George E. *A Power Stronger than Itself: The AACM and American Experimental Music*. Chicago: University of Chicago Press, 2008.

———. "Toneburst (Piece for 3 Trombones Simultaneously)." *The Solo Trombone Record*. SKCD2–3012, Sackville, 2001.

Linebaugh, Peter. "All the Atlantic Mountains Shook." *Labour/Le Travail* 10 (1982): 87–121.

Lipsitz, George. *The Possessive Investment in Whiteness*. Philadelphia: Temple University Press, 1998.

Lock, Graham. *Forces in Motion: The Music and Thoughts of Anthony Braxton*. New York: Da Capo, 1988.

Lubiano, Wahneema. "Black Nationalism and Black Common Sense: Policing Ourselves and Others." In *The House That Race Built: Original Essays by Toni Morrison, Angela Y. Davis, Cornel West, and Others on Black Americans and Politics in America Today*, edited by Wahneema Lubiano, 232–52. New York: Vintage, 1998.

Lupton, Julia. "Creature Caliban." *Shakespeare Quarterly* 51, no. 1 (2000): 1–23.

Macey, David. *Frantz Fanon: A Biography*. New York: Picador, 2001.

Mackey, Nathaniel. *Atet A.D.* San Francisco: City Lights Books, 2001.

———. *Bedouin Hornbook*. Callaloo Fiction Series, Volume 2. Lexington: University Press of Kentucky, 1986.

———. *Splay Anthem*. New York: New Directions, 2006.

Marable, Manning, Leith Mullings, and Sophie Spencer-Wood, eds. *Freedom: A Photographic History of the African American Struggle*. New York: Phaidon, 2005.

Marder, Michael. *The Event of the Thing: Derrida's Post-deconstructive Realism*. Toronto: University of Toronto Press, 2009.

Marriott, David. *On Black Men*. New York: Columbia University Press, 2000.

Marx, Karl. "Private Property and Communism." In *Early Writings*, translated by Rodney Livingstone and Gregor Benton, 345–58. New York: Vintage, 1975.

———. *Grundrisse: Foundations of the Critique of Political Economy*. Translated by Martin Nicolaus. New York: Penguin, 1973.

Mbembe, Achille. "Necropolitics." Translated by Libby Meintjes. *Public Culture* 15, no. 1 (2003): 11–40.

———. *On the Postcolony*. Translated by A. M. Berrett, et al. Berkeley: University of California Press, 2001.

McGettigan, Andrew. "The Philosopher's Fear of Alterity: Levinas, Europe, and Humanities 'Without Sacred History.'" *Radical Philosophy* 140 (2006): 15–25.

Mellino, Miguel. "The *Langue* of the Damned: Fanon and the Remnants of Europe." *South Atlantic Quarterly* 112, no. 1 (2013) 79–89.

———. "Notes from the Underground: Fanon, Africa, and the Poetics of the Real." Unpublished manuscript.

Menand, Louis. *The Metaphysical Club: A Story of Ideas in America*. New York: Farrar, Straus and Giroux, 2001.

Menninghaus, Winfried. *In Praise of Nonsense: Kant and Bluebeard*. Translated by Henry Pickford. Stanford, CA: Stanford University Press, 1999.

Mignolo, Walter D. "On Subalterns and Other Agencies." *Postcolonial Studies* 8, no. 4 (2005): 381–407.

Mondrian, Piet. "Jazz and Neo-Plastic." In *The New Art—The New Life: The Collected Writings of Piet Mondrian*, edited and translated by Harry Holtzman and Martin S. James, 217–22. Boston: Da Capo, 1993.

Moten, Fred. "The Case of Blackness." *Criticism* 50, no. 2 (2007): 177–218.

———. *In the Break: The Aesthetics of the Black Radical Tradition*. Minneapolis: University of Minnesota Press, 2003.

——— "Knowledge of Freedom." *CR: The New Centennial Review* 4, no. 2 (2004): 269–310.

———. "Nandi's Objection." In *Stolen Life*. Durham, NC: Duke University Press, 2018.

Negri, Antonio. *Negri on Negri: In Conversation with Anne Dufourmantelle*. Translated by M. B. DeBevvoise. New York: Routledge, 2004.

Newton, Huey P. *Revolutionary Suicide*. New York: Writers and Readers, 1995.

Nishida, Kitarō. "The Logic of the Place of Nothingness and the Religious Worldview." In *Last Writings: Nothingness and the Religious Worldview*, 47–123. Translated by David W. Dilworth. Honolulu: University of Hawai'i Press, 1987.

"One World in Relation: Édouard Glissant in Conversation with Manthia Diawara." Translated by Christopher Winks. *Journal of Contemporary African Art* 28 (2011): 4–19.

Patočka, Jan. *Body, Community, Language, World*. Translated by Erazim Kohák. Chicago: Open Court, 1998.

Patterson, Orlando. *Slavery and Social Death: A Comparative Study*. Cambridge, MA: Harvard University Press, 1982.

Petitot, Jean, Francisco J. Varela, Bernard Pachoud, and Jean-Michel Roy, eds. *Naturalizing Phenomenology: Issues in Contemporary Phenomenology and Cognitive Science*. Stanford, CA: Stanford University Press, 1999.

Piper, Adrian. "Cultural Hegemony and Aesthetic Acculturation," *Noûs* 19, no. 1 (1985): 29–40.

———. "Talking to Myself: The Ongoing Autobiography of an Art Object." In *Out of Order, Out of Sight—Volume I: Selected Writings in Meta-Art, 1968–1992*, 29–53. Cambridge, MA: MIT Press, 1996.

———. "Untitled Performance for Max's Kansas City." In *Out of Order, Out of Sight—Volume I: Selected Writings in Meta-Art, 1968–1992*, 27. Cambridge, MA: MIT Press, 1996.

Plato. "Lysis." In *The Collected Dialogues*, 145–68. Edited by Edith Hamilton and Huntington Cairns. Translated by J. Wright. Princeton, NJ: Princeton University Press, 1961.

"The Position of the Unthought: An Interview with Saidiya V. Hartman Conducted by Frank B. Wilderson III." *Qui Parle* 13, no. 2 (2003): 183–201.

Povinelli, Elizabeth A. "The Child in the Broom Closet: States of Living and Letting Die." *South Atlantic Quarterly* 107, no. 3 (2008): 509–30.

Pryor, Richard. *Craps*. London: Umgd. 1994.

Raiford, Leigh. "'Come Let Us Build a New World Together': SNCC and Photography of the Civil Rights Movement." *American Quarterly* 59, no. 4 (2007): 1129–57.

Rediker, Marcus. *The Slave Ship: A Human History*. New York: Viking, 2007.

Reinhardt, Ad. "Black as Symbol and Concept." In *Art as Art: The Selected Writings of Ad Reinhardt*, edited by Barbara Rose, 86–88. Berkeley: University of California Press, 1975.

Robinson, Cedric J. *Black Marxism: The Making of the Black Radical Tradition*. 2nd ed. Chapel Hill: University of North Carolina Press, 2000.

———. *The Terms of Order: Political Science and the Myth of Leadership*. 2nd ed. Chapel Hill: University of North Carolina Press, 2016.

Rodney, Walter. *The Groundings with My Brothers*. London: Bogle-L'Ouverture, 1975.

Rosen, Charles. *Arnold Schoenberg*. Chicago: University of Chicago Press, 1996.

Rosenzweig, Franz. *Franz Rosenzweig: His Life and Thought*. Edited by Nahum Glazer. New York: Schocken Books, 1961.

Santner, Eric L. *On Creaturely Life: Rilke, Benjamin, Sebald*. Chicago: University of Chicago Press, 2006.

Sawicki, Marianne. "Edmund Husserl (1859–1938)." *Internet Encyclopedia of Philosophy: A Peer-Reviewed Academic Resource*. n.d. Accessed March 25, 2013. www.iep.utm.edu/husserl.

Schürmann, Reiner. *Heidegger on Being and Acting: From Principles to Anarchy*. Translated by Christine-Marie Gros and Reiner Schürmann. Bloomington: Indiana University Press, 1990.

Sexton, Jared. "People-of-Color-Blindness." YouTube. Accessed May 20, 2013. www.youtube.com/watch?v=qNVMI30iDaI.

———. "The Social Life of Social Death: On Afro-Pessimism and Black Optimism." *InTensions* 5 (2011). Accessed November 1, 2012. www.yorku.ca/intent/issue5/articles/jaredsexton.php.

Sexton, Jared, and Huey Copeland. "Raw Life: An Introduction." *Qui Parle* 13, no. 2 (2003): 53–62.

Singh, Nikhil Pal. *Black Is a Country: Race and the Unfinished Struggle for Democracy*. Cambridge: Cambridge University Press, 2004.

Spillers, Hortense J. *Black and White and in Color: Essays on American Literature and Culture*, 203–29. Chicago: University of Chicago Press, 2003.

Spivak, Gayatri Chakravorty. *A Critique of Postcolonial Reason: Toward a History of the Vanishing Present*. Cambridge, MA: Harvard University Press, 1999.

Taylor, Cecil. *All the Notes*. Cadence Jazz Records CJR 1169 CD, 2004.

Thompson, E. P. *The Making of the English Working Class*. New York: Pantheon, 1964.

Tinsley, Omise'eke Natasha. "Black Atlantic, Queer Atlantic." *GLQ: A Journal of Gay and Lesbian Studies* 14, nos. 2–3 (2008): 191–215.

Trilling, Lionel. *The Moral Obligation to Be Intelligent: Selected Essays*. Edited by Leon Wieseltier. Evanston, IL: Northwestern University Press, 2008.

Wagner, Bryan. *Disturbing the Peace: Black Culture and the Police Power after Slavery*. Cambridge, MA: Harvard University Press, 2009.

Wall, Cheryl A. *Worrying the Line: Black Women Writers, Lineage, and Literary Tradition*. Chapel Hill: University of North Carolina Press, 2005.

———. *Incognegro: A Memoir of Exile and Apartheid*. Cambridge, MA: South End Press, 2008.

———. "The Prison Slave as Hegemony's (Silent) Scandal." In *Warfare in the American Homeland: Policing and Prison in a Penal Democracy*, edited by Joy James, 23–34. Durham, NC: Duke University Press, 2007.

———. *Red, White, and Black: Cinema and the Structure of U.S. Antagonisms*. Durham, NC: Duke University Press, 2010.

Wright, Jay. *Disorientations: Groundings*. Chicago: Flood Editions, 2013.

Young-Bruehl, Elizabeth. *Hannah Arendt: For Love of the World*. 2nd ed. New Haven, CT: Yale University Press, 2004.

INDEX

abolitionism/antiabolitionism, 90–94

Adorno, Theodor, 173, 181; jazz criticism, 79, 131, 151

Afro-pessimism: black life and social death of, 194, 195; black optimism and, 197, 234; nothingness and, 196–97, 230; positionality and, 203–4, 242; as the study of impossibility, 193

Agamben, Giorgio: animal-human life relation and, 36, 37–38; Heidegger and, 40; on naked life, 143–44, 262n6; Schmitt and Santner relation, 40–42

agency, 27, 50; political, 99–100

Algerians, 174–75, 181–82, 186–87

alienation, 82, 199; internal, 54; natal, 79, 219, 226

allegory, 47–49

Allen, Danielle, 81, 257n26, 259n59; on dark speech, 102, 105; on Elizabeth Eckford, 96, 103–4; path to citizenship, 106–7; reading of Arendt, 98–99, 108, 110–14; reading of Ellison, 97, 99–100, 110; on sacrifice, 100, 109

alterity, 6, 34, 127, 137, 138; exposure to, 39, 40; Levinas and, 5, 7–8; sly, 103–4

Althusser, Louis, 155–56, 187

Ammons, Albert, 156, 168, 170, 172

annihilation, 126, 147–48

antiblackness, 122, 204–5, 223, 226; of Arendt, 66, 82, 101, 254n4

anticolonialism, 177, 182, 185, 192; struggle of, 186, 188

antipolitics, 79, 87, 101, 104

apartheid, 60, 61, 63

apposition, 16, 93, 145, 150, 180, 211–12; to Afro-pessimism, 194; Coltrane and, 28; opposition and, 118–19

Arendt, Hannah, xii, 109, 253n1, 259n59; abolitionism and, 90–93; Allen's reading of, 98–99, 108, 110–14; antiblackness of, 66, 82, 101, 254n4; on Baldwin and love, 83–88; on belonging to the Jewish people, 253n3; black study and, 67, 72–73, 74–75, 138; Forman and, 71, 73, 139; Jaspers and, 85–86; Kant and, 93–94, 115; as a Negro mother, 76–79, 82; the political and, 101–4, 107, 194; on power, 184, 266n50; refuge for, 65; self-projective self-protection, 81, 257n28. *See also* Arendt, Hannah, works

Arendt, Hannah, works: "Civil Disobedience," 89; *The Human Condition*, 85, 99; *Men in Dark Times*, 112–13; *On Violence*, xiii, 67, 72, 80, 89–90, 92, 184, 255n7, 255n14; *The Origins of Totalitarianism*, 91–92; "Reflections on Little Rock," 75, 80, 254n6

art, history of, 63–64, 76

artist and art form, 163–66

art–life encounter, 167, 168

assimilation, 14, 81, 219; exclusionary, 14, 26, 38, 81–82; Jewish, 56–57

Association for the Advancement of Creative Musicians (aacm), 73

Ayler, Albert, 243

Brown, Wendy, 108
Buddhist teaching, 206, 208
Butler, Judith, 44–45, 77, 253n3, 262n6;
    Levinas and, 8, 26

Camus, Albert, 189
capitalism, 63, 71, 235; racial, 236–37
captivation, 33, 35, 37–39
Carr, David, 13
Celan, Paul, 55
celebration, 148, 197, 239–40, 268n95
Cervenak, Sarah Jane, 117
Césaire, Aimé, 216, 224
Chandler, Nahum Dimitri, 88, 194, 204,
    212, 262n3
charismata, 103–5
Cherry, Don, 197, 199, 201–2, 207,
    209–11
Chicago, 65–66, 137
children, 54, 77–79, 99
Chomsky, Noam, 123–26, 134–35
chromatic saturation, 168; blackness and,
    154–57, 170, 173; repercussions of, 171;
    weak/strong forms of, 153–54
chromatic space, 152–53
circle, the, 29–30, 189
citizens, 97–99, 114, 121, 133, 259n59;
    sacrifice of, 110–11
citizenship, 93, 96, 101, 106–7, 111; refusal
    of, 133; subjectivity and, 50, 136
city, 40, 41, 59, 137; cell and, 132; escape
    or free from, 171, 172; fugitivity and,
    64; outside the, 29–30, 42
civil disobedience, 67, 90, 92
civilization: blackness and, 219, 226; danc-
    ing, 1, 11, 49, 58, 60; Western, 36, 238
civil society, 195, 238–40
class status, 220
Clinton, Bill, 256n25
colonialism, 174, 177–78, 181, 236;
    French, 187
color black, the: Adorno on, 173; Ad
    Reinhardt's view of, 158–59, 162; in
    Mondrian's paintings, 169–70, 172;
    pathological as, 182; saturation and, 156

Coltrane, John, 28–29, 133, 134, 202,
    203, 222–23; exhausting the instru-
    ment, 190–91
Columbia University, 254n4
commercium, 74, 129–32, 246
commodity world, 131–32
common sense, 70–72, 78, 167
communal decision, 97
communion in pleasure, 250n32
community: art and, 166; black, 89,
    166–167, 168; sing, 130, 132, 137;
    slavery and, 95; world, 94
consciousness, 14, 15–16, 105, 109, 228,
    243; art, 80, 120; of the colonized,
    178–79; human life and, 26; metaphi-
    losophical, 23; moral, 20; national, 171,
    265n46; of objects, 32, 106; political,
    169, 179, 181–82; revolutionary, 186,
    236–37; unconsciousness and, 221;
    unified, 119, 120–21
consent not to be a single being, 81, 112,
    118, 136, 237, 240; sacrifice and, 100,
    109; of the speaker, 138
constitution, 106–8, 115
contemporaneity, 21–23, 215
Cooper, Harry, 168–69, 172
Cooper, Melinda, 246
Copeland, Huey, 143–44, 263n10
corporeity, xi–xii. *See also* body/bodies
creature–human life relation: abandon-
    ment and, 50; borders and boundaries,
    26–27, 29, 38; Celan's account, 55;
    definition, 54; the Open and, 32–33;
    the political and, 39–40; proximity
    and captivity, 36–39; the thingly and,
    52–53
criminality, 23, 36, 150, 244–45;
    anoriginal, 111, 132; anticolonial,
    177–78; colonial rule and, 181–82;
    political, 176, 182

damnation, 185, 228
Davidson, Donald, 116
Davis, Miles, 151
death. *See* life and death; social death

debt. *See* subprime debtor

decolonization, 4, 7, 103, 239

Deleuze, Gilles, 197, 198, 210, 222; on exhaustion, 185, 189, 231

democracy, 92–93, 97–100, 110, 112

Depraz, Natalie, 105

Derrida, Jacques, 11, 22, 39, 223, 226, 251n32; on lysis, 222

desegregation, 73, 77, 98, 105, 108

desire, capacity to, 196, 233–34

dialectics, 13, 14, 26, 82, 203, 250n32

Diderot, Denis, 54

difference: alterity as, 7–8; animateriality of, 11; black or Negro, 48, 143, 176; Coltrane and, 190; in friendship, 234; generativity and, 137; inequality and, 23; internal, 156, 158–59; intra-ontic, 5–7; musical, 154, 155, 156; ontological, 143; pathological and pathogenic, 194; of philosophy, 14; racial, 13, 94; radical, 249n16

dignity, 159–60, 243

disavowal, 79, 167, 180, 225, 226, 250n32; of fallenness, 23–24; of musical ends, 153; of new speech, 213–14, 216; of pidgin, 218; of things/the thingly, 10, 11, 250n17

discretion, 124

displacement, 92, 117, 147, 194, 200, 241; of binary logic, 209; dissidence and, xi; of personality, 176; relationality and, 211; technology and, 232

dispossession, 79, 95, 228, 233, 242; to claim or own, 49, 92, 185, 212, 230, 243

dissident strains, xi

Donne, John, 228

Douglass, Frederick, 68–69, 86, 217

Du Bois, W. E. B., 152, 170, 171, 213, 233; Fanon and, 204, 205, 212, 262n3; ontology and, ix, 205

Duchamp, Marcel, 163, 167, 264n23

Eckford, Elizabeth, 102, 105, 112, 114, 118–20, 123; Arendt's reflections on,

75–78, 86; face of, 88–89; parents, 104, 108; passion and passage, 79, 81–82, 95–96, 103, 107–8; performance/nonperformance, 80–81, 101, 122, 257n26

Edwards, Brent Hayes, 180

Edwards, Erica, 103

Elkins, Stanley, 90–92

Ellison, Ralph, 113, 138, 161, 226, 254n6; Allen's reading of, 97, 99–100; *Invisible Man*, 97; normative speech and, 98; notion of sacrifice, 110

empirical–transcendental entanglement, 116, 122, 123

emptiness, 39, 147, 200, 212, 222

Erskine, John, 254n4

Erwartung (Schoenberg), 152–53, 200

escape, 125, 142, 145, 177, 184, 225; from being, 23–24, 36, 64, 150; generativity as, 137; Levinas's, 18–19, 250n32; philosophy of, 2; racism and, 4; the rock of South African history, 59–61, 252n62; victory of, 172

eschatology, 209

essential disruption, 37–40, 64

Europe, 22, 32, 38, 250n32; Bible and the Greeks and, 1, 3–7, 10–12, 31; Jewish intellectuals in, 23; openness of, 35

European man, 5, 31–32, 50; discovery of, 3–4; racism and, 18; saving, 23–24, 26, 64; spirit of, 13–14

everyday life, 185, 240; *Dasein* (Being) in, 19–21, 128; Palestinian, 45

exhaustion, ix, 201, 208, 209, 225, 237; death through, 187; Deleuzean, 189–90; im/possibility of, 188, 190, 193; nothingness and, 231; thingly, 191

expansion and envelopment, 9, 19, 54; of Europe or the world, 3–4, 12, 35; failure of, 56

experience, possibility of, 105–6

exteriority, 6, 124, 127, 232; Deleuze on, 210; Levinas on, 7

external world, 24, 30, 81–83. *See also* world of things

fabrication, concept, 241–42
face, 5, 7–8; Elizabeth Eckford's, 75–78, 88–89
fallenness, 7, 22, 76, 102, 114; contemporaneity and, 21–23; damnation as, 96; *Dasein* (Being) and, 21, 128–31; of the political body, 102; into the world of things, x, 17, 18, 19, 21
Fanon, Frantz, xiii, 12, 170, 185, 197, 203–5, 207; Ad Reinhardt and, 158–59; on Algerians, 186–87; on being an object, 143–44, 147, 149; biochemical metaphors, 224; blackness and, 141, 148, 150, 161, 180, 227, 262n3; Cecil Taylor and, 159–60; colonized intellectuals and, 174, 191; on decolonization, 239; Deleuzean exhaustion and, 189–90; duty of the colonized subject, 179, 181; intrahuman theory, 248n16; on language and speech, 212–19, 226; law of motion, 180–81; on liberation of self, 226; lysis and, 221, 223; narcissism and, 220–21; phenomenology and, ix, xi–xii, 142, 147, 233, 246; Piper and, 81–82; psychosomatic pathology and, 174–78; rejection of negritude, 242; on repercussions, 171; sociogenic principles, 125, 192, 224. See also *Black Skin, White Masks* (Fanon); *Wretched of the Earth, The* (Fanon)
fantasy in the hold, 198–200, 203, 205, 208, 222, 229
Felix in Exile (Kentridge), 60–63
Forman, James, 73, 74, 95, 139; "A Black Manifesto," 71–72
fortuna, 61, 252n62, 253n63
fossil, 48
Foucault, Michel, 24, 219, 262n6; ship of fools, 198, 209–10
fraternity, 7, 113–14
freedom: artwork and, 166; community and, 167; creaturely life and, 32–33; gift of, 172; lawless, 41, 60, 181; love and, 87; mastery and, 248n11; unfreedom and, 85

French language, 214–16, 218–20, 227
Fried, Michael, 166–68, 264n24
friend–enemy distinction, 40, 221–22
fugitive movement, 142
fugitivity, 24, 39, 44, 47, 64, 180; anoriginal, 41; enclosure and, 192; Fanon and, 183; Foucault and, 262n6; love and, 88; notational, 155; ontic-ontological, 150; of things, 27, 251n32

generativity, 114–15, 133, 197; cell's, 128; nonbeing's, 224; regulation of, 231
genesis, 23, 237
German-Jewish tradition, 26, 40, 42, 44, 52, 56
gift/gifting, 103–4, 136, 148, 219, 228, 237
Gilroy, Paul, 8, 248n16
Ginsberg, Allen, 191
Glissant, Édouard, 112, 227, 237, 249n16; encounter with Braxton, 134–36
Gordon, Lewis, 201, 226, 229
grammar: general economy of, 125; jurisgenerative, 74, 123, 127, 134; materiality of, 126; refusal of, 124
Greeks, 1–4, 10–12, 23, 31
Greenberg, Clement, 166–68
Guattari, Félix, 10, 222
Guyer, Paul, 70

Han, Sora, 257n26
harmonic (in)security, 68–69
Harris, Laura, 76, 253n62
Hartman, Saidiya, 104–5, 239–40, 267n78
hegemony, 49, 239, 240
Heidegger, Martin, 6, 14, 22, 114, 232; animal captivation and, 37; *Das Ding* ("The Thing"), 145–49; *Dasein* (Being), 18, 19–21, 37–38, 128–31; emptiness and, 39; openness of, 23; Santner's reading of, 32–40; un/concealedness and, 40
Hemings, Sally, 123
heroes, 259n59
historicity, 124, 191, 215, 237; European, 6, 13–14

home ownership, 240, 245
hope, 74
Huarte, John, 124, 134–35
humanity, 7, 8, 113; European spirit and, 13–14; expelled from, 91–92; infinite, 181, 183; of man, 3–4, 19, 24, 39
human nature, 126
Huntington, Samuel, 93
Husserl, Edmund, 13, 108–9, 232–33; Levinas and, 12, 23, 35, 44; phenomenology, ix, 14, 105–6

idea, propagation of an, 3, 7
identification, 116–17
illiteracy, 102–3
imagination, 109, 168, 171, 180, 181, 207; Fanon's, 184; Kant's principles, 41, 56, 93–94; maternal, 77, 78; musical, 154; social, 107, 170
im/possibility: Afro-pessimism and, 193; colonized individual and, 174; exhaustion and, 188, 190, 193, 205; of the law, 29; weakness and, 192
improvisation, ix, 24, 95, 129, 212; blackness and, 154–55; Braxton's, 127, 132; on friendship, 197; in jazz, 131; as self-analysis, 223, 226
impurity, 22, 93, 211; internal difference and, 156, 158–59
individual–world interplay, 114, 115
individuation, ix, xi–xiii, 8, 98, 105
institutionality, 90–91
intellectuality: American, 90; black, 161–63; colonized, 174, 176, 191, 265n46; Jewish, 23; Marxian, 235; New York, 254n4
intelligence, moral obligations of, 66, 92, 254n4, 254n6
intentionality: of blackness, 148, 258n43; Husserlian, 32; phenomenologists and, 14–17; racism and, 9, 16–17, 25
interiority, 14, 36, 48, 51, 117; black, 176, 182; emptiness as, 39; Foucault and, 210; of philosophy, 11; of things, 18, 34

intrahuman relation, 248n16
Inwood, Michael, 11, 31
Irigaray, Luce, 26, 250n32
isolation, 114–15, 137, 241
Israeli-Palestinian impasse, 45

Jacobs, Harriet, 88, 172, 226
Jameson, Fredric, 235
JanMohamed, Abdul, 194
Jaspers, Karl, 85–86
jazz, 170, 192; Adorno on, 79, 131; howl, 191
Jefferson, Thomas, 123, 192
Jews, 56–57, 253n3. See also German-Jewish tradition
judgment, 33–34, 44, 209, 223
jurisgenerative principle, 44, 107, 115, 132, 134

Kant, Immanuel, x–xii, 23, 41–42, 70; Arendt and, 93–94; fearsome generativity and, 114–15; natural history theory, 46, 48–49; necessity of regulation and, 109; Piper's reading of, 119–22; purposiveness, 32, 47; teleological principle, 47–48, 56, 109, 182; understanding of the thing, 53, 149–50; Weininger's critique of, 57–58
Keeling, Kara, 146, 222, 263n10
Kendricks, Eddie, 68, 69
Kentridge, William, 58–63, 252nn61–62, 253n63
King, Martin Luther, 73
knowledge, 147, 196, 208, 228, 229, 244; of language, 124, 127; theoretical, 14, 15
Krauss, Rosalind, 58, 59, 62, 252n62, 253n63
Kunkel, Benjamin, 235

labor of the negative, 28–29, 180
Lacan, Jacques, 51, 54
Landau, Jon, 68–72, 95
language, 198, 225, 248n11; Chomsky on, 123–26; Fanon on, 213–19; Linebaugh

on, 213; music and, 127. *See also* French language; pidgin; speech

Laplanche, Jean, 54

law: making, 110, 125, 126; of movement, 142, 154, 180–81; and non-law, 43; rule of, 41, 44, 109–11

Le Guin, Ursula K., 112

Levinas, Emmanuel, xii–xiii, 35, 39, 44, 248n16; on dancing and mourning, 1, 49, 60; definition of philosophy, 25; on Europe as the Bible and Greeks, 2–4, 23; on Hitler's philosophy, 18, 23; Irigaray's reading of, 26, 250n32; McGettigan's reading of, 4–9; on phenomenologists and intentionality, 14–17; racism and, 1–3, 11, 16; reading of Heidegger, 18–22, 36; shame and, 51; understanding of the thing, 9, 10, 16–17

Lewis, George, x, 124

liberation: national, 66, 176, 177–78, 183; of self, 226

life and death, 38, 46–47, 143, 175, 230

lifeworld, 12–13

Linebaugh, Peter, 197, 212–14, 229

linguistics. *See* language

Little Rock Nine, 98–100, 103, 107, 108, 113; Arendt and, 75, 86; Bill Clinton's speech on, 256n25; Thomas Jefferson and, 123

loneliness, 96, 101, 107–8, 257n26

Lorde, Audre, 81

love, 83–88, 193

Lupton, Julia, 52, 54

lysis, 224; friendship-enemy distinction and, 222; lyric and, 216, 223, 225, 230; of morbid body/universe, 194, 207, 221, 226–27

Mackey, Nathaniel, 150, 198, 203, 224; "Dolphic Oracle," xi; "Splay Anthem," 201

making process, 146–47

Markmann, Charles Lam, 211

Marx, Karl, 21, 155, 183, 203, 236

Marxism, 235–37

mastery, 7–8, 28, 248n11

materiality, 39, 126, 131, 222, 244; of the damned, 185; social, 209; of the subprime, 246; thingly, 19

Max's Kansas City, 80–81

Mayfield, Curtis, 74, 93, 193; Landau's review of *Curtis/Live!*, 68–69, 95

Mbembe, Achille, 263n10

McClary, Susan, 152

McGettigan, Andrew, 5–9

melancholia, 49

Mellino, Miguel, 185, 190, 193, 266n52

Menand, Louis, 90, 254n4

mental disorders, 173–76, 186, 192, 265n46

metaphysics, 48, 98, 101, 108, 116, 132; of ascent, 114; biological, 32; classical, 118; of individuation, xii–xiii, 87; of sound and color, 140; Western, 64, 149, 205

minority, x–xi, 114–15

miracle, concept, 45

Mitropoulos, Angela, 246

modernity, 21–22, 118, 253n3

Mondrian, Piet, 163, 164, 167, 264n23; blackness in paintings, 169–70, 172, 173; obsession with revision, 168–69; urban victory and, 171–72; *Victory Boogie Woogie*, 157, 168, 170, 173

motherhood, 75–79, 82, 200

mourning, 1, 10, 46, 49, 59, 60

movement, meaning, 259n59

Moynihan, Daniel Patrick, 151

mu, term usage, 201–3, 205, 208–9

musical moments, 199

musical regulation, 155

mysticism, 205, 209

narcissism, 213, 216, 220–21, 225

natality, 79, 112, 193, 216, 227, 241; inalienable, 245–46

natural history, 46–49, 101, 231

naturalization, 46, 67, 85, 90, 101, 107

Negri, Antonio, 64

Newton, Huey P., 189

New York City, 170–71

internally driven, 134–35; paraontological, 79; resistance and, 44, 240; sovereign, 8, 41–43, 49, 98; state, 77
prayers, 45
preservation: of blackness, 236–37; regenerative, 197; revolution and, 184, 190, 192
Pryor, Richard, 130, 238
psychopathology, 174–79, 186. *See also* pathological, the
psychosomatic disorders, 174–75, 178
publicness, 100, 113, 115–16, 265n50; being-lost in, 129, 130; dark speech and, 102, 105; private partnership, 103, 104
purposiveness, 32, 34, 47–48

race, 22, 48, 94, 253n3
racism: failure of, 17–18; humanity of man and, 4; Levinas and, 1–3, 11; philosophy of, 64; unintendedness of, 4, 9–10, 16–17, 25; universality/universalism and, 2, 12, 24
radical art, 173
rationality, 8, 119, 121, 123; musical, 154
Rediker, Marcus, 199–200, 201
refuge, 89, 95, 114, 137, 139, 243; for Arendt, 65; in the cell, 128
refusal, 139, 148, 197, 206, 212; art's, 118; black/blackness, 90, 101, 180, 206, 230; of citizenship, 133; consent and, 212; of enclosure, 91; Fanon's, 145, 184, 263n10, 265n46; having something and, 242–43; of integration, 121; of privacy, 88; and response interplay, 45; of sociality, 100; of standpoint, 193, 223; of the state, 77
rehabilitation, 177, 180, 184
Reinhardt, Ad, 264nn23–24; antipathy to thingliness, 166–67; the color black and, 158–59, 162–63, 172; encounter with Cecil Taylor, 157–58, 159–61, 163–66; Mondrian and, 168–69, 172–73
relationality, 112, 204–6, 208, 211, 229
representation: of animals, 35; equal, 160; failed, 220; between man and world, 27–28; mastery and, 7, 26;

objects and, 149; resistance to, 28; of things, 32, 34, 147
resistance: of the artist, 61; bodily, 176; colonial/anticolonial, 178, 182; to enclosure, 94; Fanonian, 206; ontological, 12; power and, 44, 240; to racism, 11; to representation, 28; as resource, 103; revolutionary, 184; thingly, 9; without meaning, 222
Rilke, Rainer Maria, 55–56; *die Kreatur* and *das Offene*, 26–29; Santner's read of Heidegger and, 32–33
risk, 86–87
Robinson, Cedric, 246; *Black Marxism: The Making of the Black Radical Tradition*, 235–38; ontological totality, 42, 236
Robinson, Smokey, 68, 69
rock, notion of the, 59–61, 62–63
Rockman, Arnold, 157, 161–62, 165
Rodney, Walter, 191–92, 233
Rose, Barbara, 157, 159
Rosen, Charles, 152–55
Rosenzweig, Franz, 2
Rustin, Bayard, 68, 255n7

sacrifice, 226; black and white, 100, 108; democratic society and law and, 97, 109–11; heroism and, 79, 99; selflessness and, 97; the sovereign and, 98
Salanskis, Jean-Michel, 109
Salomon, Gayle, xi
Santner, Eric: on allegory and melancholy, 49; on creaturely-human life relation, 26–29, 52–55; on Jewish assimilation, 56–57; oppositional posture, 30–31; reading of Agamben and Heidegger, 32–41; reading of Benjamin's natural history, 46; reading of Levinas, 50–51; reading of Schmitt, 42–43, 44; state of exception and, 50; on Žižek and the concept of miracle, 45
savage thought, 3–4
Sawicki, Marianne, 233
Schmitt, Carl, 40, 42–44, 47